ORGANIZING DISSENT

CAN. THEORETICAL APPROACH

- HOW MOVEMENTS ARE FORMED

  WHY MOVEMENTS ARE FORMED.

- DOES THE STATE SHAPE MOVEMENTS?

  IS IT THE POLITICAL CENTRE? P.12

- PERHAPS COULD THIS BE AN ANSWER TO

  BRODIE'S DILEMMA OF NEOLIBERALISM, OR

  RATHER COMPLEMENT HER CALL FOR

  ADAPTATION? P.13

- SOCIAL CONSCIENCE + SOCIAL CHANGE VS.

  CONTROL OF IMPACT + ADVANCING

  PERSONAL GAIN P.14

  — FRAMING DISPUTES P.16

  └ ISSUE W/ RMT. — COMMON INTEREST VS =

- NEW SOCIAL MOVEMENT THEORY (NSM)

  — COMMON IDENTITY

  — NOT STATE CENTERED.

ORGANIZING DISSENT

Contemporary Social Movements
in Theory and Practice

Studies in the Politics of Counter-Hegemony

Edited by William K. Carroll

UNIVERSITY OF VICTORIA

Garamond Press, Toronto

Publisher: Peter Saunders
Editor: Robert Clarke
Typesetting and Design: Robin Brass Studio
Cover Photos: David Maltby

Printed and bound in Canada

Canadian Cataloguing in Publication Data

Organizing dissent : contemporary social movements in theory and practice :
studies in the politics of counter-hegemony

2nd rev. ed.
Includes bibliographical references and index.
ISBN 1-55193-002-1

1. Social movements – Canada. I. Carroll, William K.

HN107.074 1997   303.48'4'0971   C97-093874-4

CONTENTS

CONTRIBUTORS

Barry D. Adam teaches sociology at the University of Windsor. He is the author of *Experiencing HIV, The Rise of a Gay and Lesbian Movement*, and *The Survival of Domination* and has long been active in gay, AIDS, and Central America solidarity organizations.

Peter Bleyer is executive director of The Council of Canadians and a member of the steering committee of the Action Canada Network. From 1988 to 1990 he was Co-ordinator of the Pro-Canada Network. He is also a doctoral candidate at the London School of Economics.

William K. Carroll teaches sociology and participates in the graduate program in contemporary social and political thought at the University of Victoria. He is the author of *Corporate Power and Canadian Capitalism*.

Aaron Doyle is completing his Ph.D. in sociology at the University of British Columbia. He is a former journalist.

Brian Elliott teaches sociology at the University of British Columbia. He is the co-author of *The City: Patterns of Domination and Conflict* and *Property and Power in a City*.

Gary Kinsman teaches sociology at Laurentian University and is active in the socialist, gay, and AIDS activist movements. He is the author of *The Regulation of Desire: Homo and Hetero Sexualities*.

David Alan Long teaches sociology at The King's University College in Edmonton. Along with his active participation in the Aboriginal rights movement, he has written in the areas of religion and spirituality, science and technology, and critical pedagogy.

Warren Magnusson teaches political science and participates in the graduate program in contemporary social and political thought at the University of Victoria. He is the author of *The Search for Political Space: Globalization, Social Movements, and the Urban Political Experience*.

Dominique Masson is a doctoral candidate in sociology at Carleton University.

Jacinthe Michaud is a political scientist teaching women's studies at Glendon College, York University.

R.S. Ratner teaches sociology at the University of British Columbia.

Bob Russell teaches sociology at the University of Saskatchewan. He is the author of *Back to Work: Labour, State and Industrial Relations in Canada*.

Catriona (Cate) Sandilands teaches environmental politics and thought in the Faculty of Environmental Studies, York University. Her current research interests concern the place of nature in social and political discourse, especially as it intersects with questions of gender and/or nation. Her book *The Good-Natured Feminist: Ecofeminism, Identity and Democracy* will be published next year by the University of Minnesota Press.

Sharon Dale Stone teaches sociology at Okanagan University College, Kelowna, B.C. Recent community activities include organizing Kelowna's first Lesbian and Gay Pride Day march and celebrations in 1996.

David Tindall is a faculty member at the University of British Columbia where he teaches and conducts research on social aspects of environmental and resource problems.

ACKNOWLEDGEMENTS

Several people have been indispensable in bringing this new edition to frui-tion. The idea for a revised edition first germinated in a conversation I had with Peter Saunders of Garamond Press in 1994, and Peter has offered en-thusiastic encouragement throughout the ensuing three years. Karen Chong-Kwan and Carole Rains of the University of Victoria Sociology De-partment have given invaluable secretarial assistance, and Robert Clarke's copy-editing has once again been both sensible and meticulous. The support of the Social Sciences and Humanities Research Council of Canada is also gratefully acknowledged. Contributing authors from the first edition have put much effort into updating and in many cases reinventing their chapters, and some chapters appear here for the first time. The result, I trust, is a col-lection of theoretical and empirical reflections on movement politics and emancipatory possibilities that will be of value as we cross into the next cen-tury.

Bill Carroll
April 9, 1997

Part 1

SOCIAL MOVEMENTS IN THEORY

SOCIAL MOVEMENTS AND COUNTERHEGEMONY: CANADIAN CONTEXTS AND SOCIAL THEORIES

William K. Carroll

SOCIAL MOVEMENTS AND CANADIAN STUDIES

In recent years social movements have become a leading topic in Canadian social and political studies. Yet despite the academic interest in contemporary movements, and despite their tangible impact in day-to-day life, there has been a dearth of available texts that probe the meaning of movements in a distinctively Canadian context. The first edition of this book attempted to redress that absence; this new edition continues that project with a series of theoretical and empirical studies that have either been revised – and in some cases extensively rethought – or appear here for the first time.

In a thematic sense, social movements have long been central to the social sciences in Canada. The historical sociology of S.D. Clark focused upon the religious and secular movements that helped constitute "the developing Canadian community," particularly at the frontier.[1] The pathbreaking works of Seymour Lipset (1950) and C.B. Macpherson (1953) were centred around the prairie protest movements that arose in part out of the contradictions of Canadian capitalist development, as uneven development in both its spatial and temporal dimensions brought particularly hard times to prairie communities in the 1930s. In Quebec the francophone sociology that emerged in the mid-1960s took up the national question, an issue imbued with movement politics. Since the beginning of the 1980s, Québécois scholars have leaned towards "a sociology of praxis, of collective social action and of recomposition of subjective totality" (Juteau and Mahue 1989: 378). In English Canada, the intellectual forces that collected together to press for "Canadianization" in the late 1960s, and that consolidated the field of Cana-

3

dian studies and reshaped the agendas of sociology and political sciences, were themselves part of a social movement opposing the continentalizing impact of Americanization.

The journey "to know ourselves," as Thomas Symons (1975) aptly put it, may be yet unfinished (Hofley 1992), but sociology and political science in Canada have at least managed to hold onto a definite sense of place. This continues a long tradition of idiographic, socio-historical scholarship inaugurated by Harold Innis and other political economists of the "Toronto school," who saw in Canada a specific social and economic formation that needed to be understood in terms of its particular, historically formed features and context. In like manner, S.D. Clark – Innis's student and the first sociologist appointed at the University of Toronto – brought to his work a keen sense that to understand the role of sectarian and other movements in the developing Canadian community it was most important to chart the specific and interconnected histories of the groups involved.[2] This concern with grasping specificity has continued to distinguish Canadian scholarship from the more ambitious – and some would say imperialistic – aims of American sociology, namely, to construct universal theories of human behaviour and social relations, typically on the basis of research conducted in the United States.

In the study of Canadian social movements, the same emphasis upon constructing idiographic accounts rather than nomothetic explanations has continued to predominate. The result has been a literature organized less around theoretical issues – of movement mobilization, of the formation of collective identities, of strategic interaction among movements, and the like – than around substantive topic areas that include regional protest, labour struggles, and feminism.

As an organized discipline in Canada, sociology is a child of the post-World War II era, and given these rather shallow roots it is not difficult to trace the main lines of development in this idiographic approach to social movements. The coming of age of Canadian sociology in the late 1960s and early 1970s coincided fortuitously with the climax of a period of social movement activism in Canada and the other capitalist democracies. The cultural and political sensibilities of the generation of social scientists that would set the agenda for scholarship in the 1970s and beyond were formed within this context.[3] In contrast to the trajectory of sociology in the United States – where sedimentations from a lengthier academic history combined with the virulent legacy of McCarthyism to instil an institutional and ideological inertia against a radical turn – the agenda for Canadian sociology began to incorporate many of the concerns raised by the movements of the day.[4]

One can see this especially in the growth of a critical political-economy paradigm emphasizing the inequities of class, region, and nation, and identifying itself with the interests of the dominated.[5] By 1971 Arthur K. Davis was drawing a close connection between political-economic structure and social movement agency. His "Canadian Society and History as Hinterland Versus Metropolis" deftly wove the disparate elements of the making of Canada into a master narrative, wherein:

> Metropolis continuously dominates and exploits hinterland whether in regional, national, class or ethnic terms. But the forms and terms of domination change as a result of confrontations. Spontaneous and massive social movements in regional hinterlands or urban underclasses may force their way toward an improved status for colonials within the going system. On the other hand, metropolis-hinterland conflict may be outweighed by conditions of prosperity or by temporary alliances in the face of larger confrontations. (Davis 1974 [1971]: 452)

Davis held – and many agreed – that such a schematic model of social movement formation could highlight the relations and processes of domination/resistance that have shaped contemporary Canada, whether in the case of Canadian western settlement, Quebec-in-Canada, Canada-in-North-America, or even United States-in-the-world (453-4).

Much of the political-economic analysis that followed from the enunciation of this perspective by Davis and others was attentive both to structures of domination and to agencies of collective resistance in the form of regional, national, or class-based movements. Sheilagh and Henry Milner, for instance, in their *The Decolonization of Quebec* (1973), first presented a structural analysis of Quebec as a colonized society and then traced the social movement that was propelling the Québécois from "submission to self-consciousness." In their edited collection of essays, *Underdevelopment and Social Movements in Atlantic Canada* (1979), Robert Brym and James Sacouman joined the metropolis-hinterland perspective to a Marxist political economy of class. They asserted that, contrary to the Central Canadian stereotype:

> Atlantic Canadians *have* engaged in a wide variety of political and non-political movements to improve their lot; and if formally political attempts to improve their lot have not been as successful as in, say, the Canadian west, this is due less to any inherent conservatism than it is to the fact that the character of regional underdevelopment has, at least until recently, distributed political resources so unevenly as to militate against widespread success. (1979: 13)

However, with a few exceptions[6] Canadian social scientists tended to theorize movements as little more than the political reflex of structural contradictions defined at an economic level. In the 1970s – and well into the 1980s – theorists paid scant attention to social movements as emergent and contingent phenomena in their own right; the new political economy provided little space for theorizing movements as collective agencies grounded, to be sure, in a developing "material realm" but relatively autonomous from that realm in the identities, strategies, and organizational forms they adopted. In short, the new political economy recognized movements as forces for social change, but it explained their existence and imputed their historical meaning directly from the master narrative of political economy itself, rather than by building up an understanding through close observation and interpretation of actual movements.

In some degree, this tendency to analyse social movements by means of historical narratives that highlight their interest bases in political-economic structure was fortuitous. It meant that work in Canada retained an important sense of place, eschewing the universalizing pretensions of mainstream American sociology. It also meant that Canadian scholars working within a political-economy perspective on movements were spared the encumbrances of the major contemporaneous U.S.-based theories, which remained in play well into the 1970s. Those theories offered simplistic and pejorative explanations that viewed social movements either as unmediated responses to a collectively experienced "relative deprivation" (Davis 1969; Gurr 1970) or as symptoms of normative breakdown (Smelser 1963; Johnson 1966). The latter, Durkheimian tradition defined the collective action of social movements as a sort of mass deviance, to be categorized alongside other mass departures from consensually established norms, such as panics, crazes, and fads. Within frameworks such as Neil Smelser's theory of collective behaviour, social movements were thus constructed as "Other" to the rational, well-adjusted bourgeois individual – and the rationalized organizations – of modernity.[7] Clearly, this conservative sort of analysis did not offer much purchase to Canadian scholars interested in creating a sociology that could both interpret and criticize the character of their own society.

Yet by the late 1970s the foundations of the metropolis-hinterland perspective that had informed Canadian studies of social movements were themselves shaking. On the one hand, scholars were raising a number of concerns about the adequacy of a political economy that had at its core a reified concept of spatial relations instead of a historical concept of class relations (Carroll 1986; Kellogg 1989). On the other hand, as feminist perspectives gained prominence the adequacy of a class-based political economy was also called into question, and the need for a critical sociology and political science capable of analysing a plurality of social movements and struggles became increasingly apparent. Now-classic feminist studies of the 1970s and early 1980s adopted a political-economy framework in attending primarily to structures of patriarchy and secondarily to women's resistive agency (Smith 1975; Armstrong and Armstrong 1978; Luxton 1980). In itself, the transformative impact of this work upon such political-economic categories as (re)production, class, and state was significant (Maroney and Luxton 1987; Fox 1989). But in the 1980s an increasing emphasis was placed upon women's collective agency, as feminist sociologists sought to develop theoretical and strategic analyses of feminism as an emancipatory social movement. In *Feminist Organizing for Change*, Nancy Adamson, Linda Briskin, and Margaret McPhail (1988: 20) expressed this concern about understanding feminist praxis, and the constraints that surround it:

> We want to understand how to make change. The lack of fundamental structural improvement in the conditions of women makes us turn a critical eye on the women's movement. We are struck by the contrast between the relatively unchanging movement of today and the heady mobilizations of earlier stages. We are concerned that the women's movement has become overly institutionalized and that this may undermine our ability to achieve change in the future, especially in the fact of attacks by neo-conservatives who want to turn back the clock on the few gains we have made.

The editors of *Social Movements/Social Change: The Politics and Practice of Organizing*, a book initiated by the Society for Socialist Studies, voiced a similar desire to understand the workings of the hegemonic processes of regulation and "how we – collectively and individually – are implicated in maintaining the relations of power in society" (Cunningham et al. 1988: 13). They called for a "politics of transformation" that would challenge not only dominant interests but the beliefs and practices that sustain power in everyday life: a politics that could thereby "reflect and validate our role as agents of change rather than as simple victims in the making of history" (13).[8]

It is precisely on this question of "how to make change," of how to practise a "politics of transformation," that a careful consideration of contemporary social movement theory can be helpful. Political economy has furnished a basis for situating collective agency in a structural context; the idiographic accounts of movements that have typically proceeded on that basis have woven into narrative form much of the texture of social struggles in Canada. But these modes of analysis are rooted in a language of structure and events, not agency and strategy. In themselves they cannot provide for a theoretical understanding of movements as instances of collective agency. Important as it is to retain the insights of the Canadian political-economy tradition, it is equally important to access a language of politics, in the broadest sense, through which social activists and analysts can speak about their intersecting concerns.

One way towards that end is through listening to the movements themselves. In providing "first-hand accounts and analyses of the experiences of some of the social movements in Canada," the Cunningham et al. (1988: 16) collection enabled movement activists to speak to others in their own voices. The same may be said of the more recent collection of essays by labour, environmental, and other activists edited by Steven Langdon and Victoria

Cross (1994). Many of the contributors who follow here speak with a compa-rable authority of experience gained through years of movement activism. Yet they also draw upon the political vocabulary of contemporary social movement theory, in its various manifestations. When read not as determin-istic, predictive theory but as a set of more or less rigorous reflections upon the dynamics of social movements in the world today, these formulations also become resources for creating a transformative politics.

SOCIAL MOVEMENT THEORY AND TRANSFORMATIVE POLITICS

In both its American and European versions, contemporary social movement theory differs radically from the reigning perspectives of earlier times. The resource mobilization theories espoused by Charles Tilly (1978, 1985), Sidney Tarrow (1994b), and others have little in common with the Durkheimian collective-behaviour tradition of American sociology; the "new social movement" (NSM) theories championed by Alain Touraine (1981, 1988), Alberto Melucci (1989), and others break significantly from the struc-turalist interpretations of Marx, which were so influential in continental thought in the 1960s. Without pretending to be comprehensive I want to con-sider these approaches briefly, with an eye towards how they can contribute to a critical analysis of social movements as agencies for change.

We can, at the outset, draw two distinctions between the paradigms. Firstly, resource mobilization theory (RMT) – the predominantly American approach – focuses primarily upon *how* movements form and engage in col-lective action; the more European new social movement (NSM) formulations focus primarily on *why* specific forms of collective identity and action have appeared in late twentieth-century Euro-North American societies (Melucci 1989). By implication, RMT analyses tend to be sensitized to the specific situational context that facilitates or hinders a process of movement mobili-zation, while NSM formulations are typically more sensitized to the broad, macrosociological transformations of the late twentieth century, which pro-vide new cultural, political, and economic contexts for collective-identity for-mation.

Secondly, RMT offers a conception of movement practice that emphasizes the *shared interests* underlying the process of mobilization: in forming a movement a social group engages in the rational pursuit of its common inter-ests. NSM theory, in contrast, views movements less as agencies of common interest and more as new forms of *collective identity*, which not only trans-form people's self-understandings but create cultural codes that contest the legitimacy of received points of view (Cohen 1985).

Resource Mobilization Theory

The mobilization of a social movement is a process by which resources use-ful to a group's collective action are brought under collective control. It is this pooling of resources that enables a group to transform itself from a collection of political spectators sharing a common interest to a contending group able to pursue a shared goal (Tilly 1978). In this transformative process, social movements appear as instrumentally rational collective actors, deploying effective means to the pursuit of a shared end. On the basis of felt grievances stemming from shared interest, the constituents of a movement pool their resources, and secure other resources, in order to pursue collective goods – such as higher wages, universal daycare, and Native land claims. As resources of various kinds become pooled, a group gains the capacity to mount collective actions in pursuit of its common interest; that is to say, it becomes mobilized. RMT analysts differ in describing the kinds of resources mobilized by movements, but any reasonable list would include labour (the active commitment of constituents to work for the movement), money, land, or facilities (for instance, an office and communications equipment), and technical expertise (the skills of key activists – whether in media relations, popular education, or political strategizing; cf. Jenkins 1983: 533).

Bringing such resources under collective control, in turn, involves *social organization*, in two senses. Firstly, pre-existing social networks and collective identities are a prerequisite to mobilization. Indeed, the mobilization potential of a group is primarily determined by the extent of pre-existing social organization. Groups lacking such social networks and shared consciousness rarely mobilize, for they have no practical means by which to pool resources. Conversely, groups sharing strong identities and dense interpersonal networks are highly organized and can be readily mobilized (Tilly 1978: 62-3). Often, mobilization involves the co-optation of resources from pre-existing organizations in civil society such as churches or voluntary associations.

Secondly, social organization *results from* mobilization; that is, mobilization typically involves the creation of a *social movement organization* (SMO). Such organizations institutionalize the collective control of resources – the commitment of activists, the group's claim to other resources such as communications media (for instance, a newsletter) – and thus work to maintain the movement in a mobilized state. SMOs are "the carrier organizations that consciously attempt to coordinate and mobilize supporters" (Zald and McCarthy 1987: 339).

McCarthy and Zald's Entrepreneurial Mobilization Model
Within the resource mobilization paradigm are two distinctive schools of thought: the "professional organizer" or "entrepreneurial mobilization" model (Jenkins 1983: 527); and the "political process" model (Pichardo 1988). The professional organizer model, developed mainly by J.D. McCarthy and M.N. Zald (1973; Zald and McCarthy 1987), draws on organizational theory and Olson's (1965) rational-choice political theory. Rational-

choice theory presents a model of instrumental rationality according to which rational decision-makers base their choices on a calculus of costs and benefits. When the theory addresses the issue of resource mobilization, its key insight is that *mobilization costs something*; that is, in pooling their resources to strive for a collective benefit people forego other pursuits: they commit their time, money, or other resources to the common cause. From this premise, the entrepreneurial mobilization model constructs accounts of the practical and technical aspects of social movement formation. The costliness of mobilization makes the link between grievances or shared interest and collective action contingent upon creating the right combination of manageable costs and tangible benefits so that resources will be pooled and wielded effectively (Fireman and Gamson 1979: 9).

One consequence of focusing on the instrumental rationality of costs and benefits is a blurring of the distinction between movements and other modern forms of political action, such as the work of parties and pressure groups. Like other modern political organizations, social movement organizations emphasizing cost-effectiveness tend to adopt organizational forms that routinize the flow of resources to ensure movement survival (McAdam et al. 1988: 697). This is not to say that SMOs necessarily evolve into bureaucracies. Rather, different organizational forms are effective for different tasks. A bureaucratic structure may yield technical expertise but be less effective at mobilizing the "grassroots." A decentralized structure may be more effective at mobilizing the grassroots but less able to make timely strategic interventions (Jenkins 1983: 542).

Another implication of rational-choice analysis has to do with the recruitment and participation of individuals. Each person is viewed as a rational actor who weighs costs and benefits and chooses to participate when potential benefits outweigh expected costs (McCarthy and Zald 1977). Yet this account of the economically rational, egoistic individual immediately presents a "free-rider" problem for resource mobilization. Collective action, if successful, generates collective goods, such as improved wages or working conditions, socialized health care, or stronger regulations on pollution. Such collective goods can typically be enjoyed by all members of the movement's constituency – *regardless of whether or not a particular individual has participated in the movement.* Given the costliness of participation, it is most rational for individuals to "free-ride," to enjoy the collective benefits of movement mobilization without bearing any of the costs (Olson 1965: 11). Yet if all potential participants make this egoistically rational choice, no mobilization, that is, no movement, occurs. The standard solution to the free-rider paradox has been to consider how SMOs distribute "selective incentives" to activists, thus rationalizing their intense participation. A major means by which an SMO sustains a movement over time is through provision of these incentives to *movement entrepreneurs* – "professional" organizers, specialized in the task of movement mobilization, who invest much of their time in the movement but also reap selective benefits such as salaries, prestige, and power. A push to overcome the free-rider problem imposes organizational and technical imperatives on SMOs. To fund selective incentives such as salaries for professional organizers, an organization must tap external resources, which becomes a major preoccupation (Scott 1990: 112). The permanent and elaborate canvassing practices of SMOs such as Greenpeace come to mind.

Such organizational imperatives bring up a final claim of the entrepreneurial mobilization model, one based explicitly on the "trend of social movements" in the United States (McCarthy and Zald 1973). McCarthy and Zald argue that before the post-World War II wave of prosperity, social movements were based in aggrieved populations that directly provided their own necessary resources. The increased middle-class affluence of postwar U.S. society brought a new situation in which movements could acquire resources from "conscience constituents" – supporters who do not stand to benefit directly from the success of the movement (Zald and McCarthy 1987: 23). The rising affluence of the 1950s and 1960s thus furnished an expanding pool of discretionary income that SMOs could tap. Movements of the 1960s and 1970s, then, mobilized an affluent conscience constituency (including university students) and co-opted institutional resources from government agencies, private foundations, and even corporations. In consequence there has been an important shift in social movements. The trend is *away from* classical SMOs with indigenous leadership, volunteer staff, extensive membership, resources from direct beneficiaries, and actions based upon mass participation, and *towards* professional SMOs "with outside leadership, full time paid staff, small or nonexistent membership, resources from conscience constituencies, and actions that 'speak for' rather than involve an aggrieved group" (Jenkins 1983: 533). It is particularly in this changed context that movement leaders become "social movement entrepreneurs," endeavouring to mobilize financial resources from conscience constituents and manipulate "images of relevance and support through the communications media" (Zald and McCarthy 1987: 374).

This reading of contemporary movements can be recognized as Weberian in its basic thrust. Several of the features of modernity emphasized by Weber – the predominance of instrumental rationality in human affairs, the increasing importance of professional expertise, the creation of efficient organizational forms – figure prominently in the professional organizer model. The logic of collective action, then, follows the same logic as other practices of modernity: social movements may espouse alternative values, but in their practices of mobilization and activism they are as much prisoners of modernity's iron cage as are establishment organizations such as parties or state bureaucracies.

PRISONERS OF MODERNITY'S IRON CAGE

Tilly's Political Process Model

The second variant of RMT – the *political process model* – has intellectual roots closer to Marx than to Weber, and the empirical grounds for its account come more from the Europe of the nineteenth and twentieth centuries than from postwar U.S. society. One distinguishing feature of this approach is its historical sensitivity to the importance of the state as a centre of modern political contention. Charles Tilly, the most influential exponent of this variant of RMT, defines a national social movement as "a sustained challenge to state authorities in the name of a population that has little formal power with respect to the state" (1988: 1), and he notes that such sustained challenges can occur only where states exist. In the modern era the elaboration of a system of formally autonomous national states claiming to base their sovereignty at least partly on the consent of the governed has profoundly structured the field of collective action for social movements. On one hand, each state's claim to sovereignty on the basis of democratic consent renders it vulnerable to "concerted public displays of numbers and commitment" by dissenting groups (Tilly 1988: 3). On the other, mobilization of such collective actors has typically occurred in nationally bounded contexts within which the state constitutes the political "centre."

A key insight in the political process model is that to create change, social movements require more than a mobilization of resources: they require an *opportunity to act*. Within the context of national states, changes in the *structure of political opportunities* can have a decisive impact on the ebb and flow of movement activism (Tarrow 1994b). At different times and places the state may be particularly receptive or vulnerable to organized protest by a given contending group (McAdam et al. 1988: 699). As Gary Marx and Douglas McAdam (1994: 84) point out, "In one era, the political forces aligned against the challenger may make collective action a near impossibility. In another, shifting political alignments may create a unique opportunity for political action by, or on behalf of, the same group."

The configuration of mobilized social forces – both within the state and in civil society – provides the strategic context within which a given social movement acts. Indeed, the political process model focuses on the *strategic interaction* between SMOs, the state, and other collective actors and institutions. A good deal of strategic interaction involves various instances of *repression* and *facilitation*, as groups manipulate each other's costs of collective action, whether upwards (repression) or downwards (facilitation) (Tilly 1978: 100-1). For instance, in the 1980s the peace and anti-poverty movements in Vancouver were particularly vibrant, in part because the local labour council *facilitated* these movements by providing key resources to SMOs such as End the Arms Race and End Legislated Poverty (Carroll and Ratner 1995). But the U.S. government's outlawing of the Communist Party (CP) during the Cold War was *repressive*: it raised the CP's cost of collective action by guaranteeing that its leaders would be jailed whenever it undertook visible collective action (Tilly 1978: 100).

Over time the changing structure of political opportunities shapes the social movement sector of a given national state. In Canada, for instance, the move since the late 1970s "from consent to coercion" in the state's management of industrial relations has had a *repressive* impact on the labour movement, obliging unions to rethink their own strategies and to build mutually *facilitative* alliances with other progressive movements (Panitch and Swartz 1988, 1993; Carroll and Warburton 1995; Bleyer's chapter here). In addition movements – as agencies of change – can influence their own opportunity structures (Tarrow 1994b): the cumulative impact of environmental activism in raising public awareness in the 1970s and 1980s has made states and corporations more vulnerable to the claims of environmentalists relating to such matters as industrial pollution, wilderness preservation, and sustainable development.

The *repertoire of collective action* available to a given group is also subject to change over time. Demonstrations, strikes, and petition campaigns are forms of collective action that emerged with modernity. The strike – originally the means by which artisans threatened with proletarianization fought back by disrupting the production process and imperilling employers' profits – became the primary means by which workers advanced *new claims* regarding wages, working conditions, and employment security (Tilly 1978: 161). In the process strikes became a standardized element in the modern working class's repertoire of action. Yet depending on the structure of political opportunities, "At different times, political pressure, sabotage, demonstrations, and occupations of the workplace all become alternatives to striking. The workers' repertoire of collective action includes more items than the strike" (Tilly 1978: 166), and the same holds for other movements and other forms of collective action.

A final aspect of the political process model, implicit throughout this discussion, is its emphasis upon indigenous organization and mobilization of resources (McAdam et al. 1988: 697) – in contrast to the entrepreneurial mobilization model's emphasis upon outside leadership and resources from conscience constituents. Studies by Aldon Morris (1984) and Douglas McAdam (1982) dispute McCarthy and Zald's claim that the main impetus behind recent movements in the United States came from white middle-class liberal and elite groups. Morris shows that resources critical to the success of the civil rights movement came from within black communities, which took advantage of the pre-existing social organization provided by black churches. Invoking a Marxist analysis of power and interests, proponents of the political process model also question the claim that elite groups form an important conscience constituency for contemporary movements. Within the societal structure of power and privilege, the interests of such groups typically conflict with those of insurgent groups committed to social change. In this reading, to the extent that elite groups act to facilitate an SMO's mobilization or action, they are motivated not by a sincere sense of social conscience but by "a desire to contain or control the impact of the movement or to exploit the conflict for their own gains" (Pichardo 1988: 101).

Notwithstanding these internal disputes, RMT presents a reasonably coherent perspective within which social movements are depicted as deeply implicated in the social and political practices of modernity: in professionalization, in instrumental rationality, in formal organization, in distinctively modern repertoires of collective action, and in political opportunity structures that centre around the liberal-democratic state but span outward to include other agents in civil society. RMT offers a useful means of conceptually mapping the field of movement activism in *pragmatic* terms. That is to say, it attends to mechanism rather than substance (Eyerman and Jamison 1991: 39), to the "how" of contemporary movements – the practicalities of mobilization and strategic interaction in pursuit of collective goods. By attending to the character of a group's interest-base (never purely a matter of "objective location" but formed within the lived experiences of group members), to the nature of a group's resources and of the organizational forms within which those resources are mobilized, to the surrounding structure of opportunities for collective action (including the presence both of other mobilized groups with similar or opposed interests, and of the state) and the repertoire of collective action through which a group presses its claims, one can read a movement as a rational collective actor. By emphasizing the rationality of collective action, RMT serves to *validate* movements as credible political agencies.

In other respects the theory suffers from several weaknesses, and some of them have provoked considerable rethinking of the paradigm in recent years. Firstly, despite the virtues of an approach that recognizes the *rationality* of collective action instead of dismissing such action as governed by crowd psychology and panic, numerous sociologists have vigorously criticized the specific model of rationality embraced by RMT – rational-choice theory and its corollary in the free-rider problem (Fireman and Gamson 1979; Ferree 1992; Schwartz and Paul 1992). Each of the several grounds for this criticism calls into question the importance of the free-rider problem:

- in movement mobilization the cost/reward dichotomy becomes blurred. In addition to being a means towards a valued end, collective action can be "its own reward" in expressing the actor's deeply held values, including solidarity with others (Scott 1990: 121);
- in situations in which individuals come to share a sense of group fate, free-rider logic can be overridden by a "group logic" holding that "unless large numbers join the group effort, *nobody* will benefit" – in which case free-riding becomes irrational (Schwartz and Paul 1992: 214);

- the rational-choice criterion at the centre of RMT uncritically reflects the dominant, technocratic, and consumerist consciousness of corporate-capitalist society, yet movement activists – the principal critics of that consciousness and that society – make their choices not on the basis of anticipated personal gain but on the basis of moral commitments (Ferree 1992: 33). That is, for groups struggling for social justice the task of mobilization is not to make participation personally "profitable" to individual constituents but to promote an alternative morality that challenges the dominant calculus of selfish individualism.

RMT, then, falsely universalizes or *reifies* a certain form of rationality – the instrumental rationality of the isolated, profit-motivated individual – and misapplies this model to the sphere of movement politics.[9]

A second critique of RMT takes note of a related reification. As Myra Marx Ferree (1992: 47) indicates, "the prevalence of bureaucratically structured organizations and the individual utilitarian calculus in our society ... can make being structured like a profit-making company appear natural." In McCarthy and Zald's entrepreneurial mobilization version the formal organizations that dominate the economy and state in late modernity are reified as models for social movement organization. RMT thus contains an organizational bias that implies that "only formally organized bodies can act effectively" (Buechler 1993: 223). It tends to reduce movement politics to a slightly more exotic version of state-centred, mainstream politics, the principal difference being whether a formally organized interest group or movement organization is "inside" or "outside" the polity (Tilly 1978: 52-3). In contrast, contemporary feminism and other NSMs have been structured less around formal organizations than around "social movement communities" – informally organized networks of activists, many of them explicitly repudiating formal organization on ideological grounds and striving to create more egalitarian forms of organization (Buechler 1993). By the same token, the political-process version of RMT has an inbuilt tendency to reify the state – a formal organization *par excellence* – as the focal point of movement politics. In contrast, critics like Warren Magnusson (1990: 535) note that movement groups such as the Raging Grannies practise a lateral politics that not only avoids formal hierarchies among participants but focuses less on the state and more on extending the political and cultural sensibilities of the movement to more and more people.

This brings up a third criticism of RMT, namely its deficient theorization of *consciousness*. A highly restrictive focus on tangible *resources* has led RMT analysts to neglect the *interpretive* factors associated with mobilization (Benford and Hunt 1995: 85) – factors that take in the whole spectrum of human experience from psychology to ideology and culture. In recent years, RMT analysts have themselves been active in attempting to broaden the paradigm to take account of the social-psychological "micromobilization contexts" within which movements form and are maintained (McAdam, McCarthy, and Zald 1988).

A particularly important development in this regard is the concept of "framing." David Snow and Robert Benford (1992) define collective-action frames as emergent action-oriented sets of meanings and beliefs that inspire and legitimate social movement campaigns and activities. Simply put, such frames are interpretive schemata through which movements define certain conditions as unjust, attribute responsibility for the injustice, and point to alternatives that might be achieved through collective action (Snow and Benford 1992: 137; Tarrow 1994b: 122-3). By analysing the frames through which social movement organizations and activists define their political situations, theorists can gain insight into the cultural and psychological dimensions of mobilization. An integral aspect of mobilization involves a process of "frame alignment" (Snow et al. 1986), in which SMOs play an active role in establishing a congruence between their definitions of the situation and those of their constituencies. Without such a discursive and psychological alignment, few members of the constituency are likely to participate. That is, the human resources crucial to any movement cannot be pooled unless the organizations create a collective will to participate, and such a collective will requires a common interpretive understanding of issues, goals, and strategies. Recent research has explored the various kinds of "frame disputes" that occur between SMOs in a single movement (Benford 1993a) and the role of master frames in co-ordinating mobilization across diverse movements (Gerhards and Rucht 1992; Carroll and Ratner 1996a, 1996b).

Despite the hopeful development of frame analysis as a means of extending the paradigm, a fourth limitation of RMT has to do with its insensitivity to emergent features of social movement activism – features that may point away from the modernist practices of professional organization, state-centred campaigns, and a given repertoire of collective action. As Timothy Ingalsbee (1994: 140) writes, "Even though it was developed to explain the actions of post-War movements, RM theory has had no sense of the alternative oppositional forms of consciousness and action being created by contemporary social movements." This deficiency of RMT brings us to the alternative paradigm of New Social Movement theory, which can be read as a series of attempts to understand the specific kinds of movements – such as environmentalism, gay and lesbian liberation, and feminism – that have emerged in advanced capitalist democracies since the 1960s.

NEW SOCIAL MOVEMENT THEORIES

The various formulations known under the rubric of NSM theory replace RMT's root metaphor of "common interest" – viewed as a prerequisite to mobilization and collective action – with the metaphor of "collective identity" (Cohen 1985). NSMs are viewed as instances of cultural and political praxis through which new identities are formed, new ways of life tested, and new forms of community prefigured. Influenced by poststructuralist analyses, which view language as not simply descriptive but *constitutive* of social life (Shapiro 1981: 216), identity-based theories such as Alberto Melucci's (1989) endeavour to account for the emergent movements of the 1960s and 1970s, which seem to mark a departure from the state-centred, instrumentalist, and modernist political practices attributed to the old left.

According to Melucci (1989: 11), new forms of social control extending beyond state action have called forth new forms of popular resistance, consisting in the construction of collective identity and in the mounting of "symbolic challenges which publicize novel dilemmas and problems, the clarification of which requires new definitions of freedom and the recognition of new rights and responsibilities." Melucci supplants RMT's modernist collective actor, rationally pursuing interests on the stage of history, with a decentred view of movements as "networks composed of a multiplicity of groups that are dispersed, fragmented and submerged in everyday life, and which act as cultural laboratories" in the production of new meanings and forms of relationships (60). In this interpretation, new social movements are based not in material interest but in the *discursive practices* that construct new political subjects and create new political spaces in which to act, and may ultimately lead people "to rethink what we mean by community, or power, or reason, or passion, or consciousness, or energy, or security, or development, or democracy" (Magnusson and Walker 1988). This approach emphasizes the capacity of new movements to reshape the discursive terrain of politics in distinctive and potentially radical ways, through personal and cultural transformations that refuse accommodation with existing institutions.

Various versions of NSM theory were worked out in France, Italy, and Germany in the 1970s as intellectual responses to two historical developments. In the first place, it has become increasingly apparent that Western capitalism began to enter a new era in the 1960s and 1970s, variously described as "postindustrial," "post-Fordist," "postmodernity," "high modernity," "disorganized capitalism," and "programmed society." These appellations, though not entirely interchangeable, do highlight common themes concerning the diminution of bipolar class conflict, the growth of tertiary sectors, the expansion of cultural, consumption, and leisure activities, and especially the new types of social protest (Ray 1993: 60). In the second place, the specific events of May 1968, when students in France took the lead in mass protests while workers and Communists played a cautiously conservative role, unsettled the thinking of many European intellectuals, whose commitments to a strong tradition of Marxist theory and working-class struggle were thereby placed in question (Wallerstein 1989). The NSM theories that emerged out of this matrix attempt to account for the changed character of movement politics in the closing decades of the twentieth century, while responding to the crisis of Marxism, either by endeavouring to reconstruct historical materialism (for example, Habermas) or by explicitly breaking from Marxism and its problematic of capitalism, the state, and emancipation through collective action (for example, Melucci).

Melucci's Theory of Collective Identity

Alberto Melucci's theory of social movements and collective identity provides the best example of a clean theoretical break from the Marxist tradition. Influenced by his former teacher Alain Touraine (1981, 1988) – who is credited with having coined the term "new social movement" – Melucci's (1989) *constructivist* theory depicts contemporary movements as "nomads of the present" creating temporary spaces and identities for themselves within the complex societies of late modernity. For Melucci, the rise of complex society has meant a displacement of material production (and with it, class) from the centre of social life, and its replacement with the "production of signs and social relations" (1989: 45). By implication, power is no longer concentrated in a materially dominant class; it is dispersed across the various fields of society and increasingly is located in symbolic codes and forms of regulation. Melucci views social movements not as unified collective actors strategically pursuing their rational interests, but as variegated "networks of meaning" (1989: 58) whose collective identities are no more than tentative products of ongoing practices submerged in everyday life.

New social movements do not contest political power; their concern has "shifted towards a non-political terrain: the need for self-realization in everyday life" (1989: 23). Rather than adopt the modernist, state-centred quest for power, NSMs endeavour to *reveal and expose* "that which is hidden or excluded by the decision-making process. Collective protest and mobilization bring to light the silent, obscure or arbitrary elements that frequently arise in complex systems decisions" (Melucci 1994: 185). In exposing power, movements pose "symbolic challenges that overturn the dominant cultural codes" (Melucci 1989: 75). At the same time, the continuing construction of collective identity is also the lasting creation of new cultural practices within social movement networks. From the circulation of alternative media to psychotherapy, "recovery," and consciousness-raising, these everyday practices provide individuals with alternative ideological frames and self-understandings while furnishing the movement with a basis for solidarity and collective identity (Scott 1990: 124).

In challenging dominant codes, in constructing new identities such as the "out" gay or the independent woman, contemporary movements open public spaces free from control or repression, wherein questions surrounding ecology, gender, sexuality, and so on are rendered visible and collective. The upshot is a "democracy of everyday life" that has the potential, through movement activism, to become globalized. According to Melucci (1992: 73):

Social movements can prevent the system from closing upon itself by obliging the ruling groups to innovate, to permit changes among elites, to admit what was previously excluded from the decision-making arena and to expose the shadowy zones of invisible power and silence which a system and its dominant relations inevitably tend to create. By their action, they are already contributing to making visible the planetary challenges and to establishing a new transnational political arena in which people and governments can take responsibility for the dramatic choices that human beings are facing for the first time.

As important as these insights regarding collective identity and symbolic contestation are, Melucci's theory has been criticized by Amy Bartholomew and Margit Mayer (1992) on two telling grounds (see also Mooers and Sears 1992). Firstly, in his effort to overcome the "political reductionism" he discerns in theories like RMT, Melucci himself falls prey to a "cultural reductionism" that distinguishes too sharply between political action (which NSMs supposedly eschew) and collective identity formation (which NSMs supposedly embrace). Citing examples from the U.S. civil rights and women's movements, Bartholomew and Mayer argue that the construction of collective identity depends in part on present and past political engagements with the state. In reality, the political and cultural aspects of social movement formation are interdependent, yet Melucci's singular focus on everyday life, culture, and symbolic challenges blinds his analysis to this interdependence.

Secondly, unlike other concepts invoked to help explain the present era, such as "post-Fordism" (Ely 1993) or "disorganized capitalism" (Offe 1985a), Melucci's "complex society" fails to specify any structural relations of hierarchy and unequal power and therefore becomes "an analysis which treats codes/regulation as neutral in the sense of lacking inscription of relations of inequality and domination" (Bartholomew and Mayer 1992: 148). Such a view informs Melucci's claims that NSMs do not challenge power but merely render it "visible," and that "conflicts no longer have winners but may produce innovation, modernization and reform" (Melucci 1989: 76-8). In parting company with the historical legacy of Marxism, Melucci cedes the possibility of situating NSMs within the admittedly complex but deeply inegalitarian orders of contemporary capitalist democracies, in which political and economic power is substantially concentrated within identifiable state and corporate hierarchies.

Both major shortcomings in Melucci's theory – his cultural reductionism and his deficient concept of "complex society" – are symptomatic of a lack of *political economy* in his understanding of the context within which NSMs act. Other theories, however, do address this inadequacy, while maintaining an emphasis on the constructed and cultural character of social movement practice.

Habermas's Theory of System and Lifeworld

Jürgen Habermas, perhaps the most important German social theorist since Max Weber, has written relatively little on social movements per se. His most widely cited discussion of this topic takes up barely six pages of his two-volume *Theory of Communicative Action* (1987: 391-6). Yet his influence has been substantial. Analysts such as Arato and Cohen (1989), Friedmann (1989), Eyerman and Jamison (1991), Ray (1993), Eder (1993), and Schloshberg (1995) have pursued at length the implications of his perspective for contemporary social movements. Habermas views late modernity or "welfare-state capitalism" as a configuration of *system and lifeworld* – of macrostructures organized by markets and bureaucracies (system), and of meaningful everyday existence within "the relations and communications between members of a societal community" (lifeworld) (Hewitt 1993: 62).

Following Weber's lead, Habermas avers that the historical trajectory of the system has been towards *rationalization* in the very restricted sense of instrumental rationality. The capitalist's concern for maximizing profit and the bureaucrat's preoccupation with cost-benefit analysis are indicative of this tendency. The computer-programmed trading that in some measure drives contemporary capital markets and the obsessive concerns of most governments with eliminating state debts almost irrespective of the social consequences testify to the continuing dominance of instrumental rationality in the economy and state, which are the central components of the "system." But unlike Weber – and unlike Habermas's own critical theory forebears – Habermas argues that throughout modernity a parallel albeit suppressed process of rationalization has partially transformed the lifeworld from a sphere of meaning and identity based upon unquestioned conventions to an increasingly postconventional discursive formation, open to critical reason or "communicative rationality." A rationalized lifeworld entails a distinctive morality based not upon hierarchical authority and fixed traditions but upon self-reflexive individuals able to take the standpoint of others, aware of the relativity of personal values, and committed in their interactions to free and open discussion of issues. However, capitalism's central role in the making of modernity has given dominance to system rationality over the communicative rationality immanent in the lifeworld; indeed, rationalization of the lifeworld has been blocked in favour of its *colonization* by the money and bureaucratic power that issue from the political-economic system. Even so, critical reason grounded in a partially rationalized lifeworld has continued to constitute modernity's counterculture – "a permanent opposition to the dominant forms of instrumentality" that has surfaced in emancipatory social movements such as socialism and feminism (Ray 1993: 81). Like Karl Marx, Habermas thus argues that the possibilities for emancipation are immanent in modernity itself, but in place of Marx's revolutionary proletariat Habermas emphasizes the cumulative potential for releasing cognitive and moral learning processes within an increasingly rationalized lifeworld. "The task for Critical Theory, then, is to locate those social movements which are potential carriers of new learning potentials, which offer the capacity for widening the scope for a critical politics whilst defending endangered ways of life against systemic encroachment" (Ray 1993: 81).

At this point NSMs enter the scenario. Since the 1960s, conflicts have developed in advanced capitalist democracies that deviate from the institutionalized (and instrumentalized) pattern of electoral and trade-union struggle over material distribution. Indeed, the mechanisms of the welfare state – collective bargaining arrangements for unions and economic concessions to the disadvantaged – have muted the agency of old social movements such as the labour movement. The new conflicts appear in domains of social integration and cultural reproduction – in and around the lifeworld – and they are pursued not through statist channels but through the popular mobilization of protest. The new movements express a "silent revolution" in values and attitudes – a shift from the old politics of economic and social security to the new politics of participation, individual self-realization, quality of life, and human rights. They do not seek material compensation from the welfare state, but have to do with "the grammar of forms of life" (Habermas 1987b: 392).

Such NSMs may be defensive – in defending particularistic features of the lifeworld (for example, local community) from colonization by money and bureaucratic power; or they may be offensive, in trying out new ways of cooperating and living together, based in a communicative ethics. The offensive type is exemplified for Habermas in the universalistic emancipatory concerns of feminism, which in struggling against patriarchal oppression seeks to redeem promises of equality and justice anchored in modernity's unfinished project (Habermas 1987b: 393). Such movements are offensive in attempting to extend the public sphere – to transform hierarchical and instrumentalized social relations in the direction of communicative rationality – and thereby to democratize civil society while curbing the influence of money and power in human relations.

One can point, as do R. Eyerman and A. Jamison (1991: 89-90), to the example of the student movement of the 1960s, which involved a fundamental defence of freedom of speech and expression, a refusal to participate in the instrumentally rational "military-industrial complex," and an experimentation with new forms of learning – the teach-in, the free school, and a proliferation of alternative communications media – all under the rubric of a movement for a "democratic society." Today the same sort of democratic impulse informs many movements for local decision-making and participatory democracy – whether with regard to urban, ecological, or other issues.

Ray (1993) has noted the major weaknesses in Habermas's account of NSMs and advances a more adequate Habermasian formulation. Firstly, like virtually all the other theories, Habermas's has a Euro-North American centricity and takes as its object the nation-state.[10] Yet the system of power and money is increasingly global, and, likewise, networks of communicative action (including SMOs themselves) often cross national borders (Thiele 1993). Secondly, in asserting that NSMs are primarily concerned with symbols and identity – with the "grammar of social life" – Habermas veers towards a cultural reductionism not unlike Melucci's. As Ray (1993: 177) points out, "Not only is it difficult to separate symbolic from material objectives, but identity politics can involve a privatization of political questions into subcultural movements which eschew engagement with the state and thereby conspire in their own marginalization." Conversely, the demands of "offensive" movements such as feminism clearly concern more than a "border dispute" between system and lifeworld: they point to a structural transformation of economic, state, and interpersonal relations (Ray 1993; cf. Fraser 1989a).

The RMT and NSM formulations, then, have complementary weaknesses – RMT (particularly as represented by McCarthy and Zald) in its silence about cultural politics and communicative action; NSM theory (particularly as represented by Melucci) in its underestimation of the importance of structure in shaping movement activism. In another sense the perspectives converge in turning away from the problematic of *structural transformation* in favour of a conceptualization of activism in terms of either single-issue reforms (RMT) or the politics of everyday life (NSM theory). Yet these emphases risk losing sight of the crucial relation between political economy and political praxis.

In an era widely heralded by some and denounced by others as the triumph of capitalism, it is understandable that the question of movement activism and structural transformation might recede to the background of sociopolitical analysis: perhaps, like Weber's iron cage, capitalism is effectively escape-proof. Yet from a critical perspective, global capital's apparent triumph hardly mutes the importance of a careful analysis of capital, class, and political agency. While it is true, for example, that new social movements have been based mainly in variegated middle-class constituencies, on demographic grounds alone it is unlikely that significant social change could occur without substantial working-class involvement. Indeed, "In uncritically accepting the failure of new social movements to reach large numbers of working-class people (or treating this failure as a virtue) new social movement theory abdicates its responsibility to help the movements find direction" (Epstein 1990: 48). By the same token, in emphasizing the particularistic, fragmentary character of many contemporary movements, and in embracing their wariness to unify or even to construct a shared agenda, NSM theorists such as Melucci underestimate the extent to which these movements might share a universalist vision organized around such modernist themes as social justice and human rights (Epstein 1990: 47; Offe 1985b: 841-2; Adam's chapter here). L.A. Kauffman (1990) maintains that at

its limit the identity politics of everyday life that is celebrated by such theorists devolves to an antipolitics, with its attention to lifestyle and lack of collective organization actually mirroring the ideology of the capitalist marketplace (78). She calls instead for an approach that balances concerns about
identity "with an emphasis on solidarity, as well as with attention to other key
categories like interest and needs" (79).

On a more positive note, although analysts differ in their assessments of
the feasibility of synthesizing RMT and NSM formulations (cf. Cohen 1985;
Canel 1992; Ratner 1992; Ingalsbee 1994), the two theories do have complementary strengths. Certainly, RMT's emphasis on *social organization* as a
prerequisite to and concomitant of collective action is insightful and indispensable for a proper sociological analysis, as is the emphasis in NSM theories on *discursive struggle* as an integral aspect of movement politics. Both
perspectives also resonate in different ways with a third approach that has
proved valuable – both theoretically and strategically – in the analysis of social movements and social change: namely, the neo-Marxist problematic of
hegemony and counterhegemony, first enunciated by Antonio Gramsci.

SOCIAL MOVEMENTS AND COUNTERHEGEMONY

Elsewhere (Carroll 1990), I have argued that the conception of hegemony/
counterhegemony, which stems from Gramsci, enables social and political
analysts to build upon the insights of Marx while resisting the pitfalls of
economism, reductionism, and determinism commonly associated with orthodox Marxism. In the various essays and fragments that comprise the
Prison Notebooks (1971) Gramsci develops the conceptual architecture for a
"new politics" (Germino 1990) that recasts historical materialism as an
agency-oriented "philosophy of praxis."

Like Habermasian theory, Gramscian approaches to social movements
carry forward the classical Marxist project of *critical theory*; that is, they
refuse any sharp distinction between "fact" and "value" but instead combine
an analytical project of interpreting the world with a normative interest in its
emancipatory transformation.[11] They provide accounts of political praxis under modern capitalism that also entail normative frameworks for practising
politics. Just as Habermas's normative criterion of the "ideal speech situation" provides a basis for appraising communicative rationality (or its absence), Gramsci's vision of an alternative counterhegemony is less an *explanatory construct* than it is a *normative guide* for constructing lines of collective action. Gramscian analyses – even those like Ernesto Laclau and
Chantal Mouffe's that jettison much of the problematic of Marxism – entail a
combination of sociopolitical analysis of power/resistance and normative-
strategic commentary on the possibilities for transforming resistance in the
direction of emancipatory outcomes. In this respect, Gramscian theory differs from many of the RMT and NSM formulations whose core concepts –

mobilization, opportunity, repertoires of action, identities, codes – are meant to inform explanatory accounts of contemporary social movements.

But if both Habermas and Gramsci share a Marxist concern with not only analysing the social world but also consciously participating in its emancipatory transformation, they differ in other respects. Whereas Habermas's critical theory turns on his dual conception of *rationalization* (of system and lifeworld), Gramscian thought emphasizes the duality of *hegemony*.

On the one hand, in modern capitalist democracies "formal freedoms and electoral rights exist alongside the class inequalities of the bourgeois state; therefore relations of domination need to be sustained with the consent of the dominated" (Carroll and Ratner 1994: 5). Hegemony in this first sense refers to the practices, cultural codes, and social relations through which that consent is organized and the "system" stabilized. The bourgeoisie does not rule directly and singularly but participates as a leading social force in an ensemble of alliances with other groups, including intellectuals such as liberal economists and journalists who articulate perspectives that are consonant with the interests of capital. This ensemble of alliances constitutes a *hegemonic bloc*[12] that governs by presenting its interests as universal while selectively dispensing material concessions to pre-empt unified opposition from below. In this way, a "general interest" or collective identity is constructed that unites dominant and subordinate alike as members of the same political community. Nor is hegemony merely or even primarily a matter of state control. In Gramsci's analysis, power is both concentrated in the state and dispersed throughout organizations of civil society such as the school, church, family, and other agencies of socialization that diffuse hegemonic worldviews into daily life (Carroll and Ratner 1994: 6). This prevailing consciousness, to the extent that it is widely internalized as reflecting the natural order of things, becomes part of "common sense." When hegemony gains this kind of self-evident validity it fulfils a role that direct coercion can never perform: it mystifies power relations and public issues; it encourages a sense of fatalism and passivity towards political action; it justifies every type of system-serving sacrifice and deprivation. In short, hegemony works in various ways "to induce the oppressed to accept or 'consent' to their own exploitation and daily misery" (Boggs 1976: 40).

Hegemony in this first sense captures only part of the complex political and cultural realities of advanced capitalism, because civil society is not only a site for the organization of consent but also a field of *interest articulation* and *social struggles* (Urry 1981: 31). People's everyday lives are permeated not only by hegemonic practices that legitimate class, gender, sexual, and racial inequities, but also by acts of subversion and adaptation that can be likened to a continuing guerrilla warfare.[13] By maintaining a sense of the oppositional – of the "we" (the subordinates) who are not the same as "them" – popular-cultural resistances no doubt form "a necessary precondition, if not a necessary cause, of populist radical movements" (Fiske 1989: 161). But if resistance to hegemony remained fragmented and episodic, we would have little reason to invoke the concept of *counter*hegemony, with its hopeful prognosis for social and political transformation.

Contemporary social movements testify to the continuing relevance of counterhegemony as an orienting concept in social and political studies. As Melucci (1989: 38) suggests, a criterial attribute of a social movement is "the extent to which its actions challenge or break the limits of a system of social relations." Such challenges, such transgressions, necessarily entail a *disor-ganization* of consent, a disruption of hegemonic discourses and practices. In this sense, movements may be viewed *prima facie* as agencies of counter-hegemony. By mobilizing resources, and acting outside established political structures of state, parties, and interest groups, movements create inde-pendent organizational bases for advancing alternatives. By contesting the discourses of capital, patriarchy, industrialism, racism and colonialism, and heterosexism, movements destabilize the identities of compliant worker, subservient wife, or closeted queer, and create new ways of thinking about ourselves and the world around us. But if social movements can thus be viewed as counterhegemonic in the sense of *opposing* the existing order, a vexing question remains as to whether and how counterhegemonic politics can be defined in a more proactive, visionary sense.

Indeed, the concepts hegemony/counterhegemony have been employed in analysing movement politics and strategizing about social change in sev-eral ways. Here it is useful to distinguish the approach developed by Gramsci and elaborated by contemporary neo-Gramscians from the radical-pluralist analyses that are sometimes aligned explicitly with NSM formulations such as Melucci's. Each entails a distinctive reading of the relevance of social movements for emancipatory change in the (post)modern world.[14]

Neo-Gramscian Analysis
For Gramscians and neo-Gramscians the contradictions and crises of capital-ism limit the lifespan of any hegemonic order, and as the material basis for consent deteriorates opportunities open for constructing hegemony in a sec-ond sense, namely an alternative hegemony that unites various subaltern groups into a counterhegemonic bloc of oppositional forces committed to an alternative social vision. Such a vision frames social justice not in terms of one or another group's immediate concerns but "through a conception of the world attentive to democratic principles and the dignity of humankind" (Holub 1992: 6). Counterhegemonic politics involves both an engagement with capital and the state and a cultural politics in the realm of civil society and everyday life to build popular support for a radically democratic order.[15] Building an alternative hegemony thus entails a protracted "war of position" in which a coalition of oppositional movements wins space and constructs

mutual loyalties in civil society, the state, and the workplace, thereby disrupting and displacing the hegemony of the dominant class and its allies.

Neo-Gramscians hold that the NSMs of the late twentieth century express alternative social visions that are both symptomatic of a weakening or crisis in the post-World War II hegemonic order and imbued with the potential for a counterhegemony. The postwar era of the late 1940s to early 1970s saw the consolidation of what Gramsci presciently termed *Fordism* – a historically specific form of capitalism in which mass production and mass consumption coincided in a largely unionized workforce whose rising affluence cemented its support for a welfare-state capitalism that in turn guaranteed near-full employment and social benefits such as medicare and unemployment insurance. Thus, according to George Steinmetz (1994: 192): "Fordism was based on the centrality of industrial labor as producer and consumer. Male workers were relatively well-paid, and the welfare state propped up consumer demand during slack periods. The social movement sphere was monopolized by the official labor movement, centralized and bureaucratized labor unions; closely connected were social-democratic or labor parties engaged in neo-corporatist relations with employers' organizations and the state."

Yet while the labour-capital accord and welfare state served to organize consent to this hegemonic order, Fordism also engendered new areas of conflict as it developed, and NSMs emerged as voices of dissent – whether to the unbridled domination of nature in the mass-production system (ecology), to the enforced conformism of the male-dominated nuclear family (feminism, gay/lesbian liberation) or to the authoritarian, disabling ways in which the welfare state ascertains and serves people's needs (movements of welfare-state clients, citizens' movements for participatory democracy) (Steinmetz 1994: 193-4). In this interpretation, NSMs are not so much responses to the system's colonization of the lifeworld, but, rather, emerge among constituencies that were *left out* of Fordism's hegemonic bloc of white, male, established workers and managers (Cox 1987). As Joachim Hirsch (1988: 50) points out: "The new social movements are the real products of the social and political form of Fordist capitalism, Taylorism, mass consumption, social disintegration, normalized individualism, excessive exploitation of nature, and bureaucratization and state control. Their aim is, in sum, individual emancipation, the recovery of civil society, freedom from bureaucratic control and suppression, self-fulfillment, and 'the good life.'"

This is not to say that NSMs necessarily articulate a coherent social vision that might sustain a viable counterhegemonic bloc. New social movement politics is framed within a complex array of ideological discourses that include civil-libertarian liberalism, radical-democratic collectivism, and romantic conservatism (as in deep ecology's critique of industrialism; see Bookchin 1988). There is a political and ideological vagueness to these movements, which also suggests their capacity to yield new radical political concepts. According to Hirsch (1988: 51), "The new social movements are a contradictory battlefield in the struggle for a new hegemony."

Since the mid-1970s that field has become further differentiated. With the deepening crisis of Fordism and its deficit-ridden welfare state, and with the collapse of class compromise, new-right hegemonic projects have taken the place of corporate liberalism as ruling orientations. These projects, each with its national and even subnational specificity (Whitaker 1987; Carroll and Ratner 1989), celebrate the "free market" – and the "strong state" that is necessary to enforce the discipline of that market – as a basis for a post-Fordist historical bloc from which organized labour is marginalized in favour of flexible economic arrangements that facilitate the new quest for global competitiveness (Gamble 1988; Jessop 1988). The migration of organized labour from a core participant in the Fordist bloc to a peripheral element – or even an irrelevancy – in post-Fordism presents great challenges to the labour movement, but it also forces open new opportunities for remobilization, as Bob Russell's chapter here illustrates. In the 1990s, then, the legacy of Fordism has come to include both the NSMs that have arisen in part from its contradictions and a labour movement whose defence of rights and entitlements from the Fordist era is at the centre of resistance to the new right project (Carroll and Ratner 1995). With so many contradictions and exclusions, whatever historical bloc might be mobilized in favour of a post-Fordist regime is likely to be rather thin and potentially unstable (Cox 1987).

Claus Offe (1985b) suggests that in these circumstances the prospects for effectively advancing an alternative social and political paradigm – a counterhegemony – hinge on the nature of the alliances forged between NSMs, the traditional left, and the traditional right. NSMs appeal to diverse constituencies, including old middle-class elements (self-employed, professionals, business people), new middle-class elements (white collar employees), and "peripheral groups."[16] Depending on which of these constituencies shapes the agendas and identities of NSMs, any of three scenarios is possible. If traditional middle-class elements gain influence in framing NSM politics, the likely alignment will be with the traditional right; thus, for instance, environmentalism can be reframed within a discourse of ecocapitalism, sustainable development, and green consumerism that poses no challenge to existing power (Adkin 1992); or feminism can be recast within a "new conservative" frame that emphasizes equitable co-parenting without confronting institutionalized structures of male dominance (Stacey 1983). If the so-called peripheral groups gain influence in framing NSM politics, the likely alignment will be between traditional left and right. This would mean a renewal of the labour-capital accord in which peripheral groups remain peripheral and NSM claims are marginalized as sectarian. This scenario has been played out in the squatters' movements of urban Germany and the Netherlands (Offe 1985b), but the "ecoterrorism" practised by some direct-action envi-

ronmental groups and the separatist or "disengaged" politics of radical feminism might present other examples (Adamson, Briskin, and McPhail 1988).
Finally, if the new middle-class elements – white-collar employees particularly in the state sector – gain influence in shaping the NSM agenda, the likely
alignment will be with the left – with the labour movement and political parties
like Canada's New Democratic Party. Such an alliance, which Offe (1985b:
868) sees as "the only one of the three which could possibly lead to an effective and successful challenge of the old paradigm of politics," would require a
reframing of collective identities on both sides of the NSM/labour divide. As
Laurie Adkin (1992: 136) points out in the context of environmentalism:

> A counter-hegemonic discourse is formed by the rearticulation of ele-
> ments of existing identities, values, and conceptions of need. For exam-
> ple, it is when the "environmentalist" confronts the crisis of livelihood of
> the "worker," and when the "worker" confronts the destructive impacts of
> her livelihood that alternatives to the hegemonic model begin to be not
> only thinkable, but necessary.... As a consequence, the definition of con-
> flict changes from "environmentalists versus workers" to "those who de-
> fend the conditions for a possible and desirable life versus those who de-
> fend practices and relations that make impossible such a life.

There is some evidence that a confluence of labour and NSMs into a potentially counterhegemonic bloc may be under way. In Canada the turn of the
Canadian Labour Congress towards "social unionism" and its sponsorship of
the Action Canada Network – a coalition of labour and NSM organizations –
is indicative (Bleyer's chapter here), as is Carroll and Ratner's (1995) finding that many labour activists in Vancouver share the same sensibilities as
NSM activists regarding the importance of a politics of everyday life and alternative culture. A number of scholars have challenged the claim that the
political sensibilities and practices of NSM activists are qualitatively different
from those of "old" movements such as trade unionism (cf. Scott 1990; Plotke
1990; Calhoun 1993). The particularistic politics of autonomy, identity, and
lifestyle celebrated by theorists such as Melucci represent only one face of
NSMs, according to Barry Adam (in his chapter here). The other face is a
socialist one, not in the narrow, social-democratic sense but in the sense of a
universalistic concern for social justice produced out of the practices of new
social movements themselves. As Adam puts it here (p.53):

> This other face of new social movement mobilization includes a great
> many participants who understand their praxis within a comprehensive
> worldview that recognizes and supports subordinated people wherever
> they exist. Complex linkages already exist among feminist labour activ-
> ists, gay Third World solidarity activists, black ecologists, disabled peace
> activists, and so on, people working in organizations of more than one

movement. In addition to overlapping participants, the movements have tremendous influence upon each other in their analyses, strategies, and self-criticisms. These workers for social justice often understand themselves as socialists and represent a potential source of renewal generally ignored both by Marxism and new social movement theory.

Yet even if such commentaries invite us to entertain the possibilities of a confluence of movements around shared commitments to social justice, the challenges of building a counterhegemony are great. Although we can point to coalitions of social movements, viewed over time such coalitions seem inherently unstable and ephemeral. To what extent are such coalitions vehicles for a Gramscian "war of position," and to what extent are they mere mechanical and instrumental assemblages of convenience that decompose at the next political conjuncture (Carroll and Ratner 1989)? Put another way, to what extent does coalition politics bring a transformation of particularistic and instrumental "discourses of interests" into a universalist "discourse of rights" capable of informing counterhegemonic practice (Hunt 1990: 310)?

Then again, the pursuit of counterhegemony – of a coherent practical and ethical alternative – always carries with it the possibility of creating *new injustices*. By presenting their interests as the most universal, some movements can play a leading role that relegates others to the margins. Other groups can be left out of the "grand coalition" altogether, through exclusionary practices that may not even be evident to the activists themselves (see Michaud's chapter here). This issue has prompted some political theorists to endorse a "politics of difference" that takes NSMs' struggle for autonomy as the archetype in validating the specific claims of a plurality of aggrieved groups (Young 1990). Yet a politics of difference tends to *fragment* the social movement sector into many incommensurable units, an eventuality that may have the unintended consequence of actually reinforcing the existing hegemony (Carroll and Ratner 1994). There is no definitive solution to this quandary, but recalling Habermas's analysis of communicative rationality we can suggest that the effective pursuit of social justice within a counterhegemonic bloc requires a continuing reflexivity about the extent to which communicative practices foster equitable participation.

Radical Pluralism
In the radical-pluralist approach to theorizing hegemony/counterhegemony, the universalizing aspirations of a Gramscian (counter)hegemonic project are rejected as little more than variations on themes that have themselves been central to the hegemonic discourses of modernity. The quests for a shared vision, for a unified strategy, or for an integrated historic bloc are seen as totalizing political moves that carry potentially authoritarian subtexts. With regard specifically to contemporary social movements, there

are two versions of this argument: (1) Laclau and Mouffe's (1985) post-Marxist theory of hegemony, which breaks only in part from the Gramscian problematic, and (2) postmodern analyses such as those of Foucault, Deleuze and Guattari, and Patton, which realize a complete rupture.

In the post-Marxist version (discussed in greater depth in Dominique Masson's chapter) a poststructuralist critique of Marxism as a class-centred, essentialistic discourse leads Laclau and Mouffe to reconceptualize counter-hegemony by situating it not within the Marxist narrative of capitalism's revolutionary transformation into socialism, but within an alternative narrative centred around the struggle for democracy in the modern world. New social movements are said to mark "the emergence of new antagonisms and political subjects as linked to the expansion and generalization of the democratic revolution," a revolution that predates the rise of socialist movements but in which workers' struggles have been of "inestimable importance" (Laclau and Mouffe 1985: 166-7). A world of multiple social struggles in which identities have become unfixed contains no necessary linkages between struggles; any "unity" across struggles must be practically constructed through discursive chains of equivalence, which Laclau and Mouffe (178) term "hegemonic articulation": "It follows that it is only possible to construct this articulation on the basis of separate struggles, which only exercise their equivalential and over-determining effects in *certain* spheres of the social. This requires the autonomization of the spheres of struggle and the multiplication of political spaces, which is incompatible with the concentration of power and knowledge that classic Jacobinism in its different socialist variants imply."

Laclau and Mouffe retain much in Gramsci, including ultimately a commitment to the "ideal of socialism," which they subsume under their own master narrative of the democratic revolution (178). Yet their poststructuralist emphasis upon discursive articulation shifts the focus of analysis from the appraisal of concrete political-economic conjunctures to "the realm of the symbolic" (Bocock 1986: 106) while their critique of Jacobinism leads them to shift the meaning of hegemony from the assertion of moral and intellectual leadership within a coalition to the process of coalition formation *tout court* (Epstein 1990: 51).

Writers such as Paul Patton make a cleaner break from the Marxist-Gramscian reading of hegemony/counterhegemony. In his call for "a nomadic social theory, pluralistic and deterritorialized," Patton (1988: 30) delivers an important critique of Marxism's "will to totality," which, he holds, typically "enjoins us to address society as a whole and is accompanied by a commitment to a unitary project of emancipation that may leave no room for the specific, limited concerns of 'marginal' social movements. Alternatively, it may be applied to the dispersion of political subjects, calling for their recombination into a single, totalizing subject." The position of the totality is, according to Patton, the perspective of the state "whose duty it is to resolve conflicting interests, establish priorities, and institute hierarchies" (133). It is a position that by denying the specificity and irreducibility of autonomous social movements, by drawing those movements back onto Marxism's discursive field, militates against "the emergence of a creative radical political culture" (125), which these new movements portend. The deterritorialized alternative that Patton advocates bears a close resemblance to Melucci's (1989) view of new social movements as "nomads of the present." For the individual, this means taking the position of "the nomad – not so much the tribe as an activist in a movement, a militant on behalf of an avowedly partial perspective" (Patton 1988: 134). More broadly, and particularly in view of the difficulty of predicting from just where the forces to destabilize an entire hegemonic order might issue, Patton (131) states, "We should perhaps argue not for moving beyond the fragments toward the global politics of a new alliance but for multiplying the fragmentary effects of ... local campaigns" (cf. Rorty 1995).[17]

Patton's analysis is largely inspired by the innovative ideas of Gilles Deleuze and Felix Guattari (1987), but equally intriguing approaches draw upon the work of Michel Foucault.[18] Michael Wapner (1989), for instance, argues that in an era that has witnessed the end of grand theories and emancipatory politics, Foucault's thought furnishes a viable basis to envision strategies for social change. Foucault's *conception of power* as web-like – without any point of origin, agent, or predominant directionality – combined with his radically *decentred view of social reality* as lacking any essential, fundamental, determinate element – opens up an alternative approach to radical politics (Barrett 1991). The omnipresence of power means that no one site is privileged as a locale for political activism; hence a multiplicity of resistances is given validation within a Foucauldian perspective. Concomitantly, decentring removes the notion of necessity from social arrangements and thus "destroys the weight that guards against change: the notion that 'what is' is 'meant to be'" (Wapner 1989: 107).

Even so, with these fresh insights come difficult problems for those seeking social change. A conception of power as pervasive and ever-changing renders the idea of co-ordinated, strategic opposition problematic and makes it impossible to devise strategies for change, because "there is no target against which to organize or direct energy" (Wapner 1989: 108). Likewise, a decentred conception of the social can provide no countervision from which to critique the status quo and towards which to orient social change, and without a countervision of some sort the very reason to struggle for change loses force (Wapner 1989: 107). For Stephen Crook (1991: 158), such problems in postmodern thought pose a continuing threat of degeneration into nihilism: "When radical social theory entirely loses its accountability, when it can no longer give reasons, something has gone very wrong. But this is just what happens to postmodernism, and it is appropriate to use the over-stretched term 'nihilism' as a label for such a degeneration. This nihilism shows itself in two symptoms: an inability to specify possible mechanisms of change, and an inability to state why change is better than no change."

Postmodern accounts of contemporary social movements eschew the notion of counterhegemony as leadership – or at least as an articulated ensemble – of diverse forces in favour of the radical autonomy of movements. They reject the centring of transformative politics around a fundamental class – or at least the inclusion of that class in a strategy for transformation – in favour of a completely decentred politics that refuses to privilege any particular agent or structure. They supplant the metaphor of transformative politics as a "war of position," progressively shifting the balance of political and cultural forces in civil society, with metaphors of localized guerrilla warfare and nomadic militancy (Patton 1988: 131). Such postmodern movement politics can be called counterhegemonic only in the sense that they strive *to subvert* the hegemonic discourses that sustain subordination, not in the modernist sense of striving *for liberation* from oppression (cf. Kaufman 1994: 80). They disavow the modernist assumption that the struggle *against* the existing hegemony must also be a struggle *for* an alternative social vision. Thus, rather than espousing an approach to counterhegemony, radical pluralism ultimately becomes a position of anti-hegemony.

WHAT FOLLOWS

The chapters in this book convey a variety of perspectives from which we can understand social movements and the politics of counterhegemony in contemporary Canada. Some chapters, concentrating on issues pertaining to movements as a diverse category of praxis, are grouped under the rubric of "social movements in theory." Others, focusing on particular cases of movement formation and collective action, are grouped as "social movements in practice." The distinction between theory and practice is best grasped not as a division between mutually exclusive categories but as a dialectical relationship. Keynes is well known to have said that there is nothing so practical as a good theory; Mao held that "knowledge begins with practice, and theoretical knowledge is acquired through practice and then must return to practice."

The theoretical discussions that follow explore some of the most pressing conceptual and philosophical issues bearing upon contemporary movements. Barry Adam and Dominique Masson probe some of the implications of the turn from political economy to culture in NSM theories such as Melucci's and in post-Marxist theories such as Laclau and Mouffe's. For Adam, the new social movements have traded the old left's faith in the myth of the revolutionary break for a cool-eyed pragmatism and through their praxis have made visible a set of apparently autonomous systems of domination, including patriarchy, heterosexism, structural racism, and the domination of nature. Yet the tendency for NSM theory to deal summarily with these diverse movements seriously hampers its coherence, while its view of NSMs as primarily "cultural" occludes these movements' heavy engagements in contesting the structural power of capital and the state. The problems in NSM theory inhere in the curious way in which it has abandoned what is most indispensable in Marxism – its critical analysis of capitalism – while retaining one of traditional Marxism's least appealing features – its penchant for fitting a great variety of social movements into a very few broad generalizations (with NSMs displacing class as the central category).

Masson, likewise, argues that the turn to the discursive in contemporary social movement theory has been marred both by a lack of analytic detail on the specificity of movements' signifying practices and by an inattention to the field of power relations in which discursive struggles are mounted and have effect. She provides an instructive discussion of the three most prevalent attempts to theorize social movements' symbolic activity – Melucci's pathbreaking formulation of "symbolic challenge," Laclau and Mouffe's conception of articulatory practices in the struggle for hegemony, and the efforts of RMT analysts such as David Snow and Robert Benford to theorize the strategic use of collective action frames. Drawing upon the work of Foucault and Bourdieu, and critical discourse analysts influenced by them, she presents an alternative analysis of language and discourse that emphasizes their *performativity* in social and political struggles and their *boundedness* in constraining what can be said and done by given agents. Masson points the way towards a more adequate account of discursive struggle, sensitive to the concrete actors who produce and enunciate symbolic challenges, to the political fields and institutional sites where discursive practices occur, and to the larger social processes in which they are implicated.

From different vantage points, Catriona Sandilands and Warren Magnusson take up a key metatheoretical issue in the analysis of social movements, namely the question of how the political is to be understood in our late-modern age. Both authors provide compelling arguments against the traditional view – still influential in political science – that the political is that which is contained within or oriented towards the state, but Sandilands's discussion is grounded in her reflections on the difficulties in "politicizing the environment," while Magnusson explores the destabilizing implications of globalization for "the political," "the social," and other master categories of modern thought.

The archetypal NSM is probably, as Adam notes, the greens, so it is with some irony that Sandilands describes environmental groups – ostensibly the carriers of new codes and sensibilities – as participating in the *depoliticization* of the environment. As environmentalism has embraced a realist politics of professionalism, expert discourse, and interest-group machinations – and as green consumerism has supplanted open political conversation about environmental issues – "the environment" has become less a subject of public discourse and more an object of administration and bureaucracy, of markets, experts, and consumers. For Sandilands, repoliticizing the environment is tied up in the larger Habermasian project of resuscitating a specifically public sphere in which democratic conversation holds sway over technical interest brokering. "The political" is recognizable not as a set of contentious issues or as a complex of practices arrayed around the state, but as "a process of opening – to diverse publics, to diverse and uncertain possibilities."

Magnusson's chapter reminds us that distinctions we take as foundational – for instance, those between social order and social movements, between the political and the social – are no more than scientifically ratified sedimentations from earlier struggles. Indeed, Magnusson invites us to think of the human world not in terms of such fixed categories or "structures" but as a multiplicity of movements, some of which (for example, capitalism, statism) have amassed enough authority to secure the appearance of fixity but all of which are political in the Aristotelian sense of seeking to establish or maintain distinctive ways of life. In a world in motion, where processes of globalization have brought forward an urban system that resembles a single global city, movements move in relation to each other, thereby creating their own spaces in ways that often transcend the reified boundaries of modern politics. Ultimately, Magnusson's plea is for a critical theory that can guide political judgement in an era of new challenges and opportunities raised by the global city and the decentred state.

Together these chapters address some of the key theoretical issues in the study of contemporary social movements, while endeavouring to move beyond what the authors regard as current impasses. In quite different ways, they critically scrutinize some of the most prevalent concepts and substantive claims of social movement theory. What emerges from these encounters is a variegated call for a style of theorizing that is mindful of its own political investments, suspicious of reified abstractions, and attentive to complexities of power, discourse, and politics in a globalizing world.

The seven case studies that take up the theme of social movements in practice employ a variety of formulations to explore the organizational and discursive facets of movement politics in Canada. Bob Russell's inquiry into the prospects for labour as a social movement combines recent examples from Saskatchewan and Ontario with an informative history of Canadian labour that highlights some of the strategic dilemmas unions have faced and continue to face in their struggles with capital and the state. Peter Bleyer examines the Action Canada Network, a coalition of social movements formed initially in opposition to the Canada/U.S. Free Trade Agreement, but which has subsequently broadened its agenda to promote an alternative vision of Canada's future. David Long charts the course of the mobilization of Native peoples into an Aboriginal rights movement with international ties.

His focus on the Lubicon First Nation reveals much about the contemporary search for common ground among diverse collective actors. Sharon Dale Stone emphasizes the strategic importance of *visibility* in the amorphous but subversive struggles of lesbians, a diverse group doubly marginalized by sexual orientation and gender. Jacinthe Michaud analyses the interplay between the changing practices of the Quebec welfare state and the attempts by feminists – particularly through the women's health centres movement – to construct a counterhegemonic project that can represent the interests of women in all their diversity, without being either co-opted into dominant state discourses or excluded from wide politico-cultural influence. Gary Kinsman draws upon Dorothy Smith's (1990a) incisive analysis of the role of documents in actualizing the relations of ruling, applying her insights to the relationship between state and activists in the field of AIDS organizing. Finally, Aaron Doyle, Brian Elliott, and David Tindall make use of frame analysis in their case study of the complex interactions between the B.C. Forest Alliance and the mass media.

These case studies convey a strong sense of place that contributes to the idiographic tradition of Canadian studies in sociology and political science. In recounting the stories of the Lubicon in Alberta, of AIDS activists in St. John's, of feminists in Quebec, of counter-environmentalism in British Columbia, and of lesbians and labour activists across Canada, the chapters offer a multiplicity of vantage points on the "struggle for historicity," which is a struggle for the future of Canadian society.

At the same time the studies revisit debates around contemporary social movement theory and the politics of counterhegemony. For instance, in their respective accounts of the Action Canada Network and the Canadian labour movement, Bleyer and Russell explore the key role of labour in defending social entitlements and (prospectively) in counterhegemonic coalition formation. By the same token, Long's study of the Lubicon Cree's land rights struggle highlights the potential benefits and problems that social differences and similarities bring to social movement coalitions, and Stone argues that the lack of consensus in lesbian politics should be viewed not as a sign of failure but as a reflection of creative diversity in opinions and actions. Doyle, Elliott, and Tindall and Michaud use discourse-oriented approaches to good advantage in their respective examinations of environmentalist politics and feminism. Doyle, Elliott, and Tindall focus on a corporate-sponsored countermovement – an instance of collective mobilization in defence of bourgeois hegemony – while Michaud considers the formation of a feminist self-help discourse that is counterposed to scientific medicine and welfare-state regulation; and explores the challenge of integrating diverse identities into the counterhegemonic project.

These studies of movements "in practice" acknowledge the continuing strategic importance of the state – whether it is construed as a multiplex structure or as an ensemble of movements – yet they refuse to reduce "the political" to exclusively state-centred practices. Politics is not merely contained within a body politic. Indeed, it is inscribed upon the bodies of human agents, and no less upon the "environment" in which those agents move. Michaud and Kinsman explore the issues of gender, health, and sexuality that centre upon the politics of the body, yet they also emphasize the role of state regulation in striving to control the play of discourse and in establishing dependency relationships that constrain collective action by selectively channelling resources into state-designated venues. Sandilands contends that it is an open question as to whether "the environment" becomes a term of bureaucratic administration and marketing or an aspect of democratic conversation. Doyle, Elliott, and Tindall detail the efforts of such corporate spin-doctors as Burson-Marsteller to mobilize an anti-environmentalist discourse around a jobs-versus-trees frame, which resituates "the environment" as a term in the instrumentalist discourse of industrial production.

Although our seven case studies range widely across the terrain of contemporary movement politics, the book as a whole unavoidably leaves important areas of social struggle unexamined. A cursory list of significant movements not directly considered here includes anti-racist struggles, gay activism, the peace movement, human-rights and international solidarity groups, the antipoverty movement, a student movement showing signs of rebirth, and a nationalism in Quebec whose hegemony among the Québécois poses deep challenges to the viability of the Canadian state. These omissions are regrettable, and they underline the provisional nature of the present work, which offers no more than a few selective glimpses of the current political landscape. Perhaps the incomplete yet suggestive character of this collection will serve to inspire others to look carefully, critically, and hopefully upon the changing field of movement politics, in Canada and beyond.

Such scrutiny will find a useful point of departure in R.S. Ratner's afterword, which highlights some of our recurring themes while exploring both the challenges posed by the globalization of capital and the prospects for a democratic globalization-from-below in the form of transnational social movements.

NOTES

1. See especially the essays "Social Organization and the Changing Structure of the Community" [1942], "The Religious Sect in Canadian Economic History" [1946], and "The Frontier in the Development of the Canadian Political Community" [1954], in Clark (1968). For a thoughtful appraisal of Clark's contribution to Canadian sociology, see Harrison (1981).
2. As Clark put it in his essay, "The American Takeover of Canadian Sociology" (1976: 132): "Perhaps, in the end, what is most required on the part of the sociologist is a feel for his society. That feel can only be got by knowing its history and having a strong sense of identification with it."

3. See Kostash (1980) for an engaging if journalistic account centred around the movements and cultural politics of the times.
4. This confluence of movements and social analysis was particularly strong in the cases of feminism and Canadian nationalism. Several of the essays in Carroll et al. (1992) highlight this aspect of the formation of sociology in Canada.
5. For a thorough guide to this literature through the mid-1980s, see Drache and Clement (1985).
6. Noteworthy exceptions include Pinard's (1971) study of the rise of Social Credit in Quebec, which relied mainly upon Smelser's (1963) theory of collective behaviour; Clark's (1975) introduction to *Prophesy and Protest: Social Movements in Twentieth-Century Canada*, which drew upon Smelser's and several other American-based social movement theories; and Brym's (1978) comparative analysis of regional protest movements in Alberta, New Brunswick, and Saskatchewan, which incorporated ideas from Tilly's (1978) political-process version of resource mobilization theory.
7. There was, of course, much more to the U.S. literature than can be discussed here, and many of the formulations offer important insights when read with a critical eye. For an overview of the various theories that predominated in the United States until the late 1970s, see Wood and Jackson (1982).
8. See also the collection of essays edited by Harries-Jones (1991), which draws some important connections between advocacy, empowerment, and social movements in a Canadian context.
9. The tendency in RMT to reify instrumental rationality contrasts sharply with the use of an alternative concept of "communicative rationality" in Habermas's version of NSM theory. Cohen (1985) offers a useful comparison on this point.
10. As Fraser (1989a) argues, Habermas also fails to take account of the persistence of gendered power in both lifeworld and system – a failure that inspires Fraser to advance some important feminist reformulations.
11. With characteristic eloquence, Marx (1968: 30) first enunciated this position in his eleventh thesis on Feuerbach: "The philosophers have only *interpreted* the world, in various ways; the point, however, is to *change* it."
12. On the use of this concept in the analysis of political-economic structures and transformative movements see especially Cox (1987: 298-391).
13. De Certeau's work has been particularly suggestive in this regard. Through the "murmurings" of everyday practices, "an uncodeable difference insinuates itself into the happy relation the system would like to have with the operations it claims to administer. Far from being a local, and thus classifiable, revolt, it is a common and silent, almost sheeplike subversion – our own" (1984: 200).
14. A third approach to hegemony/counterhegemony – that of Lenin – predates Gramsci's theoretical breakthroughs. For a discussion of Leninist, Gramscian, and radical-pluralist conceptions, see Carroll and Ratner (1994).
15. The task of building an alternative hegemony affords a useful comparison between neo-Gramscian theory and RMT. One major practical barrier to such counterhegemonic formation is the permanent scarcity of resources that oppositional groups must cope with, which as RMT emphasizes leads each SMO to prioritize the immediate interests of its constituency in its work. On this score, RMT is instructive in depicting relationships between social movement organizations as a *competition* for resources and strategic advantage (Zald and McCarthy 1987; Marx and McAdam 1994: 102-4). So long as interests are defined sectorally this dynamic will tend to be operative, and cross-movement coalitions will tend to have an opportunistic, instrumental character (Carroll and Ratner 1989: 46). It is

only by consciously promoting broadly resonant counterhegemonic discourses and practices that the factional strife issuing from such competition can be significantly reduced, if not overcome. Similarly, only by promoting a compelling alternative vision to the hegemonic ideology of liberal individualism can oppositional movements overcome the barrier to mobilization posed by egoistic rational-choice logic. It is precisely in circumstances where liberal individualism is hegemonic that the "free-rider problem" is indeed a problem for oppositional groups.

16. Namely "decommodified" categories on the margins of social and political participation such as the unemployed, youth, and students. See Offe (1985b).

17. Patton's critique of Marxism has not gone unanswered. Fields (1988: 152) has replied with a "defense of political economy and systemic analysis." Among the points registered by Fields, two bear repeating here. Firstly, Fields argues that Patton's critique is fashioned around a series of unacceptable dualisms, such as that between destruction of a group's collective identity and total autonomy. Fields maintains that an emancipatory group *can* have a utopian vision without attempting to hegemonize others. "It can, indeed, be engaged in a project for the creation of a more humane world respecting 'difference.' But it cannot do this unless it transcends its own boundaries, or 'territory,' in two ways: (1) it comes to an understanding of the systemic impediments to its project, and (2) it reaches out to other groups and engages in mutual expressions of solidarity and strategic networking."

    Secondly, Fields (1988: 154) notes that the postmodern thrust towards single-issue strategic approaches to social transformation fails to challenge and may even reinforce the hegemonic ideology of liberal practicality. By the same token, "Totally disconnected efforts are more likely to be frustrated or assimilated by the dominant structures than are efforts that are part of a larger social movement." Fields asks, "What does it mean to argue for a purely local action and strategy in this world so far apart from a homogeneous, aboriginal community? It means the opposite of putting things together, the opposite of understanding how oppressions relate to and reinforce each other. It not only means difference, for one can accommodate difference with a notion of mediation. No, it also means *fragmentation*. To whom is fragmentation of the oppressed useful?"

18. Foucault has probably been the most important philosophical influence in radical-pluralist analyses of new social movements. In the contemporary resistances to the power of men over women, of medicine over population, of administration over everyday life, and so on, Foucault (1982: 210-12) saw a series of dispersed struggles revolving around the question, "Who are we?" Foucault (1984: 46) endorsed the "partial transformations" such struggles portend and advised critical thinkers to "turn away from all projects that claim to be global or radical." For a comparison of Gramsci and Foucault on the question of hegemony, see Smart (1986).

POST-MARXISM AND
THE NEW SOCIAL MOVEMENTS

Barry D. Adam

Much of the recent social theory generated around understanding the 1990s has turned from political economy to culture in identifying the forces for social change. New social movement theory, in particular, has tended to put forward a claim that advanced capitalist societies are in the midst of a historical shift from conflict and concern around issues of social class and economics to issues of culture and identity. The various "post"-al theories (post-Communism, poststructuralism, postmodernism) have typically separated new social movements from questions of political economy by placing them on the side of "culture," thereby denying the ways in which the origins, identities, and development of subordinated categories of people remain fully rooted in the dynamics of advanced capitalism.

The proposition that the new social movements represent movements of cultural defence has failed to take into account their ongoing struggles with the state and capital. It has also limited recognition of the scope of new social movement practices that exceed the conservation of culture and involve the active construction and innovation of new social relations. To confine them to a form of cultural expression is to ignore their effects on the amplification of civil liberties, on curbing the violence of state and capitalist institutions, and on more equitable distribution by employers and bureaucrats. Samuel Bowles and Herbert Gintis (1986: 177) characterize this as a project "to continue the expansion of personal rights and thus to render the exercise of both property rights and state power democratically accountable."

The implications of this shift for social theory are twofold: first, a good deal of "post-Marxist" and "new social movement" theorizing ignores or underestimates the enduring effects of the political economy of advanced capitalism in shaping the trajectory of the new social movements, thereby neglecting the strengths of certain well-established Marxian analyses; and second, at the same time, this contemporary theorizing fails to understand much about the concrete struggles of new social movement organizations, thereby displaying certain of the traits of the orthodox Marxian theories it intends to transcend. These traits include the reification of new social movements into decontextualized, monolithic categories in order to solve pregiven theoretical problems; and they include top-down theorizing, which fails to "do its homework" concerning its objects of analysis.

In other words, certain trends in post-Marxist and new social movement discourses both retain *too little* Marxian analysis, thereby abandoning the salience of the modern world system in contemporary social change, and retain *too much* Marxism in their search for new referents for old categories.

THE POSTWAR KEYNESIAN COMPROMISE

Much of the thinking in postwar political economy has turned towards accounting for the relatively stable, hegemonic form of "late capitalist," liberal-democratic societies. Syntheses of the political economy tradition offered by Jürgen Habermas (1975) and Claus Offe (1984) in Germany, and Bowles and Gintis (1986) in the United States, identify similar elements in the formula that apparently "worked" for the Group of Seven nations. According to these theories, the internal tensions of advanced capitalism have been managed over the last fifty years by a series of reforms and compromises that have institutionalized fundamental conflicts under state supervision and "bought off" potentially threatening social sectors. The containment of politics by electoral systems, the management of class conflict through collective bargaining, and the retention of a "reserve army of labour" through social welfare programs have served to restabilize modern capitalism while leaving *grandes bourgeoisies* free to wield capital at will.

But the Keynesian formula ran up against a series of limitations that called into question the stability of the "truce" among social forces guaranteed by the welfare state. The apogee of the expansionist state was marked in the 1950s and early 1960s by uninterrupted economic growth and an "end of ideology" debate. The 1970s and 1980s exposed some of the tenuousness of this arrangement in terms of impending crises in the modern world system, in state fiscal capabilities, in ecology, and in family and gender. The "mopping up" operations of the welfare state became decreasingly capable of compensating for the growing damage generated by the market, plunging even the richest governments into a deficit spiral in order to maintain health, education, and social services at 1960s levels. The globalization of production, while eroding local tax bases, sharpened international competition, leading governments to compete against each other with corporate subsidies and tax concessions to stem the export of jobs. Unbridled economic expansion began to expose just how limited were the ecological prerequisites that had been taken for granted in the construction of postwar stability.

Recent history, then, has uncovered a problematic that is both a part of and beyond the conventional framework of political economy. Upon the increasingly exposed, but once taken-for-granted, prerequisites of modern capitalist development has arisen a heterogeneous and discontinuous array of social movements with an unfamiliar relationship to the usual boundaries of production and distribution. Several trends in contemporary social theory, both "inside" and "outside" Marxism, moved to assess the displacement and proliferation of social conflicts on the multiple sites apparently exemplified by the new social movements. But much of "new" theorizing around these issues has too quickly abandoned the engagement of, for example, problems of race, gender, and ecology with the dynamics of state and capital. At the same time, political economy discourse has remained too inflexible and reductionist in making sense of the current conjuncture.

DILEMMAS OF MARXISM

These historical developments have posed a series of dilemmas to Marxian thinking since the 1960s: most notably, intensified scrutiny of the nature of the working class and its theoretical role as a subject in history, examination of the myth of the revolutionary break, a questioning of *étatisme* as a solution to capitalism, and attention to the contemporary mobilizations of people around multiple categories of subordination.

Jean Cohen (1982: 4-13) and Ernesto Laclau and Chantal Mouffe (1985) have offered trenchant critiques of the many attempts to rework and relocate the received model of working-class historical agency expressed in ideal-typical form as the nineteenth-century male, English, industrial working class of Marx and Engels. These reworkings have included a number of expansions (Erik Wright), reductions (Nicos Poulantzas), and redefinitions (early André Gorz) of an "essential" working class in advanced capitalist societies, as well as attempts to abandon it in the North in order to rediscover it in the Third World (for example, McCarney 1990). Yet the heterogeneity of the lived experiences of the inhabitants of the "working class" category has forced a reconsideration of its content and the role assigned to it by Marx in *The Holy Family*.

The lengthy decay of the Marxian concentration on the "working class" has proceeded along several lines. Gorz (1989) has pointed out the limitation of the Marxian preoccupation with workers and capitalists, in light of a widening gulf between a relatively privileged class of workers and growing numbers of people tenuously linked to or *excluded* from the means of production altogether through underemployment and unemployment. In A. Sivanandan's (1989: 11) words, alienation from the means of production also entails recognition of "the new underclass of ... ad hoc and temporary workers ... refugees, migrants, asylum seekers: the invisible workers who have no rights, no claims, no roots, no domicile, and are used and deported at will."

The "working class" experienced by its inhabitants is marked by rifts and transitions around homelessness, incarceration and institutionalization, receipt of transfer payments, ghettoization and dispossession, deskilling and skills obsolescence, and immigration status. Split labour markets, articulated around race and sex, engender life-chances experienced through the particularities of being female, Afro-American, Aboriginal, Arabic, or Latino, as much, if not more than, as a "worker" per se (Hall 1988). Out of the shifting employment patterns in modern capitalist economies has come talk of the decentred subject, the deconstruction of the class category, and the need to come to grips with diversity even in order to realize classical Marxian goals of understanding and empowering people at their workplaces.

Even among revolutionary movements, the last twenty-five years have been an era of pragmatism and reappraisal. The record of both classical and recent revolutionary seizures of the state has shown the limitations of state-directed change in the face of internal and external structural exigencies (Skocpol 1979; Wallerstein 1989a). Even thorough-going social and political revolutions face virtually insurmountable problems in reordering social hierarchies, whether because of the power of the modern world system guaranteed by imperial military forces and economic blocs, or because of the power of existing domestic social formations, which can actively or passively resist the threat of lost privilege, however small. For such revolutionary states as Sandinista Nicaragua, which pursued a pragmatic path abjuring the destruction of whole classes of people, social change came to a halt as the result of the alliance of the U.S. imperium with the local church and bourgeoisie, combined with the subsequent distress of peasants and workers who were forced to live through a decade of economic deterioration. More militant and purist solutions to these problems have resulted elsewhere in terrorist states that indulged in genocide to remove their capitalist classes, along with often sizeable sections of recalcitrant or dissenting peasants, workers, professionals, artists, and intellectuals, in the end imposing new social hierarchies that have proved both fearsome and repressive. Among revolutionary movements of the 1980s, both the Salvadorean Farabundo Martí National Liberation Front and the African National Congress steered away from the myth of the revolutionary break in favour of strategies that augmented the social, political, and economic lives of the people without presuming the immediate seizure of the state as a prerequisite. One need not embrace the postmodernist claim of a general "fall of metanarratives" to recognize the decay of the Leninist model and the multiplication of analytical and practical sites in the struggle to gain mastery over the conditions of one's own life.

Revaluation of the Marxian working class has also been set in place by popular mobilizations around other inequalities no less ubiquitous and pernicious than the alienation of labour. Immanuel Wallerstein (1989b) remarks,

"After 1968, none of the 'other' groups in struggle – neither women nor racial 'minorities' nor sexual 'minorities' nor the handicapped nor the 'ecologists' ... would ever again accept the legitimacy of 'waiting' upon some other revolution." Or in Cohen's (1982: 13) words, it was no longer enough that "other groups are left to fend for themselves or to bask in the ideological hegemony of the proletariat." New social movement theory took the step towards "a phenomenology of class, i.e. recognition of social differentiation of life chances where it exists" (Adam 1978: 128).

DILEMMAS OF NEW SOCIAL MOVEMENT THEORIES

Yet new social movement theories have scarcely remedied or replaced the Marxian dilemmas. Instead they have produced new difficulties. Much theorizing about new social movements has adopted Habermas's (1987b: 343) premise that the new social movements are all about defence against "the bureaucratization and monetarization of public and private areas of life." Alain Touraine (1988: 122) sums up the current intellectual shift: "From the industrial era we have inherited the image of two opponents, the capitalists versus the working class, confronting each other on a ground and with weapons that are those of the ruling class.... Today, on the contrary, the image that prevails is that of an impersonal and integrating central apparatus that controls, beyond a 'service class,' a silent majority, and scattered around the latter are a number of excluded, confined, underprivileged, or even denied, minorities."

Marxian analysts have critically scrutinized this image by finding the class composition of the new social movements wanting. Some non-Marxists (such as Dalton and Kuechler 1990) have jettisoned history and political economy altogether in order to locate the new social movements in a global shift towards "postmaterialist values." Both trends have generated confused discussions around a supposedly new "Identity politics." Yet what is perhaps most remarkable about both sets of commentators are their shared premises and limitations, which: (a) underplay the salience of political economy for the development of new social movement identities and activities; (b) ignore the diversity of the new social movements both among themselves and internally; and (c) become caught up in the claim of "newness" of the "new" social movements and the attendant claim of postmodernism.

A somewhat syncretic thesis on the origins of the new social movements, drawn from the work of Habermas (1975), Lefèbvre (1976), Offe (1984), Boggs (1986), and Bowles and Gintis (1986), might follow these lines: crises of advanced capitalist societies, which have been "managed" through the modern Keynesian state, have nevertheless been displaced onto crises of social reproduction. In other words, the ossification of electoral and party systems, combined with the bureaucratization of trade unions, has resulted in a displacement of political activity onto new sites which have been subject to the "monetarization and bureaucratization of the spheres of action of employees and of consumers, of citizens and of clients of state bureaucracies" (Habermas 1987b: 386). Habermas (1987b: 392), in particular, asserts that the purpose of new social movement mobilization is "primarily one of ... defending and restoring endangered ways of life," namely addressing issues of "quality of life, equal rights, individual self-realization, participation, and human rights." Habermas curiously enough exempts the women's movement from this characterization, naming it as part of the "tradition of bourgeois-socialist liberation." He then identifies an extensive list of other new social movements[1] as fundamentally *defensive* movements of "resistance and withdrawal" with "historical parallels ... in the social romantic movements of the early industrial period." These movements are further subdivided between reactionary, status defence movements, such as Christian fundamentalism and tax protests, and all other new social movements by characterizing the former as engaged in the "defence of traditional and social rank (based on property)" and the latter as "defence that ... tries out new ways of cooperating and living together" (Habermas 1987b: 394).

This defensive image appears to be widely endorsed among new social movement theorists. Herbert Kitschelt (1985; see also Eder 1985) typifies them as aiming "at incrementally limiting the expansion of commodity relations and administrative control under conditions of 'bounded rationality.'" Alberto Melucci (1980) considers them a "revolt against change directed from above" where the body is a "cultural locus of resistance and of desire ... opposed to rationalization." Carl Boggs (1986: 174) sums up the project of the new social movements as "a struggle to recover community that had been destroyed by rampant urbanization; revulsion against the worst manifestations of economic modernization and the consumer society; and a scepticism towards conventional ideologies of whatever sort – liberalism, Marxism, Leninism, even anarchism." A variant from the regulation school runs: "Their decentralised organizational form; their social heterogeneity; their fluctuating and localised targets and goals; and their predominantly antistate, antibureaucratic, and, in some sense, 'populist' character ... are reactions to the Fordist form of capitalist societalization and to the political structure of the Fordist security state" (Hirsch 1988: 49).

The search for the support base for the new social movements has produced a number of proposals usually centring around various fractions of the middle class (Steinmetz 1994: 183), although Lawrence Wilde (1990) argues for a working-class foundation. Sometimes these movements have the look of a somewhat self-indulgent, yuppie phenomenon, as, for instance, when Joachim Hirsch (1988: 50) identifies their aim as "in sum, individual emancipation, the recovery of civil society, self-fulfilment, and 'the good life.'"

Are the new social movements, then, the product of a narcissist generation, the conservators of communitarian narratives amidst the desert of debunked nationalist and communitarian codes of the nineteenth and twentieth centuries? Poststructuralist or postindustrial reasoning, which avoids the state and capital for analyses of cultural iconography, infuses this thesis in its affirmation of the retreatist-defensive image of the new social movements and in seeing their project as a politics of identity. Touraine (1988: 18) claims, "We no longer demand to direct the course of things; we simply claim our freedom, the right to be ourselves without being crushed by the apparatuses of power, violence, and propaganda." Melucci (1980: 220) finds them "not oriented toward the conquest of political power or of the state apparatus, but rather toward the control of a field of autonomy or of independence vis-à-vis the system." Habermas (1987b: 395) states, "ascriptive characteristics such as gender, age, skin color, neighborhood or locality, and religious affiliation serve to build up and separate off communities supportive of the search for personal and collective identity ... all this is meant to foster the revitalization of possibilities for expression and communication that have been buried alive." Perhaps the rise of the micronations in Quebec, Catalonia, Euskadia, the Baltic and Caucasian republics, Slovenia, and Croatia is exemplary of the collective reformulation of identity in a rationalized and anomic world. For Stanley Aronowitz (1987/88), this abandonment of universality, of the myth of progress, and of logocentrism has the earmarks of a new postmodern politics.

Yet these characterizations falter over a few basic problems. The first is a general lack of specificity concerning *which* social movements are being included in the "new social movement" category. Laclau and Mouffe's critique of traditional Marxian analyses that theorize over the heads of workers, ignoring their internal diversity and their shifting personal and collective interpretations of labour movement strategies, might equally apply to much theory about the new social movements. A good deal of new social movement discourse makes sense only as commentary on the environmental (especially the German Green Party) and, to a large extent, peace and antinuclear movements. In many instances, lip service is paid to feminism with very little direct analysis of feminist theories, issues, or struggles (see, for example, Dalton and Kuechler 1990). Beyond this core emerges a periphery of occasionally recognized movements. European writers tend to acknowledge youth and countercultural activity, alternative economic and co-operative organizations, micronationalists and regionalists, and squatters, while North Americans more often mention the black civil rights, Aboriginal, and gay and lesbian movements. Jost Halfmann (1988: 14, 33) argues that only movements of protest against the "central role of the state as promoter of risk technologies" (that is, movements against nuclear weapons, nuclear energy, toxic pollution, and genetic engineering) qualify as new social movements, while the others, who work for the "establishment of democracy through the introduction or extension of (*individual*) rights," remain "old" social movements. While much of this difference can be accounted for in terms of local salience, European disattention to local racial (Arab, *Gastarbeiter*) and gay movements and U.S. provincialism concerning Québécois nationalism as well as co-operatives are not so readily explained.

Indeed, much of the class critique of the new social movements makes sense only as an observation of the environmental and peace movements, though even then Hanspeter Kriesi (1989) makes a strong case for at least passive support for these movements among blue-collar workers and the old middle class.[2] The class critique works, as well, only by excluding trade union health-and-safety committees from the ambit of environmentalism, even though they represent one of the most sustained areas of struggle around the control of the toxic effects of industry. Class inventories of the feminist, black, or gay and lesbian movements are rare to non-existent. Though it would be surprising to see a low representation of people employed in the tertiary sector in these movements, given their overall proportion of the general population, the reduction of these movements to the class interests of the "new middle class" is presumptuous and misleading.

The tendency to deal with the new social movements summarily lumps together a great many ideological trends and organizational forms under a single banner. Combining highly professionalized and well-financed international organizations like Greenpeace with spontaneous street activists like Queer Nation greatly hampers the coherence of new social movement theory. None of these "movements" is singular or unitary in analysis, strategy, or objectives.

Finally, several observers have intervened to point out that the new social movements are not entirely "new" (Weir 1993a; Steinmetz 1994). Joseph Huber (1989) points to youth protest, the Adventists, romantic conservatives, suffragettes, and Mennonite/Quaker pacifists from 1815 to 1848; D'Anieri, Ernst and Kier (1990) mention the Oneida colony and the postwar peace movement; Kenneth Tucker (1991) makes the case for pre-World War I French syndicalism; and Karl-Werner Brand (1990) postulates a cyclical trend in the growth of these kinds of movements (see also Kauffman 1990). Indeed, a good case can be made that direct antecedents of several of the major contemporary movements were born in the decades following the French Revolution and flourished into the twentieth century. The historical amnesia that finds the new social movements "new" may arise from two sources: (a) the current crisis in Marxism, which has allowed leftist social theory to "see" movement activity around it, activity it had long discounted, and (b) the upswing of many of these movements in their "second wave" after a period of decline in the 1940s and 1950s due to Nazi extermination, Stalinism, or McCarthyism.

A dilemma of contemporary Marxism and new social movement theories turns on the problem of overcoming the partiality of a century of socialist thought. The new social movements have brought into view a variable set of apparently autonomous domination systems, which include: structural racism, patriarchy, heterosexism, the exploitation of nature – a list that could seemingly be extended to centre-periphery relationships based on ethnicity, religion, region, able-bodiedness, and more. The feminist insight that "the personal is political" challenged social theory to take account of domination and inferiorization in a wide spectrum of lifeworlds and subordinated subjectivities (Adam 1978; Boggs 1986). Michel Foucault's theory of power, while sacrificing explicit linkages with macrostructures of power in capital and the state, captured the new sense of the pervasiveness of politics in everyday, face-to-face contexts.

What has been missing from the too-strictly drawn opposition between Marxism and new social movement theory is an understanding of how the dynamics of capitalist development are engaged with the production and re-production of ostensibly non-economic systems of domination and inferiorization. One of the most sustained recent intellectual traditions to undertake this problem has been socialist feminism, which has sought to move beyond an analysis which, on the one hand, postulates patriarchy and capitalism as parallel systems in an uneasy and inexplicable "marriage" and, on the other hand, collapses sexism into an epiphenomenal effect of the re-production of capital. The domestic labour debate usefully pointed out the functionality of unpaid work done in households for the reproduction of the relations of production, but could not be extended to include the whole of the politics of gender (see Kuhn and Wolpe 1978; Barrett 1988; Ferguson 1991). Nevertheless, a fundamental point retained by socialist feminism is that the existence of gender coding in both precapitalist and non-capitalist societies does not negate the fact that gender relations require continual, day-to-day reproduction to survive and that gender distinctions have been taken up and re-created in an ongoing manner by state and capitalist relations (see, for example, Ursel 1992).

The constituencies of the new social movements have always been deeply engaged with and shaped by the actions of states and capital. William Julius Wilson's (1980) work demonstrates that little can be understood of the changing fortunes of black people in the United States without examining the changing patterns of capital movement and class alliance that have had an impact on their fates. The unprecedented growth of heavy industry in the Northern states at the turn of the century, combined with industrialists' interest in using black workers as a tool to undermine the wage demands and union activities of white workers, offered the rural poor a historical opening to improve their lot at the same time as racial distinctions were thereby renewed and amplified. The reign of Jim Crow (the regime of racial segregation) later began to decline as war production, and then postwar reconstruction, replaced the Great Depression, creating more industrial employment for black people at a time when unionization successfully came to embrace workers of both races. The civil rights movement, begun at the turn of the century, gained momentum through the improving resources of black urban churches and colleges (McAdam 1982). Still, the decline of the blue-collar sector since the 1960s has brought renewed impoverishment to many black Americans and created increasing class cleavage.

At the same time, as Michael Omi and Howard Winant (1994) argue, political economy may be a necessary but insufficient resource in the task of understanding the evolution of racial oppression. Structural racism encompasses actions of the state and its agencies, of churches and the professions, of landlords, of educational institutions, of language and the arts. All of this cultural work fed back into the split labour markets and helped to reproduce the economic realities of race and class.

The rise of the black civil rights movement, which in many ways acted as a trailblazer for many of the other new social movements in North America, is fully comprehensible only within the context of social class and political economy. At the same time, it cannot be reduced to it. Rather, it brings into question the pervasiveness of racial distinction both inside the workplace and throughout the many spheres of the lifeworld, and it thematizes the urgency of theorizing domination where it is lived.

A similar analysis can be made for ecology: the nexus between the bodies of community residents and the industries that both employ and destroy them may be direct causes in explaining ecological mobilization. But consider an example often written off as a case of "identity politics," namely, the lesbian and gay movement. The possibility of an autonomous gay or lesbian people arises only in the modern era, when kinship codes have declined as primary modes of production and distribution in the face of capitalist reorganization (Adam 1995). The mobilization of vast numbers of European and North American populations into urban, industrial employment profoundly influenced the strength and extent of familial networks, the growing independence of children from parental authority, and the refounding of marriage on voluntarist and romantic grounds. These shifts in the division of labour and in traditional family and kin structures created the conditions for the development of public spheres (first occupied by men), the reorganization of family and household as "private" and as women's domain, and the growth of new venues for intimacy, at first for gay men and later for lesbians.

RETHINKING NEW SOCIAL MOVEMENTS

Theorizing about the new social movements, then, needs to recognize that the differentiation and formation of subordinated categories of people are both a part of and apart from the political economy of advanced capitalism. How people come to *identify* themselves with some others in opposition to still other people is always a particular historical process that is not predetermined along a single political dimension, such as exclusion from production decisions, but rather follows complex patterns of inferiorization in the many spheres of life: "Only the image of self reflected by others able to influence or control one's life or survival necessarily organizes the self's priorities and orientations.... The identity of the dominated admits no complacency. It is a necessary alertness and defence" (Adam 1978: 11-12).

While the institutionalization of trade union and electoral politics has at least momentarily contained or managed conflicts on some fronts, the new social movements have arisen on a multitude of additional sites of struggle. Social and political theory of the last twenty-five years has been groping towards a language to encompass this proliferation of conflict through such theoretical initiatives as the New Left's connection of "the personal" and "the political," increasing focus on "civil society," and Foucault's paradigm of a society structured through pervasive micropolitics. The regime of violence visited upon subordinated peoples has provoked a multifaceted response in:

- the workplace and unions, where the hegemonic code has been reproduced in wage and seniority scales, in "glass ceilings" to career advancement, in health and safety regulation, in the racial and gender composition of union leadership, and in the distribution of "family" benefits;
- the streets and public places, where most often young heterosexual men have acted as the enforcers of the traditional code of privilege through rape, gay-bashing, and predation of the poor and visible minorities;
- housing and households, with their own increasingly visible regime of violence and where the marked categories of people suffer the arbitrariness of landlords, insurance companies, municipal zoning ordinances, and state supervision of the appropriateness of the composition of household members;
- the delivery of health and social services, where subsistence payments and medical care may be used to punish women seeking abortions, people living with AIDS, those living in non-"family" households, and people with disreputable disabilities;
- churches that manufacture ideological warrants for apartheid and heterosexism, for the suppression of activism among the poor, and for the "place" of women;
- the mass media, education, language, and the arts, where "inferiorized people discover themselves as symbols manipulated in the transmission of the dominant culture. Their "objective" identity lives beyond their control; the image of self, institutionalized by cultural agents, exists alien to their own experience and self-expression" (Adam 1978: 31);
- the natural environment, where nuclear technology poses total annihilation or slow poisoning, where food, air, and energy carry potential carcinogens, and global warming threatens the infrastructure of the food supply.

Although not centrally economic movements, the new social movements *do* address political economy. Their constituencies do go to work and do not leave their non-work "selves" at home when they press for equity and affirmative action programs to have, at minimum, representation throughout job hierarchies, or when they press for non-discrimination clauses in union contracts. These issues have been central concerns in the platforms of black, women's, gay/lesbian, disabled people's, and Aboriginal people's movements. Struggles against urban redlining, where local financial institutions decapitalize "at-risk" communities, directly challenge the right of banks and corporations to allocate capital along racial lines and consequently to de-develop the communities of non-white people. Struggles around the siting of toxic dumps and incinerators and around the location of environmentally predatory and polluting industries do take on the basic exercise of capitalist power.

While ambivalent about state power, the new social movements *do* address the state and are profoundly shaped by its actions. Despite those theorists who would locate the new social movements away from the state and capital (see, for example, Melucci 1980; Touraine 1985), these movements act towards the state both *defensively*, in protesting police violence, fending off state intervention in community affairs, and asserting the right to control one's own body, and *offensively*, in demanding human rights guarantees, social benefits, domestic partners' rights, wheelchair accessibility, or environmental regulation. The state is a primary and unavoidable agent in the reproduction of relations of domination in race, gender, sexuality, and environment, and the new social movements struggle actively to block and remake these mechanisms of subordination (see Donzelot 1979; Leiss 1979; Kinsman 1987; Connell 1990; Omi and Winant 1994).[3] To use Philip Corrigan and Derek Sayer's (1985: 203) terminology, new social movements arise in opposition to the "moral regulation" inherent in "state formation." Their emancipatory work focuses on "the immensely long, complicated, laborious micro-construction and reconstruction of appropriate forms of power; forms fitted to ways in which a particular class, gender, race imposes its 'standards of life' as 'the national interest' and seeks their internalization as 'national character.'"

Finally, lest the new social movements be accorded theoretical status only as phenomena of "postindustrialism" or "postmodernism," it must be noted that all of these movements have representation in Latin America, Asia, Africa, and Eastern Europe and have provoked discussions among such revolutionary movements of the "old" model as the Sandinistas and the African National Congress. Third World concerns, in turn, have their expression in the advanced capitalist nations in peace, anti-imperialist, anti-apartheid, and Third World solidarity organizations that challenge military hegemony at home.

But, although the new social movements do challenge or resist the state and capital, they also partake in and express that power field. Foucault contends that power is not simply a question of resistance and opposition to externally wielded force, but rather that "both sides" are as much *in* as *against* the power articulated through a larger discursive matrix. Just as the modern development of capitalism has both engaged and reproduced categories of exclusion, it has set in motion forces that shape the actions and identities of new social movements, posing a series of ironies and paradoxes in the determination of what is "self" and what is "other," what is "emancipation" and what is "submission." The communicative communities developed around inferiorized categories have engendered indigenous petit bourgeoisies who have often been responsible for sustaining the most durable public institutions "for" their publics. These small business people, while providing new meeting places, commodities, and services denied by the "mainstream," nevertheless frequently have a class agenda of their own that reduplicates mainstream politics, and they exert significant financial pressure on community organizations. Businesses also often provide an entrée for corporate capital to begin marketing "green" products, to promote smoking among blacks and Latinos, or to profit from sex-talk phone lines or pornography, demonstrating again Herbert Marcuse's thesis concerning the power of capitalism to absorb and commodify its opposition. As unpaid domestic labour declines in the face of capitalist valuation, feminism oscillates between affirming the trend by demanding wages for housework or state and professional childcare services or by abstaining from the trend by focusing, for instance, on cooperative child care provided by both women and men. In the absence of social reform in either direction, maids become the hidden solution to the demands of professional mobility and childbearing. Just as there can be no simplistic imputation of "resistance" or "consciousness" to workers, there can be none to the "new" constituencies.

NEW SUBJECTS IN HISTORY?

The theorists agree that the new social movements represent a rejection of the unified, disciplined, and militarized party machine oriented towards seizure of the state and enforcement of a single ideological line. Rather, the "newness" of the new social movements is in its "insurrection of subjugated knowledges" (Foucault 1980: 81), its subjectivity, "a decentered, detotalised agent, a subject constructed at the point of intersection of a multiplicity of subject-positions between which there exists no a priori or necessary relation and whose articulation is the result of hegemonic practices" (Mouffe 1988: 35). The movements rooted in micro-organizations in the workplace, political clubs, churches, sport, support and counselling centres, spontaneous action groups, and cultural projects – these are the signs of "networks composed of a multiplicity of groups that are dispersed, fragmented, and

submerged in everyday life." They are the signs of "short-term and revers-
ible commitment, multiple leadership, temporary and ad hoc organizational
structures" (Melucci 1989: 60). They are "informal, ad hoc, discontinuous,
context-sensitive, and egalitarian," without central programs or leaders who
can be held responsible for their actions (Offe 1985b: 826-31). Like guerrilla
warriors, the new social movements have developed low-cost, relatively effective, decentralized methods of outflanking a centralized, extraordinarily
expensive, high-tech adversary. Their "self-limiting radicalism" (Cohen
1985: 663) is an unsurprising tactical manoeuvre against a military-industrial
complex with virtually insurmountable weapons of social control from computer surveillance through nuclear weaponry. Their dispersion and
detotalized style, operating within everyday practice and lifeworld networks,
is perhaps the mode of politics that is comprehensible to a population faced
with enormously complex modern social systems (Habermas 1987b: 359;
Calhoun 1988: 222).

Dethroned are the chiliastic politics of the privileged moment of the revolutionary break that will "change everything." Now have come the "prefigu-
rative politics" seeking to "create and sustain within the live practice of the
movement, relationships and political forms that 'prefigured' and embodied
the desired society" (Breines 1982: 6; see Melucci 1989: 205). The new social
movement strategy works from below through "'living social change': cooperative markets, media groups and publications, bookstores, rent-control
boards, rape crisis centres, medical clinics, toxic-waste projects, research
organization" (Boggs 1986: 133).

Still, all of this talk about diversity, plurality, and decentredness does not
come to grips with widespread common dilemmas and the strategies used to
cope with them. Much of the confusion around "identity politics" reflects the
"nationalist," "fundi," or "culturalist" face of new social movements, which
valorizes difference, essentializes identity, and affirms the self. Much of the
postmodern claim postulating the fall of metanarratives, the replication of
incommensurable discourses, and the character of new social movements as
"nomads of the present" depends on conceptualizing them as an incoherent
series of particularities.

This cultural nationalism is an important, perhaps inevitable, moment in
the coming-into-subjectivity of the subaltern. Domination truncates subjectivity, hedges it in, drains it of resources and richness (Adam 1978); empowerment requires the forging together, wrenching, and re-creation of discourses that break with their predecessors. It is a process of encoding inar-
ticulate experience: not simply the adoption of a given hegemonic discourse,
but a working through to move beyond defensive and self-defeating strategies (Fanon 1967; Adam 1978; Higgins 1980; Kauffman 1990). For women,
feminism must "articulate disjunctures between dominant representations of
femininity and women's perceptions of their own lives" (Felski 1989: 230).

Black pride and gay pride reclaim and reconstitute selves limited by external hegemonies. They overwrite the silences and absences enforced by superordinate cultural traditions that give subordinated peoples impoverished resources for developing the self as a subject in the world.

Yet, for all of its worthiness, cultural nationalism is also vulnerable to the reification and spiritualization of difference, political quiescence, and courtship by the right. This trend is strongest among ethnic, Aboriginal, and micronationalities, where it can become a vehicle for semi-peripheral bourgeoisies to mobilize support around language and culture in order to form "nations," which in the end offer little gain in democracy and little challenge to the larger political order. Among new social movements, these new identities too often conceal a rehegemonization of traditional codes that reproduce exclusion based on social class, gender, race, or region. As Rita Felski (1989: 220) remarks in regard to cultural feminism, "The truth of female experience is perceived to provide an adequate basis for the development of an oppositional women's culture with little attention given to the ways in which the notion of a female reality is itself mediated by ideological and discursive systems which are neither innocent nor transparent." This tendency, which produces talk of autonomy, withdrawal, and cultural politics as the ends of new social movement activity, creates a justified disquiet among theorists aware of the movements' susceptibility to co-optation by conservative forces (see Offe 1985b: 861; Hirsch 1988: 53; Sivanandan 1989: 10).

But particularistic identity politics makes up only one facet of new social movement endeavours. More remarkable are the "socialists" born not (or at least not only) of the labour movement, but produced out of the new social movements themselves. This other face of new social movement mobilization includes a great many participants who understand their *praxis* within a comprehensive worldview that recognizes and supports subordinated people wherever they exist. Complex linkages already exist among feminist labour activists, gay Third World solidarity activists, black ecologists, disabled peace activists, and so on, people working in organizations of more than one movement. In addition to overlapping participants, the movements have tremendous influence upon each other in their analyses, strategies, and self-criticisms. These workers for social justice often understand themselves as socialists and represent a potential source of renewal generally ignored both by Marxism and new social movement theory.

These different manifestations of new social movement practice pose questions about their viability as a force for social change. Even setting aside the ideal model of the proletarian class revolution, many wonder sceptically with Wallerstein (1989b: 442) if "there is a meaningful strategy that can be constructed that involves the variegated pursuit of multiple forms of power."[4] The Nicaraguan FSLN, the Salvadorean FMLN, and the African National Congress have presented one well-tested model of the Third World grand

revolutionary coalition that pulls together a wide range of existing organizations of peasants, rural workers, urban neighbourhoods, trade unions, students, leftist political parties, dissenting clergy, cultural organizations, and
intellectuals. Social movements usually included in the "new" list, however,
have usually played a junior role, if any, in these kinds of coalitions, although
they are showing up more often in recent years. In the United States, the
1988 presidential bid by Jesse Jackson had some surprising successes in
piecing together a "rainbow coalition" founded in the black civil rights tradition, but appealing to a range of other new social movements along with economically stressed small farmers and urban workers. In Canada and Europe,
social-democratic and green parties have had modest success in trying to
"add on" to their traditional support bases. No small part of the difficulty of
drawing these movements into coalitions is their lack of central leadership
and internal incoherence. Movement organizations display a wide range of
internal structures and political orientations, from professionalized direct-
mail fundraisers cultivating a relatively passive, atomized membership to
spontaneous direct-action collectivities with little formal institutional structure. They, as well, vary greatly in their perceptions of having common interests with other movements. There is no lack of internal problems and crosscutting alliances, including major United States labour organizations co-
opted by the state to undermine their counterparts in Central America; class
biases among the new movements that ignore the plight of poor neighbourhoods or workers in one-industry towns; underrepresentation of people of
colour in the ecological, feminist, and gay movements; or sexism and homophobia among black and Latino groups.

The rainbow coalition model may not be the most effective way of creating change in advanced capitalist societies. Stuart Hall (1988: 7) offers a view
stressing communicative initiative in his definition of "hegemony" as "the
struggle to contest and disorganise an existing political formation; the taking
of the 'leading position' (on however minority a basis) over a number of different spheres of society at once – economy, civil society, intellectual and
moral life, culture; the conduct of a wide and differentiated type of struggle;
the winning of a strategic measure of popular consent; and, thus, the securing of a social authority sufficiently deep to conform society into a new historical project."

Perhaps the wisdom of the new social movements lies in working towards
a social restructuring around and under the state and capital, leading to an
undermining of their traditional social foundations and creating a need for
them to adapt to changed practices and circumstances. The new social movements are sites of active politics and creative, innovative energy for change
that express deeper structural problems. Their appropriation of rights rhetoric extends democracy beyond the electoral sphere and challenges liberal
boundaries that would contain change along the public-private distinction.

Their demands reassert claims for the good of communities against pure profit and require capitalists to respond to more of the citizenry than just their own shareholders and unions (see Carroll and Ratner 1994).

Still, a historical imponderable remains as to whether the new social movements represent a displacement of opposition and circumventing of capitalist hegemony with a potential of making "end runs" in the name of democracy, or whether they will necessarily leave the deep structure of capitalism untouched and avoid taking on the prevailing distribution of wealth and power. At this time, there is little possibility of assessing the potential for an unravelling of the contemporary impasse among states, corporations, and labour, a step that might reactivate labour movements in alliance with new social movements. At the very least, there would need to be an upsurge of the still small movement for co-operative and democratic workplaces (Krimerman and Lindenfeld 1990) and a concerted reorientation of First World labour unions at home to resist the imperial sponsorship of genocidal client regimes, while matching the internationalization of capital with global unionization abroad. For Henri Lefèbvre (1976: 36), the more optimistic forecast is possible: "The peripheries may be powerless, isolated, and destined for only local and episodic revolts, but it is nonetheless possible for them to outflank the centres, once the latter have been shaken."

CONCLUSION

Many of these debates of contemporary Marxism, post-Marxism, and new social movement theory have been impelled by attempts to come to grips with recent historical events which, over the last twenty-five years, have challenged received wisdoms of the left. Not least among these changes have been the reign of new right governments in the major advanced capitalist powers, the ossification and collapse of Soviet bureaucratic regimes operating in the name of Marxism, the rise and persistence of social movements ostensibly organized around non-class issues, and the preoccupation of contemporary political discourse with questions of gender, race, ecology, and a plethora of "particularistic" issues. I would argue that a good deal of these contemporary debates has shown too little cognizance of Marxist political economy in its understanding of social movements and yet has been too apt to resemble traditional Marxism in its tendency to try to fit a great variety of social movements into a few very broad generalizations.[5]

A genealogy of the current debates around Marxism and new social movements might begin with Antonio Gramsci's widening of the traditional focus of political economy to encompass the politics of everyday life and the role of cultural tradition and innovation in the construction of hegemony. It might be traced through Karl Polanyi's (1957: 3) *The Great Transformation*, which examined civil society as a series of movements of social protection against the corrosive effects of the market which otherwise "would have physically destroyed man and transformed his surroundings into a wilderness." For Polanyi, the destructive effect of the market extended well beyond the workplace and the alienation of labour. A half-century of Western Marxian theory about the commodification and reification of social relations lay behind Althusser's idea of "ideological state apparatuses" on the one hand and Lefèbvre's "reproduction of the relations of production" on the other, both of which sought to keep and step beyond political-economic analysis.

The practice of new social movement organizations shows both a cultural attack on the power relations contained in the code of *différance*, which assigns them the marked position of alterity, and an acute awareness and engagement with the state and capital as hegemonic forces with undue bearing upon their fates. To ignore the dynamics of capitalist development, the role of labour markets in reorganizing spatial and familial relations, and the interaction of new and traditional categories of people with dis/employment patterns is to ignore the structural prerequisites that have made the new social movements not only possible, but also predictable. Although the chiliastic faith in metanarratives and the myth of the revolutionary break have been replaced by a cool-eyed pragmatism, the new social movements nevertheless trace a direct genealogy to Enlightenment antecedents reformed in the rhetoric of "rights" and "democracy." Whether they will or can fundamentally transform the state and capital in the long run, they nevertheless embody a democratic impulse that would extend mastery over the individual's own life to more and more social constituencies.

NOTES

1. "Antinuclear and environmental movements; the peace movement (including the theme of north-south conflict); single-issue and local movements; the alternative movement (... squatters ... rural communes); the minorities (the elderly, gays, handicapped ...); the psychoscene ...; religious fundamentalism; the tax-protest movement, school protest by parents' associations, resistance to 'modernist' reforms" (Habermas 1987b: 393).
2. Eckersley (1989), for example, defends the environmental movement from the "new class" charge but nevertheless accepts the basic premise that it is a movement of the new middle class.
3. Scott (1990) also makes this point in *Ideology and the New Social Movements*, as does Weir (1993a).
4. Wallerstein tilts toward a negative answer in a later article. See Wallerstein (1990); Plotke (1990).
5. I owe this characterization to an anonymous reviewer of this paper.

LANGUAGE, POWER, AND POLITICS: REVISITING THE SYMBOLIC CHALLENGE OF MOVEMENTS

Dominique Masson

There has certainly been a sea change in social movement theory since John D. McCarthy and Mayer N. Zald (1977) bluntly dismissed the symbolic dimension of movement activity from the establishment of the "Resource Mobilization" (RM) paradigm.[1] Reducing movements' symbolic constructs to grievances and treating these as only marginal components of collective action has become indefensible today. "Neo"-resource mobilizationists, New Social Movement (NSM) theorists, and political scientists all converge now to give greater weight to movements' subjective constructions in theorizing social movement activity. Internal controversies and debates spawned by an increased recognition of the limitations of the RM model[2] have led theorists to reappraise the role of solidarities, movement goals, and cognitive frameworks in movement mobilization. The emergence of the New Social Movement approach as a contending paradigm in the field, granting a central status to the cultural and the symbolic,[3] has redirected attention toward the production of "alternative meanings," such as new identities, cultural innovations, and oppositional discourses. Political scientists, for their part, have noticeably shifted their treatment of symbolic issues away from "the history of ideas" and into the terms of representational, democratic, and identity politics.[4] As questions previously subsumed under the appellation of "ideology" and relegated to a secondary plane of explanation have come to the forefront, scholars in social movement studies are insistently called on to pay more attention to the symbolic dimension of collective action.

Yet, for all the talk about movement meanings and discursive hegemonies, subjectivities and identities, interpretive frames, and other "fightin' words" (Johnston 1992), social movement theory has remained on the whole remarkably uninterested in the specifics of movements' meaning-making practices. Also crucially lacking is a clear understanding of how these symbolic constructs operate within social struggles. How are we to describe movements' symbolic constructions, and how are we to trace the processes through which they are produced and changed historically (Escobar and Alvarez 1992: 6)? And, perhaps more importantly, how are we to analyse their workings and consequences in a field of power relations and struggles? These are all questions that ought to be asked if we are to understand, as is increasingly contended, "the symbolic" as an intrinsic dimension of the exercise of power, and of struggle over power (Alvarez and Escobar 1992; Slater 1994; Jenson 1989a; Melucci 1989).

Growing dissatisfaction with the meagre theoretical and methodological tools available to pursue this inquiry has sent social movement scholars in search of more adequate frameworks. Recent suggestions include drawing from ethnography and ethnosemiotics (Escobar 1992; Starn 1992), sociology of everyday life (Escobar 1992), postmodern and poststructuralist analyses of discourses and subjectivities (Slater 1994; Starn 1992), ethnomethodology and American sociolinguistics (Johnston 1991, 1992; Donati 1992; Larana 1994). This chapter is part of that quest. It endeavours to contribute to the current revaluation of the role played by interpretations and representations in movement activity, strategy, and politics by bringing to bear on social movement theory some propositions developed within a European tradition[5] of language studies, in particular by scholars identified with "critical" perspectives on language and discourse.

If we are, as I will argue, to take the notion of the symbolic challenge of movements seriously, we have to revisit this challenge not only as a truly political struggle, but also as a political struggle of a special sort: that is, as one characteristically fought over the modalities in which power relations are embedded and enacted through social systems of signs and meanings. To do so, we have to understand why the specifics of the language in which movement representations are couched should be considered, what exactly is at stake in the discursive struggles in which movements are involved, and how this goes beyond contests over "meanings," "naming," and "framing."

Some of the answers to these questions can be found in social movement theory's attempts to deal with movements' symbolic dimension. The three most influential perspectives are Melucci's (1989), Laclau and Mouffe's (1985), and RM theory's fast-growing literature on action frames. Yet there is also a need for a closer, more rigorous scrutiny of the role of the symbolic in movements' activity than these frameworks have so far fostered. European approaches to language and discourse, for instance, can help further our understanding of "the symbolic" as a distinct level of analysis. Scholars looking at social movements need to consider the more linguistically sensitive, empirically grounded, and politically oriented analysis advocated by these approaches.

SYMBOLIC CHALLENGE AND SYMBOLIC POLITICS
IN SOCIAL MOVEMENT THEORY

Challenging Codes, Challenging Power: Alberto Melucci

We owe to Melucci the first formulation of "the symbolic challenge" of movements. Melucci's notion of symbolic challenge is linked to his conception of power in today's societies. Melucci argues that we live in "complex societies" characterized by a heightened capacity to produce signs and social meanings. Complex societies are also characterized by a pronounced social differentiation that sets greater needs for integration and control (Melucci 1989: 45). Integration and control are exerted through signs and meanings, as these are expressed, according to Melucci, in the form of societal norms, standardized codes, and formal frameworks of administrative and technological knowledge. Indeed, Melucci's argument goes further: power in complex societies *is* "signs," power is transformed and concealed within sets of signs (76-7) that codify and regulate social relations.

Against complex societies' always expanding and increasingly anonymous forms of power, actors mobilize to regain hold of the meanings and conditions of their action. Individuals and groups mount what Melucci sees as a symbolic challenge to the dominant codes, norms, identities, and other "sets of signs" that regulate social life. This symbolic challenge encompasses two main aspects. The first is the production of alternative frameworks of knowledge and meaning in the process of collective action. The second is the experimentation of new ways of living and new forms of relationships in the daily practice of movements' "submerged networks." Moreover, the very existence of the movements is considered a symbolic confrontation with the technological rationality of the system (60). This is because movements themselves become "signs": the living proof, so to speak, of the possibility of social change and alternative interpretations of society.

By casting light on the arbitrariness of complex societies' cultural modes of regulation, movements' symbolic challenge renders visible the power inscribed in those modes (76-7). Melucci's fundamental contribution lies precisely in this notion that signs and social meanings are part of how power is exerted and, consequently, are also part of how power can be, and is, contested. Signs, meanings, and power are intimately intertwined. In Melucci's argument the symbolic ceases to be merely a portrait, a mirror of the social order, and becomes implicated in society's very ordering. Movements' attempts at reinterpreting and challenging dominant "codes" by proposing "a different way of perceiving and naming the world" (75) are to be considered, in this sense, attempts at altering not only the "symbolic" order of society, but the social order itself.

Although insightful, Melucci's conception of movements' symbolic challenge is problematic, however, regarding the interface of "signs" and power, of the symbolic and the political. Firstly, as Bartholomew and Mayer (1992) note, Melucci's notion of power is too unspecified. Crucially missing is an understanding of the grounding of movements' symbolic challenge in the fractured field of unequal power relations between people and groups of people. How particular hierarchies and forms of power relations operate – and are contested – *via* signs and meanings lingers as the theoretical and empirical question to be answered. Secondly, the symbolic challenge of movements has to be reinstated within a broader vision of the political. Melucci's too narrow understanding of politics as state-based and his erroneous view of collective action as located mostly outside politics have been criticized as unduly bounding movements to cultural venues and civil society issues. Finally, another important problem is that movements' symbolic challenges remain enacted in an essentially *expressive* manner. The existence of movements and the experiential "practice" of "the alternative meanings of everyday life" (1989: 71) are limited to *signal* ("announce," "publicize") an opposition that, within an immanent and disembodied version of power relations, is never otherwise played out.

In contrast, I contend that as a challenge to power relations, the symbolic dimension of movement activity should rather be analysed as an intrinsic part of movement politics: that is, as part of the struggles over power in which concrete actors are engaged in the variety of social sites where unequal power relations are at play. In addition, I suggest that understanding movements' symbolic challenge as being – partly – a "politics of signs and meanings" directs us towards the semiotic aspects of this challenge.[6] For it is through semiotic systems – systems of signs – that actors signify the world, constructing classifications and categories and assigning meanings to situations, groups of people, and relationships.[7] In doing so, actors actively build power structures and power relations through codes of signs (Fowler 1991; Fairclough 1992). One of the main avenues to reconceptualizing and investigating "the symbolic challenge of movements" is to analyse this challenge as a struggle whose domain is linguistic and discursive practices, and whose stake is the power relations built into them.

Laclau and Mouffe's Discursive Politics: The Symbolic as Contingent
In this perspective, Laclau and Mouffe's (1985) conception of "struggles for hegemony" throws more light on the notion of movements' symbolic challenge in terms of discursive politics. The authors strongly assert the political character of symbolic struggles. Laclau and Mouffe draw on postmodern claims that place "discourse" at the origin of the constitution of the subjects, objects, and relationships of the social. Struggles over discourse, or more largely over the definition of the meanings we attach to lived social relations, thus occupy the very centre of social conflictuality.

Laclau and Mouffe argue that social relations of power have no set meanings outside of the discourses that enable us to make sense of them. Social antagonisms, they contend, are polysemic: they can bear as many different significations (that is, meanings) as there are discourses to constitute them. The significations that do get fixed are so within discursive struggles for hegemony, that is, within struggles for the political imposition of constructed significations. The authors firmly state that neither the collective identities of the political subjects nor their projects, issues, or interests are pregiven. Rather, these are all contingent: they are not determined in advance by the social structure, but vary as a result of the discursive struggles for the hegemonic fixation of social meanings.

This fixation is always partial and tentative. Concretely, the attempts to "effect closure" on significations is realized, according to Laclau and Mouffe, through a process of "articulation." In this process, dissimilar elements are linked through discursive strategies that establish among them what the authors call "chains of equivalence." Through these chains some discursive elements become substitutable. They are also placed in a relation of difference or opposition with regard to other discursive chains. Through such mechanisms, Laclau and Mouffe (1985: 62-5) argue, identities such as "the people" or "the working class" have become tentatively fixed among the various and intersecting subject positions occupied simultaneously by any individual. Similar sequencing operations offer the potential to transfer or "displace" meanings made historically available by the liberal-democratic discourse to new areas that they resignify and politicize (154-71). The notions of hegemonic struggle, articulations, and discursive "chains of equivalences" can be useful, as the authors suggest, in tracing the constitution of coalitional politics and the emergence of new issues.

More importantly, perhaps, Laclau and Mouffe's claim about the contingency of symbolic constructions should be taken on board by social movement studies. It is worth underlining that, despite its definitively post-structuralist flavour, the view that identities, interests, and political projects are contingent rather than ascribed is also compatible with more fluid versions of contemporary Marxism. In this case, the notion of structural limits to discursive constructions is to be retained. Such limits include the weight of the past, the balance of forces, and the nature of the unequal relations of power at play (Jenson 1989a: 75). To these I would add the availability of existing meanings to signify and resignify, which is also constrained, and constraining. As a result of the combination of these factors, not all discursive constructions are possible.

This acknowledgement of the contingent character of the symbolic dimension of collective action has important implications. The definition of identities – the "self-naming" of movements – is increasingly acquiring an explanatory status in social movement theory.[8] Yet if the lived experiences of the social subjects are crisscrossed by different types of power relations, the identity of a political actor – a movement – cannot be seen as following

directly from the social structure. Heterogeneous rather than unified subjects become politically assembled under the label of a movement's name.
Peasant movements, for example, Orin Starn (1992: 93) argues, are not a
"cut-and-dried affair of class mobilization." Rather, the question of who quali-
fies as "peasant" in a given peasant movement varies and shifts according to
an internal process of political hegemony,[9] in which "negotiation, choice, and
imposition" are intertwined (96).

Seemingly similar political identities – such as "Native peoples,"
"women," or even "workers" – are not defined the same way in different
times and places, or even within movements. Criteria for inclusion and exclusion differ. We need to know the more precise terms under which a movement's "name" is defined and the meanings attached to it if identities are to
be in any way explanatory of the movement's goals, strategies, or access to
political opportunity.

Within this perspective, the construction of interests and political projects
cannot be seen as flowing directly from the choice of an identity, or a name.
If movements indeed construct claims and interests "in accordance with the
logic of [their] name," as Jane Jenson (1993: 343) contends, this very "logic"
is itself discursively and diversely constructed. Contemporary feminist
works, for instance, have clearly asserted the diversity of "women's" experiences. This diversity translates into diverse "logics," thus giving rise to the
political expression of widely diverse "women's interests" within largely heterogeneous, fragmented, and multiform "women's movements."[10]

Moreover, interests and projects are susceptible to being articulated within
and to widely different discourses, with divergent or even contradictory implications in terms of the direction of struggles (Laclau and Mouffe 1985: 168-9).
As contingency and multiplicity of possible discursive articulations combine,
movement politics acquire a more ambiguous outlook. Most movement initiatives, Starn (1992: 95) aptly remarks, "defy neat categorization as hegemonic
or counterhegemonic." The meaning of "democratic struggles" fluctuates in
the context of complex, historically specific imaginaries and is contested amid
contending discourses (Slater 1994). Contingency means that movements'
symbolic dimension bears no external guarantees. A closer examination of
movements' discursive constructions is thus in order.

Yet Laclau and Mouffe's framework is not readily applicable to the task.
Relying heavily on some of the recent developments in postmodern and
poststructuralist theory, their proposition suffers from similar ailments, in
particular an abstract approach to "discourse" (Poynton 1993). Consequently
their work has been conducive only to an impressionistic view of how different discourses and meanings jostle, merge, yield, or win in the "struggles for
hegemony."

Unspecified and detached from the concrete modalities through which
they are socially realized, discourses in this version appear utterly disembod-

ied from the materiality of the linguistic means that express them. They are also delinked from the institutional locations and the social activity that permit their existence and are the bases of their effectiveness. Despite the acknowledgement that discourses find their realization, in great part, through language, Laclau and Mouffe eschew detailed accounts of actual processes of meaning-construction in linguistic forms. Therefore they do not have much to offer, beyond "chains of equivalence" set at the level of the overarching themes of "equality," "difference," "justice," and "liberty," to probe into the specifics of the partial fixation of social meanings.

Furthermore, they lose sight of the notion that the positions, relations, and other regularities of meanings constituting discourses need to be actively enacted to take effect. Discourses are not omnipotent or agentless. Rather, they draw their authority and social efficacy only from the repeated utterance or performance of their elements by people speaking from particular socio-enunciative positions or institutions inscribed within a field of power relations. The argument that the subjects are also "constituted in/by discourses" should not detract us from concerns for agency and its exercise. This involves analysing the level of the written and spoken symbolic production by and through which concrete agents reproduce, struggle over, and alter the terms of discourses in specific institutional, political, and strategic contexts.

RMT and the Framing of Collective Action

The reappraisal of the importance of social meanings under the labels of "social constructivism" or of a revamped "new social psychology" approach has led a whole body of RM scholars to stress the role of social movement organizations (SMOs) in appropriating cultural symbols and in constructing schematas of interpretation in a way that can be made relevant for the mobilization of people, opinion, and resources. Sparked by the reformulation by David Snow and his co-authors (1986) of Goffman's concept of "frame," the recent works on framing share the assumption that people behave in accordance with a perceived reality and that these perceptions are the locus of a variety of interpretations. Proposing selective interpretations of social reality and gaining support for these become a crucial task for movement organizations.

Collective action frames are complex ensembles of meanings assigned to events, individual and collective experiences, and social situations. Theorists generally see them as including problem identification and system attributions, the definition of solutions and strategies, as well as a rationale for participation (Benford 1993b: 199).[11] Deliberate "frame alignment" efforts are made to render SMO's frames congruent with prospective participants' (or interlocutors') frames. These attempts may even include a major transformation of the initial frame (Snow et al. 1986). Although frames are constructed at the organizational level, they can also be diffused within and among movements, eventually constituting a "master frame" that makes sense of reality and organizes collective action for a whole generation of activists (Tarrow 1994a; McAdam 1994).

The main interest of the current work on "frames" and "framing" resides in its constructivist perspective, and more precisely in its concern for the *strategic* dimension of meaning-making practices at the meso-level of movement organizations. Deliberate and sometimes shrewd crafting of symbolic constructs to "resonate" with an audience is indeed an integral part of SMO's action,[12] as the case of Greenpeace's watery-eyed baby seals eloquently illustrates. The purposeful "framing" of progressive projects within the – usually much less progressive – "language of funding agencies," a familiar practice within Quebec popular movement organizations, is another example of the manipulation of messages for strategic ends. NSM-related works typically do not address these types of strategic issues in symbolic politics.

Empirical studies of "frames" are often diverted towards and reduced to a strictly rhetorical view of movement meanings. The focus rests on the "persuasive communication techniques" whereby coldly calculating movement "entrepreneurs" (Tarrow 1994a) design or manipulate (Donati 1992, Benford 1987) symbols, metaphors, and interpretive frames as "tools for detaching people from their habitual passivity" and for "transforming quiescence into collective action" (Tarrow 1992: 191). Frames then appear as customized, highly negotiable products, launched on a free market of ideas to attract reluctant individuals.

Yet, if frames indeed display rhetorical aspects, framing practices are also shaped by the wider social processes, structures, and relations of power from which they participate. And this occurs in ways that more often than not remain opaque to movement activists. Not everything is negotiable in terms of frames: there are limits to organizational framing efforts within given movements. Concerns for the role that symbolic constructions, such as frames, play in movements' strategy need to be linked with considerations for social relations of power, which RM theory consistently skirts. Frames are produced within relational limits that are also structural. The theorists have to account for the positionality of both the actor (the frame "producer") and of the "target audience" (be it supporters or state agencies) in social conflicts and in the more immediate context of their interaction. In addition, to explain why certain frames are adopted, why they "resonate" or not, succeed or not, or why they are produced at all, they should also consider the hegemony of dominant ideologies, the prevalence of institutional discourses[13] (for example, the discourse of rights), as well as movements' symbolic constructions of a higher order such as movement identities (the "logic of the name") or ideologies.

The framing literature also tends to focus on mobilizational imperatives to the detriment of movements' social change attempts in the arenas of the state and civil society. The success of the "reframing," within the Canadian women's movement, of the abortion issue in terms of "women's freedom of choice" rather than as "free abortion on demand" makes a case for the relevance of a strategic-instrumental analysis of political representations.[14] The institutionalization of particular ways of framing claims has very real, material consequences. It influences further movement action and has implications for the political system as well as for people's daily life (Mayer 1991: 469-70). The consequences of specific framings have to be assessed as part of a more politically oriented analysis of frames, which would require a detailed, discursive analysis of the language of frames – and of "counterframes" as well. Such an analysis is still an exception in the field,[15] as RM scholars' treatment of frames is too often limited to identifying "frames" without exposing either their content in terms of social meanings, or the implications of their institutionalization.

LANGUAGE-AS-ACTION: A SOCIOLINGUISTIC CONTRIBUTION

Melucci's concept of movements' symbolic challenge, then, has to be revised as a "politics of signs and meanings": that is, as a contest over how particular types and forms of power are coded, inscribed – tentatively fixed – in language in the variety of social sites involving power relations. The contingency of movement meanings, identities, issues, and interests, as well as the relational and consequential nature of movement "frames," strongly calls for a closer inquiry into the specifics of the language in which movement representations and interpretations are couched. This inquiry into the particulars of movements' meanings, naming, and framing is imperative not only to account for the variability, ambiguity, and open-endedness of the ways movement politics develop and unfold, but also because language itself possesses its own effectiveness within social relations and, thus, "merits its own level of analysis" (Weir 1995: 52).

The theoretical propositions that critical approaches to discourse analysis take as their premise – among which can be included the influential views of French social theorists Pierre Bourdieu (1991) and Michel Foucault (1984)[16] – can contribute to our understanding of how language and power are intertwined with consequences for social relations – and for movements' political action. Drawing on these works, I will present a conception of language as a mode of action in its double dimension of linguistic practice (the practice of making meaning through "texts")[17] and of discursive practice (the enunciation of these texts as a social "event").

First, I propose that we see language as a material mediation, embedding and enacting social relations of power, and whereby what we call "social reality" is – partially, at the very least – constituted, reconstituted, and potentially altered.[18] Second, I will suggest ways to further the notion of language-as-action as it can be brought to bear on movement politics, underlining some of the ways in which political actors' discursive practices "do things with language," in particular through the power of "performatives" and the "actionable" character of authorized language. Finally, building on Foucauldian insights, I will argue that language-as-action is bounded by the social "effects of closure," limiting the possibilities to signify and act on social reality. This closure is an important part of what is contested through movements' linguistic and discursive practices.

Language: From "Representing" to "Making" the World

Meanings and interpretations do not hover above people in an ethereal world of ideas, as classical or idealistic versions would have it. Nor are they encapsulated in the cognitive structures of the mind (Lemke 1990: 192-4), as many RM theorists suggest. Rather, they exist in the material form of semiotic practices, one of these being language use in the form of written and spoken utterances. The claim made by critical discourse (CD) analysts is that language is not a clear window on the world, but a material mediation through which "reality" is socially constituted and enacted. Standing between human beings and the world, language mediates in two ways: it *refracts*, and it *signifies*.

Meanings constructed in language *refract* social reality rather (or more) than they reflect or mirror it. Language is a complex and dynamic system of meaning-making resources. As a consequence, language is inherently polysemic (Volosinov 1973; Bourdieu 1991; Fairclough 1992). Much like a prism refracts daylight in different colours and directions, language has the potential to deploy a diversity of significations about a given event, action, or social situation. There is no one possible meaning for each and every one of these, but many – something that Laclau and Mouffe have also pointed out, as we have seen. This diversity is not a haphazard feature of linguistic dynamics, but is, rather, related to social structure. Language is understood as "refracting" not only in the sense that it allows the production of a variety of significations, but also in the sense that this variety is linked to the existence of different enunciative positions, taken up by concrete actors, in a field of conflictuality and unequal power relations.

Language is also conceived as a mediation because it *signifies* social reality. Language does not merely refer (Fairclough 1992: 42) to a world that would "make sense" de facto, bearing significations that only have to be "dressed in signs" to be made intelligible.[19] Rather, language is a social practice of signifying: of constructing meaning for this world. Giving this assumption its full weight implies that in "signifying the world" not only do people construct meaning, but construct social reality itself. Constructing meaning for the world is also organizing and ordering this world (Mishler 1991: 105-6; Maingueneau 1991: 196). The categories and significations constructed in language tentatively arrest the flux of lived existence by cutting "artificial slices" "from the cake of the world" (Fowler 1991: 84). Socially relevant chunks are then selectively carved out, and these chunks make up what we define as social reality, or, more exactly, "what is to be counted as real and true" (Yeatman 1990: 155, from Foucault) about this "reality." The profound heterogeneity and the power dynamics of social life imply that there are always different ways and possibilities to signify. Yet the power to impose what "exists" as "real and true" is unequally distributed among people and groups of people, and only certain significations are given broad legitimacy, and accede to dominance.

Language then appears as a meaning-making and reality-creating social practice that is intrinsically non-neutral. Language use is laced with power relations. CD analysts argue that speaking and writing practices simultaneously *embed* and *enact* social relations of power. The linguistic practices (that is, textual constructions) involved in language use are produced from particular socio-enunciative positions: there is no view from nowhere. They *embed* power relations in various ways. Text-internal forms and meanings assign and assert asymmetrical positions between language participants. They also define their identities and relationships, the actions and processes that are under the control of the agents or that are done to/imposed on them, delimiting the fields and the objects to which their interaction conventionally applies (Fowler 1991; Halliday 1989; Fairclough 1992).

It is the active *enactment* of linguistic practices – the frequent speaking and writing – that allows these identities, relations, or processes to be objectified, legitimated, and naturalized as part of the social world (Fowler 1991: 82, 94). The mundane, day-to-day, repetitive practice of language participates in the constant making and remaking of social "reality" (Fairclough 1993: 139). Linguistic practices play an important role in organizing and sustaining social structure (Fairclough 1992: 58). Language then becomes a site and stake in a struggle that aims to unmake and alter the symbolic constructions that embed, enact, and reproduce dominant power relations.

"Doing Things" with Language

Implicated in the making of social reality and its ordering, language is further conceptualized by critical discourse analysts as a mode of action on this reality. To advance our understanding of language-as-action, we need to refer to language use and to struggles involving language not only in terms of contention among different sets of linguistic practices (of power-laden, text-internal meanings), but also as *discursive practices* – the actual saying or writing of texts by social agents. Discursive practices do not only "speak of" (that is, express) and enact particular sets of textual meanings. They also "speak from" (a particular position) and "speak to" (a particular audience) within institutional and social sites located in space and time. They are "acts of language": they are events occurring in contexts and doing something in these contexts, with consequences for movement politics, wider social processes, and power relations. The notion of the *performativity* of political speech, as developed by Bourdieu, and a focus on the *actionability* of authorized language help to highlight some of the ways in which political actors "do things with language."

The conception of the *performativity* of language originates from Speech Acts Theory (Van Dijk 1985a). In the founding work of Austin (1962), performatives are understood in linguistic terms as utterances that effect what they enunciate through the very act of enunciating (Fowler 1991: 87-8). Moving beyond Austin, French social theorist Bourdieu advocates the grounding of performativity in social and political struggles. Political performatives are "statements which seek to bring about what they state" (1991: 225). They are utterances that aspire to bring into existence that which they enunciate. Performatives are central elements in the struggle to bring into existence, or force out of existence, elements of social reality. These attempts to institute social reality, or deinstitute what is instituted, are inseparable from struggles "to make and unmake groups," to impose as legitimate a vision or a revision of the divisions of the social world (221).

We can, then, analyse the expression of "collective identities" by movements, in particular, as discursive practices that do a certain number of things. First, the enunciation of movement identities is a performative act that brings into existence the actor of politics – "that who represents." At the same time, these enunciations participate in the creation of the very subject who, it is claimed, "is supposed to be represented" (Hark 1994: 3), as the pronouncement of an identity performatively states the precedence of a specific subject position over many. The enunciation of collective identities by movement actors also works towards deinstituting already instituted categories and the social hierarchies they express and enact. Simultaneously, movements' representations operate to reinstitute identity categories "under new terms" (those of a reappropriated, positive identity: Young 1990: 159-61), giving them new saliency. From "Indians" to "First Nations," from "homosexuals" to "lesbians and gays," social groups are made and unmade through movement performatives, and political actors are established. As a result, the balance of power of the social hierarchies these identities index is de facto altered.

By directly linking performatives to political struggle, Bourdieu, more explicitly than most language theorists, shifts the location of the "power of speech" from language to the agents of language. The constitutive properties of language, the effectiveness of performatives (or of any other linguistic feature), are not to be derived from linguistic constructions alone, or from the sole communication skills of the speakers. Rather, the power of language is a form of delegated power – a power bestowed on speech either by the authority of a social institution (1991: 109), or the authority of the group ("those who are represented"), which authorizes certain sets of linguistic practices by authorizing itself to use them (129).

Another way in which language functions as a mode of action is through its *actionability*. Linguistic practices are indexical of social action. Not only do they point to certain types of actions in given contexts (Lemke 1990: 189), but the social meanings encoded in language are also acted upon. This actionability is not a property of language in itself, but a property "authorized" by institutions and groups.

The way identities, relationships, and categories of the social are defined in language matters: it makes a difference for the type and direction of people's action – or inaction (Purvis and Hunt 1993: 474; Bourdieu 1982: 127-8). The war of interpretations in which movements are engaged comprises battles over the power to establish authoritative definitions that imply "acts and interventions" (Fraser 1989b: 166). Gillian Walker's analysis of the discursive struggle around the issue of wife-battering in Canada is instructive in this regard: as "women's movement activists struggled with professionals for control over the terms in which the issue was to be recognized and acted upon ... the struggle [became] one of contestation over whose knowledge will define the situation, who is to be held to blame, and *what kind of action will be taken by whom*" (Walker 1990: 18; my emphasis). Defining the issue as a "domestic dispute" locates the problem within the Criminal Code and the purview of its law enforcement agencies, whereas "family violence" channels intervention within the practices of social work professionals (11, 14). By contrast, "wife-battering" refers to Canadian women's groups' struggle for feminist services and for social solutions countering male violence.

If the constitutive character of language is the object of the struggles for the fixation of social meanings in which movements engage, it is not only from the more abstract point of view of embedding new identities, relations, and representations in "norms and codes," policies and programs, or in the "democratic project." The discursive practices of the actors also generate and enable (Weir 1993b: 242) – or, conversely, foreclose and pre-empt – social action. The legitimation, if not the institutionalization, of specific actionable meanings has consequences for the subsequent pursuit of movement politics – as well as for the daily life of people (as the example from Walker also suggests).

Language as a Bounded Mode of Action

As a social mode of action, language typically operates within limitations on the possibilities for signifying and resignifying. The limits placed on "what can be said" are also limits on "what can be done" by social agents engaged in social struggle. The bounded nature of linguistic and discursive practices is another important feature of language as a dimension of the exercise of and struggle over power. Movements' efforts to (re)constitute social reality and to impose new actionable meanings run against and have to break through these limits, or "effects of closure," embedded in language-in-use.

A first series of effects of closure are the limits placed on speech before speech can be there, limits that pre-empt the alternative to be expressed. If, to paraphrase Foucault (1984: 127), discourse, or language, is a violence we do to things/to the world, how we arrest the flux of lived existence potentially also arrests our possibilities of knowing and acting on the world within certain types of patterns. More specifically, these limits take place at the level of the *doxa*, that is, at the level of the classification schemes, categories, or relationships that are the most entrenched in what we call "common sense." Widespread and largely accepted, elements of the doxa usually go unquestioned (Maingueneau 1991: 247-8; Angenot 1989: 14, 160). Women's organizations' counterdiscourse production, with its explicit objective of "changing the mentalities" (Masson and Tremblay 1993: 177), is aiming at the doxa. Their speech repositions "women" as subjects and agents of non-habitual social processes and in new relationships with the other actors and objects of these processes. These enunciations are attempts to reopen what it is possible to say about women and what it is possible for women to do.

The existing range of meanings socially available to signify the world also forecloses the expression of the unexpressed. Some "ways of being cannot be spoken because the people who live them have no language for them" (Cain 1994: 84) and cannot be acted upon in socially transformative ways until people do have a language for them. A "labour of enunciation" (Bourdieu 1991: 129) has to occur in relation to this emergent speech. Under the efforts of the women's movement, for example, the unease, the shame, and the unspeakability of certain social situations have been (re)interpreted and (re)named. The new terms of "sexism," "sexual harassment," "marital, date and acquaintance rape," "labor force sex-segregation," "the double shift," and "wife-battery" have contributed to remake, Nancy Fraser (1992b: 179) argues, "entire regions of social discourse." In proposing new categories or new meanings to reinterpret the group's experience of the social world, as well as bringing into existence some of the ineffable (Bourdieu 1991: 129) and some of the unthinkable (Cain 1994) elements of lived social relations, movements constitute a new actionable knowledge in the form of new sets of meanings made available as a basis for political action.

Effects of closure not only operate on "speech before speech can be there," but also on the "speech that is." *Discourses* limit both linguistic practices (the textual meanings that can be enunciated) and discursive practices as events (whether and how these events can occur). There are two main avenues through which "discourse" is usually acknowledged as bringing about closure. The first one stresses the "regularities" – or fixations – of meanings in the linguistic practices associated with particular socio-enunciative positions that are also positions in a field of power. In this sense, "discourse" is usually understood as sets of conventionalized fixations that bound institutionally positioned speakers to particular ways of signifying. Discourses "define, describe and delimit what it is possible to say and not to say (and by extension – what it is possible to do and not to do) with respect to the area of concern of that institution, whether marginally or centrally ... organise and give structure to the manner in which a particular topic, object, process is to be talked about ... provide descriptions, rules, permissions and prohibitions of social and individual actions" (Kress 1985: 6-7, quoted in Yeatman 1990: 164). Discourses constrain what can be said and what can be done by given institutional actors. Discourses also impose authorized "ways of talking" about areas of knowledge or social practice on the broader institutional sites where they are hegemonic, and on the other actors wishing to intervene on these sites.

A second way in which discourses effect closure is through what Foucault (1984: 127) identifies as their "external conditions of possibility" – that is, through the rules of the discursive economies that bound the very enunciation of discourses. By this, Foucault points to the implicit inscriptions of power that make it possible or impossible for particular statements or meaning-making practices to occur at all in or from specific institutional positions. In this perspective, he sums up an ensemble of "procedures of exclusion" through which not only the objects of discourse ("what can be talked about"), but also the site – the circumstances and ways of speech, as well the speaking subject her/himself – is limited, rarefied, foreclosed.

Canadian women's movement organizations, for instance, have ventured since the 1980s on the terrain of economic policy. Their discursive interventions re-encode in gender terms the objects of conventional economic discourse such as free trade or the deficit. We can see from Brodie's (1995: 30) account that women's organizations have been so far denied the status of legitimate speakers on the institutional (state) sites in which economic policy is discussed. Their alternative discourse is dismissed and its implications therefore pre-empted. The respective range of legitimate "women's issues" and of appropriate "economic issues" remains curtailed as well. The effective closure of this site on the speaker, on speech, and on potential actionability is undeniably an expression and an effect of the exercise of relations of power.

Effects of closure on the speech "to be" and on the speech "that is" appear as much an important part of what is at stake in social movements' struggles on the terrain of the symbolic than the meanings themselves. Among the things that oppositional social actors "do with language" are discursive practices that attempt, and sometimes succeed, in opening up the fields and the sites of meaning-making production, liquefying closure and setting up new ground rules for further political action.

CONCLUSION

The recent interest in the symbolic dimension of collective action, and in its intertwining with questions of strategy and politics, is among the most interesting developments in social movement theory today. Yet, as a fair number of scholars have remarked, the field remains ill equipped to fully appreciate the role played by symbolic constructs in movement activity. The pursuit of this inquiry requires moving away from an understanding of symbolic constructions as simple "power tools" in the hands of movement activists and their opponents (as in RMT). The relationship between "the symbolic" and power is more intimate, and its reaches have further implications in terms of social life and social structure. As flagged by Melucci and explored in a more detailed manner by Laclau and Mouffe, the symbolic is more adequately conceptualized as an intrinsic dimension of the exercise of power and of the political struggles over the power to constitute social reality.

In this light, a promising avenue for social movement theory is, I suggest, to engage more extensively with the theorizing (and, eventually, the methodologies) that critical approaches to the study of language and discourse have to offer.[20] This engagement produces a revision of social movement research orientations in particular directions. Namely, it stresses the need for a politically oriented analysis of movement meaning-making practices that pays attention to the specificity of the language in which movements' meanings and struggles over meanings are couched. This is not to promote the return to a classical, fine-grained analysis of political ideologies. Nor does it amount to considering movements' struggles as a textual "contest between competing tropes,"[21] or, in a postmodern fashion, as the disembodied confrontation of contending discourses. Rather, it proposes to understand how language and discourses are implicated and put to work, as agent-driven modes of action, in political projects of dominance and change.

The action perspective I am arguing for directs attention towards analysing the linguistic and discursive practices of concrete actors interacting within a political field, and the consequences of these practices for continuity and change within wider social processes. There are two distinct, although related, components to this proposition.

First, it advocates a detailed form-and-meaning analysis of movements' linguistic practices. Here I have repeatedly made a case for the analysis of the particulars of movements' representations, underlining the contingency of movement identities and interests, the variability and ambiguity of movement projects and politics, and the relational and consequential character of frames. If language is, furthermore, theorized as a constitutive, performative, and actionable mode of action, we cannot avoid the examination of the linguistic specificity of movement meanings. What social movement research needs is not so much a "descent into discourse" as a linguistically sensitive analysis of real instances of people saying and writing things

(Fairclough 1992: 57) in the course of collective action.

Second, integral to this proposition is the recognition that text-internal analysis of meanings is not enough. Acts of language occur in contexts, and do something in these contexts. Textual meanings have to be located within the "context of situation" (Halliday 1989) and discursive constraints that bound their production and their enunciation. They must be situated within the political field and the institutional sites where they get played out as the discursive practices of movement actors interacting and struggling with other actors; and they must be examined in their outcomes and consequences in terms of subsequent political, institutional, and social action.[22] In addition, discursive practices have to be inscribed in the socially and historically located strategies and projects of the social subjects that produce them (Maingueneau 1991). Finally, these practices cannot be treated in isolation from the larger social processes that they contribute to realize, or to alter (Threadgold 1989: 103).

Placing the emphasis on a linguistically sensitive, politically oriented approach to movements' symbolic production enables a more in-depth, sharpened analysis of specific discursive struggles over meanings, namings, and framings. More fundamentally, however, and as I have tried to make clear here, a focus on the language/power relationship opens new grounds for our understanding of the symbolic challenge of movements and broadens the scope of our inquiry into the role played by "the symbolic" in the unfolding of movement politics.

NOTES

* I would like to thank Lorna Weir, Heather Jon Maroney, Antje Wiener, and William Carroll for their critical and insightful comments on earlier drafts of this chapter.

1. This dismissal has never been complete or shared by all RM theorists. Scholars from the "political process" strand (Tilly 1978; McAdam 1982; and their followers) traditionally integrate, even if often only descriptively, a concern for movement ideologies and interests in their analyses.
2. For a brief history of RMT's turn towards issues of meaning construction, see Donati (1992: 136-7) or Benford (1993b: 197-9). For a more in-depth questioning of the rational choice assumptions at the heart of the RM model, see McClurg Mueller (1992) and Ferree (1992).
3. Classic references include Cohen (1983, 1985), Laclau and Mouffe (1985), Touraine (1988), and Melucci (1989).
4. See, for example, Young (1990), Jenson (1989a, 1993), and Dalton and Kuechler (1990).
5. The field of sociolinguistics divides into two very different theoretical strands (for an introduction see Van Dijk 1985a, 1985b). The "Anglo-American" position is influenced by the ethnography of speaking and by micro-interactionist traditions. The "European" (or "Continental") tradition owes more to its engagement with early semiotics, structuralism, Marxism, and poststructuralism.
6. "Partly" because the other route indicated by Melucci under the concept of movements' symbolic challenge is the inquiry into the new "ways of life" and

"cultural models" developed by oppositional movements. Escobar (1992) and Starn (1992) propose versions of this line of inquiry.

7. Semiotic systems include linguistic as well as non-linguistic systems of signs (such as dress codes, visual symbols, and non-verbal expressions). For an accessible introduction to social semiotics and the study of semiotic practices, see Lemke (1990).

8. See in particular Melucci (1989), McClurg Mueller (1992), Buechler (1993), and Jenson (1993).

9. The idea that movement identities, interests, and political projects are the object of a process of political hegemony that occurs "internally," amid the heterogeneous subjects and organizations that compose a movement, I derive from Michaud (1992: 212-13).

10. The challenge from poststructuralism and the non-Western feminist critique has made it impossible to speak of "women," or "women's interests" in universal terms. On these questions, see in particular Riley (1988), Mohanty (1992), Nicholson (1994), and Pringle and Watson (1990).

11. This being said, the concept of "frame" remains imprecise in its uses. In a sense, "frames" have some affinity with the loose utilization of the term "discourse," as pointing to distinctive ways of using language (of saying things), either from particular socio-enunciative positions (radical feminist frame, student left frame: McAdam 1994), or adjusted to the discourses and "styles of making claims" appropriate to particular institutional sites (equal opportunity frame, rights frame: Tarrow 1994a). Such labels as "drunk-driving frame" and "auto-safety frame" (McCarthy 1994) seem closer to the understanding of frames as ensembles of "problem attribution/solution identification" templates.

12. This point is often acknowledged by movement activists. As a telling example, Benford (1993b: 202) writes that his informants in the nuclear disarmament movement "jokingly dubbed" their own consciousness-raising movies as "apocaporn."

13. The distinction between "discourse" and "ideology" is not just a matter of diverging intellectual traditions and, although often unclear, should be retained. For an overview of the question, see in particular Purvis and Hunt (1993) and Eagleton (1991).

14. On the discursive politics around the issue of abortion in Canada see Brodie, Gavigan, and Jenson (1992), and the critical review of their book by movement activists from the Ontario Coalition for Abortion Clinics (Egan, Lee, and Robidoux 1991).

15. The exception to date is Johnston (1991).

16. The schools of critical linguistics (for example, Fairclough 1992; Fowler 1991), systemic functional grammar (for example, Halliday 1989; Weir 1995), social semiotics (for example, Threadgold 1989), and the French school of discourse analysis (see overview in Maingueneau 1991) are usually identified with "critical discourse analysis" (CDA). Reference to earlier theorizing by Bourdieu and Foucault (first published in French in the 1970s and 1980s) is a feature of many of these works. For a mapping of CDA's orientations and a brief overview of the different schools, see Van Dijk (1993: 249-51).

17. My use of the term "text" in these pages is limited to its commonsense acceptation and includes written and spoken linguistic production.

18. The respective weight of language, or discourse, and of "non-discursive" practices in constituting social reality is currently the object of heated debates. Postmodern attempts to present all-encompassing versions of "discourse" as the

source of the social are resisted by most critical discourse analysts. Their position rather acknowledges that there is a dynamic, dialectical relationship between non-discursive and discursive practices, between lived existence and what can be captured by language and discourse. On this last point, see in particular Cain (1994).

19. Paraphrasing Foucault (1984: 124).
20. An overview of the methodological apparatus available for doing linguistically based discourse analysis can be found in Maingueneau (1991). Good examples of empirical works using these methods include Fowler (1991), Fairclough (1993), Van Dijk (1993), and Weir (1995).
21. A position that Tarrow (1994a: 119-21) attributes to deconstructionists.
22. See Walker (1990) for a good example of this type of work.

IS THE PERSONAL
ALWAYS POLITICAL?
ENVIRONMENTALISM IN
ARENDT'S AGE OF "THE SOCIAL"

Catriona Sandilands

INTRODUCTION: THE DEMISE OF ENVIRONMENTAL POLITICS

On April 5, 1994, a headline in *The Globe and Mail* caught my attention: "Environmentalists not seen as force in next Ontario Election" (Rusk 1994: A3). This prophecy proved distressingly true in the 1995 provincial campaign itself: despite the demise of the Ontario Waste Management Corporation (leaving the province with no policy on hazardous waste whatsoever), despite Conservative Mike Harris's commitment to gut the Planning Act (which would reopen every possible door for suburban sprawl), and despite NDP leader Bob Rae's former environmental commitment (demonstrated by an arrest over Temagami clearcutting while he was still leader of the opposition) and Liberal leader Lyn McLeod's former status as minister of natural resources in the Peterson government, an observer of the campaign would have concluded that there is no environment about which to be concerned. Planning Act aside, the Conservatives were elected *without* an environmental platform.[1]

But what really caught my attention was the article's suggestion that public political interest in environmental issues had declined dramatically since the previous Ontario provincial election. In 1995 I was disappointed to see that even the anti-Harris protest on the lawns of the provincial legislature – a protest designed to highlight the profound injustices in his agenda – failed to note his complete lack of concern over matters environmental.[2] The protest was a parody of the Tory swearing-in ceremony being held at the same time; for each "real" minister, a "community" minister stood up to present an alternative agenda. Although there was, for instance, a minister of gay and lesbian issues, there was no community minister of the environment.

While electoral campaigns are not the only, or best, sites for the politicization of environmental issues, I find this trend disturbing. A recent Angus Reid poll confirms my distress. In 1989, when asked "what is the most important issue facing the country?" 33 per cent of Canadians polled replied "the environment." In 1990 the figure fell to 24 per cent; in 1991, to 17 per cent; in 1992, to 7 per cent; in 1993, to only 4 per cent (Lintula 1994: 7-8).[3]

As the *Globe* article suggested, "The strength of the environmental movement has been sapped in the recession" (Rusk 1994: A6). While the poll showed that many people were still concerned about environmental issues – to the extent that 21 per cent of respondents said they considered themselves to be "environmental activists," whatever that may mean to Angus Reid – it is the economy that is clearly foremost in the minds of most Canadians. Said Colin Isaacs, "With jobs at the head of the public's concerns, the message that many do not want to hear is that the solution to environmental problems is to shut down industry, ban logging, and stop the development of mines" (quoted in Rusk 1994: A6). Add that widespread – if inaccurate – perception to the dwindling of many environmental groups' financial support in the recession, and we end up with a situation in which environmental issues are, apparently, seldom raised publicly, and not particularly appreciated when they are.

At the same time, the Angus Reid Poll suggests that a clear majority of Canadians say they are engaged in "green" activities, would pay more, even in these recessionary times, for so-called environmentally friendly products, and would support stiffer penalties against polluters. One in three say they would support a ten-cent deposit on all aluminum cans and a total ban on logging of old-growth forests (Lintula 1994: 7-8). Indeed, an environmental store has recently opened in my neighbourhood and seems to be doing extremely well selling hemp clothing, "tree-free" paper, key chains made from computer boards, and organic chocolate made with Oregon raspberries. So why is it, in this context of such apparently widespread concern, that the political voices of environmental movements in Ontario are, to quote the *Globe*, a "whimper"?

Important though the recession may be, it does not explain this apparent contradiction. What we need to look at as well is the status of environmental issues as *public* and *political*. Through this lens, it seems that the environment has been generally depoliticized. Specifically, it is in the move by which environmental concern can be relatively unproblematically expressed in such actions as recycling, paying deposits on aluminum cans, buying cute little green key chains, and condemning polluters and forestry practices to Angus Reid pollsters, that we see the demise of the environment as a site of genuinely political contestation.

There are, of course, significant exceptions, like Clayoquot Sound, which was considered sufficiently political to mobilize over 800 people to get arrested in the summer of 1993 and thousands of forestry workers and supporters to engage in counterprotests.[4] In general, however, a strong relationship seems to exist between how environmental issues have become routinized, bureaucratized, and individualized, and how they have become depoliticized. As Tim Luke points out, environmental issues have become much more respectable now that corporations have applied thick coats of green paint to their reputations. According to Luke (1993: 155), twenty years ago, "Any serious personal interest in the environment often was seen as the definitive mark of radical extremism," while environmentalism today has become a much more mainstream concern, and "major corporations now feel moved to proclaim how much 'every day is Earth Day.'"[5]

While corporate and state green rhetorics have had the effect of narrowing the possibilities for a more radical outlook, it also seems that many environmental groups have themselves participated in the process of depoliticization. As Laurie Adkin (1992: 150) notes, despite the wide variety of positions apparent in Canadian environmental movements – with some of them strongly oriented to revealing and acting upon the specifically political aspects of systemic environmental problems – all too few groups are willing or able to resist dominant ecocapitalist "technocratic and market-oriented" discourses. The relative absence, in much environmental discourse, of a clear idea of the political itself is thus a large part of this problem. Specifically, much contemporary environmental concern is all too easily seduced by trends towards private, often expedient and bureaucratic, solutions. One could even argue that environmental issues inhabit a discursive terrain particularly susceptible to an administrative approach, grounded more in natural science than in political science (Paehlke 1989: 273). As a result, the specifically political dimensions of environmental issues – their ability to foster collective discussion and contestation over meanings and relations – are swallowed up by instrumental, technocratic orientations. When environmental issues do contain the possibility to constitute and mobilize diverse publics this potential is seldom fulfilled, because the political is generally not located as a central element in environmental struggle. In the absence of a clear agenda of politicization, environmental issues are, not surprisingly, all too often placed behind a corporate, technocratic, and fundamentally conservative screen.

IS THE PERSONAL ALWAYS POLITICAL?

As for the question "Is the personal always political?" it should be apparent, by now, that my answer is "no." If environmental movements are to challenge the green rhetoric of state bureaucracies and corporations, it is important that their members not allow the closing of spaces of *public* contestation that such rhetorics so often lead to. If environmental movements are to bring issues to light in a way that fosters the democratic formulation and resolution of those same issues – an approach that I (and many others) consider to be vital – their members need to consider the specificity of the political and speak about the distinctiveness of a public, political realm for ecological conversation. Here, the personal cannot be always already political; to say that it is is to undermine, ironically, the necessity of democracy.

At the same time, the phrase "the personal is political" needs to be cherished. Movements for social and environmental justice rely on making links between private, personal experience and public, political action; it is from the articulation of deeply held social justice concerns with environmental issues that the movement can find its "counterhegemonic" potential, in Adkin's (1992) terms. Here, it is the empowerment of marginalized groups to "speak their experiences" that leads to politics – indeed, that leads us to challenge dominant definitions of what is said to count as a political (or environmental) issue in the first place. For example, it was through the experiences of the Innu that most of the rest of Canada heard of Nitassinan, and found out that low-level *NATO* flights were destroying both the wilderness and the Innu's health and livelihood. Against the bureaucratic machinations of Indian Affairs and Northern Development, Aboriginal self-determination and environmental degradation were politicized together. More generally, through the linkage of environmental and social justice concerns in a wide array of terrains of social life – homes, workplaces, neighbourhoods, even human and non-human bodies – we are able to reveal the inability of ecocapitalist rhetoric to speak of democracy.

So there is a tension, here. We can neither consider the boundaries of the political to be endless, thus conflating it with the personal, nor draw a firm circle around the political, thus irrevocably barring the entry of the personal. Out of this tension comes the question that will organize the rest of this chapter: how can environmentalists simultaneously retain the liberatory character of the phrase "the personal is political" *and* argue for the specificity of politics as a uniquely important terrain for the formulation and solution of environmental issues?

In the following pages I briefly examine the shape of the contemporary public sphere as a way of arguing for the need for a specifically political orientation to environmental issues. Specifically, I argue that the preservation of the political is not antithetical to the appearance of so-called private issues in the public realm. Indeed, if environmental issues are to reach their much-heralded democratic potential, there cannot be a clear line drawn around the issues that can appear as legitimately political. At the same time, politics are clearly not inherent to environmental (or any other) issues. This problem suggests a process of retrieval, or reframing, in which we can pull out the specifically deliberative elements of environmental discourses.

THE RISE AND FALL OF THE "PUBLIC" SPHERE (IN BRIEF)

If there is one thing theorists of contemporary public life seem to agree on, it is that the spheres we commonly understand as public and private are historically specific in their construction and content. The modern, Western public sphere is generally understood to have emerged out of the separation of political from economic and family life during the eighteenth century. Defined as a realm "in which the public organizes itself as the bearer of public opinion" (Habermas 1974: 50), a genuine sphere of public authority only emerged with the dissolution of embodied feudal powers and the rise of (relatively) independent parliamentary and judicial structures. As Jürgen Habermas (1974: 50) writes, "There is no indication European society of the high middle ages possessed a public sphere as a unique realm distinct from the private sphere." Rather, with the splitting of the private and public elements of feudal powers (church, princes, and nobility) space was opened for the creation of a sphere of politically deliberative life distinct from the presence of rulers.[6]

Linda Nicholson specifies this history in terms of the decline of kinship as a general principle of social organization in Western societies. From a "premodern" period of relative integration, in which kinship played an enormous role in structuring both economic and political life, modernity has produced the progressive compartmentalization of these spheres. "In this period," Nicholson (1989: 106) writes, "the decline in importance of kinship meant the emergence of a public sphere, relatively unstructured by relations of kinship, and the increased restriction of kinship to the sphere of domestic life."

The very emergence of modern, Western, liberal-democratic political arrangements is, then, predicated on the progressive separation of the state from the family and the economy.[7] This is by no means a natural arrangement, but is rather the result of a particular (bourgeois) progression by which certain realms of life have become increasingly private and others increasingly public. That this private life is also, in modernity, domestic life has nothing to do with some inherently apolitical character of either. Instead, as Nicholson's analysis shows, the terms personal and political and private and public are embedded in a complex web of power relations and are always already the subject of discursive negotiation and contestation.

The sense of artificial separation of public from private life lies at the heart of social movements' transcendence of state containers for politics (see Offe 1985b; Magnusson and Walker 1988). More familiarly to most, it also rests in the phrase "the personal is political," particularly in its original feminist usage. If there is one thread that runs through and beyond disparate feminisms, it is the sense that what has illegitimately been labelled "personal," "private," and "idiosyncratic" in women's and others' lives must be shown to be rightly political, must be brought into the public realm of collective discussion and action. The separation of politics from private life is shown, here, to be a powerful fiction, one that delegitimates not only women's experiences in particular, as beings tied to the domestic realm, but also those of other marginalized groups. These experiences are rendered, in this separation, "merely personal" (read: particular) in contrast to the "genuinely political" (read: universal) interests of dominant groups.

Valuable though these insights may be, history did not end with decline of kinship and the rise of modern liberal democracy. In particular, it is crucial for us to take into account the impact of the development of welfare capitalism on the constitution of public and private life in Western societies. Specifically, our age has witnessed the decline of both spheres: there are fewer and fewer spaces available for genuinely political action, that is, for public contestation over issues of (potentially) common concern, and, simultaneously, fewer and fewer spaces of genuine privacy and intimacy. While there is certainly good reason to celebrate aspects of the erosion of a clear demarcation between public and private – the publicization of issues around food and waste, for example, or domestic violence – there is also reason to be wary of the forms of social life that have emerged in the wake.

To Hannah Arendt, the rise of the realm she calls the "social," which we can take for the moment to mean "mass" society, has narrowed the realm of politics on the one hand, and encroached on the possibility of intimacy on the other. Seyla Benhabib (1992: 90) provides an excellent summary of Arendt's interpretation:

> The same historical process which brought forth the modern constitutional state also brought forth "society," that realm of social interaction which interposes itself between the "household" on one hand and the political state on the other. A century ago, Hegel had described this process as the development in the midst of ethical life of a "system of needs," of a domain of economic activity governed by commodity exchange and the pursuit of economic self-interest.... Arendt sees in this process the occluding of the "political" by the "social" and the transformation of the public space of politics into a psuedospace [sic] of interaction in which individuals no longer "act" but "merely behave" as economic producers, consumers and urban city-dwellers

Thus the rise of the social does not represent simply a blurring of the boundaries between public and private life – something many social movements might want to preserve as part of the democratization of everyday life (Melucci 1988) – but the replacement of both by a particular configuration of social life in which the commodity is king, and in which bureaucratic, administrative, and instrumental logics have largely replaced democratic conversations. The phrase "the personal is political" does not capture this social realm; no longer are the private and public clearly demarcated and oppositional realms to be deconstructed, but rather both are being eclipsed by a form of mass social life hostile to both privacy and democratic scrutiny.

To Habermas, the result of this process is that the "political public sphere" of the welfare state bears little resemblance to a space for public deliberation over matters of common political concern. He argues that the processes by which the public expanded beyond the confines of the bourgeoisie – with the rise of the mass politics of the press and propaganda, for example – have produced a situation in which the public sphere is simply the realm in which private interests are mediated through forcible confrontation. Deliberation is rare. In what he calls a process of "refeudalization," Habermas (1989: 236) says, "The political public sphere in the welfare state is characterized by a singular weakening of its critical functions." What should be a place of democracy, of conference in an unrestricted fashion, is reduced to a place of interest-group conflict and administration.

The rise of the social – especially its organization through commodity circulation – shows a weakening of the ability of the supposedly public sphere to either represent or produce much more than competing interests formulated without the benefit of, or accountability to, a common public. In this context, the process of politicization is not simply a question of making something appear from private life in the public realm. *Even* if many social movements reject the state as a natural container for the political, the spaces of discussion that emerge from these challenges are not necessarily political. While it is thus crucial to recognize emerging discourses around the environment as a new sphere of conversation, in new potential spaces of politics that transect the boundaries between state and civil society, it is also crucial to recognize that these discourses are not inherently political by the mere fact of their being aired. One must consider the particular character of the public life into which environmental issues are inserted, along the lines of a question Nancy Fraser (1989b: 12) asks: "What does the emergence of needs [or, here, environmental issues] imply about shifts in the boundaries between 'political,' 'economic,' and 'domestic' spheres of life? Does it betoken an extension of the political sphere or, rather, a colonization of that sphere by newer modes of power and social control?"

For environmental politics, this question requires a rethinking of the phrase "the personal is political." It is not simply the case that removing an issue from obscurity will necessarily result in its politicization, or in the extension of the political to include environmental dimensions. In the context of administrative and bureaucratic hegemony – or what Fraser calls "juridical-administrative-therapeutic state apparatuses" – it is entirely likely that the raising of the environment as an issue will result in technocratic institutionalization, rather than in democratic conversation.

The tendency in some versions of environmental advocacy (for example, some ecofeminism) to make it seem that everything is always already equally political has the effect of making us unable to respond to the contemporary erosion of genuinely democratic possibilities. Saying that the personal *is* political, in this type of usage, is not simply a rhetorical strategy designed to highlight the flexibility of the boundaries between the two moments. It becomes a statement of equivalence, and I think this equivalence is misguided, particularly when politics inhabits such a narrow band of human life. As Fraser (1989b: 76) writes: "When everything is political, the sense and specificity of the political recedes, giving rise to ... [a particular] inflection of the expression *le retrait du politique*: the retreat or withdrawal of the political."

ARENDT: COMMUNITY, ACTION, AND THE PUBLIC SPHERE

In environmental politics, it is thus important not just to make the personal political, but also to make the *political* political. In other words, if environmentalists hope to raise issues in a way that produces some form of democratic conversation, and not simply technical interest-broking, they also need to think critically about resuscitating a specifically public sphere, and to place such an analysis at the centre of their discourse. In Habermas's terms, the defining character of the (bourgeois) public sphere is that private individuals deliberate about matters of *common* concern that transcend individual interests, and in a common forum accessible to all; commonality acts to defend the specificity of politics against the incursion of private interest-broking and serves to define the boundaries of the political. The question for environmentalists becomes: how to produce "commonality" as a central feature of environmental politics and at the same time respect the political possibilities of "the personal"?

Given this formulation of the question, it is perhaps ironic that I choose to turn to Arendt for an understanding of the specificity of politics to carry back to environmentalism. As numerous feminist thinkers point out (see Honig 1995), Arendt's understanding of public life is highly problematic for its rigid delineation of appropriate *contents* that de facto preclude the appearance of the body, the private, and, potentially, nature itself in its guise as the ground of the spontaneous and cyclical processes of biological necessity.[8] This problem is certainly important, but what is also apparent in Arendt, and what is of more relevance to my argument here, is the possibility of reading her understanding of politics as a desire for a particular character of conversation. While I can do no justice here to either the subtleties or the contradictions apparent in her thought (on the contradictions, see especially Passerin d'Entreves 1994), I would like to pull from Arendt the possibility that the specificity of politics can inhere in its form rather than in its content or space.

Briefly, Arendt understood "the human condition" as divided into three essential activities: labour, work, and action. In *The Human Condition* (1958: 7) she argued, "Labour is the activity which corresponds to the biological process of the human body" and "work is the activity which ... provides an artificial world of things." Finally, "Action, the only activity that goes on directly between men without the intermediary of things or matter, corresponds directly to the human condition of plurality." In her description of the rise of "the social," she sees the potential for "action" sorely circumscribed by the increasing dominance in interactional space of issues deriving from the realms of work and labour. In the revitalization of action, one needs to defend it from the appearance of needs, the body, and biological inevitability. If plurality is the human condition of action, only in the transcendence of inherently private necessity does the possibility of plurality, the recognition of commonality, emerge.

While we do need to halt the particular *retrait du politique* apparent in the decline of the specificity of politics, and while commonality is clearly a political condition, it is a mistake to attempt to delineate, against the labours of most contemporary social movements, the appropriate contents of politics once and for all, as if such a gesture were an adequate defence in the face of declining possibilities for a public sphere (to do so would also be to accept the neoconservative rhetoric of "special interest groups"), and as if commonality were not a discursively, politically produced understanding. Commonality is not inherent to an issue, but is rather the *product* of precisely the discursive deliberation that the public sphere is supposed to foster. As Fraser (1992a: 130-1) notes, there is no particular relationship between content and commonality; it is precisely this question with which we enter the public sphere:

> There is no way to know in advance whether the outcome of a deliberative process will be the discovery of a common good in which conflicts of interest evaporate as merely apparent or the discovery that conflicts of interest are real and the common good is chimerical. But if the existence of a common good cannot be presumed in advance, then there is no warrant for putting any strictures on what sorts of topics, interests, and views are admissible in deliberation.

But it is possible to read Arendt differently, to remove from her politics its banishment of the private and focus on its distinctive promise. The first thing to be noted in this rereading is that, for Arendt, politics appears whenever people act together in concert over issues of common concern: no particular geographic place is attached to this conception of the public realm, unlike, for example, in the libertarian municipalism of Murray Bookchin (1987, 1989).[9] Arendt (1958: 98) wrote: "The *polis*, properly speaking, is not the city-state in its physical location; it is the organization of the people as it arises out of acting and speaking together, and its true space lies between people living together for this purpose, no matter where they happen to be. 'Wherever you go, you will be a polis.'"

The polis inhabits diverse topographies; the point is not to carve out a singular space of politics, but to insist on the particular, if transportable, character of action. Thus, the second point: action, to Arendt, involves a particular process of self-disclosure through speech, a process by which human beings come together and engage in speech and deeds in the presence of others, in the realm of the "world." In this process, people reveal "who" they are, as opposed to "what" they are (the latter, categorical activities associated with labour and work, hence her banishment of their contents). In action, people come to be constituted as individuals beyond their "private" identities or interests; this constitution creates the condition of plurality, the recognition of commonality, the sense that "we are all the same, that is, human, in such a way that nobody is ever the same as anyone else who ever lived, lives, or will live" (1958: 8).

Action is about "new beginnings," about transcending inevitability and creating anew the possibility of freedom.[10] It is also about a process in which the appearing actor is opened to the presence of multiple others, thus becoming something new through political appearance itself. To Arendt, this possibility is foreclosed by the appearance of issues from the private realm of inevitability. But *if* we understand political life as defined by a *character* of uncertainty and openness, rather than by a set of topics that appear as already open – in other words, by insisting that not just the outcomes but also the origins of politics cannot be known in advance – then the very process of opening up an issue to public scrutiny gives it the potential for a distinctively political character. In Arendt's terms, this opening requires the possibility of a diverse range of individuals constituting themselves in relation to the issue under consideration. In my terms, this does not preclude the appearance of any contents, but only requires that the orientation to uncertainty and openness produces a willingness to transcend private interests in favour of their public reconstitution as "common" matters.

We can thus argue that there can be no inherent content to politics, including environmental politics, because politics itself is the constitutive moment: the act of bringing something forth for public discussion *is* the act of politics.[11] To predefine an appropriate realm of discussion is to close off the possibility of its constitution. As Benhabib (1992: 195) writes, "The struggle to make something 'public' is a struggle for justice – thus, the process can never be complete: there can be no agenda to predefine the topic of public conversation." To make the environment (for example) specifically political is, thus, to open it to a contestation whose outcome cannot be known, to produce a situation in which actors can produce themselves in relation to a matter of common concern.

From this skeletal reading of Arendt comes the conclusion that politics involves a particular character of conversation in which issues "come to light," not simply out of obscurity but also *into* a process of scrutiny in the presence of others, in which the outcome of the conversation cannot be known in advance. Political actors are created in the political process; private interests are not the stuff of political conversation, as each must take on the character of openness and uncertainty that action requires. In a sense, politics as a character requires the continual development of new commonalities, new places where "the personal" is redefined so that it will speak to a common terrain, new places where precisely that common terrain is redefined so that it will be open to the personal.

DEPOLITICIZING THE ENVIRONMENT

There is, then, nothing inherently political about the raising of environmental issues, because it is not the issue that lends itself to a private or public existence but the character in which it is discursively produced as a subject of common deliberation. The environment is neither inherently public nor inherently private; the point is to argue for the need to develop its political character as a unique and important part of environmental transformation. The key, here, is to push for a process of opening – to diverse publics, to diverse and uncertain possibilities.

Against the notion of a singular public sphere in which commonality is defined once and for all as encompassing an already apparent set of universal issues (for example, the clearly problematic environmental rhetoric of "we're all in the same boat"),[12] and against the related notion that the public sphere is necessarily a space of relative homogeneity, hostile to the appearance of difference (for example, "save the earth first, social justice later"), a focus on the character of politics suggests the possibility (indeed, necessity) of multiple environmental publics in a wide variety of spaces in both the state and civil society. Yet this character of politics retains a specificity: everything is not always already political, and the necessity of opening spaces of apparently private life to scrutiny remains an important environmental democratic project.

This character is under threat in contemporary environmentalism. If the political involves the opening of issues to scrutiny and uncertainty from a wide variety of constituencies, reshaping the constituencies themselves in the process, the political character of environmental issues is being sorely circumscribed. Specifically, environmentalism has lost its public and contested character, its ability to produce common ecological discussion, and this has happened through various processes that have made its appearance, among other things, subject to expert and individualized response. These technomanagerial discourses close off the ability of individuals to constitute themselves and their concerns in relation to others. Where "the environment" is defined by experts, and where personal responses to that predefined environment remain solidly located in the private realm, individuals gain few opportunities to come together and to see their environmental concerns as producing/reflecting a commonality.

The environment may be omnipresent as a topic of concern, but its political potential is under threat because of how the issues are approached and acted upon. Although issues continue to be raised (not insignificantly, through natural science), once raised they are passed over to panels of experts – planners, waste managers, engineers – with expediency taking absolute precedence over public discussion, over the light of scrutiny. Part of this desire for expediency resides in crisis-talk ("the planet must be saved in the fastest way possible"), and part of it resides in the expert and professional relations generated by environmentalism.

Joni Seager (1993: 185) writes of an "ecology establishment," of legions of environmental professionals seen as experts.[13] Environmental problems are all too often directed to these people, which has the clear effect of both narrowing the interests (gendered or racialized, for instance) represented in discussion and stripping issues such as urban planning from community involvement. As a result, in the absence of an open public appearance, citizens have little chance to produce their private interests in a way amenable to the formulation of commonality. Instead, environmental problems remain in the formulations and institutions of the "ecocrat." Numerous constituencies feel themselves unrepresented in environmental discourses, at least in part because their knowledges and problems have not contributed to the formulation of what constitutes a common environmental concern.

This tyranny of expertise certainly appears in such arenas as environmental impact assessment hearings. Such hearings regulate the segments of the public allowed to have interests related to the issue under consideration (for example, intervenor status). Here, clearly, "some interests are greater than others." As Mary Richardson, Joan Sherman, and Michael Gismondi (1993) indicate, for example, risk science plays the dominant role in determining "environmental impact," and not the citizens who will be impacted. In addition, the appearance of such hearings as "public" erodes the possibility of the formation of a democratic or discursive public that could discuss or produce some commonality. The only way anyone can speak at many of these hearings is as a representative of a group with an interest that the hearing process has deemed legitimate. The delineation of the public solely in terms of (certain) private interests circumscribes both commonality and representative diversity. More broadly, in the process of formulating the problems in the first place such processes close off collective contestation. The moment at which the definitional process is closed to contestation is the moment at which the political recedes.[14]

A corresponding moment in the depoliticization of the environment is the rhetoric suggesting, "It's the individual who makes the difference" (a rhetoric that we now, not coincidentally, see taken up by Ontario Hydro and numerous "ecocapitalist" ventures). When recycling, composting, and carrying your own cloth bags to the store count as significant environmental actions, the space of politics, of collective discussion, of contestation, is grossly narrowed (see Luke 1993; Sandilands 1993). So long as environmentalism is relatively easily incorporated into daily routines, its more radical proponents do not have the chance to pose difficult questions to the public, thus prompting deliberation. So long as individual actions stand in for political discussion, The Body Shop will be the most public forum in which environmental issues are raised; action will be replaced with consumption. Insofar as individuals are lured into a place where intervention into the personal stands in for action, it seems highly unlikely that action, the "work" of offering up for scrutiny painful and difficult environmental issues, will occur without a concerted effort.[15]

Through both professionalization and individualization, the environment, as a potential subject of political discourse, dissolves into a series of isolated semi-private spheres. We have little chance to engage in a collective process of connection, to constitute ourselves in relation to the underlying processes of environmental degradation that public, democratic discussion of the issues might reveal. Indeed, Peter Swan (1993: 202) argues that depoliticization is not accidental: "The promotion of co-operation between government, industry, and environmental groups, is one element of a 'discourse of reprivatization' that represents an attempt by ... industries ... to retain or extend control over the environmental agenda in Canada." In response he suggests the specific development of *oppositional* ecopolitical discourses, a process of reframing and reopening, of the reinvigoration not just of discussion but of a sense of controversy lacking in much contemporary environmentalism.

It seems apparent that the environment is losing its distinctively public and contested character through the process that Swan accurately labels "reprivatization." Where once "environmentalist" was a relatively radical subject-position, a place from which to begin controversy, it is now a very banal label. As Neil Evernden (1984) notes, even the language of "the environment" is problematic. It constitutes nature as a terrain that simply reflects human interests and has already been colonized and routinized by the language of planning and impact assessment. In other words, the environment has, in Arendt's terms, come to inhabit the murky realm of the social, of administration and bureaucracy, of markets, experts, and consumers, which narrows the possibility for both genuinely public, and genuinely private, appearances. The spaces of (public) politics and (private) wonder are both being colonized.[16]

REPOLITICIZING THE ENVIRONMENT

What I would like to suggest is that it is from precisely *the personal* that a revitalization of environmental politics may be possible, which is one of the reasons why we must consider the flexibility of the boundaries between personal and political, the uncertainty of content as well as outcome. The rising of new issues into sight, into potential spaces of public scrutiny, signals a process by which the environment has not already been completely reprivatized. If we can show the potential political *character* of these issues, their public contestation is possible.

The personal, here, cannot be mistaken for so-called identity politics, in which the validity of political speech resides in the identity of the speaker, rather than in the political process itself. It is important to consider the movement between personal and political as one recognizing mutual influence and interdependence, rather than as one irretrievably privileging private identity as the basis for politics. The point is not to reify individual or group interests, but to formulate particular positions with reference to an agenda of commonality beyond individual participants' interests, at the same time as that commonality is subject to open contestation (see Laclau 1992).

For example, waste incinerators can become political, can be wrested from the grasp of expert "risk" discourse, if the personal effects of health problems can be shown to be collective and controversial, if it can be shown that a variety of interests is not being represented or formulated in current policy. The political promise lies not in a simple enumeration of health problems of particular constituencies, but in the raising of a multiplicity of health issues that both connect and transcend particular groups. Another example: food can be taken from the realm of consumer decision-making and transformed into public debates around everything from irradiation to factory farming, so long as it can be shown that "eating green" is not enough and that a collective process of problematizing food *systems* is necessary.[17] In this case, the constituencies formulated can include non-human groups (as in animal rights), but the general point is that elements of both collectivity and specificity can be raised through the concerns of multiple constituencies, in a way that shows the need for action beyond the private sphere.

In these two examples (and there are many others), spaces of potential controversy exist that have not yet been completely bureaucratized. A wide array of positions is yet to be formulated in relation to common problems. To get the political going, we must take such personal issues and translate them into a specifically political language, against therapeutic, individualistic, corporate, or bureaucratic discourses. While the contents of public discussion cannot be known in advance, it is reasonable to argue that the environment can, if raised as a simultaneously common and specific terrain of controversy, produce a diverse and polyvocal public.

Problematic though liberal-democratic notions of rights and justice may be in other respects, particularly when applied to non-humans, they may be part of a process by which the political and connective character of otherwise private and isolated issues can be constituted. Swan (1993: 205) writes: "Rights are relational in the sense that they are connected to each other in chains of relationships.... Defined in this manner environmental rights claims represent the 'right to have other rights,' and thus contribute to the ongoing democratic debate about exactly what should be considered as legitimate objects of public debate in contemporary society."

Despite the limitations of any democratic approach that does not consider the non-human actors in environmental decision-making processes, the language of rights is, in the context of a liberal-democratic political milieu, a useful starting-point.[18] The point, here, is to take the personal and reveal its potentially political character through specifically political discursive constructions. The appearance of the environment through discourses around rights and justice shows both a distinctively public construction and the potential of linking struggles together into a radical movement that transcends particular constituencies.[19] From the politicization of multiple, personal struggles comes the possibility of both collective action and a progressive deepening of democracy to include a wider range of positions and issues, including a concern for the non-human. But much environmentalism often fails to engage in this process. Content to rely on experts, on individual change, and on relatively polite negotiations with industry, controversy and politics become sunk in the quagmire of efficacy and professionalism.

As I have argued elsewhere (1995), it is particularly in the connection between environmentalism and social justice that the radicalness of environmental politics may be constituted. If the environment is not going to disappear as a political subject altogether, marginalized communities' knowledges of environmental degradation and disenfranchisement must together form the basis of a revitalized environmental agenda, one that challenges the form and contents of politics itself in addition to the adequacy and representativeness of current policies.

So-called "environmental justice" politics are organized precisely around this formulation (see Bullard 1990; Hofrichter 1993; Merchant 1994).[20] This broad grassroots movement has raised an enormous array of issues,[21] and the diverse constituencies involved *always* aim at raising community-based issues of health, resistance (for example, to the siting of major environmental facilities in poor communities of colour), representation, and inequality – and adding them to an agenda that would critique the ability of existing policy processes to deal with those issues fairly, democratically, and *justly*. Grounded in intensely private experiences of (for example) cancer, birth defects, poverty, and disempowerment, environmental justice politics insists that issues obscured by expert discourses and inadequate representation of disenfranchised communities in environmental policy processes must be opened, democratized, and always related to a conception of justice that transcends the needs or interests of any particular community. The point is not simply to stop X facility or regulate Y's pollution; the point is to reveal the systemic relations that lie behind these isolated problems and to call for a coalition of diversely situated communities to challenge these relations as a whole. In other words, the environment is produced as a matter of common concern because of, and not in spite of, its private experience. What "justice" will be is left open for community interpretation, even as each community understands itself as oriented to a broader "justice" principle.[22]

While there is no guarantee that such a formulation will not *ever* dissolve into interest group conflicts, the language of rights and justice suggests the need for both discussion and the (re)formation of some sense of political community around environmental issues. Against Colin Isaacs, for whom it seems hopeless to reformulate popular rhetoric around environmental issues, I suggest that the linkage of personal environmental concerns through the language of social justice shows environmentalists a way towards being a political force again. The political potential of environmental issues does not reside in the issues themselves. The work is in their production *as* political. As Arendt (1958: 3) wrote: "There is no reason to doubt our present ability to destroy all organic life on earth. The question is only whether we wish to use our new scientific and technical knowledge in this direction, and this question cannot be decided by scientific means; it is a political question of the first order and therefore can hardly be left to the decision of professional scientists or professional politicians."

NOTES

I would like to thank Alicja Muszynski for her insightful comments on a much earlier incarnation of some of these ideas, presented at the 1994 Learned Societies meetings in Calgary. I would also like to thank Solomon Chrom for asking the very significant question about the "rhetoric of efficacy."

1. After their election, the Harris government quickly scrapped the Interim Waste Authority, gutted the Planning Act, and "opened Ontario for business."
2. The protest (June 26, 1995) was organized by a variety of different groups concerned about workers' rights, welfare reductions, discrimination against gay men and lesbians, employment equity, and all of the other NDP initiatives that the Conservatives virtually obliterated. It was called "Embarrass Harris" and attracted about 1,000 people.
3. Other recent polls have suggested conflicting opinions. What seems to be the general pattern is that people are "concerned" about the environment, but that they rank it far below unemployment and other economic issues in terms of political priority.
4. In Ontario, it may be that Temagami will similarly heat up again as a political site. Harris has declared the region "open for business," and a coalition of environmental groups is mounting a renewed campaign to protect the region from this "opening."
5. A recent example: Pollution Probe claimed Petro Canada as a major supporter of "Bike to Work Week."
6. Claude Lefort argues that the "emptying" of the place of power is a specific characteristic of *democratic* political arrangements; the public sphere I describe is, certainly, based on a primarily liberal-democratic understanding.
7. Here, of course, one must also speak of the increasing dominance of "the economy" over the other two. While it is not my purpose here to paint a full pic-

ture of the relations between capitalism and (liberal) democracy, it is important to note that the "disappearance" of public life in general, and of environmental publicity in particular, is always already located in the context of the erosion of the public spaces of politics by capitalist economic interests or, as Habermas puts it, of the colonization of the lifeworld (which also includes the family) by the system (which also includes the capitalist state, relatively distinct from politics). See Habermas (1981).

8. For example, as Drucilla Cornell (1991) notes, Arendt's perfect *polis* is only possible through the exclusion of a needs idiom, which, by many definitions, includes nature. If the *polis* is the realm of true action, and if action (defined as unpredictable) is specifically set against nature (defined as inevitable), then issues from the so-called naturally inscribed private realm cannot possibly appear as political.

9. Bookchin is relatively unique among environmentalists in his call for the centrality of democracy to ecological politics. While his work remains important for this (and other) reasons, I find in Arendt a clearer understanding of politics as a relationship, a process, and a character.

10. For Arendt, the possibility of new beginnings is part of the essential human quality of "natality," the fact that people are born anew into the world and can create themselves (and the world) anew through action (but only action).

11. It would, however, be reasonable to argue that current social relations make certain issues more amenable to politicization than others.

12. As someone once said, we may all be in the same boat, but the majority of people in it are travelling in steerage.

13. Seager also speaks, significantly, of the class, race, and sex biases in this ecology establishment. Not only are the natural sciences seen as the "true" source of "objective" knowledge of the environmental crisis, thus devaluing the environmental expertises of disenfranchised communities, but the professionalization of the environmental movement more generally tends to reinforce what Seager calls white male privilege.

14. Numerous other examples exist of places in which the potentially political character of an environmental issue is undermined by the professionalization of its advocates and/or some similar process of narrowing of the scope of discussion to reflect limited interests. The dominant language of environmentalism itself can be hostile to "non-expert" formulations. When problems are defined in terms of CO_2 emissions, regional holding capacities, complex food chains, and polysyllabic chemical compounds (not to mention the rarefied languages of economic externality and risk), it is not surprising that people tend to turn their concerns over to experts.

15. This argument also suggests the need for a genuine "private" life of nature; many people are fed up with what might be called an invasive, "environmentally correct" stance. When people feel guilty about using styrofoam cups, it becomes highly unlikely that they will be willing to talk about environmental politics.

16. This chapter will not go into detail about the need for "private" experiences of nature, but one could, here, see deep ecology or phenomenology as exemplary descriptions of a private life of/with nature. It is important to note that this private experience lies at the core of a more adequate public representation of nature, but that it does not replace it. Still, not all "privates" are created equal; the lifeworld is, after all, being colonized by the system, and perhaps a counterpart to the politicization of nature is a renewed understanding of the place of private experience.

17. This is happening, to a certain extent, with the public debate over Recombinant Bovine Somatotropin (rBST), more commonly known as Bovine Growth Hormone.
18. One of the most common critiques of "rights" discourse is that it tends to individualize political discourse in a manner particularly unsuitable to environmental concerns. I, following Swan, see rights as importantly relational, although I do not believe that rights are the only useful discourse through which to politicize environmental concerns.
19. Of course, as critiques of "rights" discourses suggest, there is also a need to reformulate political language itself so that different constituencies can find themselves "recognized" politically.
20. One group in Ontario that has taken the principles of environmental justice seriously is the Women's Network on Health and the Environment (WNHE). This organization grew out of a prior campaign (by WEED, the Women and Environments Education and Development Foundation) on chlorine bleaching of so-called "feminine hygiene" products, and a serious concern with the relationship between organochlorines and breast cancer. WNHE's newsletter now includes both materials specifically related to breast cancer and a wide variety of other environmental (and other) issues understood as related; the January 1996 newsletter included a critique of Ontario's disastrously undemocratic Omnibus Bill (Bill 26).
21. The environmental justice movement was born out of concern for the particular effects of environmental degradation on poor communities of colour. Based largely in the United States, but making promising inroads into Canada, environmental justice politics insist that disenfranchised communities struggle against economic inequality, political disenfranchisement, and environmental degradation.
22. One of my favourite slogans in this vein plays on the much-derided phenomenon known as NIMBYism, for "not in my back yard." Through an understanding of racialized and economic inequalities in, for example, the siting of toxic facilities – PIBBY, or "put in blacks' back yard" – comes the realization of commonality, or NIABY, "not in anyone's back yard."

GLOBALIZATION, MOVEMENTS, AND THE DECENTRED STATE

Warren Magnusson

When we talk about social "movements," what is it that moves, and in relation to what? Do we have some "fixtures" in mind when we speak about movements? If so, what are those fixtures, and what do we mean by suggesting that they are stable in relation to the movements? Does globalization refer to a process of *de*stabilization, and, if so, what is being destabilized: the fixtures or the movements (or both)? Why do we describe globalization as "economic," but call movements "social"? What do we mean by the economic and the social, and how do these things relate to the "political"? Is the political what relates to the state, and, if so, is *that* what is being destabilized (Maier 1987; Howard 1989; Crick 1993)? Is the destabilization of the state (or "society" or "scientific knowledge") what poststructuralists and postmodernists have in mind when they talk about "decentring" (Magnusson and Walker 1988)? What does it mean to decentre something?

To raise such questions is to incite the wrath of many social scientists and political activists. The empirical social sciences maintain a great resistance to "conceptual quibbling," especially when it seems to destabilize the categories commonly used for critical analysis (Connolly 1983). Shouldn't we just *get on* with the work, and not fuss so much about our methods and concepts? Won't the ordinary ways of thinking about movements, politics, state, and society just *do* for our purposes? Many political activists certainly think so, but it is our responsibility as academics to pose questions that cannot easily be addressed in the context of a political struggle. In any case, there is good reason to think that the conceptual issues raised above are pertinent to political struggles in the world today. Inevitably we understand those struggles through categories inherited from the past, and when those categories are ratified by "social science," they have an even greater weight. It is difficult to think clearly about our own experiences when our minds are clouded by

94

scientifically ratified categories that have the status of unquestionable truths. We need to recognize that these categories are actually the remains of old political struggles.

My purpose here is not to answer all the questions I have raised, but instead to suggest that the answers we normally take for granted are quite inadequate. Ultimately, I point towards a different way of thinking about social movements. I refuse the two distinctions that enable us to talk about social movements in the traditional way: the distinctions between social order and social movements, and between the political and the social. These distinctions get in the way of realistic thinking about politics. The very idea of social science is at odds with political understanding, and we need to foreground the political if we are to make sense of the world we live in—a world best understood as a global city, a city that is itself an ensemble of movements that make up our way of life. Following Louis Wirth (1937), I designate that way of life as "urbanism." Unlike him, I suggest that urbanism can only be understood as a political phenomenon, and that we need to relate to that political phenomenon. Current theories of globalization (Robertson 1992; Waters 1995; Knox and Taylor 1995) – and their reverse, ideas about decentring – point towards that phenomenon, but give us few means for understanding it. This lack is related to the tendency to depoliticize everything we analyse scientifically. Consciously or unconsciously, we conceal the politics of our analyses – sometimes by offering misleading shows of our political commitments – in order to conceal the politics of the phenomena we are analysing. Learning to problematize these practices, in ourselves and others, is a great part of the political struggle.

Let me stress that I am engaging even here in an intellectual/political movement, which sets some established categories in motion and throws up some possibilities for further reflection. Some of the arguments I only hint at, and the lines of thought are tentative. This meandering approach, then, touches on a number of topics but leaves others aside, and I invite readers to address the gaps for themselves. I have organized the discussion under a series of headings that refer to the key ideas that (I believe) need to be reexamined. What appears under these headings may seem arbitrary, but I hope that the method in my madness will become apparent before I reach my conclusion. So, let us begin with the motivating concept of this book.

THE IDEA OF A SOCIAL MOVEMENT

"Movement," as we usually understand it, presupposes a fixed point, surface, or object in relation to which the movement occurs. The earth moves around the sun; I run up the stairs or down the street; my lungs expand and contract. When we talk of "social" movements, we are apparently assuming that they occur in relation to a comparatively stable frame, environment, or structure, and that the movements move in relation to this object of stability. Judging from the social science literature, it seems that the relevant social fixtures are the ones that hold people in place in a social order. These are the laws, customs, structures of government, hierarchies of status, differences in wealth and income, and other features of society that people often complain about. Apparently, a social movement is something that challenges the "social order," whatever that is (Tarrow 1994b; Touraine 1995).

If we were to take social movements on their own terms, it would be hard to specify the social order in a way that would cover all the cases. Every social movement tends to have a different conception of the fixtures it is moving against. Socialism, environmentalism, and feminism are far from the same in their aims and objectives; more different still are the various religious and nationalist movements. One way of understanding this is to say that every movement defines its *own* time and space: that is, it locates itself in relation to certain fixtures of social reality, gives an account of its own origins, defines for itself a terrain of struggle, and projects into the future a vision of what the world should be like. So, for instance, Quebec nationalists take the founding of Quebec in 1608 as a point of origin and tell a story that focuses on the Conquest in 1759 and the subsequent (unsatisfactory) constitutional "settlements" from 1791 to 1982, as well as the struggles of the *"patriotes"* from 1837 to the present. This narrative situates the movement in a particular time and space, which is quite different from the one socialists have in mind when they talk of the struggle to overcome capitalism, or the one feminists refer to when they raise the age-old problem of patriarchy.

If it is true that every movement moves against something different, then the problem of generalizing about social movements is severe. The surprising thing is that many analysts assume that there is ultimately a *single* fixture against which contemporary social movements are struggling. This single fixture is variously conceived, in accordance with the analysts' own convictions. Thus, socialists imagine the fixture as capitalism, feminists think of it as patriarchy, and environmentalists as human domination over nature. In the belief of these analysts – who ultimately identify with particular social movements – the central fixture against which all the "progressive" movements are struggling is the one that stabilizes oppression in its various forms (Young 1990). Move this fixture, and everything else begins to move; keep it steady, and everything is held in place. If this is so, there is a *centre* to the politics of social movements, a centre that may be revealed analytically but that in practice has to be discovered politically. Based on this view, things really start cooking politically – that is, qualitative change is in prospect – when the movements get their acts *together*. It is possible on this view to distinguish between fundamentally *reactionary* movements, which altogether mistake the sources of domination and oppression, and fundamentally *progressive* movements, which identify at least some of the real obstacles to human emancipation.

Both the movements and the analyses I am referring to resonate with the emancipatory dreams of modern liberalism. However, they can also display a certain ambivalence towards modernity, which is expressed in common ideas about recovering lost alternatives or redefining human relationships. These ideas evoke what Peter Laslett (1983a) once called "The World We Have Lost." Many people suffer from acute nostalgia for life as they imagine it in the unspoiled wilderness, the traditional neighbourhood, the little fishing village or farming community, or other settings outside of or prior to the familiar forms of urban life. An even stronger reaction against contemporary trends may be expressed within religious movements that pose transcendental alternatives and offer people hope of complete redemption. Whatever their other-worldly objectives, such movements promise substantial changes in the way we live on Earth. By contrast, traditional nationalism is in many ways the least challenging of contemporary movements. Nationalist movements demand a place in the sun for a particular people, whose aspirations can be met within the established international order. However, some nationalist or particularist movements do challenge the system of sovereign states quite directly. This is the case for movements of indigenous peoples, which seek cultural autonomy and self-government (Tully 1995) but reject the model provided by the modern nation-state (either because it is impractical for them, or because it does not conform to their own traditions). Similarly, people such as gays and lesbians, who have a strong sense of identity and community despite being dispersed throughout the world, may only be able to achieve their aims by securing *universal* rights.

That some fixtures of modernity are more important than others – in the limited sense that they hold more in place – seems obvious, although few analysts would agree on exactly which of these fixtures is *most* important. Within the social movements that command our attention in this book, there seems to be an oscillation between two poles. At the one extreme is what we might call a particularist radicalism, which constitutes itself within its own space and time and imagines itself capable of self-transformation. Thus we have people creating their own communities and attempting to free themselves by their own actions from the strictures imposed by the rest of the world. From the outside, such people may seem vain and self-delusive: unable to see how they are repeating the practices they seek to escape or unable to appreciate the effects of their actions outside the bounds of their own imaginations. Such communities have a tendency to treat everyone outside them as an actual or potential enemy and to suppose implicitly that this condition of enmity will prevail indefinitely. At the opposite extreme is the feeling within social movements that everyone really is *the same* – that all people are one, in principle, and that, since what *we* believe is true for everyone, there really is nothing legitimate outside our movement. Such an attitude can lead to violent or insensitive behaviour. In any case, a universalist or totalitarian vision usually involves the idea that the fixtures that dominate us form a single ensemble, which is subject to complete or at least fundamental transformation. Thus the centring of movement activity seems to follow from a certain conception of its object.

The idea of *fundamental* social change was at the heart of the eighteenth-century conception of a "revolution" (Tilly 1978). The French "revolutionaries" became enamoured with the thought that they could overthrow the fixtures of the *ancien régime* and establish the basis for a new society. As they imagined it, nothing would remain the same once the old regime had been replaced. Moreover, they sensed that, although the revolutionary movement could proceed in many venues (from private households to coffee houses and assemblies in the streets), the movement would remain incomplete if it did not transform the state. As the centre of sovereign authority and thus of both armed force and legal regulation, the state was a nexus of resistance to revolutionary change. It had to be overcome, or transformed into a centre of revolutionary change. Thus, the impetus of revolutionary action was towards the state as the fixture that held things in place. Following the collapse of the French Revolution, analysts broadened and deepened their understanding of what was involved in a genuinely revolutionary change. In particular, Marx and his followers came to understand that capitalism held society in place, and that the state was a superstructure that secured capitalism (McLellan 1977, 1988).

However subtle the theory of revolution became, it nonetheless tended to assume that the state posed a unique obstacle to change. Ultimately, theorists believed, the state had to be transformed, or there would *be* no revolution. Thus the moment at which the state fell to the revolutionaries could be conceived as the moment of revolution. It is no accident that we identify 1789 and 1917 as the dates of the French and Russian Revolutions respectively, for these were the years in which the old regimes (meaning the old states) collapsed.

What I am suggesting, then, is that the idea of a social movement is closely connected with the older idea of "a revolution." As a result, the idea of a social movement bears with it the intellectual baggage that we have come to identify with revolutionary (or more generally "progressive") thinking over the last century and a half. It is caught up in the notion that there is a fixture or social order susceptible to transformation by the action we associate with rebels and revolutionaries, resisters and protesters. Generally the state is conceived as the key fixture, in the sense that it is the immediate object of political action. This is so even in revolutionary theories like Marxism: theories that suggest that the state simply secures relations of domination rooted in something else. To a large extent, the other progressive social movements tend to mimic Marxism (and socialism more generally) in putting the state at the centre of their political activity. Political as opposed to merely cultural or social action seems to involve a focus on the state, in the sense that it is oriented towards changing laws, public policies, governments, or institutions of government.

We need to ask why this is so. Is it simply a matter of realism for people to conceive of politics in this way, or does this supposed "realism" work ideologically? Are we being deceived about the actual locus of politics?

THE IDEA OF THE STATE

Whatever the eighteenth-century revolutionists intended, they set in train a series of movements that delegitimated previous political structures and established the idea that legitimate governments derive their authority from the people. The effects of these movements have been felt throughout the world, and the process of democratization (if we can conceive it so) has by no means run its course. So-called progressives have been especially eager to pursue democratization and thus to work within the processes that it seems to entail, including the struggles to gain the vote and to mobilize people for democratic elections. The processes also include efforts to influence governments and legislatures, to make law and public policy sensitive to popular needs and interests, to secure rights for ordinary people, and to extend public services to them. At its extreme, such a politics entails a revolutionary challenge to the government and hence to the state itself. Most democratic activists have believed that the people need to form a party of their own if they are to bring about a transformative change. No matter how much social movement activity exists, the terrain of politics seems to slope towards the state. Serious activists are thus drawn into the domain of party politics, where the object of state power is explicit.

This centring process is always resisted within a social movement. By definition, a social movement is within civil society, and thus it appears to be outside the state (Cohen and Arato 1992). Within that exterior domain of social life, the movement is likely to understand itself as one of popular redefinition. People in the movement are supposed to slough off the strictures of the existing social order, discover or recover what is authentic and true, act boldly in their own interests and for the sake of the world, and thus to renew or revolutionize themselves. From this perspective the fixtures preventing people from becoming what they should be are deep within them: these fixtures, above all, must be shifted. To the extent that a social movement is informed by such a perspective, it tends to turn inward. However, in a dialectical reversal, such inward-turning often results in an outward explosion of energy, and in this context "realists" within the movement suggest that it cannot achieve its outward objectives unless it organizes itself in relation to the state. The transformation of the state thus appears as the ultimate objective of outward, political action.

"Realism" within the politics of social movements is akin to "realism" in international relations. The latter view (which is still dominant among students of international relations) is that in the anarchic world of nation-states it is inevitable that each state will pursue its own interests without much regard to higher ideals (Walker 1993; George 1994). It follows that one should not expect demands to "outlaw war" or to enforce "universal human rights" to have much effect, unless they can be related to the interests of the most powerful states. The so-called realists believe that, despite the emergence of a globalized economy and an international civil society, world politics still consists primarily of relations between states – relations that have to be modelled in terms of complementary and conflicting interests. This view implies that the inevitable centre of citizen action in world politics is the state: to be effective globally, people have to influence their own governments. This is the flip side of the view that domestic legislation (or public policy more generally) depends on state action, and thus that the inevitable political centre of a social movement's activity is the state in which the people concerned reside.

Contemporary political space appears to have a particular shape, and this *ideologically shaped appearance* has profound implications for how we think about politics. The world is apparently divided into sovereign states, which collide with one another in international relations; but each of these sovereign states is constituted – by definition – as an autonomous political centre. Thus, to be effective (realists say), a social movement must organize itself not in accordance with its *own* conception of space and time, but rather in accordance with structures for politics that are already given. Amnesty International or Greenpeace International may be able to act globally in certain ways, but for practical purposes the organization has to divide itself into separate national organizations, which can lobby the governments concerned, raise money, and appeal to national publics. It seems that even relatively innovative organizations like these have to function within the pre-existing political spaces, spaces defined by the system of sovereign states. The spaces available also have their own temporality: each state has its own history, its own internal narrative, its own way of regulating the times for political action. As a result, a politically engaged social movement must take account of the legislative cycle, the electoral cycle, the routines of administrative and judicial decision-making, and much else within the countries where it is engaged. In consequence, a profound tension always exists between the timing and spacing of the movement itself – its own conception of when and where it is acting in its movement for change – and the political grid it confronts in the form of the state.

Given the other "sovereignty" that movements must confront—the sovereignty of "the individual"—the inward turning of movements is crucial to success. What many fail to notice is that the sovereignty of states actually mimics the supposed sovereignty of individuals – and vice versa (Walker

1993). In the modern liberal imagination, states or individuals are supposed to be autonomous beings, free to rule themselves in accordance with their own lights. (A "people" in the fullest sense has to be constituted as a state – something of which Quebec sovereigntists are constantly reminding us.) In the rhetoric of sovereignty, a person's or a state's desires are supposed to be respected because they belong to the individual concerned. What I want or what my state wants is supposed to be a reflection of needs or interests that are constituted from within. It is not for others to say whether these desires/ needs/interests are authentic or appropriate. What I say that I want or think is to be taken as given, and the same is true for what states want or think. Thus, on this view, relations between individuals or relations between states have to be conceived as *external* relations, in which interests are potentially at variance.

For social movements, this is a problematic conception, because they want to put what is internal to individuals or states at issue (Melucci 1989). The presumption is that states/individuals have been fixed in particular forms and are now held in relations of domination that give the lie to the idea that what is expressed by a particular individual or state is an authentic representation of what lies within. Rather, what we express is supposed to be an effect of the systems of domination that hold us in thrall. Generally, we say what is expected of us, and we also *want* what is expected of us (to the delight of advertisers). If we are to become different, we have to challenge what we are internally or be challenged in that internal terrain. Insofar as social movements mount such challenges, they disrupt the sovereignty claims of both states and individuals and hence are engaged in a "revolutionary" politics.

There can be no doubt that a social movement expressing an alternative vision of human life is on a dangerous and difficult political terrain. It is challenging the fixtures within both the individual and the state, and as such it is doubly at odds with the dominant order. This is why social movement activism so often conveys the sense of a life on the edge. As an activist, one is balanced precariously between the forms of life implicit in an alternative vision and the ones imposed in the dominant order. To imagine that the dominant order is on the verge of transformation, or to think oneself into a place where nothing outside really matters, is to ease the psychological tensions involved in living on the edge. However, there is liable to be a violent oscillation between political "realism" and political "idealism." Those who opt for political realism are liable to be condemned for "selling out," while the others will be accused of self-indulgent withdrawal from the real world. This tragic cycle, which forms the stuff of the morose reflections of ex-activists, is not one that can be broken by retracing the old paths under new colours. More fundamental rethinking is required, and this will take us into the domain of the state's significant other: civil society.

THE IDEA OF SOCIETY

It may not be apparent to sociology students that the idea of "society" is parasitic upon the notion of the state, a notion that began to take shape in sixteenth-century Europe – originally in Italy, and later in France, England, and Holland (Vincent 1987). It took almost four hundred years for the state to acquire all the features we are now familiar with. Significantly, the science of sociology first developed in early nineteenth-century France, amidst the ruins of the *ancien régime* and within the bosom of an increasingly self-confident modern state (Heilbron 1995). It was the state that was understood as the ultimate source of order within a society; in a sense, the state *constituted* a society legally and politically. The external boundaries of a society were those of a state, and the laws, institutions, and practices of the state itself provided the form of order that made that society distinctive. As Hegel put it, the state was the ground and completion of civil society (Knox 1967). Europeans generally believed that to become modern was to become like them – and that in the long run other peoples and cultures would have no choice but to become modern (if only because the Europeans intended to impose this modernity upon them). A society that wanted to become modern had to constitute itself as an independent state, which could function on a par with the European states. This meant developing similar institutions and thus establishing a similar relation between state and society.

It is hard to exaggerate the extent to which we take statehood for granted and use the system of states to define separate cultures, economies, societies, or even languages. Thanks partly to the legal barriers that states create, it is difficult to collect information about people that is not precoded state by state. Look for unemployment statistics, for instance, or data about attitudes towards legalized abortion. Will the figures come with labels like "American" or "French" already attached? Usually they do, and this is because so much of the information is collected for purposes of government (or purposes of influencing government). Most of the rest is generated for marketing purposes, and as such may identify population groups in a different way. In reality, however, marketing regions tend to be regions of states, and so data of this sort is usually precoded in state-centric terms. (People in Metropolitan Toronto are a subcategory of "Canadians.") As a result, it is difficult to think about the world generally without slipping into comparisons between states. One slides easily into the assumption that each state is a separate society, with its own economy and its own culture, as well its own laws and political institutions.

We make another slide as well, and this is into the assumption that, since the state is the source of order, society is the source of disorder. (No wonder that the early students of social movements regarded them with such distrust.) Now, of course, sociologists go to great trouble in showing that societies are held together by things other than the state, but the implicit assumption is usually that without the ordering force of the state the other sources of order within society would be insufficient of themselves. In a sense, the state is the necessary ground and completion of the project of social order. Thus, we can begin from the state, within the boundaries it establishes, to sketch an answer to the question of how a society hangs together. This implies in turn that the internal boundaries generated by the separation of the state from society are to be understood as inevitable features of a modern social order. There must be a sphere of law and government, political institutions, and public administration, a sphere separate from the domain of civil society. In turn this implies that there must be separation between the economy and politics, for the production and distribution of goods and services involve activities that are distinct from the business of governing. Similarly, we can distinguish family life, or social activity, or cultural expression, and see that it is something apart from the state. It becomes possible soon to delineate a number of separate spheres of life, and to develop for each a science that analyses it. This seems to have been the project implicit in the development of the modern social sciences.

At this point we might pause and ask ourselves why these sciences are called "social" and not political or economic or cultural. What is it about the social that can command such privilege? Ironically, it seems to be that the social lacks specificity: it is what is left over when we have already talked about economics, politics, culture, geography, and psychology. But this characterization of the social as a remainder allows for a sort of reverse disciplinary imperialism: the economic, the political, and so on are reconceived as aspects of the social, to be understood by a sociology that puts the other social sciences in their appropriate places. This allows for a mode of analysis that leaves open the question of where the ordering principles of society are, or what form they take. One does not have to assume a political or an economic or a cultural determinism when one adopts the perspective of the social. But a subtler displacement is also at work in this perspective. Heretofore – that is, prior to sociology – the science of the whole had been conceived as philosophy or theology or history or jurisprudence or political economy. The first two of these five forms of thought had pointed towards a metaphysical understanding of human reality; the last three pointed directly or indirectly towards political understanding. The shift towards a science of society was away from philosophy and politics and towards a domain of human existence that could be understood naturalistically, thus completing a movement already implicit in the concept of "political economy," a concept that itself tended to collapse politics into economics. In the ancient world Aristotle insisted that the economic had to be understood in relation to the political, and the political in relation to the philosophical, in a hierarchy of understandings that reflected the hierarchy of ends in human life (Barker 1962). The displacement of this hierarchy by a naturalistic science of society

– either in the guise of an independent sociology or of an ensemble of social sciences, each with its specific field of interest – in itself entailed a different way of thinking about politics.

In this new way of thinking (now so old to us that we forget any alternative ever existed), "politics" is a special sort of activity, separated off from other things that people do. The domain of the state (or activity in relation to the state) is the home turf of politics. We identify activity in other domains as political insofar as it mimics the forms and practices of politics on its home turf. For instance, we look for conflicts of interest and value that put rules of social practice into question, examine patterns of domination and resistance, attempt to explain co-operation and conflict. In this way we can identify politics wherever we choose to look in civil society. Such a parasitic conception of politics leaves in place the assumption that political action is epiphenomenal – in other words, that what people do politically can be explained by forces at work outside politics. This is the tendency of all forms of naturalistic explanation, a mode of explanation implicit in the idea that a complete science of human life is necessarily social rather than political.

Perhaps I can make my point clearer by referring again to Aristotle. In his lectures on *Politics* (Barker 1962), Aristotle notes that the science of politics is properly conceived as the *master* science. (Perhaps this is why political scientists still read Aristotle, while sociologists have given up on the practice.) For him, this idea follows quite directly from his understanding that politics is concerned with the development and implementation of the principles necessary for the good life, in all aspects of life within a self-sufficient community. To Aristotle, a polis (what we might call a city-state) was a complete community, whose way of life or principles of organization were always at stake politically. To be active politically was to be engaged practically in the question of what form the polis should take and how that form could be preserved or implemented. Nothing was outside politics, because the question of politics was the question of how we should live. Thus we might have other sciences – he might talk of rhetoric or military leadership, we might say sociology or economics – that might properly inform our political science, but the centrality of political science followed from the fact that the other sciences were to contribute to political judgement. The need for political judgement was not only an unavoidable human need, but one that reflected the highest of human capacities: the capacity to establish a way of life for ourselves, and to govern ourselves in accordance with the principles we had established. What centred the various sciences (including what we call the natural sciences) was this need for political judgement. These sciences were useful insofar as they helped us decide what we had to do, and the greatest questions we had to decide were political (that is, they related to our lives as a whole or in their full complexity).

This interpretation of Aristotle suggests an important distinction between a politics centred on the state and a politics centred on the problem of judgement. The state is conceived as a set of institutions standing over and apart from society. As such, it appears as a fixture, and politics seems like an activity related to that fixture. By contrast, a judgement-centred politics has no necessary spatial location: or, to be more accurate, its space expands indefinitely to encompass the whole, and then folds in on itself in particular locations. A judgement-centred science or philosophy (the distinction between the two becomes immaterial in this context) tends to focus all inquiries on the ultimate question: what is to be done? This is a question that can be posed locally or globally, and, wherever it is posed, it points beyond itself to the other locations where it is addressed. Insofar as this political question is displaced in favour of naturalistic explanation, the science in which we are engaged is reified and depoliticized. The further we go along such a path, the more difficult it becomes to recognize our own political assumptions.

This brings us back to the question of a social movement. At the beginning of this chapter I raised the question of why we called these movements *social*. The answer that is emerging is that this conceptualization allows us to displace and repress the knowledge that these movements are political. I suspect that if Aristotle were around today and were asked to identify the major venues for political action, he might well point to the activities of social movements. He would not separate these movements off from what we call political parties, because he would want to say that between them the parties and the movements were engaged with those questions of the whole that he considered political. He would be troubled by how we separate *social* movements from *political* parties and thus imagine the movements as existing in a domain apart from the state.

If Marx could also rise from the dead, he might point out that it was the very separation of the state from society, so typical of the bourgeois era, that had fixed or reified politics in a form that made it difficult for people to recognize the breadth and complexity of their political activities (Marx in McLellan 1977: 39-62). He would not be surprised that, in a capitalist world, people act politically without having any idea of what they are doing.

THE IDEA OF THE GLOBAL

An obvious difficulty with Aristotle's analysis is that he fixes politics within the polis. His ideal was of a self-sufficient city-state, not too small to be independent but not too large to be known properly by its own citizens. For him, citizenship was something that should only be conferred on the masters of households – not on women or slaves or servants or dependents. Moreover, the polis was to be fiercely independent – prepared for war if necessary (one of the reasons why Aristotle thought of citizenship as naturally male). As a result, the polis was like a protected enclosure: set off from other such political communities and guarded against the intrusions of women, children,

workmen, and others who were deemed incapable of rational political judgement. Although open debate and considered judgement on human affairs as
a whole were supposedly at the centre of politics, that centre was constituted
as a citadel fortified against the wrong people.

By comparison, the modern state seems much more open and inclusive.
Citizenship is available to everyone, and states are spread out over huge
tracts of territory with millions or even hundreds of millions of inhabitants.
Thus, the masses and the strangers, the low-born and the poor, the feminine
and the juvenile are all included within the politics of the state. As a result we
are able to delude ourselves into thinking that we have created a world of
democracies, in which all people can participate as equals in the key decisions affecting their lives.

This delusion is nonetheless hard to sustain in face of our growing awareness of globalization. Formerly separate societies, economies, and cultures
are now so closely integrated that the putative sovereignty of states seems
increasingly illusory (Gill and Law 1987; Waters 1995). Every time we have
an election or discuss public policy in our own country, we have to pretend
that we are autonomous even though we know we are not. We have to leave
aside matters that can only be addressed by wider global or regional institutions. So we are faced with a "sovereignty" that says: "You Canadians are
completely autonomous. You can organize your country however you like,
live in accordance with your own laws and by your own values. No one will
interfere.... Unless, of course, you decide to do something that *we* think
might affect our security or diminish our prosperity or threaten our investments, our markets, or our access to your resources. You can pursue whatever economic policies you like, provided they conform to the guidelines established by the bond-rating agencies in New York and London (and further
elaborated by the Organization for Economic Co-operation and Development, the International Monetary Fund, the World Trade Organization, and
the G-7). Of course, your social policies can also follow whatever principles
you choose, provided you can finance them within the fiscal limits required
by multinational corporations and international investors – and so long as
you ban the drugs we want to ban, control the environmental hazards we
want to control, and so on. We'll even let you into the inner circles of global
policy-making, if you keep your economic and social policies within the
bounds we want, and supply troops for the peacekeeping missions we have
decided upon, and generally act like good global citizens. So, you see, you're
completely free to do what you want."

Are there echoes here of the familiar promise of freedom that we make to
the young? "You can be anything you want to be – provided that you have the
talent, get yourself a first-class education (of the specified type), hustle your
butt in the marketplace, work sixty or seventy hours a week, save your
money, invest wisely, and – most importantly – do exactly what other people

want you to do. *That's* freedom." Somehow, neither freedom nor sovereignty is quite what's it's cracked up to be, either at the personal level or at the national.

In fact, these collective and individual rights – to be what we want to be and do what we want to do, as communities or individuals – are bound up with some formidable social disciplines. We have to learn to think in a certain way, and to act in accordance with that thinking. Even to go to the store and buy milk involves a number of disciplines that we have learned very well – to keep to the sidewalk and not intrude on other people's property, to refrain from taking (without paying) any of the things laid out on the shelves of the store, to accept or reject what is on offer without complaint, to hand over our money and accept our change: in other words, to be respectable customers, who acknowledge private property and abide by the laws of the market. These disciplines are so deeply ingrained that we are scarcely aware of them. As my example indicates, the disciplines imposed by the state are as nothing in our daily lives compared to the ones required by the market. To get and keep a job, to sell ourselves or our services at good prices, to *be* marketable commodities so that we can *have* marketable commodities: these are stern modern imperatives.

Much of what people have in mind when they talk about "globalization" is the intensification of market pressures, pressures that force open protected local markets and at the same time require people to sell what was not previously marketed. All activities – including artistic creation, scholarly research, charitable service, and public deliberation – are now considered to be marketable commodities, which ought to be supplied in the forms and quantities demanded by willing buyers. There are fewer and fewer places to escape from the dictates of the market, unless one has already been a success on the market, or can claim inherited wealth. To merit a decent life, one must have worth on the market, and to have worth on the market one must become what the market demands. (So a market-conscious person really should avoid the unpopular diseases and disabilities, for which there are no telethons.) Of course, a real freedom is involved in being able to spend or give money as we choose, and being allowed to compete in any business or for any occupation that attracts us. But this freedom is the sunny side of the totalitarianism of the market: the flowers on our chains, as Rousseau put it a couple of centuries ago. By enslaving ourselves to the market, we get access to what the market offers, but at the price of becoming what the market demands. There is no guarantee even then that the market will have use for us: the market has already dispensed with a large part of the African population.

For more than twenty years the major governments in the Western world have been trying to cut back public expenditures, privatize public services, and reorganize government on market principles. There has been a good deal of resistance to this process, and the process has been slow as a result.

However, the trend has been accelerating in the 1990s. Significantly, the agenda of neoconservatism has been adopted by most of the socialist and social-democratic parties. The theme of domestic politics in almost every country is the one enunciated so succinctly by British Prime Minister Margaret Thatcher in the early 1980s: "There is no alternative." Since there is no alternative, the point of political activity seems increasingly obscure, and it is not surprising that voter participation is declining, that people are becoming more alienated from their governments, and that new oppositional movements are again expressing the sort of anger and vengefulness once associated with fascism. When the popular desire for revenge is more apparent than the desire for liberation, optimistic talk about the positive features of contemporary social movements seems touchingly anachronistic. Can movements be anything other than punitive and destructive when "there is no alternative" to the totalitarianism of the market?

To put the issue so starkly is to remind ourselves that, when we invoke the "social" in the context of a political analysis, we are referring to whatever has been expelled from the realm of respectable politics. Social movements express the goals, identities, aspirations, and resentments that have not been completely incorporated into the routines of day-to-day politics within the state. Thus the movements always represent a threat of some sort to the good order of the state. We should not delude ourselves into thinking that what has been excluded is necessarily benign, although we should be able to see that the relentless restriction of political opportunity implicit in the globalization of the market is a major source of popular desperation. In a perverse cycle, political exclusions themselves produce the desperate behaviour that justifies demands for more exclusions. It is worth remembering at this point that one of the great themes of neoconservatism in the 1970s was that we could no longer afford democracy, because the people expected government to spend more money than capitalists were prepared to allow (Crozier, Huntington, and Watanuki 1975; King 1987; Gill 1990). The solution proposed was to put legal limits on public spending, borrowing, and taxation, and to force governments to put as many services on the market as possible. *Voilà*, the politics of the 1990s. If we are to break the vicious cycle of political restrictions, we need to globalize our politics so that we can deal constructively with the forces that are impoverishing our lives and producing the violence that we can sense around us.

Unfortunately, it is difficult to know what such a globalized politics would involve. I have no simple answers of my own, but I do think that we have to make a conceptual shift from our state-centric conceptions of society and politics, economy and culture. For me, this process is eased when I begin thinking of the world as a huge city, with economies, cultures, and systems of governance that recall the patterns of the great metropolises of the past and present (Magnusson 1994). In such metropolises, there is no state that provides an overarching order: rather, it is the life of the metropolis that encompasses the activity of state agencies and puts them in play in relation to a variety of other activities. To analyse such political complexity, we have to remember that the phenomena we are observing are not fixtures but movements. These movements interact in complicated ways – in fact, in such complicated ways that the interaction probably cannot be conceived as occurring within familiar four-dimensional space. (This is the Einsteinian conception, in which time is the fourth dimension.) Because every movement creates its own space-time, we have to imagine interaction in a global *hyper*-space (Kaku 1994), which has many more than four dimensions and allows for regional autonomies that, although relative and limited, are nonetheless real. How one is to act politically in such a global hyperspace is not immediately apparent, but we may get some clues from thinking about the nature of the city – and more particularly from reflection on urbanism as an "architectonic" social movement.

THE IDEA OF URBANISM
In 1937 Louis Wirth wrote what was to become the most widely cited article in American sociology: "Urbanism as a Way of Life." He was trying to make sense of the difference between modern U.S. society and the old world that was passing away. He did not necessarily applaud what was going on, but he could see that the Chicago he was familiar with was fundamentally different from the forms of society still existing in the U.S. countryside. He did not think that terms like capitalism or industrialism fully represented or explained that difference, so he hit on the notion of "urbanism as a way of life." When I first encountered Wirth's article, I thought it was vacuous – and so it still seems, in many respects. But I now find the concept of urbanism increasingly helpful in conceptualizing the global realities to which we must relate politically. Several important insights are buried in Wirth's concept:
(1) what is dominant is not a structure, but a movement (urbanism);
(2) this movement is to be understood as a "way of life": that is, holistically; and
(3) the movement somehow encompasses other movements, such as capitalism and industrialism (to which we might add scientism, liberalism, and statism).
Wirth's big mistake was to understand the architectonic movement of urbanism naturalistically rather than to conceive of it as a political movement (Castells 1977; Smith 1979). A political movement is something that can be contested from within and without.
Thinking about urbanism in the widest terms, we can see that it is at least as old as the ancient civilizations of Egypt and Iraq: it has been with us in some form for thousands of years (Mumford 1961). Urbanism is older than modernity, older than capitalism. The outward explosion of the Europeans in

the sixteenth century, the revolutions in commerce and industry in the seventeenth and eighteenth centuries, the consolidation of industrial capitalism and European imperialism in the nineteenth century, and the successive reorganizations of the world economy and the state system in the twentieth century certainly have involved profound qualitative changes in the conditions of human life. It is not my purpose to suggest any explanation for these changes, and it is certainly not my view that urbanism of itself "caused" anything else. My point, rather, is that in retrospect we can see that the way of life that has emerged from these changes – and that was foreshadowed long before – is urbanism. Moreover, it is now becoming apparent that we all live in a giant city of global scale.

No one particularly intended to create a global city, and it was not apparent until recently that such a thing was possible. Nonetheless, the impetus in this direction can be detected in the processes to which Marx and Engels drew attention many years ago (McLellan 1977). Those were processes of material production, whereby successive generations of people in different parts of the world attempted to provide for their own subsistence, and developed new needs as they did. In turn these new needs induced further inventions, and so on, in a continuing cycle. Whether or not people really meant to, they have been gradually changing the world to suit themselves. Thus, they have been humanizing their own environment, so that the world in which people live today is already in large degree the effect of earlier human actions. The semi-conscious effort to make the world into a place that suits us ultimately takes the form of urbanism: a way of life in which people concentrate in cities and towns, which are connected to one another by various means, and from which people appropriate the surrounding countryside and natural wilderness. In the end, what is outside the urban is what has yet to be fully controlled. (Commercial farming, forestry, fishing, and wilderness tourism are all obviously urban activities. From an urban perspective, earlier forms of these activities appear like primitive efforts that have been brought to completion by urban enterprise.) At a certain point – the point we have now reached, I think – it becomes apparent that the urban system is so dense that it no longer makes sense to think of cities as separate from one another. What we used to call cities are more like particular districts of a single, global city, which extends to the most obscure corners of the earth.

Many will cringe at this description, which echoes the Marxian celebration of human capacities and refuses the idea that there are natural limits to the human world. The point, however, is to suggest that any limits we impose on our own activities have to make sense from a human perspective. Such limits are not given naturally: they are developed politically. If this is so, there is little to be gained from imagining that wilderness reserves or fishing villages or tribal communities or family farms are somehow outside the urban. As the Walt Disney Corporation could explain, every one of these "places" –

real or imaginary – has a vital role to play in marketing the products de-manded by urbanites (Zukin 1991). Moreover, the place of these places within the larger whole is determined by a politics that we can sensibly des-ignate as "urban." Urban politics in this sense is not a politics confined to municipalities, nor is it peculiar to places where the density of human settle-ment is especially high. Rather, the politics of the urban is the politics that relates – critically or supportively – to the practices by which we humanize our environment. The urbanites who go to the forests of British Columbia and sit down in front of the logging trucks are involved in a form of urban politics: they want the fact of their protest flashed across screens around the world, and they are hoping for decisive remedial action from the urban cen-tres of power. They are acting from within to secure a natural "outside" that puts appropriate limits to human endeavour.

To think this way about what we are doing is to emphasize that none of us are outside the practices by which we are destroying the natural wilderness, enslaving ourselves to the market, excluding the socially marked minorities, acting violently, and otherwise behaving in ways that moralists label inhu-man. Since we share in the responsibility for the dreadful things that are hap-pening (as well as in the credit for human achievements), there can be no honest politics that fails to remind us of this responsibility. Urbanism is *our* way of life, and it is our responsibility as humans to recognize how we are liv-ing, to take responsibility for what we are doing, and to consider what we can do politically to improve our own practices. In this context, we need to recog-nize that we are involved in a number of activities, the most important of which we can conceive as social movements. These movements are not nec-essarily directed at particular fixtures. On the contrary, they create their own spaces in relation to other ongoing activities. In truth, the human world is a world in movement in which the apparent fixtures are just sedimentations or reifications of earlier movements. Movements move in relation to one an-other, and not in relation to stable fixtures.

So, how are we to think of the state, or the market, or patriarchy? There is only one possible answer: as movements. Conceived as a fixture, we can im-agine the contemporary economy as "the market" or "the globalized mar-ket." Conceived as a movement, the same phenomena appear as capitalism. That capitalism is a movement (and that Marx, for instance, conceived it so) is quite apparent, not only because capitalists (like other movement activ-ists) spend huge amounts of time and money on publicizing their cause or organizing political parties, but also because the institutions and practices produced by capitalism are constantly changing. Capitalism is not some fixed thing: it is a movement that brings people in relation to one another in particular ways and encourages them to respond creatively to the con-straints and opportunities that arise in consequence. The forms of political, social, and economic organization that are most conducive to capitalism are subject to constant revision, and so it is always a mistake for critics and opponents of capitalism to suppose that the form fixed for now will still be there in ten or twenty years. We might say the same for statism, patriarchy, racism, or any of the other movements that have been subject to criticism or resistance.

To understand statism as a movement is particularly important, for it is in and through this particular movement that we come to understand politics in a particular way. It is important to recognize (*pacem* Marx) that statism is not simply an effect of capitalism. Statism emerged as a consequence of sixteenth-century humanism, and took particular hold on the Western political imagination as a consequence of the seventeenth-century wars of religion. It may be well to remember in our own age of religious fundamentalism that statism was and is a movement *against* such fundamentalism and in favour of a particular form of civilized political order. One of the questions we have to face today is whether statism remains the most adequate response to the dangers of religious warfare, or whether we must act to transcend the movement altogether. Certainly, the proliferation of states and interstate institutions in the twentieth century suggests that statism will continue to be a powerful movement for the foreseeable future. It is less clear what other movements will be producing alternatives.

THE IDEA OF THE POLITICAL

Lurking in this analysis is a concept of the political that has yet to be articulated with sufficient clarity. If we accept the idea that what appears to us is an ensemble of movements – some more important than others, but none of them with the capacity to determine the whole completely – the politics that must concern us is *within and between movements*. But, what is it to say, "politics"? If politics is not simply what relates to the state (or what mimics activity in relation to the state), what is it? What are we saying when we declare that a particular problem is political, or when we label our own actions as political interventions? What is the point of thinking politically rather than socially?

As indicated above, concepts like judgement and responsibility seem to be intimately associated with the notion of politics (Crick 1993). To act politically is to take responsibility and to exercise judgement. But, in relation to what? The simplest answer is, "In relation to everything." The political is what exceeds the merely economic, the merely social, the merely moral. It is the domain in which we are obliged to relate economics, morality, religion, identity, and much else to one another. It is the domain in which the rules of judgement, the boundaries between one thing and another, are always in question. These matters are in question because they have no universally satisfying answers, and because the political is the locus for resolving differences that cannot be resolved by applying the established rules. The political is always a domain of uncertainty, negotiation, deliberation, compromise – and violence. That we could constitute the political as a domain without violence is a recurring dream, but violence is always in the shadows, always a problem (and an option) that must be considered. Politics is always difficult and always dangerous (if only for the people excluded from it). To draw attention to the political character of our activities is to remind ourselves of our own violence as well as of the ideals we pursue. It is thus to insist on our responsibility for our own actions and on the need for judgement in these matters.

So conceived, politics is the creator and destroyer of boundaries. Political activity may produce the boundaries between one country and another or between the state and civil society, but political activity also puts those boundaries into question. If I am right about how we now live in a global city, the familiar boundaries of modern politics are now contained within a way of life that washes over them. The world contains a proliferation of political authorities, each of them liminal; that is, every authority sits uneasily at a boundary, pointing beyond itself into the world as a whole. The municipality is paradigmatic in this respect: modern states are like municipalities, and not the other way around (Magnusson 1996). This is a reflection of the illusory character of state sovereignty. The key point is that the domain of the political is a global hyperspace that we have barely begun to conceptualize. It is time that we got down to this conceptual work: the task is eminently practical.

Part 2

SOCIAL MOVEMENTS IN PRACTICE

REINVENTING
A LABOUR MOVEMENT?

Bob Russell

Within the "new social movement" genre, most discussions of social movements studiously avoid treating contemporary labour movements seriously. Indeed, within contemporary social theory, labour and the study of working-class social movements are now downright unfashionable topics of discussion.

One reason given for this disenchantment with labour is the disillusionment that set in following the failure to realize transformative projects in the late 1960s and early 1970s, with the waves of wildcat strikes in North America and the factory occupations in Western Europe (Crouch and Pizzorno 1978). Then, in the 1980s, came the defeats and setbacks visited upon many national labour movements, including the de-unionization of most of U.S. society (Freeman and Medoff 1984; Goldfield 1987; Weiler 1990; Wrenn 1985), the historic defeat of the miners and the quiescence visited upon Britain (Hyman 1986), and the decline in strikes and militant action in other settings, including Canada (Panitch and Swartz 1993).

In turn such failures have often been traced back to an institutionalization of employment relations and a bureaucratization of the labour movement over the entire postwar era (Aronowitz 1973). Having seemingly been transformed from an original social movement to a special-interest group, in its current bureaucratic guise labour is no longer capable of mounting more than symbolic opposition to an agenda it no longer controls, and on behalf of social actors it cannot presume to speak for (Palmer 1992). Adding to the dilemma are changes in capitalism itself, including the movement out of industrial Fordism, which allegedly robbed an oppositional class politics of much of its force (Hobsbawm 1989). In these accounts the homogeneous industrial working class of a bygone Fordist era has been replaced by the segmented, diffuse identities of a postmodern world (Harvey 1989).

None of these admittedly stylized arguments is incorrect on its own, but as a whole they have led to some unwarranted inferences. In all of this, class realities, state power, and the labour movement in particular have not only been eclipsed, but have also often entirely disappeared (Gortz 1982). Not only has attention, with some justification perhaps, been drawn elsewhere, to other currents of opposition and identity, and to other terrains of struggle, but the labour movement *qua* social movement has largely been denied. In other words, although labour may still have a vestigial institutional presence, as a social movement force it can now safely be ignored. In its place we find various other social movements, which bear few organizational affinities to labour. The most contentious implication of the new social movement litera-ture is that it is pointless to raise the issue of a labour movement in the con-text of contemporary social protest: labour movements are no longer impor-tant enough to draw into current analyses of social change; they are a spent force. Furthermore, no particularly useful function can be served by study-ing labour movements in the analysis of new social movements, which rep-resent different interests with different organizational formats, modes of mobilization, and operational strategies.

Further reflection, however, reveals the weaknesses of these assertions. At a theoretical level, employment relationships, which include labour-market conditions, the labour process, industrial relations, and unemploy-ment, remain vital components of identity, community, and social life.[1] In-deed, it is difficult to take up the issues of gender, racialization, the environ-ment, or peace in a serious fashion without bringing the employment rela-tion back into the analysis (Wood 1986; Williams 1983).[2] Nor can we auto-matically assume that class identities subscribe positions with respect to other focal points. Tom Dunk's investigations into class and environmental attitudes, which illustrate the complex and nuanced mediations that forestry workers bring to environmental concerns, and Roger Keil's study of work-ing-class environmentalism as expressed in Toronto's Green Work Alliance both serve as important correctives against what could be termed a new form of reverse class reductionism that is often associated with certain streams of post-Marxian analyses (Dunk 1994; Keil 1994). William Carroll and R.S. Ratner, in ongoing research, have also detected a substantial over-lap between labour activism and participation in other social movement activity (Carroll and Ratner 1995). At the level of organizations, recent cam-paigns such as those run by the Canadian Automobile Workers on domestic violence and the United Steelworkers on racism in the workplace give practi-cal expression to the fundamental links between labour markets, the struc-turing of work, and extraworkplace forms of oppression.

Locating labour movements vis-à-vis other social collectivities ought also to be viewed as more than a case of arcane theoreticism or antiquarian curi-osity. Thus, while giving due attention to labour's significant defeats and set-backs in the last twenty years, beginning with the federal wage-control program in 1974, one would still be hard-pressed to find levels of resistance to match those expressed in the 1972 Quebec Common Front general strike or the 1983 British Columbia Operation Solidarity movement.[3] And although expressions of resistance on this scale remain periodic, the "cultures of solidarity" (Fantasia 1988: 199) that inform them, as well as everyday workplace relationships, should never be dropped from our analysis of dissent.[4]

Finally, there is the argument that labour is to be distinguished from the "new" social movements along a number of important dimensions, including forms of internal organization, goals and objectives, and relationships with other social forces. In these respects, labour has been written off as an "old" social movement, a product of modernity, with all of the encumbrances this origin entails. Counterpoised to the rational bureaucracies of trade unions, then, are the radically democratic politics of the NSMs, the decentring of law, politics, and the state, and struggles to realize personal autonomy in lieu of grand hegemonic visions (Laclau and Mouffe 1985; Gortz 1982). Despite this, nagging doubts remain. The stylized objectives of today's social movements – "struggles for 'the reappropriation of time, of space and of relationships in the individual's daily experience'" – have a familiar ring to them (Canel 1992). The advocacy of participation for its own sake and democratic, egalitarian procedures remain contested issues within many unions and their locals. Finally, and perhaps most importantly, the question of periodicities has been neglected (Weir 1993c). Do the new social movements have radically different agendas that qualitatively distinguish them from the labour movement, or are they new iterations on older organizational themes? As long as students of social movements give short shrift to class-based collectivities and the history of the labour movement, we shall never have a satisfactory response to this query.

The Canadian labour movement, not unlike its counterparts elsewhere, has passed through a series of phases, but there has been nothing inevitable about this sequencing: it is the product of conscious choices, usually rendered in the context of internal debate, shaped by strategic interaction with other parties, and subject to unanticipated outcomes. In other words, a binding "iron law of oligarchy" has not necessarily been at work here (Michels 1949). Far more important, and absolutely essential for an understanding of this history, is the role of the modern state. More than any other factor, the state has shaped the modern labour movement, partially determining what it would become, but, perhaps more importantly, overseeing what it would not be. Following from this, if we review its periodicities, at least in some of its guises, we can more clearly see the resemblances between the labour movement and mobilizations of more recent vintage. We will also see that we should not downgrade the role of the state and politics in any account of this one social movement. Furthermore, the centrality of the state has not necessarily been at labour's behest, but rather is something that has confronted this social movement as a practical "precondition." Thus, whether as an adjunct to the liberal laissez-faire era, or as the Fordist welfare state, or finally as the strong state prop in a free economy, the state is a practical reality confronting labour, and most other social movements that I can think of. No matter how much new social movement theorists may desire to wish politics and the state away, it remains, in this era of global capitalism, a determining presence that agencies of social change are bound, sooner or later, to come up against in their strategic calculations.[5]

PARADOXES OF THE PRESENT

What do trade unions do and how do they do it? This simple question is quite revealing for a "take" on the contemporary labour movement, its strengths, and weaknesses.[6]

Much of the day-to-day politics of trade unionism involves policing collective bargaining agreements as they pertain to the interests of individual members. In practice this entails hearing out complaints, deciding whether they are justiciable under the terms of the agreement, and attempting to resolve the relevant issues, either through various stages of formal complaint up to legal arbitration, or through dissuading members from continuing with "hopeless" cases. Grievances relating to issues such as assignment of overtime, bumping and bidding rights, and work and holiday scheduling are the mainstays of this sort of activity. As well, new managerial initiatives, more common in periods of corporate restructuring, such as revamped payment structures (profit-sharing, gain-sharing) or new training programs, may be taken as affronts to existing arrangements and hence made subject to group grievances on behalf of the local union as a whole.

All of this assumes the existence of a collective bargaining agreement, a "woolly" document that is generally renewed every two to three years by local managements and unions with, or sometimes without, the help of paid professional staff. Quite frequently, prior to the onset of collective bargaining, local unions will elicit opinions and preferences through short membership "surveys," after which informational meetings will be held to update members on management offers and garner membership views on prospective settlements or the desirability of job actions. Most of this work is done by volunteers – members of bargaining committees, grievance committees, occupational health and safety committees, and so on. In addition to normal work schedules, such participation does not allow for a surplus of discretionary time.[7] Should such exist, however, there are always positions to be filled in local union area councils, on municipal and provincial labour councils, and in politics proper (NDP local constituency executives, for example). In other words, union activism tends to be demanding and all-inclusive.

Things were not always such. The present institutionalization of labour affairs assumes, amongst other things, a regime of regularized collective bargaining, a highly juridified state of industrial relations, a formal division between workplace representation and political representation proper, and, for highly involved activists, a relatively inclusive trade union culture that may have overall exclusionary implications. Additionally, such patterns are repeated over and over again from one community to the next, as part of a highly decentralized industrial relations practice in Canada.

Each of these traits may be taken as militating against large-scale, timely, and decisive mobilization at the same time as they have given workers a voice at the point of production. Grievance machinery for so-called "rights disputes" has been substituted across Canada for the right to strike during the term of a collective agreement (Haiven 1990). Rather than being a venue for collective action and solidarity, disputes are channelled into individual complaints. As a result, grievances have been largely individuated, filed by the aggrieved, only to disappear into lengthy, formalized adjudication processes that largely remain the preserve of legal experts (Clement 1981).[8] Similarly, collective bargaining has become increasingly formalized, in the production of discourses that relate to conditions of production. The hundreds of collective agreements to be negotiated every two to three years become a main order of business on many union calendars. Finally, even the nature of union organizing has changed considerably. In an insightful comparison of two union locals separated by thirteen years from respective founding points, Don Wells demonstrates how union organizing in the 1940s sprang from local, internal plant initiatives with some aid from international union offices, while in the 1950s organization drives were directed from those very same offices with temporary assistance from a minority of workplace activists (Wells 1995). The change in part reflects the development of a whole jurisprudence on union "recognition" and certification procedures, which again have tended to remove organization as a local movement initiative. Instead new organization becomes subject to a body of rules pertaining to required levels of authorization, voting procedures, rights and challenges, all of which require specialized knowledge. This has undeniably altered the nature of trade unionism. Organization increasingly reflects the prerogatives of existing unions branching out to unorganized work sites. Such "campaigns," as they are referred to, are either launched directly by the parent body on behalf of a work site or may be petitioned for by a group of workers who "wanted to be organized." In either case initiative lies somewhere beyond the immediacy of plant, office, and community, a trait bolstered by legal prohibitions against "campaigning" on employer premises (Drache and Glasbeek 1992).

Such practices led to what contemporaries then referred to as "responsible unionism," a term very much in vogue when modern industrial unionism came into its own in the mid-1940s. But this approach also entailed a more passive form of unionism, in which direct member control was increasingly moderated by management from above. Wallace Clement captures part of this dynamic when he writes that for many, "the union is like an insurance policy; they hope they will not have to use it, but they are happy it's there if they really need it" (Clement 1981: 333-4).

Such contradictory effects, which involve both democratic participation and a rich associational life for a small minority of members and passivity for many, became apparent in one local studied, in which collective bargaining had reached an impasse with a private-sector corporation. Typical of the times, the dispute entailed a change of corporate direction in management practices. The company wanted the union to support a new continuous improvement plan that would be accompanied by the introduction of a gain-sharing scheme. The union was leery, fearing that continuous improvement would translate into employment loss and that gain-sharing would be at the expense of employment and wages. As a result the union wanted improvements in layoff language, retraining provisions, and some retroactive gain-sharing in acknowledgement of previous improvements. A further novel suggestion that gain-sharing proceeds be set aside in a retraining fund had been previously vetoed by the company.[9]

In meetings with shop stewards, members of the bargaining committee conveyed the impasse and explored the levels of support for job action among members.[10] Based on the meeting, members obtained a consensus to move ahead with a one-day study session to be held before the pending summer maintenance shutdown. This plan would increase the impact of the action on the employer (in lost production), while minimizing wage loss for the employees. Legally, however, the local had to observe a notice period of forty-eight hours before any type of job action, including a twenty-four-hour strike, could be set in place. Additional complexities entailed getting notice to and scheduling the action over two shifts, and maintaining the powerhouse operations over the course of the strike. For these reasons the union's staff representative was sceptical that a newly elected local executive could execute the planned action, even though the bargaining unit employees wanted to strike while it was strategically most advantageous. In short, the local faced formidable logistical obstacles posed by mandatory legal requirements, shift work, "essential services," and company production schedules (the maintenance shutdown). Executing even a brief job action that conformed to the limitations of the law and modern production norms had turned into a time-consuming affair.

In the end, and in a testimony to local democracy, the strike action went ahead as intended. To accommodate the shifts, the local planned three separate "study sessions" to take place following the mandatory notification period. Through a combination of telephoning members, patrolling the entrance to the company facilities to turn workers back, and word of mouth, the local achieved a successful shutdown.[11] The three study sessions were well-attended but short affairs, lasting no more than an hour each. Union spokespersons updated members on the most recent proposals and fielded questions dealing with job security, layoffs, pensions, restrictions on supervisors doing out-of-scope work, and the length of the contract.[12] They also made clear that the workers were fulfilling their moral obligations by attending one of the meetings and that they ought to take advantage of the rest of a free day while the bargaining committee returned to its deliberations. Participants were assured that this brief display of collective determination had made a difference: "it had caught the company's attention."

Indeed, this was the case. Negotiations, which had been languishing, were put on the fast track, with managers called back from summer vacation. Within a week the local was ready to go forward with a ratification vote on a contract that did not include the worrisome continuous improvement program or the gain-sharing plan. The contract improved on seniority, layoff, and recall language as well as the pension plan, although criticisms from the floor on these issues were still rife.[13] At the end of the day, 83.8 per cent of those in attendance had cast ballots in favour of the new two-year agreement.

As union-management disputes go this conflict was largely unexceptional, but precisely for that reason it captures, in a microcosm, many of the ambiguities of the contemporary labour movement. First of all, the conflict remained a small local matter, isolated from similar establishments and almost identical issues in the same industry and region. For that matter, workers and their organizations throughout the world are being confronted with similar managerial initiatives pertaining to new forms of work organization and payment systems (Katz 1985: 198; Kochan et al. 1986: 198; Piore and Sabel 1984; Russell 1995, 1997). In this instance a union local briefly mobilized a collective effort to resist changes that were deemed detrimental, and again one can hypothesize similar situations reoccurring many times over. However, even this effort required an inordinate number of hours of preparation to meet legal regulations for a one-day show of solidarity. While corporate initiatives were turned back, gains on seniority and retraining language, as well as pensions, remained marginal. In other words, this was principally a defensive struggle, undertaken in relative isolation. Finally, and within the next ten months, the company unilaterally went ahead with its own gain-sharing plan and attempted to introduce a "competency development program" of peer review assessments as part of the continuous improvement agenda. Continuous improvement, although delayed through membership resistance, was far from dead. In terms of images, then, we are left with a small, isolated struggle that involved a flicker of mobilization and a great deal of time spent in ensuring its legality. Participation was mixed with control and internal politics. The objectives were largely defensive, and the results uncertain. These features were not happenstance, but are, rather, one face of a system of regulation that encompasses the modern labour movement.

LESSONS FROM THE PAST

Things were not always such. Labour historians have referred to the existence of a "movement culture" in late nineteenth-century Canada. I would
extend this time line further, until 1921, and would then go on to delineate
three additional, distinct phases in labour's history (see Figure 1).

By the term "movement culture," historians are referencing "a process of
working-class self-activity that took the collectivist impulses of labouring experience and shaped them into a reform mobilization" (Palmer 1992: 127).
Critically, this movement culture was concerned with surmounting socially
constructed oppositions that had either been inherited from the past and/or
actively reproduced by industrial capitalism itself. Its first expression came
in the Knights of Labour of the 1880s, which organized on a scale not to be
duplicated again until the Second World War (Kealey and Palmer 1987: 63-6).
Through the Knights, "Long-standing points of division within working-class
life – skilled versus unskilled; male versus female; Protestant versus Catholic
– were opposed by the Order's conscious and persistent attempt to construct
an alternative vision of the possibility of solidarity" (Palmer 1992: 131).

Nor was this an isolated (or utopian) endeavour. If anything, efforts to
create an inclusive, holistic movement were redoubled between the 1880s
and 1919, first with the Industrial Workers of the World and later with the
One Big Union movement. Despite their differences, each of these efforts
arose from a similar lineage and aimed at similar objectives that, if anything,
were expanded as time went on. First, significant sections of the labour
movement sought as a desideratum a social inclusivity with respect to such
socially constructed identities as skill level, gender, industrial affiliation,

Figure 1
Canadian Labour Movement:
Defining Phases

| Syndicalism –
working class
alternative
political-economy | Trade union co-
determination | Trade union
interests/
lobbying | Trade union
coalitional politics |

One Big Union;
Economy & State

Labour   State   Business

Business
State
Labour

Labour   New Social Movements   State   Business

1890–1921   1937–1947   1950–1975   1983–

occupation, and ethnic background. This goal posed a stark challenge to existent forms of organization, which took the capitalist labour market and its many divisions as a given and hence remained sociologically exclusive. Second, the tasks of a labour movement did not end with mediating the employment relationship. Again, the movement posed nothing less than an alternative working-class political economy in which trade unions would assume an overtly political, as well as economic, centrality in social organization. In practice this push involved tempering emergent capitalist social relations with the moral economy of community and class (Thompson 1964).

Written off as millenarian and hopelessly impractical by some (Bercuson 1978), such experiments were never given a chance to succeed or fail on their own merits; one after another they were suppressed out of existence by a combination of employer resistance and state hostility. For their part, employers refused to have anything to do with the organizations, refusing recognition, dialogue, or dealings. In this they were actively abetted by state officials, who openly favoured existent craft unions to the exclusion of alternative organizations when it suited political priorities (Russell 1990: ch. 5). Suffice it to note, then, that we are still in need of a more nuanced and sophisticated critique of the historical possibilities, as well as inherent limitations, of working-class syndicalism than has so far been offered.

The fate of the syndicalist organizations speaks to an essential dilemma faced by social movements in general. Namely, in the absence of an extension of legitimacy by other powerholders in society, a collectivity will find it difficult, if not impossible, to move towards the realization of its goals. In the case of the early labour movement, the withholding of recognition and the boycotting of all proceedings by the owners of capital left labour without an interlocutor. In most cases such unilateralism spelt defeat. But the extension of legitimacy often comes at a price, which is the trade-off/dilemma often confronted by social movements – evident in the next phase of labour movement activity.

Legitimacy is ultimately about the bestowal of recognition, and as such is constitutive of a deeply political decision. To bring it about, the recognition often entails state sanctioning. For the labour movement this official approval was expressed in various pieces of twentieth-century legislation that compelled the recognition of autonomous worker organizations and a duty to negotiate fairly with them. This was the essence of the 1935 National Industrial Relations (Wagner) Act in the United States, the 1944 Wartime Labour Relations Regulations (PC1003) in Canada, and the Canadian Rand Formula of 1946. The U.S. NIRA provided the essential model. The product of a strike wave, which was itself provoked by the failure of previous New Deal legislation to guarantee rights to collective representation, the aptly named Wagner Act provided for the certification of trade unions with exclusive representation rights at the individual plant level, following a demonstration of majoritarian support. Customarily, the signing of union membership cards by a majority of workers at a site is taken as sufficient evidence to warrant certification, and the union agent is then granted exclusive bargaining rights for that industrial "jurisdiction."[14]

Certification implied legal recognition of the union by all parties to the employment relation. Hence, under the NIRA employers had a duty to bargain in good faith with the chosen union representatives of the workforce with the intention of reaching a mutually acceptable collective agreement. According to the framers of the NIRA, such processes were intended to provide for macroeconomic stability as well as reductions in social conflict. This was precisely the stamp of legitimacy that had been wanting. Events would trail in Canada, but by 1948 Canadian labour had, if anything, a more conducive labour code than its counterpart in the United States. In particular, the 1946 Rand solution to a strike at Ford Canada moved to provide certified unions with income security through the automatic checkoff of dues, a demand that had been around since the beginning of the century. By virtue of the formula, once a union had demonstrated majority support and been duly certified, all members of the bargaining unit, whether or not they belonged to the union, were required to contribute to its upkeep. In effect this guaranteed a solid resource base for trade union functioning.

Judgements as to the overall effect of these political accords on the labour movement vary widely. Some critics have argued persuasively that Wagnerism effectively ensured a deradicalized labour presence. In the first instance, state authorities were given the power to ultimately determine the boundaries of emergent industrial unionism through the certification mechanism (Klare 1978; Tomlins 1985). The localism (that is, decentralized plant-level unionism) that had been a dominant feature of North American industrial relations was given further impetus, thereby reinforcing tendencies to a fractured labour movement (Millar 1980). Meanwhile, subsequent judicial interpretations of the Wagner Act functioned to reward "responsible" union behaviour, while denying benefits under the act to militant unions that were strike-prone or that disregarded the sanctity of corporate property through such acts as worker occupations (Harris 1982; Klare 1978).

In the Canadian context, the quid pro quo was, if anything, more obvious. In return for the protocols of union recognition, the employer duty to bargain, and security of union funding through Rand agreements, unions ceded the right to strike over such items as working conditions during the term of the contract. Organized resistance could only be proffered on those infrequent occasions when the labour contract had expired, while all other discontent was funnelled through the legal maze of "rights arbitration."

As a result, recent historiographic and legal opinion has stressed the disciplining effects of state intervention on the labour movement. Union recognition and union security were exchanged for far-reaching managerial rights protocols and the arbitration of conflict (Warrian 1986), thereby leaving employer power modified, but essentially intact (Millar 1980). As succinctly summarized by one observer, "Government legislation underwrote the gains made by organized labour ... but in so doing ... it channelled that power to minimize its potential to disrupt" (Fudge 1987: 221). For some, then, this exchange constituted a "counterfeit liberty" – "what the state offered workers and their organizations was ultimately no more than the opportunity to participate in the construction of their own subordination," an opportunity the trade union movement readily tapped into (Tomlins 1985:327). Others, however, who are also part of a renewed historiographic research effort, dissent from these evaluations. Thus, for the "labor movement of July 1935, the Wagner Act cost nothing and promised vast gains," one writer noted. "The Wagner Act was so advanced and the protections it guaranteed workers and unions so fulsome that it carried the potential to transform radically the American social and economic order" (Dubofsky 1994:129-31). Others have also joined in arguing that, if nothing else, Wagner-type legislation was certainly supportive of a burgeoning labour movement (Brody 1980:ch. 3; Montgomery 1979:ch. 7).

My own reading of the evidence suggests the existence of societal crisis and concomitant political openings. The eventual framework of the so-called postwar accord was far from preordained. Rather, the ongoing "exchanges" between labour, the state, and business were fluid in their unfolding and often unanticipated in their outcomes (Russell 1990:ch. 6). It is also the case that based upon past experiences, the goals of the labour movement had undergone alteration since 1919. In lieu of the substitutionalism that characterized syndicalism, we find a different kind of social unionism, developing in both the interwar and immediate postwar periods, premised upon forms of societal co-determination. How else would one describe the 1946 demands of the United Automobile Workers for a 30 per cent wage hike with no increase in the price of product associated with it along with demands for public scrutiny of corporate ledgers? (Brody 1980; Harris 1982; Lichtenstein 1982). This, and numerous other examples of demands for joint industry production boards during World War II, and concerted economic planning initiatives in the postwar era ("win the peace programs"), indicate that social unionism was not immediately eradicated in the aftermath of the new labour regime (Dubofsky 1994). In effect, labour called for a determinative influence over macroeconomic employment levels, social welfare policy, and corporate pricing and profit rates. Only once these goals proved to be beyond the strategic capabilities of the labour movement did labour fall back into a regime of localized collective bargaining, or what is commonly referred to as Fordism, supplemented with occasional forays into political lobbying and electioneering (Yates 1993). While political initiatives such as the Wagner Act and the Rand Formula were certainly conducive to this result, they did not uniquely predetermine it.

THE NEAR FUTURE

The debate on the implications of Wagnerism is not merely of historiographic interest. It forces the issue of state reform and social movement experience squarely back onto the analytical agenda. Furthermore, it has returned to haunt the contemporary labour movement as has no other issue. Today's movement is now explicitly confronted with the dilemmas posed by a heritage of regulation and reform.

In the first instance, this question has been posed by labour's response to the crisis of Fordism, constituted as it is by job loss, high unemployment, falling real wages, and fiscal liabilities. Work reorganization, demands for trade union concessions, and an absence of tangible gains at the bargaining table have certainly removed some of the lustre from routine collective bargaining, while the abandonment of Keynesian welfare policies by social-democratic parties has added to the sense of crisis within contemporary labour movements. In Canada these pressure points have resulted in emergent cleavages, which have centred around a critique versus a defence of the postwar status quo. Although the positions taken overlap to a considerable extent with the divisions between private-sector and public-sector unionism, this is far from a perfect fit. Indeed, two private-sector unions, the Canadian Auto Workers (CAW) and the United Steelworkers (USWA) have assumed leading roles in framing the divergent positions.

Each of these pressures has come together most tellingly in the old industrial heartland of Ontario, where a novice NDP government confronted a precipitous slide into the worst depression since the 1930s. Encapsulating the sense of confusion spawned by these events is an Ontario Federation of Labour document that cogently observes that the social-democratic government responded to the crisis by initiating "the most anti-worker intrusion into free collective bargaining in Canadian history, while at the same time legislating the most progressive labour legislation in North America" (OFL 1993). The anti-worker intrusion refers to Bill 48, the so-called "Social Contract," which unilaterally overrode existing collective agreements to impose a three-year wage freeze and mandatory unpaid leaves on the public and parapublic sectors (Panitch and Swartz 1993). The progressive legislation refers to Bill 40, which reformed the province's industrial relations legislation and, among other things, introduced modified anti-scab measures and made other favourable extensions of existing legislation (Russell 1996: 185-6). In essence, then, we have witnessed both an extension of Wagnerism combined with a crisis of Fordism, the political-economic regime that framed the postwar model of industrial relations. These highly contradictory developments have evoked latent tendencies within the labour movement that are worth examining in further detail.

The peak organization, the OFL, reflecting the diversity in its membership, has issued a confused response to the prevailing dynamics. On the one hand, it asked that support for the social-democratic NDP be revoked until collective bargaining rights were restored in the public sector and Bill 48 nullified. In lieu of electoralism, the OFL urged a fuller development of coalitional politics, that is, broad-based alliances that would keep the pressure on governments to fulfil their popular commitments (OFL 1993). On the other hand, the Federation proposed to contest incumbent MLA renominations, challenging all government members who supported the social contract. In other words, while calling for increased labour participation within the Ontario NDP, via the nomination process, the house of labour also pledged itself to a boycott of the 1995 provincial election and indicated an intention to siphon resources away from the party towards community-based social movement groups.

Although the OFL does not specifically indicate potential coalitional partners in its documents, the Canadian Auto Workers union has refined its position on movement politics to a greater extent. Its disaffection with "labourism" and party politics predates 1993 and the social contract. While the union has consistently had a more ambiguous relationship with the NDP, serious disenchantment set in with the party's lacklustre challenge to the Free Trade Agreement in the 1988 federal election (CAW 1994b). Since then the union has moved to distance itself from the party, in the process assuming a more critical, autonomous position.

The Auto Workers union itself has also undergone important changes. First of all, the union is no longer principally a union of autoworkers. Embodying emergent economic trends, the CAW has grown to be the largest private-sector union in Canada, mainly through a series of dazzling mergers over the last decade. Such significant entities as the United Electrical Workers, the Mine Mill and Smelter Workers, the Brotherhood of Railway Trainmen, Industrial Mechanics (CAIMAW), airline workers (CALEA), and fisheries workers have entered the union.[15] Organizers portray this as the formation of "one big (general) union" within the CAW, a definite movement towards labour unity (CAW 1994a). However, this development contains two portents: the formation of one big union that could represent a new counter-hegemonic force in society; or the creation of a bureaucratized general union that is all but immobilized by its own aggrandized dimensions.

While undoubtedly there are pressures in the latter direction, it is fair to say that CAW growth has been framed within a larger self-perceived shift in the nature of unionism that brings into play the notion of a "movement politics." This represents a redoubling of efforts to construct a new brand of social unionism. While social unionism is characterized as taking the union into the community through the pressing of extraworkplace demands, movement politics, as characterized by the CAW, involves bringing the community into the union. Thus it is not so much about joining others "as recognizing these coalition partners to be either other workers (unorganized, unemployed,

visible minorities, women, immigrants), or people involved in other dimensions of our lives (... public health, the environment ... the school system ...)"
(CAW 1994a). The union itself again becomes a broad centre of political resistance and mobilization both inside the workplace – through, for example,
challenging the reorganization of labour processes around models of lean
production – and, more significantly, in the community – through the creation of "Area Action Groups" open to a wider constituency, of both local union representation and community participation (CAW 1995).

In this conjunction, two initiatives are of particular note. The first is a campaign to redistribute work (CAW 1993), which comes out of a recognition of
the tremendous disequilibrium that corporate flexibility and post-Fordism
have brought to labour markets. Thus side by side in the emerging economies, we find unemployment, contingent employment, and huge quantities
of non-voluntary (and voluntary) overtime.[16] While demands for the regulation of working time are almost as old as the labour movement itself, in the
current context they have been lent a new narrative. Reductions in work time
are not simply justified by the large increases in productivity that have en-
sued since the last reductions some fifty years ago, but are also an equity
measure, reducing the overwork of some and the unemployment of others
in one measure. The CAW would implement these steps through the introduction of "guaranteed training allowances" in collective agreements, essentially establishing the right to enhanced skills and analytical training for employed workers, while unemployed personnel would replace workers on
training sabbaticals (CAW 1994c).

The second campaign ostensibly targets state monetary policy and the
ensuing austerity measures dictated by that policy. This initiative makes the
link between the deconstruction of the welfare state and increasing levels of
worker insecurity, as a means of generating a wider audience for employee
concessions, but reaches beyond immediate union members by targeting
banks and other national financial institutions. Among potential actions pertaining to this project the union has identified the picketing of banks and the
occupation of properties that banks have listed for foreclosure action, the
publicizing of bank profits and exports of loan capital abroad through advertising campaigns, and mass pickets of parliamentary constituency offices in
support of a lower interest rate/higher corporate tax policy (CAW 1995).

The potential for each of these strategies to constitute a broader-based
resistance front in the community undeniably exists. Mobilization on behalf
of reduced working hours has definite implications for employment levels
and the unemployed, although it deals with the issue of unemployment in a
somewhat indirect fashion. To date the unemployed themselves remain unorganized, although the pending implementation of workfare programs in
several provinces provides a medium for addressing this issue directly. So,
too, an alternative economic agenda directed against monetary policy and

the banks has considerable potential for forging ties with homeowners (many of whom may also be union members), farmers, and small business people. Although one should never belittle expressions of local solidarity and their importance in building enduring ties, nevertheless at this time it is difficult to envisage moving beyond occasional demonstrations towards a more sustained and winnable confrontation over this issue. Clearly, unions will also have to develop other strategies for keeping the pressure on.

The new directions taking shape also have immediate political implications, which have in turn become the most contentious issue within the labour movement. For organizations identifying with a movement politics, new initiatives have been necessitated first and foremost by the international crisis in social democracy. The disenchantment with traditional labour politics extends beyond specific tensions within the NDP, which are only symptomatic of a broader fault line that has also been registered in New Zealand, Australia, the United Kingdom, and France. In each instance social democracy has been progressively marginalized with respect to the emerging post-Fordist economy and its fallout of unemployment and immiseration. As a political movement, it has been unable to build upon the disruption and anger generated by massive destabilization. Owing to this, members of the so-called "Alliance" (the CAW and several large public-sector unions) are no longer content to "contract politics out" to professional social-democratic parliamentarians. Instead, they are arguing that unions must reappropriate politics as direct organizational actors rather than as mere institutional supports for party structures. As one publication stated, "The point is not to push the role of parliamentary politics aside, but to broaden the definition of what politics is and what it should include" (CAW 1993: 23).

No one should underestimate the potential significance of such a shift in direction. This rethinking represents a serious critique of existing relationships within the labour movement and between it and the state. Because of this, such positions are in the process of being contested by other strategies that seek to extend tripartite co-determinative relations with governments and business. For unions such as the United Steelworkers, the crisis in the public realm has been created by the unprecedented erosion of employment in the private goods-producing sector. Consequently, solutions to labour's problems must begin with regeneration in that domain. Specifically, greater levels of co-operation are required, as evinced in the formation of joint sectoral frameworks to oversee the implementation of a new industrial strategy, replete with comprehensive retraining, and the development of new labour-based investment tools and ownership forms ("Rethinking Our Mission" 1993).[17] Such initiatives, however, require political support, and the NDP remains the only political agent even remotely interested in overseeing this type of agenda. As a result, downgrading the linkages between the labour movement and social democracy is a self-negativizing proposition, or, as registered in one response to the OFL resolutions on the issue, "Renewing the party is one and the same mission as renewing the Canadian and Ontario labour movements" ("Rethinking Our Mission" 1993: 25). In this scenario, then, while coalitional politics are not to be entirely ignored, neither can they be allowed to displace the more traditional forms of labour partyism for fear of placing the very philosophical core of the labour movement at risk, subordinating it to the single-issue politics of selected social movements ("Social Coalitions Versus Social Democracy" 1993).

Such contemporary divisions within the labour movement raise anew the vexatious strategical issue pertaining to relations between social movements and the state. While one charter looks at decentring parliamentarianism, although certainly not the state, as a means of reviving political unionism, the other raises the possibility of tripartist co-determination. Clearly, important, unsettling questions remain unresolved in both positions.

For those who would pursue a deepening of the Wagner/welfare regime, there is an unwillingness to confront the untenability of classical social democracy in a post-Fordist world. Corporatist solutions have floundered since the collapse of the social contracts at the outset of the crisis in the early 1970s (Panitch 1979). There are few grounds for optimism with respect to reviving this model under current circumstances, which have led to a steady accretion of power to large business interests in the interceding twenty years. In the 1990s theoretical advocacy of co-determination and co-operation sits uncomfortably astride practical and deserved cautions with respect to workplace restructuring and the larger corporate agenda (USWA 1991,1992).

Anyone attempting to move beyond the industrial relations mould of Wagnerism finds uncomfortable dichotomies, as, for example, between advocacy on behalf of participation in local economic renewal boards and challenges to the greater corporate agenda (CAW 1993). Nevertheless, the appreciation that "We are now ripe for a resounding rollback and defeat or the beginnings of a revival" is a frank admission and a fruitful starting point for renewal (CAW 1995: 1). So too are the distinctions being made between social unionism and movement politics and the implications of this for trade union behaviour. Readers of these chapters cannot, I think, be indifferent to either the debates that are currently under way within the labour movement or, for that matter, the practical conclusions that this movement will help to fashion.

NOTES

1. Important theoretical exposés on this point include Wood (1986) and Wright et al. (1992).
2. As Williams (1983: 172, 163) notes, "There is not one of these issues which, followed through, fails to lead us into the central systems of the industrial-capitalist mode of production and among others into its system of classes." Furthermore,

"The point at which particular interests, properly brought together, can be seen to be a general interest is the moment of socialism."

3. On British Columbia's Operation Solidarity/Solidarity Coalition see Palmer (1987) and Shields (1988).
4. The significance of such "local" cultures of resistance and solidarity has been given renewed emphasis by Fantasia (1988).
5. Polanyi (1957) was one of the first social theorists to unravel the critically important role of the state in an ostensively libertarian social order. For a recent restatement of the compatibilities in neoconservatism between an open economy and a strong state presence, see Gamble (1988), as well as Mooers and Sears (1992). The opposing view is found in Magnusson (1992) and Magnusson and Walker (1988).
6. The following observations are largely the product of field research being conducted by the author. They are based on an investigation of five local union branches in a primary Canadian industry. The five local unions referred to are all affiliates of the United Steelworkers, representing employees in the mining industry.
7. On the demanding nature of union work as it pertains to paid staff, see Stinson and Richmond (1993).
8. Interviews with unionized mine workers indicated that two-year backlogs of grievances were not uncommon. In some cases, workers were unsure what had happened to grievances that they had filed; that is, whether they had been won, lost, "traded away" in collective bargaining, or were still awaiting resolution.
9. Interview with local president and union staff rep., July 1, 1994.
10. Executive/Shop Stewards Committee Meeting, July 18, 1994.
11. The company also made it clear that it would send any workers who showed up for work home, as management did not want further complications with the union over this issue. For its part, the union indicated that anyone who did work over the course of the study sessions would be subject to fines equalling the amount of wages earned. Executive Meeting, July 19, 1994; Study Session, no.1, July 21, 1994.
12. Study Sessions, no. 1 and 2, July 21, 1994.
13. Ratification Meetings, no. 1,2, 3, July 27, 1994.
14. Somewhat later the National Labor Relations Board began to insist upon representation elections in addition to card signatures. This put an end to so-called automatic certifications, which still exist in Canada.
15. Autoworkers are now outnumbered by a ratio of 3 to 1 in the CAW. Since the mid-1980s the union has lost 56,000 members partially through closures and downsizing, but has picked up 37,000 new members through organizing drives and acquired over 85,000 members through mergers (CAW: 1994a).
16. The literature on flexibility is large. For pieces that examine specific labour-market effects, see Atkinson (1984), Harvey (1989), MacDonald (1991), and Shields and Russell (1994).
17. The text refers to two documents: "Rethinking Our Mission in Ontario: A Discussion Paper for Union Leaders," and "Social Coalitions Versus Social Democracy." The authorship for both papers is not indicated in the copies circulated, although the positions taken up presumably speak for a number of private-sector unions that have been opposed to the directions pursued by the "Alliance" and OFL. Much of this agenda was also shared by elements within the Ontario NDP government and its policy branches (Wolfe 1992: 198).

COALITIONS OF SOCIAL MOVEMENTS AS AGENCIES FOR SOCIAL CHANGE: THE ACTION CANADA NETWORK

Peter Bleyer

The Action Canada Network (ACN) is generally regarded as the most important manifestation to date of coalition-formation among the progressive social movements and groups that in Canada have come to be collectively known as the "popular sector."[1] First formed in 1987 as the Pro-Canada Network by groups opposed to the proposed Canada-U.S. Free Trade Agreement (FTA), the Network today includes more than forty-five national groups and provincial coalitions.

The experience of the Action Canada Network presents a valuable case study for addressing both the potential and the limitations of movement coalitions as agencies for social change. What lessons about the prospects for such a project can we glean from this particular experience? And what value do the theoretical approaches to social movements have in the study of an existing social movement coalition?

THEORY AND SOCIAL MOVEMENTS

In the 1960s and 1970s the emergence of student, anti-racist, and environmental movements and the resurgence of the women's movement set the stage for a series of fundamental reassessments of traditional views on agencies for social change. Within the pluralist paradigm, "resource mobilization theory" (RMT) developed as a challenge to the dominant social-psychological approaches to collective behaviour. The classical definition of social movements as products of dysfunctional or irrational collective behaviour was refuted. Instead, social movements were viewed through the optic of an analysis that combined organizational theory with a rational-choice model.

Concomitantly, the intense experience of movement activism and its problematic relationship with the traditional political agencies of the left, trade unions, and political parties sowed the seeds for a reaction in the 1970s against an orthodox Marxist view of collective behaviour. The label "new social movement theory" is now attached to the wide variety of perspectives that share a number of basic characteristics. Firstly, they challenge, each in its own way, the privileging of class as the fundamental societal cleavage and therefore the primacy of the working class and the labour movement as agencies for social change. Secondly, they view "new" social movements as constituting a clear break with the forms and practices of previous collective actors, specifically, the labour movement. Thirdly, having broadened the range of groups relevant to social and political change, they focus on the particular and distinct identities of these actors.

A significant number of "new movement" or "identity-oriented" theories see this newly recognized plurality of social movements and struggles as necessary *and sufficient* for effecting social change. From this perspective, the coalescing of movements – particularly under the mantle of a preconstituted socialist project – runs the risk of betraying the radicalism implicit in this diversity (see Magnusson and Walker 1988: 46). Many socialists, in contrast, argue that an articulation of this plurality of struggles is absolutely necessary. They focus on the importance of linkages between new social movements and working-class struggles if a political project is to become transformative.[2] Historically, socialist alliance strategies have ranged from the communist antifascist popular front to the electoral alliance politics of social democracy (Przeworski 1980). Another approach has evolved, at least on the theoretical level, out of Gramsci's analysis of the political and ideological formations that reproduce capitalist economic power. From a "neo-Gramscian" perspective a counterhegemonic political project necessitates much more than electoral pacts or superficial alliances. It requires the construction of a historical bloc: "a strategic alignment of classes, class fractions and popular groupings whose interests and outlook are realized within the project and whose coalescence establishes 'an organic relation between base and superstructure'" (Carroll and Ratner 1989: 30).

Unlike its pluralist predecessors, resource mobilization theory (RMT) does provide useful tools for the study of social movement coalitions. Yet its rational-choice model of agency entails an excessively economistic assessment of coalition formation: it views movement organizations as coalescing solely as a function of anticipated resource maximization. The implication is that competition between movements is as likely as co-operation (Klandermans 1989: 304, 1990: 125). While the coalescing of social movements and their organizations is undeniably influenced by considerations of resource maximization, this narrow economism denies the possibility that ideological affinity or commonality of interest might also underlie this process.

Despite this major shortcoming, RMT provides a valuable framework for the study of coalition formation. Its fundamental strength as an approach informed by organizational theory is the focus on linkages that can be discerned from the examination of social networks, organizational dynamics, and political processes. A number of theoretical concepts specifically reflect this concern, including the "alliance system," "multi-organizational fields," and the attempt to contextualize the phenomenon of contemporary social movements in a society-wide manner as part of a "social movement sector."[3] Also, because of its combination of organizational and historical analysis RMT leads to the identification and highlighting of contemporary similarities and historical continuity between and among movements.

To apply these theoretical frameworks to the case of the Action Canada Network, we must first consider the political and economic context within which the ACN developed: the crisis and restructuring of capitalism in Canada; and the challenges raised for the Canadian popular sector.

THE POPULAR SECTOR: FREE TRADE AND THE FORMATION OF THE PRO-CANADA NETWORK

By the mid-1970s the Canadian economy was exhibiting all the symptoms of exacerbated structural crisis. Double-digit inflation and unemployment had combined with plummeting productivity rates to bring growth to a practical standstill. The growing crisis only intensified the increasing disappointment of labour and community groups with the Trudeau Liberal government as that administration moved from wage and price controls to 6 and 5, substantial public spending cuts, and a tight money policy. As the crisis reached new depths with the full-fledged recession of 1981-82, the Liberal government abandoned its fledgling attempt at a nationalist resource-based strategy built around the National Energy Program (NEP) (Warnock 1987: 41; Brodie 1990: 181).

The recessionary gloom of 1982 set the stage for the important 1983 New Year's statement by the Canadian Conference of Catholic Bishops (CCCB). The Bishops' statement, "Ethical Reflections on the Economic Crisis," was openly critical of the monetarist direction of government economic policy. It also went beyond this critique to propose, firstly, the basic principles of an alternative economic strategy and, secondly, a political strategy emphasizing coalition-building (CCCB 1983). As Remi De Roo, then Chairman of the Social Affairs Commission of the Canadian Conference of Catholic Bishops, explained: "What we hope to do ... is contribute to the building of a social movement for economic justice in Canada. And there are signs of great hope, signs that people from so many walks of life and such a cross-section of interests can come together to look at what can be done – in solidarity and co-operation – to build this kind of social movement" (De Roo 1983: 7).

The Trudeau government's own reaction to the failure of its economic strategy in the midst of the recession was the appointment, in November 1982, of the Royal Commission on the Economic Union and Development Prospects for Canada, headed by Donald Macdonald. The Macdonald Commission process and its final report played key roles in the forging of the logic that was eventually to lead to the formation of the Pro-Canada, later Action Canada, Network (see Drache and Cameron 1985).

By the time the Commission issued its report in fall 1985, the Mulroney Conservatives were in power, committed to an agenda of spending cuts, deregulation, and privatization. At the urging of an increasingly mobilized business community led by the powerful big-business lobby group Business Council on National Issues (BCNI), the Commission had made itself the carrier of the neoconservative response to the crisis (Langille 1988). As a result its recommendations for resolving Canada's economic woes by increasing the role of the market and radically reducing state intervention in the economy were in perfect step with the new government's agenda. The Macdonald Report's recommendations paid little notice to the dozens of presentations made by popular-sector groups during the hearings. This avoidance was most clear on the issue of free trade: despite being roundly panned by popular-sector groups, a bilateral trade agreement with the United States became the centrepiece of Macdonald's plan. The final result was the public drawing of clear lines of demarcation between a neoconservative corporate vision of Canada and a "popular-sector" perspective. Furthermore, with free trade clearly hitched to the corporate wagon, the "popular sector" had an issue it could rally around.

The 1984 election of the Mulroney government followed by the Macdonald Report's recommendations in 1985, on top of the recession of 1981-82 and the monetarist turn of the later years of the Trudeau government, provided plenty of incentive for growing co-operation between popular-sector groups. Relationships, from the interpersonal to the interorganizational, developed throughout the late 1970s and early 1980s, leading, for example, to instances of common-front bargaining within the labour movement, coalition work by labour and community groups around issues ranging from pay equity to the proposed Arctic Pipeline, and broad-based co-operation and campaigns on peace issues. The most important example of coalition politics in this period was the formation of the Solidarity coalition in British Columbia in summer 1983 (cf. Palmer 1987; Carroll and Ratner 1989).

In the period following the issuing of the Macdonald Report a series of developments in the popular sector set the stage for the formation of the Pro-Canada Network. In November 1987 the Working Committee for Social Solidarity, composed of the representatives of a number of trade unions and women's and church organizations, and with strong participation from Quebec, issued a Declaration: "A Time to Stand Together ... A Time for Social Solidarity." Its stated goal was to help create the "political and social vision required in order to provide a framework of analysis, avoid co-optation by governments and business, and foster an alternative social and economic policy agenda for popular-sector groups" (Working Committee for Social Solidarity 1987/1990). While the political agenda was being advanced on this front, a series of consultations and conferences convened by the interchurch coalition GATT-Fly provided the space for the further development of the trade-policy content for the popular sector's position (GATT-Fly 1987b).

On a parallel track, the increasingly clear continentalist orientation of the Mulroney government and its corporate allies was reviving some of the nationalist sentiment more or less demobilized by the Liberal government's own initially nationalist response to the economic crisis. A month following the release of the Macdonald Report, the Council of Canadians (COC) was founded in Ottawa. Prominent Canadian nationalists pulled together by Mel Hurtig, a Western book publisher and former organizer of the Committee for an Independent Canada, committed themselves to "creating the most widely-based coalition possible of Canadians in favour of maximizing Canadian cultural, economic and political sovereignty and autonomous development, and to work for a consensus among Canadians for this goal" (Council of Canadians 1986).

In general, then, what emerges is a picture of growing co-operation within the popular sector. While there were certainly hiccups, the outline of a national process and an increasingly central policy focus were taking shape. Different constituencies and their organizations – women, farmers, church activists, and seniors, along with labour – were progressively uncovering the implications of free trade for their sectors.[4]

The Pro-Canada Network

In April 1987 the Council of Canadians convened the "Canada Summit," better known as the Maple Leaf Summit, as a counterpoint to Ronald Reagan's and Brian Mulroney's "Shamrock Summit." Close to one hundred representatives of thirty-two national organizations, including the Canadian Labour Congress (CLC), National Action Committee on the Status of Women (NAC), the National Farmers Union (NFU), and GATT-Fly came together to share their respective concerns about the project that was rapidly moving to the top of the Conservative government's agenda: the proposed Canada-U.S. Free Trade Agreement. By the end of the day they had agreed to continue working together in opposition to free trade under the umbrella of the Pro-Canada Network.[5]

At the Network's first "Assembly" in October 1987, representatives of national organizations were joined by representatives of provincial coalitions. The presence of groups already engaged in cross-sectoral campaigns in their own regions, such as the Saskatchewan Coalition for Social Justice, the Coalition against Free Trade (Ontario), and the Coalition québécoise en opposition au libre-échange, altered the nature of the Network and provided for more direct links to activists in their communities. The Assembly became the Network's decision-making body, while a steering committee with representation from key national organizations and the Quebec and Ontario coalitions provided an institutional existence between assemblies.

Initially the Pro-Canada Network operated principally as an "information-sharing" network, formalizing and improving communication between sectors and organizations. Following on the model of the Maple Leaf Summit, sectoral groups brought forward their concerns and shared their respective analyses and strategic priorities around the growing free trade debate. The Free Trade Action Dossier (later the Pro-Canada, and then Action Canada, Dossier), launched for the Network by GATT-Fly in May 1987, became a key communications tool.

As the proposed Free Trade Agreement was concretized in the fall of 1987, the Network's role began to shift into a more proactive gear. The development of a collective analysis process was a key element in this formative stage. An analysis team composed of academics and researchers from a variety of sectors and movements came together. With their wide-ranging expertise and direct involvement in specific sectors they undertook a quick but systematic critique of the FTA's preliminary text. Their analysis was circulated to groups participating in the Network and beyond in a variety of formats.

Building on the collective analysis process, the Network undertook a number of actions aimed at forcing the Conservative government to call an election before signing the agreement. Following a lobby of the leaders of the federal opposition parties involving an unprecedented number and range of sectoral leaders, the Network initiated a National Day of Action on June 12 around the theme "Let Canadians decide!" During this period the Network and its member groups also supported the Liberal Senator's stalling of the FTA implementation legislation (C-130).

Next came the Network's baptism by fire: the 1988 federal election campaign. Developing relationships and a novel process were subjected to the hectic cut and thrust of electioneering. The Network continued its co-operation with the opposition parties, offering briefing sessions and materials to their candidates. Its information-sharing focus was put to the test. Internally this involved helping member groups to co-ordinate and publicize their actions, trying to eliminate duplication and increase effectiveness in the process. Externally the Network carried forward the anti-free trade message in a variety of ways, including public events (ranging from large rallies to press conferences on specific aspects of the FTA) and the mass distribution of literature (pamphlets, fact sheets, broadsheets) by member groups. The highlight was no doubt the distribution of over two million copies of the cartoon booklet, "What's the Big Deal?"[6]

LIMITATIONS AND POTENTIAL OF COALITION POLITICS

Coalitions per se are not new and do not necessarily herald a move to a more radical, transformative politics. Indeed, they have typically formed as the ultimate stage in a defensive political project. Traditionally, coalition-building, like other expressions of solidarity, gets its initial impetus from the appearance of a perceived threat. Coalitions, then, are most often conceived as defences against excessively authoritarian and reactionary policies, governments, or regimes.

In a contemporary conjuncture so strongly marked by the increasing globalization of capital, the sense of powerlessness and therefore the defensive reaction of subordinate groups are amplified. On the one hand, the potential to construct a cohesive progressive project "in one country," until now largely unexploited, seems drastically curtailed. On the other hand, the ability to win policy reforms within the state appears to have been dramatically reduced as well.

In many ways the ACN fits quite comfortably into this framework. The Network's creation was a direct response by threatened constituencies to the Conservative/corporate free trade initiative, which was itself easily comprehended as part of the concretization of a wider neoconservative agenda. More generally the formation of a network of popular-sector groups was a reaction to the growing collective organization of capital on the political scene, of which the formation of the Business Council on National Issues (BCNI) in 1976 was the key moment (Langille 1988).

Socialist critics of coalition politics point out that the need to maintain a working defensive unity inevitably drives coalitions to lowest common-denominator agendas. Indeed, the ACN has not been immune to this dynamic. For example, in the early stages of the free trade debate, trade policy alternatives were considered and might have been advanced more readily had there been a broad consensus among member groups. The absence of a consensus is probably best exemplified by contrasting the positions of the CLC and GATT-Fly on international trade. The Canadian Labour Congress had traditionally supported the principle of free trade, and despite its strong stand against a bilateral FTA it initially supported a continuing liberalization of trade within the multilateral GATT framework.[7] GATT-Fly (later renamed the Ecumenical Coalition for Economic Justice), firmly rooted in ecumenical development and solidarity work, was, as the organization's name implied, among the most visible and active exponents of trade self-reliance in Canada. Its long-standing record of involvement in trade debates around the GATT gave it substantial credibility (GATT-Fly 1987b). Through a process of discussion and negotiation a working compromise was nonetheless fashioned between these divergent perspectives, as was later to happen between other coalition partners on other issues such as taxation and the constitution.

For the ACN, moving on to other issues beyond free trade also meant reaching past the defensive aspect of coalition politics to begin to exploit the potential for a transformative political project implicit in solidarity. To accomplish this expansion, solidarity coalitions have to go beyond both a single-issue focus and the simple aggregation of sectoral groups and their particular struggles and concerns.

The ACN clearly moved partway down this road. Indeed, explicit collective decisions did shift the Network's agenda beyond the "single issue" of free trade. The relative ease and success of this broadening of political consensus owed much to the very nature of the Free Trade Agreement. Free trade was a "single issue" unlike any other, because the FTA was itself a distillation of a broader dominant socioeconomic agenda and as such opened the door to an aggregation of the concerns of many sectors of Canadian society. Nonetheless, the post-election Assembly's decision, in December 1988, to broaden the Network's mandate to oppose the neoconservative agenda was not predetermined by the nature of the FTA. Chances were good that having fulfilled, however unsuccessfully, its initial mandate (to call for and then fight an election on free trade), the Network would now close up shop (Pro-Canada Network 1988).

Three important factors undergirded the decision to not only keep the Network alive but also broaden its mandate and resource base. Firstly, the corporate sector's spirited and very public fight during the election campaign exposed, in a dramatic fashion, the class nature of Canadian society and the place of the FTA in capital's broader zero-sum game plans for the future (Fillmore 1989). Secondly, the positive experience of co-operation between popular-sector groups ensured this transition. This was no small feat in the complicated context of an electoral campaign, which typically spells marginalization for non-party political organizations. Finally, disappointment with the NDP's inability (or unwillingness) to effectively mobilize on the free trade issue served as a further incentive for continuing extraparty organization.

The reaction of the more narrowly nationalist member groups to the election results was particularly instructive. The Business Council for Fair Trade, formed by small and medium-sized firms, had always been a marginal participant in the Network's activities, and after the election it ceased to participate.[8] The Council of Canadians could be expected to continue its fight against free trade: after all, what other path could an explicitly nationalist group take? But many of its 10,000 to 15,000 members at the time were powerfully influenced by the experience of the free trade fight, and as a result the COC supported a broadening of the Network's mandate beyond a nationalist focus.

With a broader mandate in place, the Network selected priority issues and strategies to fulfil the twin goals of (a) confirming and carrying forward this new consensus and (b) advancing into a new phase of campaigning that would combine opposition to government initiatives with the building of a popular base for an alternative agenda. The impatience of the Conservative government and the business community alike to move forward with their own agenda probably helped to advance the mandate-broadening process within the ACN. In the wake of the election the Network made concerted efforts to link co-ordinated fightbacks against government initiatives with discussion of policy alternatives (Pro-Canada Network 1989). A first attempt, the "Alternative Budget Popular Planning Process," focused on formulating popular-sector demands in advance of the 1989 federal budget.

The next step in this process was the Campaign for Fair Taxes, aimed at linking extreme popular dissatisfaction around the proposed Goods and Services Tax (GST) with the discussion and promotion of progressive alternatives for revenue generation. The campaign signalled the popular sector's recognition of the need to advance an alternative agenda and provided the Network with a central focus for its activities. In a successful if non-traditional mobilization, more than two million Canadians signed cards supporting the campaign over the course of two days of activities in workplaces and communities across the country. While the GST was not stopped, a noticeable shift in the tenor of public debate occurred as the campaign gathered momentum through 1990. Until then the debate had been framed as a conflict between the right and the far right as the Mulroney government weathered the anti-tax ravings of the National Citizens' Coalition and the Fraser Institute. By fall 1990 the NDP had won election in Ontario based on a platform – "The Agenda for People" – that included "fair taxation" as a prominent plank.

The gradual opening of the ACN's agenda was undertaken carefully. There was a conscious attempt to avoid the lowest-common-denominator trap by relying on a dynamic process driven by the shared experience of participating groups and, crucially, by consistently maintaining the Free Trade Agreement as a point of reference. Tying the GST and other issues to free trade was in any case far from difficult.

The broader agenda brought with it outreach to new groups. For example, in mobilizing a response to the 1989 federal budget, which included severe cuts to Canada's foreign aid program, discussions with the international development agencies Oxfam Canada and InterPares led to those organizations joining the Network. The Campaign for Fair Taxes reactivated participation by organized seniors in the Network and brought other important groups, including the Canadian Federation of Students, into the fold.

Increasingly called upon to co-ordinate fightback campaigns against Tory cuts, the ACN also developed an innovative approach to promoting solidarity between the users and providers of public services. In summer 1991 the Network planned the signing of solidarity pacts by seniors', students', and anti-poverty groups with the striking Canadian Union of Postal Workers

(CUPW). While these groups declared their support for CUPW's objectives, the postal workers agreed to continue to deliver essential mail such as pension, UI, and welfare cheques for the duration of the work stoppage. During the subsequent national strike by members of the Public Service Alliance of Canada (PSAC), the ACN also co-ordinated a number of solidarity activities between federal public-sector workers and members of organizations in other sectors (ACN 1992b: 6).

The North American Free Trade Agreement

The onset of negotiations towards a North American Free Trade Agreement brought a new urgency and renewed energy to the Network's activities. Unlike the first campaign against free trade, a prerequisite for taking on NAFTA was the development of close ties with popular organizations in Mexico and indeed in the United States. After initial contacts in 1989 under the auspices of the ACN-sponsored Common Frontiers project, relations with Mexican trade unions and citizens' groups multiplied as opposition to corporate continentalization picked up steam. Sharing across borders was not limited to analysis of trade deals. Just as the PCN was being relaunched as the Action Canada Network in April 1991, Mexican free trade opponents representing more than a hundred groups were forming the Red Mexicana de Accion Frente al Libre Commercio (RMALC). The structure of the new Mexican network paralleled that of the PCN/ACN, and some of its founders identified the Canadian network as a model (Sinclair 1992: 137-8).

The ACN developed ambitious plans for mobilizing to unseat the Conservative government and block NAFTA (ACN 1992c). A coast-to-coast caravan gathered voices of opposition to Tory policies, and the call once again to "Stop Free Trade" culminated in a major CLC-sponsored rally on May 15, 1993. Close to 100,000 trade union and community activists gathered on Parliament Hill during what would prove to be the high point of this second phase in the anti-free trade fight. Despite high hopes, the eventual impact of the ACN and its member groups on the election campaign was far more limited than it had been in 1988.

STRUCTURE, PROCESS, AND THE MOBILIZATION OF RESOURCES

Any examination of the ACN experience should also consider specific questions of organizational process and structure. Indeed, the coalition model adopted by the ACN had a number of built-in tensions, the most apparent one involving the traditions and concerns of the labour movement and community groups. "New movement theory," for instance, emphasizes the differences between old and new social movements, and evidence supporting this emphasis certainly exists. From organizational structures and meeting procedures all the way to policy, there are important differences between trade unions and, for example, environmental groups.

There are, nonetheless, also important parallels, for example, in the extent to which the direction of labour or community groups has been influenced by participation in bipartite and tripartite structures and by the lobbying function these groups exercise on behalf of their respective constituencies. Moreover, the Canadian case provides evidence that seems to contradict some of the basic tenets of NSM theory, particularly its excessively unified and homogeneous definition of *"newness"* and its tendency to overlook *continuity* between old and new movements. "New movement theory" tends to overstate the "cultural revolutionary" aspect of new movements at the expense of their concern with the "defence of real social consumption" (Olofson 1988: 26). As a result, the theory tends to exaggerate differences between old and new movements and ignore existing or potential points of common interest.

The Canadian women's movement provides a particularly vivid example. Itself a coalition of more than four hundred women's groups, the National Action Committee on the Status of Women engages in a radical critique of political/cultural practices and in the development of alternatives (such as feminist process); but it pursues with equal vigour the defence of gains that women won in the heyday of the postwar Keynesian welfare state. The "new" aspect of its politics explains the positive and transformative impact that women and NAC have had on the labour movement's internal processes. The "old" aspect is reflected in the growing co-operation between NAC and the labour movement on issues ranging from equal pay to choice.

The ACN itself has served as something of a laboratory in which "old" and "new" organizational traditions and decision-making styles have been absorbed and to some extent reconciled. Individual participants with backgrounds in a variety of sectoral movements as well as histories in the personal and interorganizational relationship-building that has characterized the Canadian popular sector over the last two decades have played an important role in this process. Moving beyond the traditional "resource mobilization" concern with leadership as a factor in social movement development, the notion of "bridge-builders" seems to better describe both the alternative leadership style and the intersectoral process these actors are engaged in (Brecher and Costello 1990: 335). It is a co-operative, horizontal approach to leadership, focusing on making links between different groups and struggles. The significance of leadership in the process of coalition-building would become most apparent with the departure of long-time Network chair Tony Clarke at the end of 1993. As practitioners of an alternative style of leadership, Clarke and other movement "bridge-builders" face the added challenge of resisting the pull of traditional politics and its preferred leadership style. The loss of Clarke's tremendous ability to facilitate consensus was a major blow.

If RMT's approach to theorizing leadership seems inadequate in light of the ACN experience, its overriding emphasis on the maximization of resources has considerable relevance to the Network's brief history. In the first place a glaring contrast exists in the level of resources available to different groups within the ACN: ranging from the CLC's annual seven-figure budget and dozens of staff to the activist group Rural Dignity's hand-to-mouth existence. Indeed, participation in the Network creates the opportunity for groups to maximize resources. The collective resource base of the Network, however meagre, allows poorer community-sector groups to participate in campaigns and take more effective stands on issues that might otherwise be beyond their reach. And with a broader definition of resources a much more complete picture of the "maximization" process can be drawn. For example, for larger labour affiliates, at whose expense the collective financial and material resource base of the Network is largely achieved, the maximization of what might be termed "less tangible" resources is a benefit (Klandermans 1990). They gain access to more extensive communication and research networks, a deeper pool of skills and experience in these areas, and a broader base of support for their own sectoral struggles.

But the ACN is engaged in more than merely expanding the range of resources being maximized; its approach to building a coalition includes the more or less explicit and direct *redistribution* of resources within the popular sector. This is most plainly evident in the relatively informal and sometimes erratic "pay as you can" membership fee structure that provides the bulk of the ACN's small operating budget. Participating groups contribute financial resources, and where this is impossible they provide materials, equipment, or in-kind services on the basis of their ability to pay. More fundamentally, this limited redistributive function reflects the attempt to overcome the problems historically associated with labour-dominated coalitions, or for that matter with any relationship between unequal partners.

Similarly, the ACN's survival has been premised on the credibility of its consensus-building process with participants. In the context of past experiences with coalition politics, which had left a sour aftertaste with many, a number of substantial tensions have to be mediated. Firstly, the historically more powerful and activist labour movement could not dominate – or be seen to be dominating – the process. Past experience had shown that merely relying on secretariats set up by labour for broader groupings was not a good starting point. Secondly, a successful pan-Canadian coalition needed to recognize and attempt to mitigate regional power imbalances. Thirdly, a coalition model built on two types of components, national organizations and provincial coalitions, would further reflect the stresses within the Canadian federal system, bringing together, around the same table, leaders of national organizations, for the most part based in Ontario, with their own members active within less resource-rich provincial coalitions.

This series of tensions, however difficult to negotiate, also forms part of the driving force behind the ACN's survival. The presence of different regional, political, and organizational components has provided an internal "reality test" of sorts. More importantly, diversity of participation in a process that strives for new democratic norms offers the opportunity to move beyond the redistribution of resources to the reconstruction of political identities.

ACTION CANADA AND CANADIAN POLITICS

A series of specifically Canadian characteristics posed important obstacles to the development of the ACN. Sheer geographic expanse alone poses important logistical limitations; and effective pan-Canadian campaigning is hampered by the nature of political jurisdictions, specifically the "binational" federal system. The difficulty of dealing with provincial jurisdictions of varying size and economic strength and with other regional differences is further amplified by the unresolved co-existence of two nations (as well as the First Nations) within one federal state. By its very nature the fight against free trade was bound to run up against this factor and, consequently, the broader question of Canadian identity. The revitalized Canadian nationalism of free trade opponents outside Quebec contrasted sharply with the approach taken by the Coalition québécoise en opposition au libre-échange and other free trade opponents within Quebec. As the ACN was to discover, mobilizing progressive nationalist opinion in a "binational" state and avoiding internal antagonism are no simple tasks.

In another respect, however, the ACN contributed tangibly to a reconstruction of political identities by broadening the scope of legitimate political activity and discourse. In a Canadian system dominated by brokerage politics and "first past the post" polling it has been argued that the "growth of citizens' groups challenges the legitimacy of the party system," as these movements seek to "enlarge the parameters of what is considered political" (Galipeau 1989: 411). But for individual movements and groups, achieving such dramatic results in the face of a firmly entrenched parliamentary system is a daunting task. The presence of the ACN has at least begun to provide space for groups at the federal level to move beyond lobbying and participation in bipartite and tripartite forums to collective political action. Similarly, the Network has fostered the development of a collective public profile for the Canadian popular sector. While this process began long before the formation of the Pro-Canada Network, the consistent presence of a cross-sectoral, cross-country coalition has significantly advanced it.

The ACN has also equipped popular-sector groups with a common voice vis-à-vis political parties. In a parliamentary system that insists on dragging parties away from movements, this is an important development. Building on the legitimacy first gained through the early analysis done on the FTA, and enhanced by the ability to deliver during campaigns (as with the mobilization of support for the Liberal Senators during the Senate hearings on the GST), the ACN developed strong working relationships with both the

Liberal and New Democratic parties. These relationships, in turn, helped to legitimate the Network as a bonafide political actor.

The results of the 1993 federal election campaign, however, dramatically altered the ACN's "political opportunity structure." The Network had been organized to oppose a Conservative government clearly tied to the neoconservative or corporate agenda, and now that administration was replaced by a Liberal government led by Jean Chrétien. The "new boss," it seemed, was very much the "same as the old boss," as the Liberals first proceeded to implement NAFTA, which they had pledged at minimum to renegotiate, and subsequently moved ahead with a raft of measures – privatization, cuts to public services, deregulation – far outstripping anything their predecessors had attempted. With the Liberals now in power, the task of opposition was left to two new major parties, the Bloc Québécois and the right-wing Reform Party, neither of them a likely ally for pan-Canadian progressive social movements. Finally, the consignment of the NDP to the parliamentary minor leagues effectively delegitimized progressive policies and discourse, creating an atmosphere far less propitious for the Network's activities.

These developments raise the issue of the relationship between the ACN as a coalition of movements and the NDP as a social-democratic party. As Carl Boggs (1986) documents in the case of its European representatives, modern social democracy has entertained a love/hate relationship with social movements. Mirroring Bogg's conclusion that the relationship becomes more difficult as social-democratic parties win electoral office, the NDP's relationship with progressive social movements became strained in the run-up to the 1988 federal election, undoubtedly the party's closest brush to date with federal power, and plunged to acrimonious depths with the imposition of the "Social Contract" on public-sector workers and the abandonment of a number of prominent campaign promises by the Rae NDP government (1990-95) in Ontario.[9] For those on the pro-NDP end of the subsequent rift in the labour movement, the existence of coalitions, and the ACN in particular, became a handy scapegoat for all that ailed the social-democratic party (McLeod 1994).

During the 1980s and into the 1990s, under the leadership of the likes of Ed Broadbent and Bob Rae, the NDP was hardly a prototype of dynamic internal policy and political debate, even compared to the weak contemporary standards of international social democracy. The CCF's dynamic relationship with prairie populism, radical evangelicalism, and labour activism and the more recent case of the Waffle faction were little more than fading memories. But the development of the ACN to some extent reinstated the movement/party dynamic that traditionally drives social-democratic and socialist parties in their more radical periods. As a result the NDP was faced, in the form of the ACN, with the co-ordinated and autonomous voice of Canada's progressive social movements. The experience of coalition-building also in-

fluenced labour activists and leaders who were prominent in the NDP, raising the prospect of a more movement-oriented NDP leadership. Unfortunately, the subsequent experience of the NDP in power in a number of provinces, and particularly in Ontario, and the party's less than auspicious efforts
at the federal level underlined the party's continuing shift away from its activist roots.

THE FUTURE OF COALITION POLITICS

The Action Canada Network, as a cross-country coalition of progressive
movements that has broadened its agenda beyond a single issue focus, has
had an important impact on politics in Canada. Most significant is the nature
of the process the ACN has engaged in. Indeed, consensus-building seems
far too limited a description for a process that has grappled with a series of
profound tensions, not least of them being the difficult relationship between
unity and diversity highlighted by new social movement theory. The Network has strived to ensure that a plurality of social identities and struggles is
not subsumed whether in discourse or organizationally. It has attempted to
constitute a new democratic practice that respects difference but understands the importance of a unity built through collective cultural, social,
ideological, and political struggle. This process reflects new social movement theory's concern with the ideological construction of identities, albeit
with an important corrective: it points explicitly to the roots of identity formation in *struggle* – in each movement's own struggles, in struggle between
movements, and eventually through their joint struggles.

The ACN, like the broader story of the Canadian popular sector of which
it is an important chapter, points out the problems inherent in the rigid distinction that new movement theory tends to draw between new and old
movements. Furthermore, the development of the Network and its member
groups provides little evidence for the argument that class – and working-
class politics specifically – has lost its relevance. To the contrary, the free
trade debate saw collective opposition to capital and its agenda reach new
heights, while the ACN process itself points to the crucial place of an activist
labour movement in any potentially transformative political project. Similarly, while the ACN experience affirms the resource mobilization theory's
emphasis on organizational linkages, it fundamentally challenges the narrow
economistic rationale that RMT accords for coalition formation.

Despite all the potential it has exhibited to date, whether the ACN will
become the core of a truly counterhegemonic project not only remains to be
determined but must also be subjected to a healthy dose of scepticism. The
process adopted by the Network has markedly improved on more traditional
hierarchical alliance structures. In so doing it has opened the way to the
gradual reconstruction of the political identities of participants and perhaps
to the construction of a new collective identification around which any new

"historical bloc" must be built. But *process*, while necessary, is not sufficient. It must be accompanied by an evolving alternative *agenda* if it is to overcome the limitations of defensive politics. For the Action Canada Network this is a particular problem, because the core of the critique of free trade was the defence of the Canadian Keynesian welfare state against the encroachment of the unconstrained North American free market. This core was both for better and worse, because, as Leo Panitch (1989) has pointed out, and subsequent developments have demonstrated, the success in imposing this kinder, gentler definition of Canada as a premise in the debate set the terms for future defensive struggles against the corporate agenda.

Certainly, overcoming the predisposition for subordinate groups to adopt defensive strategies and agendas is no simple task. In its work around the Charlottetown referendum in 1992 and in its opposition to NAFTA, the ACN did begin to correct a number of the weaknesses apparent in the initial campaign against free trade. The battle against a continental trade pact demanded increased co-operation with Mexican and U.S. activists and began the consolidation of a new continental arena for progressive movements. As the ACN's own publication the *Dossier* put it, our "zone of political activity is no longer our country – it's our continent" (ACN 1992b: 11). The refounding of the Pro-Canada Network as the Action Canada Network in April 1991 was an attempt at a progressive resolution of Canada-Quebec relations and a better integration of Québécois groups into the Network's activities.[10] Subsequently, the ACN and its member groups played an important role in putting asymmetrical federalism and a three-nations formula on the constitutional agenda in the run-up to the Charlottetown referendum (ACN 1992a: 1-3). And yet despite these and other developments the Action Canada Network cannot be said to have successfully seized the challenge of providing a space in which alternatives for a new social, economic, and political democracy can be elaborated and advanced.

Given the potential for domestic and international alliances in this era of corporate globalism, the ACN appears to be, at best, treading water. Since 1993 its member groups have accorded often lukewarm support to campaigns aimed at exposing corporate power – for example, "Where's the Wealth?" – and projects such as the development and delivery of workshops on coalition-building for local activists. Participation in the ACN's process has declined, raising some doubts as to its credibility and, consequently, its ongoing viability. The Network's more recent problems point to the contingent nature of the development of agency, while comparison with the successes achieved in opposition to the Canada-U.S. FTA draws our attention to the continuing importance of structure in the form of social and economic developments.

While the "coincidence" of a severe economic downturn and a constitutional showdown in the early 1990s might have been a fruitful terrain on which to challenge and extend the boundaries of political and economic democracy, the events led instead to a further shift to the right – with the complicity of social democracy. Whether or not the Canadian popular sector succeeds in pushing back the tide of reaction, the Action Canada Network will stand as an innovative and hopeful example of the potential that social movement coalitions hold as agencies for social change.

NOTES

1. Drache and Cameron (1985) used the term popular sector as a collective description of the many non-corporate interest groups and social movement organizations that presented briefs to the Royal Commission on the Economic Union and Development Prospects for Canada in the early 1980s.
2. Boggs (1986, particularly ch. 6) emphasizes the need for a convergence of movements and their struggles. New social movement theory, particularly the "discourse theory" version proposed by Laclau and Mouffe (see, for example, 1985, 1987; and Mouffe 1988b) elicited a large critical response. Particularly interesting arguments are made by Rustin (1988) and Osborne (1991).
3. First developed by McCarthy and Zald (1977) as a composite picture of social movement industries (SMI) and social movement organizations (SMO) in a given society, the definition of the social movement sector is further developed by Ash-Garner and Zald (1987) and Tarrow (1988, 1989).
4. For a good example of this process, see Bashevkin (1989) on the National Action Committee on the Status of Women's speedy and in-depth engagement with the issue of free trade.
5. The Council of Canadians' spring 1987 *Newsletter* includes the text of the unanimously endorsed *Canada Summit Declaration* as well as a full list of Summit participants.
6. Christopher Waddell wrote in *The Globe and Mail* (Oct. 26, 1988) that the "widely circulated pamphlet against the agreement by the Pro-Canada Network has had a major impact on voter impressions of the deal."
7. See, for example, the CLC's 1986 leaflet *Canadian Labour's Alternatives to the Mulroney Trade Policy*: "The CLC has long been a proponent of GATT and freer trade through multilateral negotiations.... We should continue our efforts to increase our exports to Europe, the Third World and the Pacific Rim, especially Japan and China. We know that it is extremely difficult to break into these markets because of language and non-tariff barriers. But we are not satisfied that enough effort has gone into opening them up, either through the GATT or through trade delegations to these countries."
8. See the Business Council for Fair Trade's Mission Statement in *The Fair Trader*, issue I, vol.1 (February 1988).
9. The extent of the strain on the relationship was reflected by the tensions that developed between the NDP and the labour movement. See CAW President Bob White's "Lost Opportunity: Letter to NDP Officers and Executive Members," Nov. 28, 1988.
10. The refounding of the PCN as the Action Canada Network involved more than a change of name. The structure of the Network was changed to better accommodate participation by popular-sector groups from Quebec. At the same time efforts were made to increase participation by First Nations organizations and "equality-seeking" groups. But by 1995 neither Quebec nor First Nations groups were regular participants in the ACN's activities.

THE PRECARIOUS PURSUIT OF JUSTICE: COUNTERHEGEMONY IN THE LUBICON FIRST NATION COALITION

David Alan Long

Contrary to popular conception, the history of Native-state relations in Canada suggests that our country is less than deserving of the title "peaceable kingdom." This is not to say that diversity among people living in Canada has been unimportant to this country's heritage; the appreciation of regional and sociocultural differences has long been a hallmark of the Canadian landscape. Nonetheless, the considerable distances that separate most of Canada's 600 Native communities from other Native and non-Native communities, as well as their myriad cultural and structural arrangements, have contributed to geographical and social isolation for these peoples. Consequently, it might seem surprising to find meaningful similarities of experience and perspective among Native peoples in Canada. That certain fundamental similarities do exist is less surprising when we begin to examine them in light of the history of colonialism in Canada – as well as in the light of a number of important developments involving Natives and their supporters who, through organized dissent over the past thirty or so years, have fundamentally challenged Canada's image as a peaceable kingdom.

Organized dissent on behalf of Native people in Canada has taken the form of court challenges, lobbying efforts, and protests of various sizes, types, and intensities. Although historically the public appears to have given minimal support for Native interests in Canada, this began to change towards the end of the 1960s. During this time, growing numbers of Native and non-Native people joined forces in a strategically organized, spiritual, and cultural revolution against the unjust fate shared by a majority of Native people in this country (Long 1993: 15-16). One of the more striking developments in the Native movement in Canada has been the worldwide coalition support for the Lubicon First

Nation. Indeed, as we shall see, efforts by people representing diverse perspectives and interests to challenge the governments' treatment of the Lubicon testify to the broad base of organized support for the Lubicon and other Native people in Canada. Nonetheless, there is also evidence to suggest that differences in perspective and interest among Native and non-Native supporters of the Lubicon have made it difficult for coalition supporters to think and act in concert. In other words, although the appreciation for and mobilization of social differences bring strength and vitality to the counterhegemonic activities of coalition and movement supporters, such differences also bring uncertainty and the potential for dissent.

My general, theoretical concern here is to understand the potential problems and benefits that social differences and similarities bring to coalitions and social movements. My specific concern is to examine how spiritual, cultural, economic, and political differences and similarities interact in relation to the Lubicon Lake First Nation coalition in Canada – to gain a broader understanding of the emergence, growth, and potential demise of the Native movement in general and the Lubicon coalition in particular. Given that coalition and social movement activities do not emerge in a vacuum, understanding their ebb and flow means taking into account the pressures on coalition and movement participants from the past as well as the present, and from within as well as from without.

THE SOCIO-HISTORICAL CONTEXT OF NATIVE/STATE RELATIONS

Pre-Contact Aboriginal Conditions

Academics tend to agree that most pre-contact societies of Aboriginal peoples were well organized, culturally distinct, and economically viable.[1] Indeed, it was the "intelligent manipulation of nature backed by supportive social structures" that "made survival possible under extremely difficult conditions" (Dickason 1993: 30). The picture of life in the Americas painted by the early explorers was quite different from the life experiences of indigenous peoples. While explorers wrote of a New World, the Aboriginal peoples had for thousands of years built great civilizations, developing agriculture into a science, producing artists, mathematicians, and deeply spiritual, philosophical thinkers. Moreover, the organization of Native societies in pre-contact Canada varied with the conditions faced, from the bounty of the Pacific coast through the marginal subsistence conditions of the north-central region to the relative stability of the eastern woodlands (Dickason 1993: ch. 4). And although Native peoples have never been culturally or organizationally homogeneous, their long history reflects certain shared, fundamental ways of being and doing (Svensson 1979: 434). In general, their approach to life was holistic: that is, they saw all details of life in relation to one another (Dickason 1993: 79-80).[2]

Early Postcontact Relations

Since the turn of the century, scholarly estimates regarding the size of the indigenous population of pre-Columbian North America have varied between one million and ten million; today, the general consensus is that between two million and five million people were living north of the Rio Grande by the end of the fifteenth century (Cornell 1988: 51-3). By 1650, 85 to 90 per cent of these people had been wiped out through disease, massacre, and suicide. For those who survived this holocaust, life changed profoundly. Initially the fur trade provided a substantial increase in goods and income in eastern and northern Canada, and many Native peoples benefited from their relations with the European traders, who depended on their expertise in trapping, hunting, and knowledge of the territories (Rich 1991: 158-68). However, rising competition in trade also increased the divisions between already divided tribes (Adams 1989: ch. 3). Moreover, when the fur trade went into decline, difficulties arose among those Native peoples who had become dependent upon European goods (Dickason 1993: 192-6).

The most profound effects of European contact followed the signing of treaties. The settling of Europeans in western and northern regions led to agreements and treaties being made with various tribes. Although treaties before and after Confederation involved different concessions, most of them arranged for First Nations peoples to cede their interest in large tracts of land in return for reserves, along with small annuities, the right to hunt and fish on the reserves or on unoccupied Crown land, the right to limited educational services, and, in treaties negotiated after Treaty 6 (1876), the provision of a medicine chest (Taylor 1991: 208-10). By Confederation Canada had a fully developed Indian policy adapted from the French, British imperial, and colonial governments and already administered by the Crown Lands Department (eventually to become the Department of Indian Affairs and Northern Development – DIAND). The last of the eleven numbered treaties was not signed until 1921, but Native peoples had begun to mobilize in response to problems associated with the policies and practices of the colonizers long before then.

Indeed, organized, sometimes violent political action by Native peoples started well before the turn of the century, as evidenced by the Red River conflict of 1869-70 and the Northwest conflict of 1885. Judy Torrance's (1977: 476-7, 488-9) contention that Canadian governments have historically responded promptly and decisively to violent political actions was illustrated early on by the deployment of some 8,000 troops, militia, and police to Saskatchewan during the 1885 Northwest conflict (Miller 1991: 252). This and other examples of overt hegemonic activity on the part of state representatives made it increasingly difficult for First Nations people to effect meaningful social and political change. For example, following the Northwest conflict, Assistant Indian Commissioner Hayter Reed drew up a list of fifteen recommendations that supported almost total suppression of Native political activity. One of Reed's proposals, that it be illegal for Indians involved in the Northwest conflict to be off reserve without a pass signed by an Indian department official, was soon applied to all Indians (Stonechild 1991: 274). Eventually it also became illegal to use band funds for political organization (Cardinal 1969: 103). Moreover, any legal action that First Nation peoples might have wanted to initiate was undoubtedly stifled by the fact that, until 1961, it was illegal for lawyers to represent Indians in actions against the Crown. Despite such obstacles, Native peoples in Canada engaged in numerous organized violent and non-violent political activities during the early part of this century. Indeed, by engaging in many and various expressions of counterhegemonic activity throughout the century, Native peoples and their supporters illustrated that the ways and means of colonialism in Canada were anything but immutable.

In a way similar to other counterhegemonic movements, the emergence and growth of the Native movement during the 1960s were facilitated by structural factors, including the recruiting of broad-based support among Native and non-Native people, effective mobilizing of scarce resources, and diligence at addressing divisions that threatened to fragment movement solidarity and delay or attenuate potential successes (Long 1993: 15-16, 5-6, 1992: 126-7). Although effective organizational strategies have contributed to the growth of the Native movement in Canada since the early 1960s, the experiences and perspectives of Native peoples have been central to the direction of the movement over this time. Current ideas and activities of movement supporters are therefore both an outgrowth of seeds sown in the past and a sign of creative adaptability over the past three decades; the militancy of certain factions within the Native movement has a precedent in Aboriginal warrior societies of the past; the nurturing of alliances with non-Native peoples and the professionalization of movement activities illustrate the ability of movement supporters to adapt to current, often volatile, social contexts (Long 1993: 16); and the concern of many Native women to be protected by the Charter of Rights and Freedoms, at least until agreement can be reached among Native peoples on the meaning of traditional ways and the implications of self-government, reflects the belief of some Native people that the past can be honoured without losing a critical perspective on current experiences, conditions, and aspirations (Hammersmith 1992).

Bureaucratization of Native/State Relations

In general, political activity and organized interest and pressure aimed at bringing about change in the Native-state relation subsided in the 1950s and early 1960s. Nevertheless, a number of developments in the 1960s were important catalysts for the resurgence of both violent and non-violent efforts at social change on the part of Native people and their supporters. One was the establishment of the National Indian Brotherhood (NIB) in 1968 as the first national organization run by and for Canada's First Nation peoples. Although the organization's turbulent history was largely a result of disagreements over funding and agendas (Ponting 1986: 40-1), NIB board member Harold Cardinal (who was also president of the Indian Association of Alberta) noted that the creation of the NIB was a turning point for Native peoples in Canada (Cardinal 1969: 107). Unlike provincially based Indian associations, the NIB was the national, autonomous social movement organization needed by movement supporters for sustained mobilization. Along with serving as a national clearinghouse for information on developments involving Native peoples, the NIB embodied a new development in the history of the organization and mobilization of Native peoples in Canada. As a national organization, the NIB provided the large-scale structural mechanism necessary for the strategic organization of movement activities. Moreover, the Native-run NIB brought a degree of unity to the efforts and perspectives of Native people across Canada.

The second major focal point for the organized mobilization of Native interests and movement identity was the introduction of the 1969 *White Paper* by Minister of Indian Affairs Jean Chrétien. For Aboriginal peoples in Canada, the *White Paper* symbolized the many problems associated with colonization. Native leaders from across Canada immediately and categorically rejected what they termed the genocidal implications of the *White Paper*, and in 1970 adopted the Indian Chiefs of Alberta's position paper, *Citizens Plus*, as their alternative vision of the state. Scott Hunt, Robert Benford, and David Snow (1994: 191-2) view such developments in terms of the process of motivational framing, asserting that the process stabilizes social movements by allowing for a social construction and avowal of common motives and identities among movement supporters, which in turn serves as an impetus for collective action.

As an outspoken representative of two of the most recognized Native organizations in the country, Cardinal was both hopeful and wary. On the one hand, he viewed the NIB as vital to the strengthening of Native identity in Canada. On the other, he was compelled to warn state representatives that failure of the NIB and other similar organizations, especially if Canadian governments were at fault, could result in Aboriginal peoples "taking the dangerous and explosive path travelled by the black militants of the United States."

We can and we have watched black riots in the United States and we can and we have pondered their lessons. Our people have seen the methods used by other groups in similar situations, and we have measured their successes – and failures. We are learning from others about the forces that can be assembled in a democratic society to protect oppressed minorities. These things, too, are our classrooms now and our textbooks. And we are learning our lessons well. (Cardinal 1969: 107, 108)

In the wake of the failed Indian policy of 1969, the attitudes and activities among Natives and their supporters began to reflect a growing self-confidence, which was further reflected in the popular support for organized grassroots activities such as the Native People's Caravan and the often unpredictable, controversial, though communally well-supported, actions of the Canadian chapters of the American Indian Movement (Long 1992: 129-30).

Post-1970s Lobbies and Protests
Numerous violent political incidents involving AIM and other Native organizations during the 1970s and 1980s seemed to fulfil Cardinal's prophecy. It is important to note, however, that most of these incidents were strategically planned: they were not the spontaneous, unexpected occurrences that media and state representatives have often made them out to be (York and Pindera 1992: 414-18). Moreover, Native people often initiated actions only after exhausting other more legitimate means of attempting to bring about change.

By the mid-1970s the idealistic radicalism that had blossomed in the late 1960s and early 1970s had begun to wane. In its stead was an emerging bureaucratic revolution, evidenced by Natives and their supporters developing more socially and politically astute tactics and strategies that took seriously the practices and interests of those being lobbied. This "professionalization" of Native leaders, supporters, and organizations during the 1970s revolutionized Native/non-Native relations. From the perspective of Canadian politicians and Indian Affairs bureaucrats, changes in Native organizations from an issue-oriented to a more bureaucratic, institutionally based structure provided those organizations with a degree of bureaucratic credibility (Frideres 1988: 282).

However, the compromises that often accompany bureaucratization also led to growing frustration among Aboriginal peoples and their supporters who had been trying to bring about radical political and social change. Increased frustration and aggression towards the state were especially apparent during the 1970s and early 1980s, when a large number of articulate, outspoken Native people began graduating from Canadian and U.S. universities.[3] Armed with a rediscovered respect for the spiritual and cultural dimensions of their traditions and histories, many of these educated young leaders joined with others in blending and alternating legitimate and illegitimate organizational goals and techniques (Frideres 1988: 269). Supporters of Native rights could now be expected to intersperse their peaceful lobbying, negotiating, and demonstrating activities with violent political action. Although the targets of their non-violent and violent actions have varied – including logging and other private companies, the military, non-Aboriginal communities, and at times factions within their own communities – the primary concern of these and other Native movement supporters over the past thirty years has been to challenge the policies and practices used by state representatives to gain Native consent to state rule.

Challenging the state has been both difficult and costly, however, largely because of the internal colonization that has affected every area of Native life. The Canadian state has adopted several policies and practices of internal colonization, including publicly supporting Native sovereignty by negotiating treaties with First Nations peoples while at the same time assuming the fundamental principle of Crown sovereignty (Boldt 1993: 5); manipulating sentiment through guilt management by painting a particular picture of state-Native relations (Boldt 1993: 18-21); the social and geographical isolation of Native people on reserves (Dickason 1993: 257); residential schooling and political co-optation of key Native leaders (Hammersmith 1992: 55); manipulation of the discourse used in Native-white relations (Jensen 1993: 350-2); and widening the division between bands and tribes by sponsoring competitive, specialized funding programs for community development projects and research into specific tribal histories for land claims arguments (Frideres 1988: 286). For well over a century, Aboriginal peoples in Canada have not had meaningful control of their lands, funds, business interactions, or educational, social, community, and local-government activities. Although the federal government's stated goal for its Native wards has long been full and equal participation in Canadian society, the route of separate development enshrined in the Indian Acts of 1876 and 1951 served to perpetuate their political, legal, cultural, and social marginality (Erasmus 1989: 295). But despite their colonially enforced marginality, Native peoples have continued to organize, often in protest, against the policies, legislation, and practices of European colonization (Long 1995: 48).

The most widely publicized Native action in the past thirty years was the Oka Crisis.[4] During the summer of 1990, the Mohawks of Kanesataké engaged in an armed standoff with the Canadian military on the grounds that the extension of a local golf course onto their land would break an agreement between the government of Quebec and the Mohawk people. This confrontation received unprecedented national and international attention (York and Pindera 1992), but it was by no means the only occasion in Canada on which police and/or army personnel were dispatched to quell potential Native uprisings (Long 1992: 127). Recent examples of such conflict include the thirty-day armed standoff in fall 1995 near Gustafsen Lake, B.C., between the RCMP and about thirty Shuswap Indians fighting for land that the Shuswap claimed was sacred Native land. Around the same time the RCMP shot and killed a seventeen-year-old Native youth involved in a blockade in Ipperwash Provincial Park, Ont.[5]

These and many other examples illustrate the preparedness of Aboriginal people and their supporters to engage in counterhegemonic activity. Various expressions of social and political activism also highlight the tension that has characterized Native-state relations since the arrival of the European explorers. In response to increased activism involving Native peoples and their supporters, the RCMP described the Native movement in 1974 as the single greatest threat to national security. Although this may now be viewed as a rather gross overstatement, what the RCMP does appear to have understood was that those with relatively little power can and do resort to violence in attempts to bring about change (Gurr 1970: 210-12). By contrast others, including Prime Minister Trudeau, dismissed the early militant outbursts as insignificant actions by a small and desperate group of extremists (York 1989: 251). While the Trudeau assessment may have contained a grain of truth – certainly many such incidents did reflect a degree of desperation – a more critical interpretation would view Native political violence as a calculated response by Native peoples to bring to light the injustices perpetuated by their social, economic, legal, and political inequality.

As members of a contemporary social movement, Aboriginal people and their supporters have recognized the importance of mass media coverage of their activities.[6] The media serve to bring added attention to the concerns of movement activists and possibly help to cultivate a broader support base (McCarthy 1994: 147-8). For example, in 1993 members of the Peigan First Nation in central Alberta focused national attention on their grievances against the provincial government and members of the local community by organizing a violent protest against the building of the Old Man River Dam. Consequently the mayor of a nearby town cancelled a ceremony scheduled to celebrate the opening of the dam because he and others "feared for their lives."[7] Although accounts vary as to what happened and why, Native leader Milton Born with a Tooth was eventually convicted on five counts of dangerous use of a firearm. No doubt such militant, sometimes violent, political actions have often angered those whose interests they threaten, but they have also enabled Native peoples and their supporters to draw local, national, and international attention to their experience of colonization and desire for change (Lennarson 1991). Recent national press coverage of the election of the Grand Chief of the Assembly of First Nations, as well as continuous, in-depth coverage of Native protests and blockades during the fall of 1995, testify to the status the press now grants to Native activities.[8]

Regardless of how these people and their supporters have acted over the past three decades, their experience of oppression and injustice has contributed to the flow of tears and the shedding of blood in the name of Canadian sovereignty. Nonetheless, it has taken over thirty years of both non-violent and violent activity by Native people and their supporters for other Canadians to ask why many Native people in this country continue to live in such bleak conditions and what the response to those conditions should be. Given the size and increasing relative growth of a young Aboriginal population in Canada, as well as the awareness that most Canadians now have in relation to the socioeconomic conditions of life experienced by Aboriginal peoples in this country, the prophetic words of Harold Cardinal (1969) and Georges Erasmus (1989) may come to fruition sooner than later. Given current Native demographic trends, it seems evident that political violence will escalate if state representatives continue to ignore the structurally induced marginality of Native peoples (Long 1995: 45-52). Granted, not all Native people in Canada have chosen or will choose the same path of counterhegemonic resistance. Nonetheless, continued alienation and a sense of relative socioeconomic deprivation among young militant Native people, coupled with a lack of movement in Native-state dialogue, will undoubtedly continue to fuel their discontent.

AN OVERVIEW OF THE LUBICON COALITION

Historical Context of Coalition Support

According to John Goddard (1991), the dispute between members of the Lubicon Lake First Nation and federal and provincial government representatives is one of the most long-standing land-rights disputes in Canadian history. For a variety of reasons, the Lubicon were not included in an 1899 Treaty signed by the federal government and numerous other Cree bands in northern and central Alberta and as a result were ignored by government representatives until band status was granted in 1940. Although the government of Alberta agreed to provide about sixty-five square kilometres of land for a reserve at that time, the land was never transferred to the Lubicon. During the 1940s an Indian Affairs official by the name of Malcolm McCrimmon removed more than seven hundred people from the treaty lists of Northern Alberta, eliminating those people's rights as Indians and cutting the Lubicon membership list almost in half.[9] Furthermore, oil exploration and production in the area began in the late 1950s. In the early 1960s, residents of a Lubicon community in Marten River were moved to nearby Cadotte Lake to allow oil companies to begin drilling. Although many residents were reportedly unhappy with the move, Marten River was bulldozed before the people were able to return home (Goddard 1991).

In 1977 the passing of retroactive legislation by Premier Peter Lougheed enabled the government of Alberta to win a court case against the Lubicon, who were still attempting to fight oil development on land they claimed was theirs. Despite warnings of "genocidal consequences" from the World Council of Churches and other church groups, and growing national as well as international coalition support, the Alberta government continued to fight against the Lubicon. Along with its federal counterparts, the Alberta government ignored the report by federal Justice Minister Davie Fulton, which stated that a generous approach be taken in settling such a "grave injustice." But the Alberta government did accept the ruling of an Alberta judge against the claim by members of the Lubicon Lake First Nation that their way of life was being destroyed. The judge stated that development on Lubicon-claimed land affected only a few individuals. The Lubicon countered the federal government's eventual offer of $45 million in 1988 by making a detailed request for $70 million. Lubicon Chief Bernard Ominayak met with government representatives on numerous occasions to resolve the dispute, although these meetings failed to bring about a satisfactory resolution.

During this time international attention began to focus on the plight of the Lubicon. Coalition support for the Lubicon grew in response to a massive publicity campaign by the Toronto-based Friends of the Lubicon (FOL). The campaign successfully raised awareness that the harvesting of trees on Lubicon-claimed land by the multinational corporation Daishowa Forest Products was destroying both the land and the Lubicon way of life. While support for the Lubicon grew rapidly, the interests and activities of coalition supporters did not emerge in a vacuum. The coalition is in many respects a microcosm of the movement of Native peoples throughout the world, a movement embodying the spirit and vision of those who for centuries have opposed colonization. Understanding the strength of coalition support for the Lubicon thus means taking into account how and why potential supporters identify with the people, ideas, and activities that make up the coalition in the first place, which in turn necessitates examining the particular beliefs, perspectives, and interests that have informed the historical and cultural movements of Native peoples and their supporters.

Although countless conflicts have arisen between Native and non-Native people since the days of first contact, the willingness of people to align themselves with the Lubicon coalition does not merely depend on supporters having a clear understanding of the place of Native peoples in Canadian history. Even those unfamiliar with the specific history and circumstances of Native peoples in general, and the Lubicon in particular, are probably aware of the presence of dissatisfied Native peoples in Canada during the past few decades. The growing awareness throughout Canada of Native issues is both a reflection and result of media coverage of Native issues and activities, regardless of whether or not people agree with the actions of Elijah Harper, the Mohawks of Kanesataké, and other Native people. But unfortunately for Native people in Canada, mass media coverage of Native issues and activities, according to Marc Grenier (1992: 274), "has probably operated more as a steadfast obstacle to ... mutual cultural acceptance and co-operation."

Grenier's findings suggest that increased public awareness of Native issues has not coincided with a deepening of knowledge and understanding in relation to Native demographics, nor has increased awareness generated support for Native peoples in Canada.[10] In fact, J. Rick Ponting (1990: 22) found that support for certain Native issues had eroded slightly between 1976 and 1986. While non-Native Canadians supported Native aspirations for self-government and Native land claims, support of demands by Native people for special privileges actually waned (Ponting 1990: 27). Ironically, part of the difficulty in mobilizing support for the Lubicon and other Native peoples is a consequence of growing recognition among non-Native Canadians that Native issues now touch all areas of Canadian life. Increased awareness of the complexity of Native issues and interests, rather than spurring more interest and involvement, can and often does reduce grassroots coalition support. As Peter Hamel (1994: 35) notes, it is much harder to mobilize people around the constitution than it is to mobilize them around a pipeline or a dam. Continued apathy on the part of non-Native people in Canada towards Native issues also suggests that colonial attitudes die hard. The problem, however, is not reducible to media manipulation of Native issues or racist apathy on the part of non-Native Canadians. Although many people continue to ignore or oppose Native interests, others actively support them. Clearly, factors other than media framing or one's racial/ethnic heritage contribute to support for the counterhegemonic visions and activities of Native peoples and their supporters.

International Context of Coalition Support
While disputes over political and legal interests and spiritual or material visions have given shape to the Lubicon coalition in Canada, two global, crosscutting, socio-historical movements have been equally important to the emergence of the coalition: support for the rights of indigenous peoples; and protection of the environment. Although the boycott organized against Daishowa by the Friends of the Lubicon emerged within Canada, international support for the Lubicon suggests the existence of similar coalitions and movements elsewhere. And although coalition supporters and opponents outside of Canada may have little or no direct contact with the Lubicon, they are informed by global awareness and activity networks that seek to redress the myriad of problems associated with colonialism and environmental degradation. The theoretical and political significance of these global movements is that they provide two master frames of reference that Native and non-Native people throughout the world use in relation to the plight of the Lubicon. Some of the more prominent, internationally based Lubicon coalition organizations that are part of the worldwide indigenous peoples' movement include: Coordinated Indigenous Affairs Working Groups (Belgium), National Christian Council (Japan), Innu Support Groups (Netherlands), Munich Society for Endangered Peoples (Germany), Plains Indian Cultural Survival School (U.S.), Working Circle for North American Indians (Vienna), and Survival International (London). Coalition organizations with an environmental agenda include: German Green Party, Rainforest Action

Group (Europe), Friends of the Earth (U.S.), Iwerliewen (Luxembourg), Big Mountain Action Group (Germany), Synesthetics, Inc. (U.S.), Bund (Germany), and Greenpeace (U.S.). Although coalition support obviously ebbs and flows, well over one hundred separate organizations have supported the Lubicon over the past ten years.[11]

Although certain differences in perspective and interest among counter-hegemonic agents would appear to make it difficult for coalition members to construct stable plausibility structures, Hunt, Benford, and Snow (1994: 186) assert that social movement actors tend to cluster around relatively stable, socially constructed identity fields: protagonists are supportive of movement values, beliefs, goals, and practices; antagonists stand in opposition to the efforts of protagonists; and audiences are uncommitted or neutral observers. Even though these categories appear to have a degree of malleability, the actual experiences, perspectives, and involvements informing the identities of coalition antagonists, protagonists, and observers are much more precarious and fluid (Gusfield 1994: 64-5). Even David Snow and Richard Machalek (1984: 176-7), who understand personal identity discourse as a phenomenon that is "redefined continuously in light of new experiences," provide a rather simplistic model of identity integration and disintegration. Taking into account the different perspectives and interests of those involved in the Lubicon coalition challenges the view that the degree of commitment expressed by coalition members is merely the result of these people making informed, rational choices. One of the keys to understanding the makeup of the coalition thus depends on a closer examination of how and why actors actually support it.

Supporters' Perspectives on Coalition Involvement
The problems associated with colonialism and the efforts by Native people and their supporters to address them are often understood in primarily political and legal terms. For example, Sally Weaver (1981) sees it as both possible and desirable to acknowledge the special status of the original occupants of a territory in a manner that aims at restoring unique political and legal rights and entitlements of Aboriginal peoples. Accordingly, she asserts that the most critical issues associated with Aboriginal rights pertain to the establishment of separate political and legal jurisdiction, and of a land base. Many Lubicon coalition supporters view the problems of the Lubicon within this type of political and legal framework, and much hegemonic activity by federal and Alberta government representatives has historically targeted the political and legal interests of the Lubicon. However, Lubicon supporters working primarily within this perspective do not fully understand or identify with the fundamental concerns and claims of the Lubicon. Focusing on political, legal, and even land issues is vital, though the essence of Lubicon identity rests on the spiritual and cultural dimensions of Lubicon life.

In contrast to those who focus on the political and legal dimensions of hegemonic struggles, Alain Touraine (1981) has argued that historical conflicts between hegemonic and counterhegemonic representatives are fundamentally conflicts between alternate visions of the state. In this respect, Native people have developed an alternative vision for their place in Canada by defining their political and legal concerns and activities in spiritual terms (Long 1992). Generally speaking, many Aboriginal people acknowledge that a balanced life honours the laws of both the spiritual and physical dimensions of reality (Bopp et al. 1984: 27). In defining the political concerns of Native people in fundamentally spiritual terms, Stan McKay (1992: 30) notes: "The vision that moves us in the struggle toward aboriginal sovereignty is integral to our spirituality. The elders speak to us of our need for balance between the physical and spiritual aspects of our being. They would caution our political leaders not to become so caught up in the struggle for power that they compromise the spiritual heritage that shaped our being."

McKay's comments suggest that coalition supporters' ability to understand the concerns of the Lubicon means acknowledging that the political struggle for Lubicon sovereignty, while undoubtedly giving a certain physical contour to the spiritual vision of the Lubicon, has itself emerged out of a spiritual vision. Comments and activities by supporters representing the Oblate Missionary Society, the United Church of Canada, the Aboriginal Rights Coalition, the Edmonton Interchurch Committee for Aboriginal Rights, the Society for Endangered Peoples, Catholic Action for Native America, and many other similar organizations suggest that an awareness of the relationship between spiritual and political visions is vital for those whose concerns transcend mere control over physical or cultural resources. In a letter to Prime Minister Brian Mulroney, representatives from Catholic Action for Native America stated, "It is unfortunate that ... the government of Canada ... refuses to accept the legal and moral implications of the fact that the Lubicon nation has never ceded any of its ancestral territory."[12] These and other such groups view the pursuit of justice for the Lubicon as the spiritual tie that binds many coalition members.

Visions of and for social change in relation to the Lubicon can also take on physical contours. For example, a 1993 press release from the Rainforest Action Group (RAN) warned, "If the Alberta government doesn't significantly modify existing agreements with Daishowa and Al-Pac – which is majority-owned by Mitsubishi – we will at the request of provincial environmental groups call for a worldwide boycott of tourism in this province until changes are made which could begin as early as 1994." RAN support for the Lubicon in the form of an Alberta tourism boycott was based on its concern over the enormous area covered by logging agreements (about one-third of the province), the fragile ecosystem in the province with its shallow soil and short growing season, Al-Pac's newly begun production of pulp and paper, and the pace of logging. The focus of RAN and similar groups is thus not primarily to protect the political, legal, or spiritual interests of the Lubicon, but to fight against abuse of the environment and to "help groups develop nondestructive, sustainable, alternatives that will provide Albertans with jobs while protecting their beautiful, vital and fragile world."

Inviting difference is thus an important dimension of coalition activity. In contrast, new social movement and resource mobilization theorists tend to assume that people in a given movement coalesce around ideas and practices representing similar interests, whether these are religious, political, or economic. It is then a short theoretical step to presume that movements have homogeneous, overarching systems of belief and practice that embody their essences. However their successes or failures are then explained (such as their historical truthfulness or illusory character, effective mobilization of resources, control over the contents, ways, and means of particular cultures by historical agents battling over hegemony), social movements presumably manifest certain socially accepted goals, interests, and practices that can be defined and quantified by the neutral, objective observer. Along with Stuart Hall (1988) and Ernesto Laclau and Chantal Mouffe (1985), Antonio Melucci (1989: 18) notes that neither social movements nor the many coalitions that comprise them are concrete, homogeneous entities. According to Melucci, the apparent absolute unity of movement identity is more a social science construction than a reality for movement participants. Just as there are beliefs and practices that serve to unify coalition supporters, so too there are beliefs, interests, and practices that potentially divide them. In contrast to the apparently monolithic social systems they defy, coalitions and social movements invite the inevitable cultural and structural changes that occur when differences are taken seriously.

REASONS FOR COALITION INVOLVEMENT

Differences in Beliefs, Perspectives, and Interests

Given their historical and sociocultural differences, it is difficult to identify what ties Lubicon coalition supporters together. Important in this regard is distinguishing between the discrete beliefs, overarching worldviews, and concrete interests of those involved. Generally, Lubicon coalition members believe that the Lubicon deserve to be treated in a just manner by governments in Canada and that government representatives should do their part in settling the Lubicon land claims. However, coalition supporters such as the Society for Endangered Peoples, the Innu Support Groups, the Austrian Society for Endangered Peoples, the Working Circle for North American Indians, the Assembly of First Nations, the Aboriginal Rights Coalition, the Native Women's Association of Canada, and the National Association of Japanese Canadians view the government's "abuse of this small group of aboriginal people [as] an outright violation of nationally and internationally accepted human rights principles."[13]

Other coalition members emphasize that the injustice experienced by the Lubicon reflects that hegemonic agents are more concerned with economic gain than respecting the relationship between humans and their natural environments. Such environmentally focused groups as the Rainforest Action Group, Earthkeepers, Greenpeace, Friends of the Earth, Iwerliewen, Big Mountain Action Group, Synesthetics, Friends of Athabascan Environmental Association, Northern Light, Environment Probe, and even the rock group Syren assert that the physical environment ought to be respected and nurtured. Although these supporters of the Lubicon coalition also share a desire to protect the environment from what they regard as the destructive log-harvesting practices of Daishowa, their primary interest is to "protect and preserve wildlife and the natural environment."[14] Outside of their involvement in the Lubicon coalition, many of these organizations engage in international lobbying efforts to establish parks and animal sanctuaries. In contrast, the Lubicon wish to negotiate a land-claim settlement with the provincial government of Alberta and the federal government of Canada that would essentially allow them to do as they wish with their land. Thus, although environmentally concerned coalition members support the Lubicon, it is not difficult to envision a future clash between these same environmentalists and the Lubicon over the appropriate use of land that may be granted to the Lubicon at some point in the future.

As Peter Berger and Thomas Luckmann (1967) note, overarching meaning systems are often made up of such discrete beliefs. Plausibility structures, which are malleable systems of belief and practice, enable the Lubicon and coalition supporters to make sense of the Lubicon situation in broad, everyday terms. The Lubicon-focused plausibility structure that coalition supporters operate within is informed by religious, environmental, business, philosophical, and economic interests and perspectives. While allowing the participation of people with different assumptions and definitions of the situation is the lifeblood of a given coalition or counterhegemonic movement, there are dangerous consequences to inviting such differences.

The Problem of Difference

Representatives of the Edmonton Interchurch Committee on Aboriginal Rights, the Aboriginal Rights Coalition, the Assembly of First Nations, and the Native Women's Association of Canada view what happens politically and legally to the Lubicon in spiritual terms.[15] Environmental groups often use similar language, although their primary concern is to raise awareness of environmental degradation as a consequence of human activity and to stress that humans must learn to respect the natural environment. In contrast businesses such as Roots Canada, Knechtel's Grocery Wholesaling, and The

Body Shop assert that Daishowa's logging practices are unacceptable because they contribute to the degradation of the environment, which also occurs at the expense of the Lubicon's well-being. In a somewhat different vein, organizations such as Kentucky Fried Chicken, Maison Du Fromage, YWCA, and *NOW* magazine supported the coalition boycott of Daishowa paper products because of the corporation's apparent concern to make money with little or no regard for protecting basic human rights.

A number of businesses that joined the coalition boycott did so to prevent similar boycotts against their businesses. In November 1991, for example, the Toronto-based Pizza Pizza chain initially refused to "take sides" in the Lubicon dispute. Representatives of the company stated that they were convinced that Daishowa was negotiating with the Lubicon and the government of Alberta in good faith. Their discussions with FOL boycott organizers lasted for over three months between November 1991 and January 1992. During this time, Pizza Pizza was a target of the boycott. Although Pizza Pizza representatives eventually joined the Lubicon coalition by honouring the Daishowa boycott, the changing tone and contents of letters from the company's president to FOL representatives indicate that their interest in doing so was primarily an economically motivated business decision.[16]

That there are often major differences among coalition supporters has significant implications for understanding the perspectives and activities of counterhegemonic agents. One implication is the need to recognize that although Lubicon coalition supporters have many different reasons and interests for their involvement, such differences may or may not contribute to a weakening of coalition efforts. Nonetheless, failure to take the diversity of coalition and movement supporters into account can lead to a distorted, even mythical view of coalitions as seen by the movements belonging to them. Since even the smallest coalitions give expression to a diversity of beliefs, perspectives, and interests that are themselves open to challenge and change, counterhegemonic coalitions and the larger social movements around them are inherently fragile phenomena. We thus distort both the "inner integrity" as well as the social struggles of coalition supporters and larger social movements when and if we portray them as anything less than highly complex social phenomena reflecting the coming together and movement of diverse sociocultural histories. In this regard the crystallization of beliefs, sentiments, and activities into what we have referred to as the Lubicon coalition is much more than a collection of people fighting against injustice. Both the coalition and the Native social movement more fundamentally represent the dynamic movements of diverse people who have decided to contend for their alternate visions of the state. That counterhegemonic agents agree on certain fundamental issues and interests does not guarantee success, for equally fundamental concerns and interests can easily become sources of division and conflict. Indeed, the hegemonic agents' often successful application of divide-and-conquer tactics attests to their understanding that support for counterhegemonic coalitions and movements is a precarious phenomenon.

Even though hegemonic forces may appear monolithic, they also contain individuals and groups holding many different beliefs, perspectives, interests, and goals. Because those in various hegemonic camps undoubtedly have different reasons for supporting the status quo, their unity and apparent immutability are potentially subject to the same disruption and change that threaten the coalitions and social movements they oppose. In short, although social movements appear to be a case of "us against them," unity among supporters or opponents of large-scale social change is a precarious phenomenon. Predicting the directions that hegemonic or counterhegemonic activities will take in relation to the movement of Native peoples in Canada is therefore difficult for a number of reasons, including the subtlety and diversity of social action, disagreements within hegemonic and counterhegemonic camps over beliefs, perspectives, tactics and goals, and the frequent lack of predictable, concrete public support for hegemonic or counterhegemonic ideas and activities.

CONCLUSION

Native peoples in Canada have been socially and politically active for thousands of years, and the countless expressions of counterhegemonic activity involving them and their supporters are much more than idiosyncratic, knee-jerk reactions to isolated experiences of government or corporate colonialism. For a variety of reasons, Native peoples in Canada continue to choose different paths of resistance to state-induced hegemony. The development of a militant agenda that expressed itself in an often violent manner during the 1970s and into the 1980s was for many Native people a matter of survival (York 1989: 260-1). During the 1990s, violent confrontations between Natives and state representatives at Oka, Gustafsen Lake, and Ipperwash Provincial Park illustrate that Native involvement in militant, counterhegemonic activity is likely to continue. Clearly, such militancy is in contrast to the more diplomatic resistance exhibited by Native MP Elijah Harper in his stand against the Meech Lake Accord in 1991.

In general terms, the Lubicon coalition and the Native movement involve the strategic actions and reactions of those who want to challenge ideas, policies, laws, and organized activities that perpetuate injustice against Native people in Canada. But differences in thought and action among coalition and social movement supporters and opponents in Canada and throughout the world suggest that the types and degree of diversity in hegemonic and counterhegemonic camps are as important to the success or failure of social movements and coalitions as their unity. Understanding counterhegemonic movements thus means recognizing that people in both camps believe many different things about the nature of human life, have very different perspectives on the purpose of human life and why they support or oppose a specific social movement, become involved in counterhegemonic or hegemonic activities for a wide variety of reasons, and often have very different interests at stake in the success or failure of a given social movement.

Social movements and the many coalitions that give them much of their definition and "movement" must therefore be understood as historical phenomena in which countless factors interact. Understanding why coalitions and larger social movements exist, fail, or succeed depends on understanding them in historical context and examining the interaction of their particular social characteristics. Of these, a close examination of differences within hegemonic and counterhegemonic camps, as well as the global interaction of crosscutting movements and coalitions, is particularly important for understanding the success or failure of a given coalition or movement. Making sense of the Native social movement in Canada means placing it in the context of the complex history of Native-white relations both before and after Confederation, of the particular beliefs, perspectives, and interests of the people involved, and of how supporters and opponents are linked to those who support or oppose the more global, crosscutting indigenous peoples and environmental protection movements.

Counterhegemonic actors face particular difficulties in their efforts to mobilize and maintain large-scale support for their alternate vision(s) of the state. Clearly, sustained counterhegemonic activity is not the sole determining factor of success for coalitions and social movements. Mobilizing and maintaining large-scale support for alternative visions of the state form a complex, precarious task in which counterhegemonic agents must take into account the problem of hegemonic and apathetic forces from without, as well as potential sources of division and conflict from within. Moreover, given the profound differences in the perspectives and interests of Lubicon coalition members and Native social movement supporters, active support for the Lubicon and other Natives will most likely wane with the settling of Native land claims. The same diminution of activity will undoubtedly occur as other Native concerns and interests are addressed to the satisfaction of those involved.

The potential dissolving of support for the Lubicon or other Native peoples thus raises the important theoretical question of how social movement researchers ought to understand and explore the relationships between social systems, social movements, coalitions, and individual social actors in an increasingly globalizing network of counterhegemonic activity. In a world in which active support for counterhegemonic visions can apparently emerge as quickly as it can disappear, social movement theorists must take seriously the complex, precarious nature of hegemonic and counterhegemonic identities. The same can be said for state representatives who want to prevent the violence and confrontation that has characterized much of Canada's past and to work towards a common, peaceful, and just vision for the country's future. In brief, healing past wounds and building a vision of hope will occur to the extent that state representatives listen to the experiences, perspectives, and concerns of Native people in Canada.

NOTES

1. Any account of the development of relations between Native and non-Native peoples in Canada is a selective, interpretive act. Divergent non-Native contributions include Moore's (1991: xxxix-xlv) chronology of events, York and Pindera's (1992) detailed journalistic history of relations between the Mohawk people living in Quebec and government representatives, and Miller's (1991) scholarly historical reader on Indian-white relations in Canada. A number of different perspectives and insights offered by Native writers include the emotionally charged book by Adams (1989), the spiritually and politically engaging oral historical account of Silman (1987), and Dickason's (1993) thorough history of Canada's founding people.

2. As Dickason (1993: 67-69, 79-82) notes, Native systems of social control did not always work perfectly within or between bands and tribes: taboos against killing did not prevent intertribal fighting.

3. Ironically, most of the leaders of the Pan-Indian (political) movements that rose to prominence during the 1970s and early 1980s were the products of state-sponsored, church-run residential schools (Tennant, 1990: 81, 139-40).

4. As equally important as what happened at Oka, Clayoquot Sound, Ipperwash, and elsewhere is how and why the mainstream media selectively cover Native news. See, for example, Grenier's (1992: 273-99) critical analysis of media framing of "the Oka crisis."

5. That the national chief of the Assembly of First Nations, Ovide Mercredi, met with the Shuswap to persuade them to resolve their dispute with police peacefully illustrates that Native peoples can and do disagree over strategies and tactics to effect change. Although Mercredi agreed with the Shuswap that Natives in Canada have long experienced injustice, his statement to them and the media was, "I disagree with the use of violence as a means of getting justice" (*The Edmonton Journal*, Aug 25, 1995, p.A3). In an interview on CBC-TV's *The Journal* (Sept. 11, 1995), Mercredi clarified his position. He stated that while he supports peaceful negotiation, politicians and others in Canada need to be aware that the escalation of violence by militant Natives is understandable and warranted if state representatives continue to refuse to take the concerns of Native people seriously.

6. "Understanding Media: Effectively Communicating the Vision of Aboriginal Canada," First Annual Conference, Sept. 21-22, 1995, held in Vancouver, B.C., is the most recent illustration of Native peoples in Canada developing a critical, pragmatic awareness of the role of mass media in their lives.

7. Reported in *The Edmonton Journal*, June 25, 1993, p.A5.

8. A striking example of media-framing occurred during a CBC-TV *Newsmagazine* interview involving Hannah Gartner and Ovide Mercredi (Sept. 11, 1995). To Gartner's question of how he was dealing with Native protesters essentially ignoring and undermining his authority as Grand Chief at Gustafsen Lake, B.C., and Ipperwash, Ont., Mercredi responded angrily by saying that was not how he saw it at all. He then "re"-framed recent militant outbursts by Native peoples in

terms of their frustration with the Canadian governments' refusal to meet with him and other Native leaders to discuss Native self-government, land rights, and other points of dispute. Mercredi also noted that Native leader Georges Erasmus had warned the government in the 1980s that militancy among Native youth would increase if state representatives failed to negotiate in good faith with Native leaders.

9. This was clearly in the government's interest, because the amount of land and money offered by the government to settle Native land-rights disputes was (and continues to be) tied directly to the number of band members on the band membership list.

10. Ponting (1990) found that non-Native Canadians support Aboriginal self-government, more Native representatives in federal and provincial politics, and even an autonomous Native justice system. It also appears, however, that these respondents had very little substantive knowledge in relation to Native issues, or how such changes would affect them personally. As Schwartz and Shuva (1992: 211) note, one reason that the measurement of public resonance with a given organization or movement can be a misleading indicator of constituent support is that it "cannot tap a vital ingredient of successful mobilization – the commitment by members to work actively for the movement."

11. Not to mention local and regional chapters of major organizations and individuals not formally aligned with such organizations. These movement supporters offer invaluable tangible support to the Lubicon through letters to editors, attending and promoting fundraising activities, and honouring boycotts in their everyday lives. Gusfield's (1994: 64-6) distinction between linear and fluid social movements is useful, though it seems more useful to recognize linearity and fluidity in all social movements.

12. Letter, Jan. 14, 1993.

13. Letter, National Association of Japanese Canadians to Prime Minister Brian Mulroney, May 10, 1993.

14. Letter, Big Mountain Action Group to Daishowa, April 16, 1993.

15. We must be careful not to oversimplify the workings of the Lubicon coalition by suggesting that all those with spiritual (or other) perspectives share the same material visions and interests. As Hamel (1994: 22-3) notes, religiously based coalitions are not exempt from experiencing intense conflict and debate from within over concrete interests and goals.

16. Press release, Friends of the Lubicon, Jan. 28, 1992.

FROM STEREOTYPES
TO VISIBLE DIVERSITY:
LESBIAN POLITICAL ORGANIZING

Sharon Dale Stone

In 1988 the Secretary of State Women's Programme issued new guidelines about eligibility for funding. Formerly, lesbianism per se had not been a barrier to funding, and in the early 1980s a few explicitly lesbian groups had received grants from the agency. The new guidelines disqualified projects that promoted a view on lesbianism. The guidelines – the result of pressure from the anti-feminist organization REAL Women – served as a powerful reminder that in mainstream society, tolerance for lesbianism can never be taken for granted and that gains won through struggle can always be rescinded.

Representing a move towards "the production of a specifically anti-lesbian rhetoric" (Herman 1994a: 87), the Secretary of State's dictum can be understood in at least two ways. It can be taken as evidence of how powerless lesbians are in mainstream society; how easy it is for the mainstream to define lesbian existence as despicable. But it can also be understood as evidence of the successful mobilization of lesbians for lesbian power.[1] Before the phenomenal growth of the lesbian and feminist movements in the late 1960s and early 1970s, lesbians were largely irrelevant to the mainstream. By 1988 lesbians were perceived as a visible threat. Collectively, we have come a long way.

It is popular for both lesbians and non-lesbians to argue from a liberal point of view that society ought to practise tolerance towards lesbians. According to this line of argument, lesbians are just like everyone else – save whom we sleep with, and that aspect of our lives should be no one's business but our own. As such, lesbians do not represent a threat to society. From this perspective, it is irrational to either hate or fear lesbians.

From a different perspective, however, the targeting of lesbians by REAL

Women, which argues for the supremacy of the patriarchal and nuclear family, was not irrational. As the Furies collective argued more than twenty years ago, lesbian existence challenges the institution of compulsory heterosexuality (see Bunch 1987; see also O'Brien and Weir 1995); and as the Supreme Court of Canada recently argued, it is reasonable to exclude homosexuals (presumably, a term meant to include lesbians) from the definition of "the family," which is seen as "the fundamental unit" of society (*The Globe and Mail*, May 26, 1995: A3).

How did lesbians and the issue of lesbianism move from being irrelevant to the mainstream, to being so visible that a department of the federal government saw fit to pronounce on the issue of lesbianism? That is the central question addressed here. In answering it, I trace highlights of a history of lesbian organizing in Canada – that is, highlights as seen from my perspective as a white, relatively privileged lesbian feminist and academic, active in the lesbian movement since the 1970s[2] – and I point out strengths and weaknesses in various manifestations of lesbian versions of counterhegemonic politics in Canada.

On one level, an analysis of the history of lesbian organizing in Canada might suggest that to the extent that there is an autonomous movement, it is too caught up in identity politics or too fragmented and ideologically divided to represent an effective counterhegemonic force. I challenge this negative assessment of identity politics, in an analysis that owes much to the work of Shane Phelan (1994). Based on what I see of lesbian organizing past and present, I argue that widespread social change can be achieved in the absence of centralized organizations working to foster unity and promote common goals. Indeed, in a heterogeneous society, such change may even be facilitated when a movement is not constrained by the desire to offer a unified voice to the public at large.

A PERSPECTIVE ON THE HISTORICAL DEVELOPMENT OF LESBIAN POLITICAL ORGANIZING

Scholars generally agree that lesbians, qua lesbians, have not always existed (see, for example, Ferguson 1991). Women have always engaged in sexual relations with other women, but in Western societies, before the end of the nineteenth century, the category "lesbian" did not exist as a way of differentiating between women. The invention of "the lesbian" as a totalizing identity occurred within the context of the popularization of the work of nineteenth-century sexologists who sought to categorize and classify human behaviour, and within the context of changing social conditions that provided large numbers of women with the possibility of supporting themselves independently of men (Faderman 1981).

Only in the twentieth century have social conditions allowed for the possibility of developing a lesbian identity (D'Emelio 1983). Early on in the cen-

tury lesbians in the United States developed an identity that placed "the lesbian" in opposition to nineteenth-century conceptions of true womanhood,
but that nevertheless relegated lesbian existence to the margins of the mainstream, with lesbians conceptualized as not "normal women."

Negative as it was when first conceived, the conceptualization of "the lesbian" as a distinct identity was a necessary precondition allowing lesbians to
recognize each other as such and organize as lesbians. Historical research is
beginning to expose the existence of lesbian communities and networks
throughout most of this century (for example, Faderman 1991; Kennedy and
Davis 1993; Lesbians Making History 1989; Weissman and Fernie 1992).

As members of lesbian communities and networks, many lesbians participated in the creation of a distinct lesbian culture in opposition to dominant
heterosexual culture, although not all self-identified lesbians were aware of
or desired to participate in this oppositional lesbian culture. By the 1940s a
visible lesbian culture centred in bars had emerged – a culture in which
members were expected to take on either a butch or a femme identity. This
was also a culture that supported not only the public visibility of lesbians who
either would not or could not adopt stereotypically feminine behaviours and
mannerisms but also the claiming of social space for lesbians (Kennedy and
Davis 1993: 373). Generally participants did not understand themselves as
engaging in politics or understand their insistence on self-expression as a
political act. Nevertheless, especially considering the context of the rise of
ideology supporting women's sexual repression, and rhetoric supporting the
patriarchal nuclear family, the existence of the culture was profoundly political. In the 1940s and 1950s, participants in this culture, as Elizabeth
Lapovsky Kennedy and Madeline D. Davis argue in their study of the formation of a lesbian community in Buffalo, New York, succeeded "in forging the
consciousness that was to become, a decade later, central to gay liberation –
that gays and lesbians should end hiding and demand for themselves what
they deserve. This consciousness in the large lesbian and gay subcultures
throughout the country provided an environment for the rapid spread of gay
liberation and in many cases actually provided some of the impetus for the
movement" (378).

The numbers of pre-Stonewall activists were minuscule, but in the 1950s
and 1960s lesbians and gay men fashioned themselves as homosexuals deserving of rights. By 1969 the American homophile movement had already
achieved significant successes (see D'Emelio 1983). In Canada the Vancou-
ver-based Association for Social Knowledge (ASK) existed from 1964 to 1969
and published a newsletter distributed across the country (Kinsman 1987).

It is sometimes popular to argue that the gay liberation movement was
born of the ashes of the 1969 Stonewall Riots. One must take care, however,
to remember that the Stonewall Riots were preceded by almost twenty years
of political organizing (Adam 1987; D'Emelio 1983). Gay liberation was able

to spread quickly because it could build upon the groundwork laid by the pre-existing homophile movement. Throughout the 1960s the homophile movement had become increasingly radical. In 1968, for example, a year before the Stonewall Riots, the North American Conference of Homophile Organizations adopted the slogan "Gay is Good" (D'Emelio 1983: 199).

In the first few years of the gay liberation movement, lesbians and gay men made common cause. To the extent that lesbians participated, they did so as gay women who saw their fate as tied to that of gay men (cf. Bearchell 1983). As the 1970s wore on, however, growing numbers of lesbians became increasingly disillusioned with the male-dominated gay liberation movement.

By 1970 conditions were ripe for the emergence of a new kind of lesbian: the lesbian feminist who identified more with the growing feminist movement than the gay liberation movement. Feminism's analysis of sexism as the locus of female oppression struck a chord for many of the lesbians who had been active in the homophile and gay liberation movements and had experienced the sexism of the male leaders. Indeed, as early as 1966 the lesbian periodical *The Ladder* began reporting news of the women's liberation movement and discrimination against women. As Rose Weitz (1984: 241) argues: "Thus, *The Ladder* implicitly suggested that lesbians share a common fate with all women and should work for both women's and homosexual rights. This in turn provided the necessary precondition for the subsequent feminist redefinition of lesbianism."

In 1970 the lesbian feminist emerged into public, representing a decisive break from the past. That year the new political stance was theoretically represented by the widespread publication of the influential "Woman-Identified Woman," which defined a lesbian as "the rage of all women condensed to the point of explosion" and argued:

> As long as women's liberation tries to free women without facing the basic heterosexual structure that binds us in one-to-one relationship with our oppressors, tremendous energies will continue to flow into trying to straighten up each particular relationship with a man....
>
> It is the primacy of women relating to women, of women creating a new consciousness of and with each other which is at the heart of women's liberation, and the basis for the cultural revolution. (Reprinted in Grevatt 1975: 443-4)

The authors of "Woman-Identified Woman" were white lesbians from the working and middle classes. Some of them had roots in the older homophile movement, and most of them had been lesbians before becoming feminists (see Grevatt 1975: ch. 3), which meant they differed significantly from younger lesbians who, as the 1970s wore on, developed a militantly separatist ideology.

By the mid-1970s, lesbians from the pre-Stonewall days were outnumbered in the lesbian feminist movement by those who had come to identify as lesbian as a result of exposure to feminist ideology. For many of these new lesbians, their lesbianism was inseparable from their feminism. Fed up with the sexism of gay men in gay liberation groups, and fed up with the lesbophobia of feminist groups, many left both groups to devote their energy to a politics of lesbian separatism. The Furies collective expressed a basic message of this early lesbian separatism: "Lesbianism is not a matter of sexual preference, but rather one of political choice which every woman must make if she is to become woman-identified and thereby end male supremacy.... Lesbians must get out of the straight women's movement and form their own movement in order to be taken seriously.... Lesbians cannot develop a common politics with women who do not accept Lesbianism as a political issue" (Berson 1988: 26).

Separatism became increasingly synonymous with lesbian feminism and community-building – the project of creating a Lesbian Nation.[3] Lesbian organizations espousing a separatist politics were created in a variety of cities across North America. In Canada, a well-documented case is that of the Lesbian Organization of Toronto (LOOT), which existed from 1976 to 1980.[4]

Arlene Stein (1992: 34) points out, "In the 1970s ... becoming a lesbian meant coming into a community committed to some shared values," which was true for lesbians who were open to adopting feminist values in general and lesbian separatist politics in particular. It was not true, however, for lesbians who did not accept or agree with those values. A sense of excitement and euphoria over building something entirely new pervaded LOOT, and it could be difficult for members to notice that most lesbians were not part of this fairly homogeneous group. Especially in light of cross-Canada and cross-North America connections, fostered by periodic national and regional conferences and by a lively and growing lesbian feminist press, it could be difficult to grasp that many lesbians felt alienated from lesbian feminist politics. Yet, in 1979, there were only four hundred card-carrying members at LOOT – a tiny minority of lesbians in Toronto.

To the extent that it was noticed that older lesbians or lesbians into butch/femme roles did not seem to be interested in LOOT, it was generally assumed that they suffered from false consciousness about their lesbianism. Lesbians active at LOOT thought of themselves as a vanguard and expected newcomers to adopt their politics. As a result LOOT gained a reputation of being full of militant separatists, and many lesbians felt unwelcome at LOOT.

To its members LOOT could, at times, seem like the centre of the universe, but of course it wasn't. In the late 1970s in Toronto alone there were a variety of groups, such as the Community Homophile Association of Toronto, Lesbian Mothers' Defence Fund, Wages Due Lesbians, and there were lesbian bars. And, of course, for those with no connections to the urban lesbian or gay communities, neither LOOT nor any other group welcoming lesbians was easy to find.

Many lesbians were either explicitly left out by the new lesbian feminist ideology and practice, or they didn't feel welcome: butches and femmes; lesbians of colour; lesbians with disabilities; lesbians who loved their male children; lesbians who enjoyed the company of men; lesbians who worked politically with men; lesbians who were not feminists; and any lesbian unwilling to privilege her lesbian identity. In this respect, LOOT expressed an identitarian politics. As defined by Shane Phelan (1994: 76): "Identitarian politics presumes that common action must be based on an identity among partners; for example, the belief that only lesbians can be trusted to work for lesbian concerns is not identity politics, but is identitarian."

Based as it is on the affirmation – even celebration – of sameness, a crucial part of identitarian politics is the creation of an identitarian community, which involves the idealization of community. As Iris Young (1990: 227, 234) explains:

> This ideal expresses a desire for the fusion of subjects with one another which in practice operates to exclude those with whom the group does not identify. The ideal of community denies and represses social difference, the fact that the polity cannot be thought of as a unity in which all participants share a common experience and common values....
>
> The most serious political consequence of the desire for community, or for co-presence and mutual identification with others, is that it often operates to exclude or oppress those experienced as different. Commitment to an ideal of community tends to value and enforce homogeneity.

In 1979 Sasha Lewis published a study on "lesbian life today," based on interviews with self-identified lesbians in the United States. In deciding whom to interview, she said she "was looking primarily for diversity," yet she defined diversity very narrowly as encompassing "older women and younger, women who had just discovered their affectional preference and those who had lived with it for decades, women who were devotedly monogamous and women who lived and espoused other relationship styles" (6).

Lewis said nothing about racial or class diversity, lesbian mothers, or disability. She further noted, "The lesbian subculture is ... appropriately defined by an overwhelming commonality of experience," so that lesbians across the country would "probably" have had a coming out experience that is "fundamentally the same" (7). Lewis's comments betray a profound ethnocentrism; it has never been true even in the United States that all lesbians share "an overwhelming commonality of experience." Nevertheless, they indicate the extent to which lesbian feminists succeeded in creating a distinct culture and transmitted that culture far and wide, a conclusion bolstered by studies about 1970s lesbian feminists in places as varied as San Francisco (Wolf

1979), a town in the U.S. midwest (Krieger 1984), a city in the U.S. southwest (Lockard 1985), Christchurch, New Zealand (Dominy 1986), and Toronto (Ross 1995). Despite great geographical diversity, the communities discussed fundamentally shared the same lesbian feminist culture – the same commitment to privileging a lesbian identity to the exclusion of any other identity.

By 1980, when LOOT collapsed due to lack of money and lack of energy on the part of the core collective, the relatively homogeneous group of lesbians associated with it could congratulate themselves on having created a lesbian feminist community. LOOT had nurtured lesbian musicians, and the feminist Womynly Way Productions and Atthis Theatre, dedicated to producing lesbian theatre, were started at LOOT. The group Women Against Violence Against Women was started by lesbians from LOOT. As well, LOOT had provided countless lesbians with an opportunity to "come out" into feminism, rather than into a bar. Although numbers remained small, the active members of LOOT successfully created a counterhegemonic culture.

Whereas the dominant society followed the medical lead in conceptualizing lesbians as "sick," lesbian feminists reconceptualized lesbianism as a positive identity they could take pride in. In the 1970s they theorized heterosexuality as an oppressive institution upholding patriarchy and conceptualized lesbian existence in terms of resistance to patriarchy. In so doing, they expanded upon the accomplishments of the homophile movement. They established the conditions that would in future decades make further lesbian visibility possible and allow lesbians to publicly take pride in a lesbian identity.

Although 1970s lesbian feminists were not representative of all lesbians, they did politicize their marginality. In a different context, bell hooks argues that marginality needs to be conceptualized as "a central location for the production of a counterhegemonic discourse that is not just found in words but in habits of being and the way one lives." By focusing only on themselves as lesbians and by valuing a lesbian identity, lesbian separatists created a "radical perspective from which to see and create, to imagine alternatives, new worlds." For this reason, hooks argues that marginality needs to be seen not as something to overcome, but "as position and place of resistance" (hooks 1990: 149-50)

CHALLENGES TO THE LESBIAN NATION

In the early 1980s the earlier vision of Lesbian Nation began to unravel – at least in Toronto[5] – as lesbian feminists were challenged to deal with their exclusionary values and practices. For example, in one of LOOT's last newsletters, Lilith Finkler (1980) wrote about feeling she had to deny her Jewishness to participate in the community. Years later she spoke of being unable to explore and own all of her various identities within the context of lesbian feminism. Whereas she had once called herself a lesbian separatist, she said she could no longer deny important parts of herself (Ross 1995: 222).

Another example of lesbians speaking out about exclusion is found in a transcript of a 1983 conversation between lesbians of colour in Toronto, in which they speak of their experiences of racism in contacts with white lesbians. One noted: "When I do tell white lesbians/straights that I am a lesbian, I am met with curious disbelief. Or they begin to regard me in a sexually racist way – I'm exotic, a novelty, a toy" (Lesbians of Colour 1991: 163). Another said: "Most of us also live in the lesbian sub-culture, but we also live in a whole other mainstream society and we are people of colour and so it makes absolutely no sense to only function on the premise that you work only with women or that you only address women's problems" (Lesbians of Colour 1991: 165).

By 1979 many lesbian feminists in Toronto were becoming increasingly disenchanted with organizing in a lesbian-only context. That year a group of lesbian feminists turned their attention to the largely heterosexual feminist movement and founded the national feminist periodical *Broadside*, which was published throughout the 1980s. Others became involved with feminist organizations such as the newly founded Feminist Party of Canada (FPC) – although the FPC did not last more than a few years.

The early 1980s also saw the publication of several anthologies of writing by women of colour, which discussed racism and anti-semitism in the feminist and lesbian movements. The earlier, narrow vision that all lesbians could be united solely on the basis of their lesbianism was becoming increasingly difficult to sustain. The limits of an identitarian politics became increasingly clear as lesbians who had never privileged a lesbian identity began to be heard, while lesbians who had once privileged a lesbian identity began to rethink earlier ideas. As well, in the aftermath of the 1982 Barnard Conference, the "sex debates" rocked feminist and lesbian communities across North America (see Vance 1984), and lesbian feminists began to talk about the formerly taboo subject of sexual practice. Lesbians who identified as either butch or femme began to break the silence they had maintained during the 1970s, and other lesbians organized groups based on their interest in S/M sex.

In Toronto the last gasp of lesbian feminist organizing was represented by Lesbians Against the Right (LAR), which was formed in 1981 and disbanded in 1983. In its short history LAR organized a lesbian visibility march, several demonstrations, and established a lesbian presence in a number of progressive groups in Toronto (Stone 1991). LAR ultimately foundered due to its inability to develop a long-term strategy and its narrow vision of a united lesbian front. LAR asked lesbians to privilege their lesbianism, so it is not surprising that, as lesbians not connected to LAR began to focus on other aspects of their identities, LAR became increasingly irrelevant to a changing social and political environment.

The last binational lesbian conference held in Vancouver in 1981 concluded with plans for another conference in 1983, but that conference never took place. By 1983 conservatism was on the rise across Canada, and with a new maturity former lesbian feminists/separatists were seeing more clearly that lesbianism alone did not represent an adequate basis for unity. As Nancy Adamson (quoted in Ross 1995: 216) expressed it, "I became very cynical about the possibility of organizing on the basis of being a lesbian. I wasn't convinced that being lesbians *was* a basis for organizing, and I'm still not."

In Toronto many lesbian feminists became involved in the gay liberation movement. In 1980, for example, former LOOT members became involved with gay men in Gays and Lesbians Against the Right Everywhere (a forerunner to LAR); some joined with gay men to organize Toronto's first Lesbian and Gay Pride Day in 1981; and later some worked to establish links with the International Gay Association. Among other things, lesbian feminists worked with gay men in the peace movement (Gay/Lesbian Action for Disarmament – GLAD) and in municipal politics. Lesbian feminists were also increasingly willing to identify with gay men, as evidenced by their enthusiastic participation in the Gay Community Appeal of Toronto; and gay men were becoming increasingly sensitized to issues surrounding lesbian difference. In 1983 lesbian feminists helped found the national lesbian and gay magazine *Pink Ink* as an alternative to the older *The Body Politic*. Although *Pink Ink* collapsed in 1984, many of its workers reorganized to create the longer-lasting magazine *Rites: for lesbian and gay liberation*. The editorial of *Pink Ink*'s first issue stated: "A primary commitment of *Pink Ink* is the equal involvement of men and women in all aspects of the magazine.... While lesbians and gay men share a common oppression, we will also address the oppression of lesbians as women."

The editorial reflected the increasing openness of some gay men to a feminist analysis of lesbian oppression. This openness, which was not in evidence in the gay liberation movement of the 1970s, was made possible by the work that lesbian separatists had done to differentiate themselves from gay men, form an understanding of themselves as female, and develop their own distinct voice. In the early 1980s lesbian feminists were prepared to bring that distinct voice to gay liberation and insist upon being heard. As Becki Ross (1995: 204) says, "The sheer increase in numbers of out lesbian feminists meant that political dykes no longer had to fight for a voice inside either mixed gay/lesbian groups ... or straight feminist organizations."

In 1985 the DisAbled Women's Network (DAWN) was formed, and by 1987 there was a viable national organization and active DAWN groups in almost every province. Lesbians with disabilities, tired of being excluded from the feminist and gay liberation movements, had helped found the new organization. Other lesbians eagerly joined DAWN groups across the country. Before long, lesbian members of various DAWN groups had set up lesbian caucuses, forcing the heterosexual majority to address lesbian issues and deal with their lesbophobia (cf. Doucette 1990; for a history of how DAWN organized, see Stone and Doucette 1988). Lesbians in DAWN represented one more group committed to organizing on the basis of shared multiple oppression, and one less group interested in privileging a lesbian identity to the exclusion of any other identity.

ORGANIZING IN THE 1990S

In 1987 lesbian attendees at a national feminist conference joined together to found the National Lesbian Forum (NLF), the first national lesbian organization in Canada. The NLF was intended "to work for increasing lesbian visibility and ensure that lesbian issues were discussed in both the feminist and the gay rights movements" (Paquette 1990: 226). One of the NLF's first acts was to join the National Action Committee on the Status of Women (NAC) to promote lesbian visibility in Canada's largest feminist organization.

Aside from the visibility afforded by having a lesbian organization listed as a member of NAC – which in itself was important and symbolic – and aside from organizing workshops on lesbian issues at some feminist and gay conferences, the NLF accomplished little. The NLF never organized a lesbian conference, worked only sporadically to raise lesbian issues in the gay rights movement and feminist organizations, and, indeed, never significantly expanded its membership base beyond the small group of lesbian activists across Canada who were connected with it in the first place. In the end the NLF continued to exist for only a few years. There did not appear to be more than a handful of lesbians who were interested in or able to muster the energy required to maintain a national lesbian organization. As well, the 1988 decision of the federal Women's Programme effectively cut off the possibility of funding for lesbian groups. Without access to funding from the federal government, the NLF was ultimately unable to martial the resources that might have allowed it to autonomously mount a national campaign on lesbian issues.

It has been access to limited funding that has allowed the Lesbian Issues Committee (LIC) of NAC to exist since 1985. The LIC produced a popular leaflet, "Do You Know a Lesbian?" offering suggestions for becoming comfortable with lesbians. According to Anne Molgat, who has many years of experience with LIC and NAC, the leaflet has been the most widely distributed of all of NAC's leaflets (interview, Aug. 28, 1995). In recent years, however, the LIC has focused on education and action within NAC rather than working to raise the profile of lesbians in mainstream society. As an underfunded committee of a larger feminist organization (which is itself underfunded), LIC does not have the financial resources that would allow it to work to galvanize lesbians across the country. Certainly, LIC's activities within NAC have done much to raise awareness about lesbian issues, but LIC does not carry the potential of mobilizing large groups of lesbians in mass action across the country.

In the 1990s, aside from the problem of funding, there appears to be even less interest in national organizing than there was in previous decades. There are no lesbian periodicals that are national in scope, and there is no formal network to connect lesbians across Canada (though many lesbian activists across the country know each other and keep in touch through informal means). The focus in the 1990s is on local organizing and action, and there is ample evidence of this activity in cities across Canada.

While it would be difficult to argue that lesbian separatist thought and action flourishes as much in the 1990s as it did in the 1970s, it is nevertheless true that lesbian separatism is, in diverse locales, alive and well. With notable exceptions (for example, the radical lesbian collective Amazons d'hier, Lesbiennes aujourd'hui (AHLA) in Montreal,[6] and other collectives in the United States), lesbian separatists are not for the most part organized as such. Yet, whether working collectively or as individuals, lesbian separatists are building upon the basic separatist premise of the need to separate from men in order to focus attention on their own needs and create for themselves a better, lesbian-positive world. To this end they are producing books and periodicals offering sophisticated and cogent analysis, keeping alive in their writings a vision of a world in which lesbianism is normative. Moreover, lesbian separatist activists across North America, whether or not they are organized as such, are working to create and expand lesbian-only space. In short, lesbian separatist ideas no longer inspire mass-organization efforts, as in the 1970s, but those ideas are continuing to be developed, refined, and hotly debated by lesbians everywhere.[7]

Although it is not possible to accurately determine the characteristics of lesbian separatists, casual observation suggests that they tend to be over the age of thirty.[8] In other words, younger lesbians generally do not seem to be attracted to the adoption of a lesbian separatist identity. There are, of course, many exceptions, but at least in large cities it seems that most younger lesbians have little interest in engaging in debates with separatists or working with them to further a specifically lesbian agenda for social change.

Many writers are calling the 1990s the postmodernist age, meaning that the search for truth and stability has been deemed naive. The modernist attempt to create fixed identities has been supplanted by the celebration of the contingency of identities. The postmodern ethic celebrates continually changing identities and the ability of actors to alternately create and then reject ever-new identities in keeping with social circumstances. Postmodern theory sees the old lesbian feminist/separatist attempt to define a lesbian by delineating her essential characteristics and then sorting out the "real lesbians" from others as hopelessly misguided. Academics in the new queer theory, at least, no longer believe in the value of such essentialist, either/or thinking. In queer theory, as in lesbian and gay studies in general, adherence to either/or thinking has for some time been considered a mark of simplistic, unsophisticated analysis; a mark that distinguishes bad theory from cutting-edge theory.

In her critique of queer theory, Rosemary Hennessy (1993: 968) notes, "The social is consistently conceptualized as only a matter of representation, of discursive or symbolic relations." There is "the assumption ... that the social forces shaping sexual subjectivities are exclusively a matter of cultural representation," but, as Hennessy argues, "The construction of sexual subjectivities involves more than culture alone." To adequately theorize the construction of sexual subjectivity, Hennessy argues for adopting a materialist feminist conceptualization of "the social as an economic, political, ideological order in which difference is enacted as dominance" (970).

Queer theory is mostly not concerned with material reality or with questions related to political organizing or political goals. To the limited extent that queer theory addresses politics it argues that identity politics is doomed to failure because of the instability of identity. As Sherri Paris (1993: 986-7) points out: "This failure is presumed rather than argued, and the possibility that political failures have specific material or historic causes rather than ultimate ones does not seem to cross anyone's mind. The conclusion that politics is impossible thereby becomes inescapable, as it has been for conservatives since Edmund Burke."

Indeed, queer theory conceptualizes politics as discourse (Paris 1993: 988). To this extent, queer theorists are not talking about the same world in which grassroots lesbian activists struggle for material change. In the world of grassroots activists, meanings are not understood as uncertain or provisional, they are concrete and confining. To the extent that queer theorists refuse engagement with this world, Paris charges that they are talking to themselves. Thus, it is not surprising that queer theory has not captured the imaginations of grassroots lesbian activists.

As a critique of the identitarian urge to create fixed identities and a politics based on sameness, queer theory has a place. At the same time, it loses its relevance to politics in the material world by refusing to acknowledge the material reality of oppression. Queer theory does not allow for the possibility of oppressed peoples making common cause based on a provisional identity. There is no recognition of the strategic value of asserting an identity for the purpose of mobilization against oppression.

What *has* captured the imaginations of a lot of young lesbians, along with many lesbians who have always felt excluded by extreme expressions of lesbian feminist ideology, has been the idea of adopting a self-consciously queer identity, as opposed to a "lesbian" identity. The term "queer" has a long history vis-à-vis lesbian and gay oppression. In the past it was used by heterosexuals as a term of insult. In the 1990s the term is being proudly claimed by people who exist in opposition to a hegemonic heterosexuality. Many lesbians are attracted to the potential inclusiveness and non-essentialism of a new, self-conscious queer identity.

Especially within the context of debates among lesbians about how to define a lesbian – debates that have continued for a quarter-century – the affirmation of a lesbian identity can seem limiting. As a sign of the times, my lesbian studies students in 1990 (in the big city of Montreal) were excited and intrigued by the 1970s debates about how to define a lesbian. By 1993 my lesbian studies students (still in Montreal, but now many of them identified as bisexual) were alternately bored and impatient with these old debates. They saw the attempt to fix identity as irrelevant to their lives and the new, postmodern times.

For some queer-identified lesbians, the term "lesbian" can evoke stereotypical images of a lesbian separatist who is preoccupied with policing the borders of a mythical lesbian community, ensuring that only "real lesbians" are allowed in. For the most part, queer-identified lesbians make a conscious decision to disassociate themselves from this stereotypical image of a lesbian.[9] Rather than spending time delineating the essential characteristics of a lesbian, they are interested in celebrating not only lesbian diversity, but also the diversity of human sexual expression (for lesbian attitudes towards the adoption of a queer identity, see Smyth 1992: Stein 1993; Onstad 1994).

Thus, taking on a queer identity symbolizes, for many lesbians, a conscious rejection of labels that appear limiting and, at the same time, a conscious embracing of fluidity and diversity. Often, embracing a queer identity is in itself considered to be a political act. As British queer activist Cherry Smyth (1992: 28) notes, "Queer is welcomed as breaking up lesbian and gay orthodoxies and making possible new alliances across gender and other disparate identities; it is claimed by some as neutral in terms of race and gender."

Smyth (1992: 21) quotes Linda Semple, who says, "I also use it [queer] externally to describe a political inclusivity – a new move towards a celebration of difference across sexualities, across genders, across sexual preference and across object choice."

In terms of the debate about whether homosexuality is essential or socially constructed, queer-identified lesbians mostly take the side of the social constructionists. They reject an essentialist view of lesbianism as transhistorical, natural or pregiven – "the idea that there is a 'lesbian essence,' something objective that lesbians have in common that makes them lesbians" (Card 1995: 17). Instead, they mostly recognize sexual identity as situationally and historically contingent, so that the identity claimed by anyone at any particular time depends, to a large extent, on the language available (discussions of "the essentialist/constructionist debate" can be found in Duggan 1992; Fuss 1989; Escoffier 1990).

The year 1990 saw lesbian and gay AIDS activists in New York City give birth to the group Queer Nation. The original idea was to fight homophobia and promote visibility using confrontational tactics (Chee 1991). Queer Nation groups quickly spread in cities across the United States, and into Canada and England. More and more, the Queer Nation idea caught the imagination of those who were simply fed up with being polite; the counterhegemonic potential of a diverse group of people united in action under the common identity "queer" appeared great. As Steve Maynard (1991: 18) points out, "Presenting ourselves to the world as a unified national carries a certain power."

Yet, as Maynard also suggests, the homogeneity and exclusivity implied by the concept of nation work against a recognition of significant differences among queers. As groups developed in the early 1990s and attempted to deal with issues such as sexism, racism, and classism, the potentially revolutionary identity of "queer" turned out in practice to have an almost exclusively white, middle-class and male face (Maggenti 1993: 249; see also Cosson 1991; Maynard 1991; Smyth 1992). Smyth asks, "Isn't setting up a lesbian caucus ... admitting that the agenda is controlled by men's concerns?" She argues:

> While queer raises the possibility of dealing with complex subjectivities and differences in terms of gender, race and class, it also risks not trying hard enough to resist the reductive prescriptiveness some of us suffered in feminism and the uncritical essentialism that privileges the queerness of gay white men. While it offers lesbians an escape from unilateral lesbian orthodoxy into a more pluralistic and flexible politics, there is a danger of losing sight of the progressive aspects of feminism, which gave many of us the courage to speak....
>
> Until queer politics visibilises white lesbians and black lesbians and gay men, it still privileges the experiences and agendas of white gay men.... Queer will fail if it fails to address the relevance of identity politics. (Smyth 1992: 30, 35, 58-9)

Phelan (1994: 153) notes that although the term "queer" carries the potential of forging a coalitional identity, queer politics generally lacks a feminist understanding of lesbian specificity. In this absence, she says, lesbians become colonized. In a critique of the concept of queer nationalism, she argues:

> To the extent that queers become nationalist, they will ignore or lose patience with those among them who do not fit their idea of the nation. This dynamic in nationalism will always limit its political usefulness. The only

fruitful nationalism is one that has at its heart the idea of the nonnation –
the nation of nonidentity, formed not by any shared attribute but by a conscious weaving of threads between tattered fabrics. And at that point, why
speak of nations? Alliances are not nations, and need not be to be strong.
(Phelan 1994: 154)

It is also important to recognize that, as fervently as many contemporary
lesbians proclaim their adoption of a queer identity, the phenomenon of
queer organizing remains primarily tied to big cities that contain large and
diverse groups of people who are marginalized because of their sexuality. In
smaller cities and towns, and in rural areas, lesbians do not have the same
access to an understanding of themselves as queer. This is all the more true
for young lesbians (and gay men and bisexuals). For example, in Kelowna,
B.C., the few young lesbians I know are unequivocal in defining themselves
as lesbians. There is not even room in their world to be bisexual, let alone
queer. One could take a place in the ivory tower and criticize them for their
essentialism, yet one must acknowledge that much of what goes on in a big
city – including the debates – is often irrelevant to life in a more circumscribed context.

In any case, organizing around the concept of Queer Nation did not last
for more than a few years in Canada. Today, in cities across Canada, lesbians
are organizing as Lesbian Avengers. Founded in 1992 in New York City, "The
Lesbian Avengers is a direct action group using grass-roots activism to fight
for lesbian survival and visibility" (Schulman 1994: 290). Eschewing ideological debate, Lesbian Avengers groups are especially interested in confrontational politics, in the tradition of ACT-UP groups. The founders have produced a Lesbian Avenger Handbook, which gives details on how to start a
lesbian direct action group and provides crucial details on all aspects of engaging in direct action.

The idea of Lesbian Avengers has caught the imagination of lesbians
across North America, much as the idea of Queer Nation did a few years earlier. Unlike Queer Nation, however, the Lesbian Avengers is explicitly and
unapologetically lesbian. And for many lesbians, this is its main attraction.
Tired of being overshadowed by gay men, or of being confused with gay
men, the women in Lesbian Avengers are interested in establishing a visible
and unmistakably lesbian presence.

As of August 1995, about seventy Lesbian Avengers groups had formed
around the world. In Canada they exist in many cities, including Ottawa,
Winnipeg, Vancouver, and Victoria. Most of the Canadian groups had
formed only within the past year and were still too new to have planned and
carried out significant actions. The Victoria group, for example, formed in
the spring of 1995, had done little besides provide marshalling for Lesbian
and Gay Pride Day.[10] But Lesbian Avengers in Victoria and elsewhere were

hopeful about the future, confident about their ability to attract more and more lesbians to promote lesbian visibility.

It remains to be seen whether these new direct-action groups will have an impact upon the social and political climate, but possibilities for the future appear to be bright. In the early 1980s right-wing forces were not as widespread or as organized as they are in the 1990s, and the threat they represented to lesbian existence was not quite as tangible. All this has changed, and the New Christian Right with its anti-homosexual sermonizing is growing every day. Moreover, after almost a decade of Conservative rule in Ottawa, with a current Liberal government that does not appear to be friendly towards lesbians, and in the wake of disappointing decisions from the Supreme Court of Canada, politically aware lesbians are conscious of living in a social and political climate that makes the hostility of the early 1980s seem tame.

In the absence of a well-entrenched lesbian movement to nourish counter-hegemonic thought, this hostile climate might be enough to scare lesbians into keeping quiet about the issue of lesbianism. Collectively, however, lesbian feminists have been asserting lesbian pride for more than a quarter-century, and stories of lesbian resistance and survival are revered in lesbian folklore. These traditions have been inherited by the lesbian activists of the 1990s. There are too many lesbians who are proud of their sexual identity, too many lesbians connected to each other both locally and across great geographical distance, and too many lesbians willing to work for collective survival, for lesbians to be collectively silenced into complicity with the heteropatriarchy.

There is a great deal of lesbian political activity occurring across Canada in addition to the organization of Lesbian Avengers groups. In Winnipeg, Manitoba (1991 population, 652,354), for example,[11] lesbians are very visible at the Gay/Lesbian Resource Centre (GLRC), which not only offers various forms of social support to lesbians and gay men, but is also actively reaching out to and educating the general public about lesbian and gay issues. Recently the GLRC has organized educational panels in high schools, and currently the GLRC is embarking upon a project of anti-homophobia training with the medical community.

In 1991 lesbians in Winnipeg organized the Coalition of Lesbians on Support and Education (CLOSE), a group that has done much to break the silence about violence in lesbian relationships. Across Manitoba, CLOSE has been instrumental in reaching out to and educating social service workers in general and women's shelter workers in particular about the needs of lesbians who use their services. As well, Winnipeg is home to two lesbian artists who call themselves Average Good Looks and have created billboards with political messages. For example, one billboard prominently displayed in a busy location carried the message "Lesbian is not a dirty word." Altogether, lesbians have over the past decade become increasingly visible in Winnipeg, and more and more of the general population are becoming sensitized to lesbian issues.

In Victoria, British Columbia,[12] despite the relative smallness of the city (1991 population, 287,897), lesbians have been able to support their own monthly publication, *LesbiaNews*, since 1988. In a recent issue, a former editor of *LesbiaNews* wrote that she has moved "from a belief in the importance of community to a belief in the importance of community visibility. Simply to publish a dozen blank pages with the word Lesbian across the top would be a political act, an act of defiance" (Perks 1995: 2).

Since at least the 1970s a relatively large lesbian population has existed in Victoria, and there are signs of lesbian political activity becoming even more visible than in the past. For example, aside from the presence of the Lesbian Avengers, lesbians were the core organizers of Victoria's first lesbian and gay pride march in 1994 – and, as evidence of the heightened political consciousness of lesbians, there were more lesbians than gay men in attendance.

Other cities, large and small, also have vibrant lesbian organizations and individual lesbians dedicated to lessening lesbian oppression. Moreover, unlike the case in the 1970s, in the 1990s it is often lesbians who are in leadership positions in organizations that are putatively lesbian and gay. Indeed, it is often lesbians who are taking the initiative for forming such organizations. An entire book could be filled with a discussion of current political activities in which Canadian lesbians, qua lesbians, are active. Following, nevertheless, is a brief sampling of activities engaging lesbians outside large cities in Canada.

- In Halifax, N.S. (1991 population, 320,501), the Lesbian Health Collective (LHC) was organized in 1994. In April 1995, in co-operation with Planned Parenthood, the LHC held a one-day Lesbian Health Clinic.[13]
- In New Glasgow, N.S. (1991 population, 9,905), lesbians were primarily responsible in 1994 for creating a group called "The Homosexualist Agenda" (THA), in the wake of homophobic remarks from the area's Member of Parliament, Roseanne Skokes.[14] THA's mandate is to "create a broad-based collective movement for social justice and equality." THA has since organized two rallies in New Glasgow and in June 1995 organized a lesbian, gay, and bisexual parade in New Glasgow, attended by close to one hundred people. As in Victoria, B.C., more lesbians than gay men attended New Glasgow's parade.
- In 1995 in North Bay, Ont. (1991 population, 55,405),[15] two lesbians were instrumental in organizing Gays, Lesbians and Bisexuals of North Bay and Area, a group that so far attracts mostly lesbians. One of this group's more political activities was the organization of a group of lesbians and gays to march in protest at the office of Mike Harris, the leader of the Ontario Progressive Conservative Party (also the MPP for North Bay).

- Not far from North Bay, in Sudbury, Ont. (1991 population, 157,613), a lesbian is president of the Sudbury All Gay Alliance (SAGA), a group that in April 1995 organized Sudbury's first ever Lesbian, Gay and Bisexual Conference. One of SAGA's concerns includes educating the broader community.[16]
- In Ontario la Collective lesbienne has existed since 1993, bringing a lesbian presence to la Table féministe francophone de concertation provinciale de l'Ontario, and other groups of francophone feminists in Ontario. In addition to raising awareness in the francophone community about lesbian existence, this lesbian collective has spoken out on how the law affects lesbians and has participated in a number of feminist political activities.[17]
- In Kelowna, B.C. (1991 population, 111,846), lesbians are working with an anti-racist group to educate the public about lesbian and gay oppression.

Several cities in Canada have explicitly lesbian radio shows on a weekly basis. For example, "Dykes on Mikes" has been regularly broadcast from Montreal for many years, as has "Dyke Dimensions" in Victoria. These lesbian productions broadcast information about lesbian concerns and activities. Among other things, they allow lesbians isolated in their homes to learn about lesbian culture and politics. Their very existence is testament to the ability of lesbians to sustain a vibrant, counterhegemonic culture.

Perhaps the most impressive success story in Canada in the 1990s is the case of the Lesbian Caucus in Montreal, which organized in June 1993 to ensure that lesbians were represented as such when the Quebec Human Rights Commission (CDPQ) carried out a public inquiry about violence towards lesbians and gays (see CDPQ 1994; also Demczuk 1994).[18] As soon as the decision was announced, the Lesbian Caucus began organizing to encourage lesbians to prepare submissions to the CDPQ. A letter to this effect was distributed to groups and individuals across Quebec.

By the time of the public hearings in November 1993, the Lesbian Caucus had gathered twenty-two submissions in addition to its own lengthy presentation to the CDPQ (which received a total of seventy-five briefs). The entire affair was well covered by the mass media, and with sympathy. Moreover, thanks to the work that the Lesbian Caucus carried out with journalists from mass media outlets, the media reports often discussed the distinctiveness of lesbian realities.[19] In the end the Lesbian Caucus could take credit for a special reference in the CDPQ's report to lesbian realities as distinct from gay men and for the CDPQ directing six of its forty-one recommendations specifically towards addressing lesbian oppression.

At the time of the CDPQ inquiry some lesbians eschewed the effort as reformist and therefore refused to participate. Nevertheless, the CDPQ's public inquiry into violence towards lesbians and gays represents a historically significant recognition of society's responsibility towards its lesbian and gay citizens – and it was made all the more significant by explicit recognition and attention to the distinctiveness of lesbian realities.

FROM STEREOTYPES TO VISIBLE DIVERSITY

As a group lesbians have moved from a position of invisibility in mainstream society to a position of relative visibility. Today lesbians are active and visible in a variety of progressive social movements, working on a variety of projects. These include, for example, "AIDS activism ... alternative publishing, literacy advocacy, fiction writing, feminist teaching, counselling and healing, 'third world' solidarity work, pay-equity lobbying, cooperative housing, performance art and cultural production, local antiracist action, antipoverty organizing, the environmental movement, feminist service groups such as rape crisis and battered women's centres, self-defence, book selling, and safe-sex education and outreach" (Ross 1995: 221). Moreover, in all of this work with others, lesbians are increasingly willing to be open and vocal about their sexual identity – sometimes to the point of being vocal about working from an explicitly lesbian perspective and demanding that lesbian issues be addressed by co-workers.

Currently, feminist and gay liberation movement activists generally show the greatest willingness to listen to lesbian voices and add specifically lesbian issues to their agendas. Indeed, to the extent that the general public is cognizant of lesbian concerns, this awareness is in large part due to the willingness of feminists and gay liberationists to make specific reference to and publicize those concerns.

At the same time, it would be a mistake to assume that either the feminist or gay liberation movement addresses lesbian issues and the specifics of lesbian oppression satisfactorily. In the case of the feminist movement, although lesbian issues are discussed and many organizations have lesbian committees and caucuses, the goal of addressing the specifics of lesbian oppression has never been a priority for the movement as a whole (cf. Collectif d'amazones d'hier, lesbiennes d'aujourd'hui 1986/87; Michaud 1992: 213).

Similarly, the gay liberation movement has, over the past quarter-century, been increasingly willing to make a point of distinguishing between lesbians and gay men (hence, most groups that used to be named "gay" have been renamed "lesbian and gay" or "gay and lesbian"). Most of the general public are now aware that there is a difference between lesbians and gay men, even if unaware of what exactly that difference is beyond the difference of gender. Nevertheless, just as in earlier decades the gay liberation movement as a whole continues to frustrate lesbians, because it rarely moves beyond paying lip service to lesbian specificity.[20] With this in mind, and considering "the gendered power imbalance that functions to disempower lesbians vis-a-vis men," Diana Majury (1994: 304) has recently questioned the extent to which it is legitimate to posit the existence of "a lesbian and gay movement."

Majury (1994: 301) argues that lesbian oppression is "about hetero-sexualism, about sex and sexism and women's resistance," unlike the case for gay men, who are oppressed because of sexual practices. That is, even when gender is the only difference between a lesbian and a gay man, "a lesbian's experience of inequality is very different." For example, lesbians are "likely to be in a worse economic situation," many lesbians are centrally concerned with the issues of reproduction and child custody, and physical and sexual violence is inflicted upon lesbians and gay men differently (Majury 1994: 306-7). In a similar vein, Ross (1995: 6) points out: "lesbians have stood and continue to stand in a different social position with regard to official sexual discourse, legislation, and police practices than have gay men.... The state sanctioning of the male-dominated, heterosexual nuclear family and of the corresponding forms of masculinity and femininity figure centrally in the social organization of lesbian lives."

In general the failure of either the feminist or gay liberation movements to adequately address the specifics of lesbian existence and lesbian oppres-sion means that many lesbians continue to be attracted to a politics of lesbian separatism that places lesbians at the centre of analysis. As Charlotte Bunch (1987: 190) wrote almost twenty years ago, "Separatism is a dynamic strategy to be moved in and out of whenever a minority feels that its interests are be-ing overlooked by the majority." Yet it must not be forgotten that lesbians have gained (limited) legal recognition and rights over the past twenty years through their participation in the feminist and gay liberation movements. In recent years, for example, the Women's Legal, Education and Action Fund (LEAF) has intervened in legal cases affecting lesbians, and LEAF has con-sulted with lesbians about strategy (see LEAF 1993). Moreover, when the Quebec Human Rights Commission in 1977 became the first in Canada to prohibit discrimination on the grounds of sexual orientation, lesbians gained equally with gay men and other sexual minorities.

Lesbian separatist praxis has matured since it first flowered in the 1970s, when large numbers of lesbian feminists were focused on "the ideal of a cul-turally and ideologically unified Lesbian Nation" (Stein 1992: 35), and when lesbians were least visible to the mainstream. In the 1970s many lesbian feminists focused on the project of creating a lesbian community, which would support a new definition of lesbianism grounded in feminist analysis, support the positive valuation of this non-medicalized lesbian identity, and support lesbian feminists as they worked to create their own distinctive voice.

This was, to be sure, an important political project. Arguably, had lesbian feminists not taken the time to build a supportive base (importantly, one that supported only a minority of lesbians)[21] and develop their own analysis of their situation, they would not have been able to be as effective as they have been over the past decade in having their voices clearly heard by heterosexual feminists and gay men. Certainly, lesbians have been successful in encouraging both groups to advocate on behalf of lesbians. Nevertheless, the development of a stable community was also a project that led many lesbian feminists to turn inward and advocate a rigid lesbian separatism. Accordingly, little or no attention was paid to working to change mainstream society. For the most part, being visible to mainstream society was not a political priority.

Even in the 1970s, however, not all lesbian feminists were opposed to prioritizing lesbian visibility. It has never been possible to present lesbian feminists as a seamless whole. In early 1978, for example, when Anita Bryant was in Toronto to preach against homosexuals, a group of lesbian feminists debated the usefulness of getting involved in a public campaign against her. Some argued the importance of publicizing a lesbian feminist response, and others took a more separatist stance, arguing that it would be better to ignore Bryant and "pay attention to other needs in our community ... It's a matter of priorities" (quoted in Ross 1995: 164). As it turned out, many lesbian feminists joined with gay men to publicly protest against Bryant's message. When Ross interviewed some of these women more than ten years later, they recalled "the exuberance engendered by such historically unmatched visibility" (Ross 1995: 162). Indeed, as a result of such empowering experiences, more and more lesbian feminists came to recognize the advantages of working to promote increased lesbian visibility in mainstream society.

It would be naive to think that lesbian oppression will disappear once all lesbians have come out of the closet and become visible to mainstream society. Nevertheless, lesbian visibility is counterhegemonic in more ways than one. As Michelle Caron (1994) points out, we are tolerated only so long as we do not affirm our sexual identity.[22] The invisibility[23] of lesbians in mainstream society not only serves to uphold a perception of hegemonic heterosexuality, but also serves to keep lesbians from finding other lesbians,[24] and it can lead to lesbians doubting the reality of lesbian existence.[25] Indeed, according to Caron, the rendering of lesbian invisibility represents one of the most important mechanisms of lesbian oppression.[26] Similarly, Lynne Pearlman (1994: 461) argues, "Heteropatriarchal dominance flourishes with lesbian erasure; that is why a conspicuous lesbian presence is so critical to lesbian survival." Thus, lesbian visibility needs to be recognized as an important political strategy that works to undermine heterosexual hegemony.

In recent years popular magazines such as *Newsweek*, *Vanity Fair*, *Vogue*, and others have published articles about lesbians. There has been a made-for-TV movie (*Serving in Silence: The Margarethe Cammermeyer Story*), and from time to time Hollywood produces movies about lesbians (cf. Nadeau 1995). Mainstream society has begun to notice lesbians. For the most part, though, attention has been focused on de-emphasizing the threat that lesbian existence represents to the heteropatriarchy and emphasizing how lesbians are "just like everyone else." This type of visibility is useful to the extent that it forces non-lesbians to take note of lesbian existence and lets isolated lesbians know that they are not alone.

At the same time, it is not helpful to promote only one image of lesbianism. Rather, as Phelan (1994: 96) argues, "Visibility ... must be the visibility of *lesbians* in our irreducible plurality." Indeed: "The most striking thing about lesbians is not our difference(s) from heterosexuals or something distinctive about lesbian cultures and communities; it is our diversity."

Lesbians have always been a diverse group, living in a variety of places in a variety of ways. Until the 1980s, however, when lesbians began speaking out about their differences from each other and began organizing around their differences *as lesbians*, lesbian diversity was not evident to more than a minority of people. In the 1990s, with lesbians in all their diversity active in a variety of issues and movements, it has become more difficult for anyone to assume that all lesbians conform to a stereotypical image. There is no national organization, no central body to process information and issue directives about implementing a specifically lesbian political agenda. This lack of centralization must not, however, be construed as a failing of the lesbian movement.

Aside from the observation that it is difficult to imagine what a specifically lesbian political agenda would consist of (others who make this point include Cooper 1994; Herman 1994b), it must be recognized that different lesbians face different kinds of oppression. Lesbians are far too diverse a group to ever be able to come together and agree on what needs to be done to overcome oppression. In what sense would it be progressive for all lesbians to reach consensus on political strategy or goals? Given lesbian diversity, it would seem that rather than unifying lesbians to create a concentrated power bloc, any move towards attempting to reach consensus would lead to elitism and leave too many lesbians out in the cold.

This conclusion can be drawn from a cursory look at the history of lesbian feminist organizing since the 1970s, which led in the 1980s to the rise of a range of new lesbian groups focusing on ways of integrating a lesbian identity with other identities. In the 1980s many lesbians who had felt excluded by lesbian feminist/separatist rhetoric came into their own. The power of their voices and their words made it difficult for lesbian feminists to ignore them. Today, as Stein (1992: 52) points out, "Many women who felt excluded by an earlier model of identity now feel that they can finally participate in politics on their own terms." It has become clear that an unsophisticated politics of common action based on common identity is naive and unworkable.

Many lesbians have come to reject a simplistic identitarian politics in favour of embracing a more mature form of identity politics – a politics that asks lesbians to do political work based on shared commitments rather than shared identity. Bringing a lesbian identity to political work remains crucial, but there is a new recognition of a diversity of lesbian identities, so that not every lesbian attaches the same meaning to her lesbianism.

The lack of centralization in the Canadian lesbian movement needs to be seen as a strength. It is not the case that all lesbians, or even most lesbians, agree on what needs to be done to overcome oppression. In the absence of a central organizing body, there is no need for lesbians to try to convince each other of the rightness of their views. There is room for a diversity of opinion and a diversity of actions. Thus some lesbians choose to work in coalition with gay men, and some work with gay men because they see no separate lesbian interests but identify completely with the agendas of gay men. Some lesbians choose to work in coalition with feminists, and some work in the feminist movement because they are interested in advancing the interests of all women and not just lesbians. Some lesbians choose to work in a myriad of other venues, for a myriad of reasons. The main point is that lesbians are doing this work as visible lesbians.

Lesbians continue to be oppressed in a variety of ways, for a variety of reasons. Yet we also continue to find each other and join together. Sometimes lesbians come together only to support each other in friendship networks; at other times lesbians join forces and speak out about their oppression. The scope of lesbian activities across Canada speaks powerfully about the strength of a counterhegemonic lesbian consciousness that is spread across the country by word of mouth, in publications, and over the airwaves. Lesbians are organizing on an ad-hoc basis to address specific and pressing issues and to meet current challenges to their well-being, however they choose to define it. Whether lesbians are self-consciously engaged in political work or not, in a patriarchal, heterosexist society, the very act of naming themselves lesbian is counterhegemonic. In this sense, simply *being* lesbian is a political act.

Given the odds that are stacked against us (cf. Rich 1980), we must celebrate the variety of ways in which lesbian life flourishes. For those who would stamp out lesbianism,[27] visible lesbian diversity makes it all the more difficult to remove the lesbian option from public view. Power, as Phelan (1994: xvii) points out, is diffuse, and so must resistance be diffuse.

The lesbian movement, an amorphous movement of consciousness, is not centralized. It cannot be pinned down to any one centre, and this is its strength. A lesbian resistance that is monolithic, or a monolithic counterhegemonic politics, cannot adequately address lesbian oppression. In the 1990s lesbian feminist organizing has a predominantly diffuse and partitioned character (Ross 1995: 221). All told, that is surely how it must be if lesbians and their movement are to continue flourishing.

NOTES

1. I use the term "lesbian power" instead of "lesbian liberation" because, as argued by Phelan (1994: 124, 120), "The answer to [scientific/medical discourses] is not 'liberation,' the absence of restraint, but is power: the power to define ourselves, to describe our lives, and to be heard." As well, lesbians need "increasingly visible entry into and transformation of a system not designed by or for lesbians. This visible entry is inseparable from the project of power."

2. This is a particular perspective among many possible perspectives. For example, a lesbian of colour and/or a lesbian with no connections to the city of Toronto would no doubt offer a different perspective.

3. Readers may notice a certain confusion between the terms "lesbian feminism" and "lesbian separatism," which points to my own ambivalence about the possibility of categorically defining the differences between the two terms – an ambivalence historically reflected in lesbians' everyday speech and writings (for example, see contributions in Hoagland and Penelope's (1988) *For Lesbians Only: A Separatist Anthology*. I am persuaded by explicitly lesbian separatist arguments that what has become the heterosexual feminist movement was originally separatist in intent. As Sarah Lucia Hoagland (1988a: 6) points out, "It is erroneous to regard separatism as coming out of feminism ... rather, feminism has developed away from separatism."

    In this chapter, I generally use the term "lesbian feminism" when intending to point to lesbian activity that is consciously feminist yet not necessarily directed towards or intended to benefit other lesbians only. I use the term "lesbian separatism" when intending to point to lesbian activity that is specifically directed towards the improvement of lesbian lives. Certainly, Lesbian Nation was a separatist project. Thus, even though lesbians in the 1970s who were engaged in the project of community-building mostly defined themselves as lesbian feminists, they were actually engaged in a lesbian separatist project, and they often subscribed to a lesbian separatist ideology. For this reason and for the purpose of this chapter, I define them as lesbian separatists.

    At the same time, readers should be aware that not all of those whom I define here as lesbian separatist would necessarily recognize themselves as such, while not all of those whom I define as lesbian feminist would necessarily agree that they do not subscribe to a lesbian separatist politics. In general, I believe that the term "lesbian feminist" is often preferred over "lesbian separatist" because the former references a heterosexual movement, while the latter references a movement of autonomous females focusing on themselves. Lesbian separatism is a politics that profoundly threatens heterosexual hegemony and patriarchal relations.

4. In the following discussion I draw on this literature about LOOT and lesbian feminist organizing in Toronto. Space prevents a discussion of the rich culture created by LOOT members; for such a discussion, see Ross (1995). It is important to note that members of LOOT were almost exclusively white and young. This highlighting of activities in Toronto is in no way meant to suggest that little of note was happening elsewhere in Canada. Indeed, since the 1970s significant activity has taken place in cities such as Vancouver, Edmonton, Saskatoon, Winnipeg, Kitchener, Ottawa, Montreal, and Halifax. Rather, I focus on Toronto because of my own intimate knowledge of activities there during the late 1970s and the 1980s, and because I am able to draw on Becki Ross's (1995) detailed study of LOOT. For information about activities in other places, see back issues of *The Body Politic* (1971-87), *Pink Ink* (1983-84), and *Rites* (1984-92).

5. As one example among many of lesbians outside Toronto organizing in the 1980s: in May 1983, as lesbians in Toronto were giving up on autonomous lesbian organizing, lesbians in Vancouver organized the first ever B.C. Regional Lesbian Conference, which was attended by six hundred lesbians from across the province. Conference organizers worked to make it inclusive of lesbians of colour and accessible to women with disabilities. Another indication of the different energy level in Vancouver was the publication of the popular workbook on lesbian organizing, *Stepping out of Line* (Hughes, Johnson, and Perrault 1984).

6. AHLA differentiates itself from U.S. lesbian separatism by also arguing a need to separate from the feminist movement, which is dominated by a heterosexual agenda; see Brunet and Turcotte (1988).

7. The journal *Lesbian Ethics*, which is devoted to discussing lesbian separatist ideas, has published continuously since 1984, while in recent years books advancing lesbian separatist philosophies have been published by, among others, U.S. writers Sarah Lucia Hoagland (1988b), Jeffner Allen (1990), Julie Penelope (1992), and Marilyn Frye (1992), the British writer Sheila Jeffreys (1993), and the French writer Monique Wittig (1992). As well, several lesbian-only festivals take place on an annual basis in the United States (also attended by Canadian lesbians), and in recent years, a lesbian-only festival has been held in Quebec.

8. This assertion stems from personal observation. It is always risky to generalize from casual observation, because a subjective social location necessarily limits what one can see.

9. Despite the popularity of this image of lesbian separatists, it has never been an accurate characterization of more than a minority of lesbian separatists (cf. Ross 1995: 209).

10. Thanks to Lisa Lander, who organized the Victoria chapter of Lesbian Avengers, for information about the Lesbian Avengers.

11. Thanks to Catherine Taylor and Lee Waytkiw for information about Winnipeg.

12. Thanks to Debbie Yaffe for information about Victoria.

13. Information from the Atlantic Canada newspaper *Wayves*, June 1995: 7. Thanks to Gary Kinsman for sending me a copy.

14. Thanks to Catherine Hughes for information about THA.

15. Thanks to David Rayside for information about North Bay.

16. Thanks to Gary Kinsman for information about Sudbury and for sending me copies of SAGA's newsletter, *Northern Pride*.

17. Information from the Ottawa feminist newspaper *Hysteria/Hystérie*, Spring 1995: 4. Thanks to Barb Freeman for sending me a copy.

18. Thanks to Irène Demczuk for providing me with information and documents about the Lesbian Caucus.

19. For example, even the sensationalist tabloid *Journal de Montréal* carried (Nov. 15, 1993) an article by Claire Harting, "Une mère lesbienne n'est past une mauvaise mère" ("a lesbian mother is not a bad mother").

20. As a case in point, Majury (1994: 306) points to controversies over lesbian representation within the Ottawa-based organization Equality for Gays and Lesbians Everywhere (EGALE). Similarly, Ross (1995: 7) argues, "The inclusion of lesbians in one seamless, undifferentiated gay/lesbian movement, community, or minority obliterates and distorts the specificity of lesbian lives."

21. Several commentators note that in the 1970s lesbian feminist thought had a hegemonic status within a lesbian environment. Ross (1995: 55), for example, writes, "A particular definition of 'lesbian feminist' came to assume a certain, though not uncontested, hegemony." As well, Stein argues that in the 1970s, les-

bian feminist activity had a centre to it. She explains (1992: 37) that "while it was never unified," the lesbian feminist movement "did have a hegemonic project. It was, firstly, an effort to reconstruct the category 'lesbian,' to wrest it from the definitions of the medical experts and broaden its meaning. It was, secondly, an attempt to forge a stable collective identity around that category and to develop institutions which would nurture that identity. And thirdly, it sought to use those institutions as a base for the contestation of the dominant sex/gender system."

22. This is my translation of Caron's words: "Nous sommes tolérées en autant que nous n'affirmons pas notre identité sexuelle" (1994: 271-2).

23. Rather than "invisibility," Caron advocates using her term "invisibilization" to draw attention to the fact that lesbian invisibility is a consequence of an act of invisibilization, an act produced by a subject. In her words, "L'invisibilité des lesbiennes est conséquente d'une action d'*invisibilisation*, d'une action produite par un Sujet" (1994: 274).

24. Statement based on my translation of Caron's words: "Ces images [de lesbiennes] confrontent non seulement la perception hégémonique de l'hétéro-sexualité mais elles ont aussi l'avantage de rendre un grand nombre de gais et de lesbiennes visible à eux-mêmes" (1994: 272).

25. Statement based on my translation of Caron's words: "L'invisibilisation constitue le moyen de cacher notre existence de lesbiennes non seulement aux yeux des autres mais il nous fait aussi douter nous-mêmes de nos réalités" (1994: 285).

26. Statement based on my translation of Caron's words: "Notre invisibilisation a représenté et représente toujours un mécanisme privilégié, sinon le mécanisme principal de notre oppression" (1994: 273).

27. I am thinking not merely of those who are "uncomfortable" with lesbianism, those given to making homophobic remarks, or those who refuse to countenance discussion of homosexuality in public schools. I am thinking especially of those members of the New Christian Right who, in pamphlets and speeches, advocate death to homosexuals. These people, who are disinclined to tolerate the existence of all non-heterosexuals, are growing in numbers.

ON COUNTERHEGEMONIC FORMATION IN THE WOMEN'S MOVEMENT AND THE DIFFICULT INTEGRATION OF COLLECTIVE IDENTITIES

Jacinthe Michaud

Any study of the discursive formation of political forces of resistance must look at the elements that have the capacity to enlarge and deepen the potential for counterhegemony (Mouffe 1992; Ferguson 1991: 242). Many studies have focused their attention on the centre of political platforms, on common elements of feminist politics and social contexts that must be reached to maintain a minimal consensus (Adamson, Briskin, and McPhall 1988; Egan 1987). To counter and resist hegemony, the feminist movement in the Western world has concentrated its action on a series of issues and created political platforms that have become the basis for a feminist analysis of women's oppression. The issues, such as reproductive freedom and reproductive control through technologies, inequality between spouses, poor working conditions in both paid and unpaid work, and sexual and physical violence, are understood to be present and problematic in the lives of women regardless of their origins.

However, creating an effective counterhegemony depends on consensual practices that more fully integrate collective identities in the struggle against systems of oppression, a process that will renew its core discourse. For instance, women of colour, lesbians, women with disabilities, and women living in poverty are all living in realities that are different from one another and are different from those shaping the lives of white and middle-class women. The realities of these diverse groups of women bring perspectives to the core discourse that can deepen feminist understandings of such social issues as control over women's bodies, violence, and job discrimination. Po-

197

litical forces against racism, homophobia, heterosexism, classism, and ableism demand that feminist organizations develop a politics of resistance that enables them to better respond to multiple systems of oppression. Furthermore, the claim for visibility and representation (Young 1989) should not be politically reduced to a mere aggregation of specific concerns that leave intact any existing political platform. To that effect, it must be recognized that the formation of a hegemony within the women's movement is highly debated as well (Ship 1991; Collins 1990; Martin and Mohanty 1986).

The object of this chapter is to understand the process of counterhegemonic formation in relation to the welfare state system while taking into consideration its potential to integrate collective identities that evolve at the "margins" of the main political platform. Marginalized elements of feminist politics do not lose their autonomy of speech and their autonomy of action. Elements of discourse, even in the most repressive state of marginalization, never disappear from history (Hall 1986: 14) but continue to evolve and change with time because their identities are never fixed or achieved once and for all. Autonomy of speech and autonomy of action mean also that the margins are able to create a genuine feminist politic that is disruptive and transformative of the main feminist platform.

The first part of this exploration involves looking at the dynamic of consensual practices in relation to counterhegemonic formation. Two elements are central to this dynamic: the formation of a new state hegemonic discourse concerning women, which can be observed through welfare state policies; and the feminist counterhegemonic discourse that has emerged in response to that state discourse. The second part of the discussion involves looking at one provincial network of a women's organization in Quebec – the "Regroupement des centres de santé des femmes" (Health centres for women) – to illustrate a process of feminist counterhegemonic formation in response to scientific medicine and the health-care system. Relevant to this process is the active presence of the marginalized elements of feminist politics that are working from the margins to renew this feminist counterhegemony.

HEGEMONIC FORMATION ON WOMEN'S ISSUES
AND FEMINIST COUNTERHEGEMONIC RESISTANCE

The process of creating a feminist counterhegemonic consensus involves a multiplicity of definitions around politics of resistance and a variety of political ideologies that aim at social changes, as well as ways to carry this diversity of perspectives through the field of institutional politics. In this regard, the women's movement is confronted with the new trends in state hegemonic discourse that re-create the notion of women as a social category in need of state protection (Lamoureux 1989; Jenson 1989b; Fédération des femmes du Québec et al. 1988).

The notion of a social category in need of protection necessitates some explanations. Using the example of the abortion debate, for instance, Janine Brodie (1992: 61) explains that two types of arguments contributed to the debate of pro-choice MPs in the House of Commons in July 1988, after the Supreme Court of Canada had struck down the abortion law earlier that year: "one pragmatic and sociological and the other rights-based" (72). Of interest to Brodie is the "meaning of abortion" in political debates and how different arguments for the pro-choice position carried a very different representation of women. The pragmatic and sociological argument, for instance, carries a representation of women as victims in which "women are largely passive and in need of protective legislation" (74). In contrast, arguments based on women's rights give a representation of women based on the autonomy of a political subject free of the moral or sociological conditions used in the former argument (77). Sometimes the action of separating victimization from autonomy happens outside the world of institutional politics – although often in relation to it – and emerges from within the women's movement itself (Milan Women's Bookstore Collective 1990: 78). The interaction of feminist counterhegemony and state hegemony reveals a field of confrontation in which different forces within civil society struggle for control over the means of regulating women's lives.

The Dynamic of Consensual Practices

With the current resurgence of the concept of hegemony and of hegemony theory, the debate has moved towards the possibility that leadership and consent to social change might be achieved not by a historical bloc organized around the leadership of the working class, but by other progressive forces seeking a radical transformation of power (Bocock 1986: 12). This shift represents a break with the concepts of leadership and consent found in Marxist theory, which emphasizes unity on two levels: first, around the ruling class in the case of the bourgeois class seeking absorption of the entire society to its "cultural and economic level" (Gramsci 1992: 260); and second, around the working class as the central entity capable of undertaking the revolutionary task of overthrowing the capitalist mode of production and achieving an advanced socialist society.

The approach emphasizing the diversity of experiences and identities owes much to the work of Ernesto Laclau and Chantal Mouffe (1987). Their critique of the central position given to the working class opposes the vision that this class is the central force for social transformation, the "historical subject" owning an "ontological privilege" in the leadership of a mass movement (56). Their dismissal of this reductionism is based on an understanding of the increasing fragmentation of the social sphere and "of a indeterminacy of the articulations between different struggles and subject positions" (13). Their task is not to dismiss the reality and the visibility of fragmentation and the multiplicity of subject positions, but to find new possibilities for articulation of those elements (12).

For Laclau and Mouffe (1987: 105) the process of articulation among diverse elements composing subject positions is central. They warn against the possibility of re-creating any kind of centralism given to collective identities that could arise from the perspective of dispersion, fragmentation, and the multiplicity of subject positions (121-2). Their claim is a claim for the reconstitution of a new consensus among all those disparate elements into a reconstitution of hegemony, seen here as the centre of a given discourse, in which differences among them will be recognized, allowing a possibility of conflict within a field of open and fluid boundaries that will make the practice of hegemony possible (135-6). Concerning their definition, it is unavoidable that in this process of articulation the identity of any given subject position is modified, transformed. Laclau and Mouffe recognize the difficulty of their articulation resulting from every group's struggle to preserve its own autonomy. For them, the notion of identity is not incompatible with hegemony, because autonomy and specific identity are never achieved and are not given "once and for all."

> The feminist or ecological political subjects, for example, are up to a certain point, *like any other social identity*, floating signifiers, and it is a dangerous illusion to think that they are assured once and for all, that the terrain which has constituted their discursive conditions of emergence cannot be subverted. The question of a hegemony which would come to threaten the autonomy of certain movements is, therefore, a badly posed problem. Strictly speaking, this incompatibility would *only* exist if the social movements were nomads, disconnected one from another, but if the identity of each movement can never be acquired once and for all, then it cannot be different to what takes place outside it. (140-1)

Practically speaking, not all elements that compose the potential of feminist discourse can be integrated within the counterhegemonic consensus. The particular process of creating organizational networks around specific issues or solidarity coalitions for general purposes is always confronted by the multiplicity of definitions on the politics of resistance and the large spectrum of political ideologies that aim at social change. The diversity characterizing the women's movement can be discerned along three different dimensions, each suggesting great potential that can be used to challenge state hegemony.

First, one must take into consideration the multiplicity of definitions and politics of resistance. Women's core demands in the 1970s and 1980s brought to the forefront a long list of issues, such as abortion, control over reproduction, family norms, all forms of sexual and physical violence against women and children, compulsory heterosexuality, sexual identity, self-help, sexual division of labour, sexual and racial discrimination, unpaid women's work, and sex equality within the family and the private sphere.[1]

Second, there is a difference of opinion on the most appropriate organizational forms and strategies for achieving autonomy and control over oneself. We might include in this dimension the notion of the feminist collective (Anadón et al. 1990: 57) and the evolution of feminist organizations from pressure groups to service groups addressing women's specific needs. One also finds diversity in the various approaches to networks and coalitions, ranging both from the networking of regional and national organizations around specific women's issues (Vickers 1989) to women's political struggles for the building of solidarity coalitions within the movement itself around general issues, and from small networks built regionally and/or nationally to participation in large solidarity coalitions around issues shared with other social movements (Adamson, Briskin, and McPhail 1988).

Third, there is the spectrum of ideological positions within feminist discourse. From the politics of activism for social, political, economic, and cultural reforms to the radical politics of direct action – refusing all participation in institutions and aiming to put into place alternatives that will enhance women's autonomy – there exists a variety of political ideologies concerning how a specific organization will construct its relations with the welfare state.

In all of these discursive dimensions of difference within the feminist movement, the building of solidarity and consensus among several women's organizations sets in motion a variety of ideological tendencies aimed at creating a convergence of interest or at least reaching solidarity at the level of organizational forms, as in the formation of a network. Reaching a consensus that cuts across the three dimensions of diversity at work within the women's movement becomes a difficult task. More often than not, women's groups are achieving and maintaining political and organizational consensus on minimal grounds, and, in such a context, issues related to identity politics of race, ethnicity, sexual orientation, or ability raise the spectre of disruption of the achieved consensus (Michaud 1995: 164).

This problem illuminates the kind of difficulty that the women's movement encounters when groups of women constituted around identities such as race and sexual orientation are organizing themselves to respond to their specific oppressions (Durocher 1990; Collectif d'amazones d'hier, lesbiennes d'aujourd'hui 1986/1987; Dûcheine 1986/1987; Monique et al. 1982). The reality and the demands of women concerned with identity politics evolved apart from the demands that motivated the coming together of women's organizations willing to defend their interests in relation to the welfare state, and, by extension, the kind of reforms, policies, and social programs they wanted to introduce or maintain. It is not that constituted collective identities are not concerned with political strategy aiming at social reforms, it is that they are concerned with the lack of representation they encounter within social movements, such as the women's movement, that proclaim to fight all sorts of discriminations. A much broader consensus is possible if there is space for identity-based groups to make their claims visible and defend them in a way that demonstrates their significance to the broad feminist counter-hegemony. Still, such inclusion requires a qualitative transformation of feminist counterhegemonic positions, which involves redefining the way in which feminist organizations tend to defend their interests in relation to hegemonic formations.

The New Trends in State Discourse on Women

If we look at changes in the state discourse on women's issues, we can observe many significant shifts now enshrined in law, policies, and social programs. To illustrate those changes, Heather Jon Maroney (1988) demonstrates how reforms arise from the integration of feminist demands through state administrative bodies such as the "Conseil du Statut de la Femme" (CSF). Maroney's work demonstrates that the Quebec women's movement has successfully achieved a major shift in legal discourses within the political scene. The CSF "has developed a close relation with sections of the women's movement, has carried out a comprehensive review of governmental policy, and has shown in its criticisms a real political independence from governing parties" (26). Maroney indicates a significant "historical shift in the legal form of gender structures," which has ideological and political implications. The masculine subject is no longer explicitly the primary political subject. "(The we) interpellated by public political discourse has moved from being explicitly and then implicitly masculine to become implicitly and then explicitly both masculine and feminine." These changes also indicate that women as a collective force have been able to impose their demands within the political arena, forcing the state to adapt its strategies and to compose a new hegemony around "egalitarianism" (27).

Nonetheless, what is the real content of the new "egalitarianism" adopted by the state? At which level does the state meet the demands of the women's movement, and which parts of the movement are represented through public administrative and state structures?[2] When the concept of equality is applied to women, there are at least two sets of problems that cannot be overlooked. One is the use of a gender-neutral language that, when applied in the context of the family policy,[3] to use one example, has the effect of undermining the particularity of women's lives in the private sphere. A second is the several ways of being equal: equality of rights before the law, equality of economic power and/or political influence, equality in social relations, equality in gender relations, and so forth.[4] These variations shed light more on the different locations of power and states of inequality than on the condition of equality itself (Marcil-Lacoste 1987). When the normative applications of the notion of equality cannot be met, state intervention into women's lives is legitimated in the name of help and protection, and welfare policies are presented as bridging the gap between states of unequal conditions. Under this egalitarian ideology, the kind of equality that the state offers to women means the institutionalization of a state of inequality while espousing the objective of reaching a point of an acceptable "minimal equality" (Henderich 1989).

Social programs for protection and the redressing of women's unequal status are considered necessary before women can become potential equals to men in the public sphere. These policies and programs are not formulated from the perspective of the autonomy of the person. They are formulated instead to enhance women's capacity to perform their work in the public and domestic spheres, while minimizing the impact of poor living conditions on their lives (Acker 1989). The Quebec family policy, for instance, encourages two-parent families in which both parents cope with family obligations and share their time equally between professional and parental work (Acker 1989; Secrétariat à la famille 1989; Gouvernement du Québec 1987: 7). This new model reinforces the norm of compulsory heterosexuality and privileges certain lifestyles, educational patterns, and patterns of individual competition and consumption. Yet old definitions of normality and deviance remain unchanged. The fact that new family policies have come to recognize both the existence of other family units and the unwillingness of a large number of women to have children does not transform the traditional norm of the heterosexual family unit.[5]

Such has been the state response to women's demands during the last two decades, cleverly adapting ideological and political discourse from the past to fit the reality of the present. When feminist discourse first arose within the political arena, it had to counter a vision of women's representation based on a perception of their roles and capacity that deemed them unequipped for the political sphere and excluded them from it (Regroupement provincial des maisons 1990). State response represents an amalgamation of other discursive representations of women, sometimes in confrontation with one another and carried on by different groups – feminist, fiscalist, familialist, and so forth – already in place or newly emerged within the field of institutional politics.

When we consider the dynamic happening in this field of institutional politics, it is important that we see the dynamic of every social force, in which legitimacy, debated issues, and choice of policy are determined for transformation (Jenson 1991, 1989b, 1986). The state plays two roles in the process: first, distributing a legitimacy that will limit the number of actors, using its own legitimate power to set the agenda for debated issues and choice of policy and to determine the course of action towards achieving meaning; and second, as a participant, considering that its own legitimacy is never completely achieved and can only be reached through its representation of social forces struggling for meaning within civil society. As such the state should be seen as a participant among others, involved in the process of achieving the construction of meaning, making alliances with selected social forces and conflicting with others, defending its own interests (Franzway, Court, and Cornell 1989; Hall 1984).[6]

THE HEALTH CENTRES MOVEMENT FOR WOMEN STRUGGLING WITH THE INCLUSION OF COLLECTIVE IDENTITIES

Health centres constitute the smallest network of women's service groups in Quebec.[7] However, the unique experience of health centres is characterized by the creation of a site in which women can find a complete range of alternative services in the areas of abortion and self-help practices. Compared with what women can expect from traditional medical establishments, women's clinics have developed their own genuine medical infrastructures and provide women with alternative and feminist-oriented health care.

In relation to other women's service groups in general, health centres positioned themselves in a somewhat different way towards governmental apparatuses, in particular the Ministry of Health and Social Services. In contrast to other networks (shelters for women, the network against sexual violence, and the large women's centres network), the health centres movement is concerned not only with the state-controlled health-care system but also scientific medicine, against which it has directed its most radical critiques. Therefore, it is possible to find within the health centres' political platform an interesting and complex position of participation/non-participation with this system.[8] The health centres movement tried to differentiate itself from scientific medicine at the same time that it was caught in the dynamic of participation for reforms and policies (Bégin 1989).

Health centres in Quebec enjoyed moments of high visibility, political mobilization, and growth, but were also hurt by periods of stagnation and decline. Their discourse on self-help politics shaped a specific feminist framework within which those clinics were organized. However, the concept of self-help needs to be analysed not only in terms of its content but also in terms of its relationship with diverse groups of women.

Self-Help: The Discourse
What feminist health activists claim they are doing within health centres is directly related to their analysis of scientific medicine and the health-care system, the ideas they have about what kind of transformation is needed, and the kind of democratic process they want to introduce within the system as well as within civil society (Regroupement des centres de santé 1991; O'Leary 1986; Saillant 1985; Comité de lutte pour l'avortement libre et gratuit 1978). According to feminist ideology, the politics of self-help is based on the autonomy developed through the acquisition of individual and collective knowledge leading towards control over women's bodies (Boston Women's Health Collective 1971). It is the belief that if women are well informed about their anatomy and physiology, they can make their own choices regarding

their health, their reproductive lives, and the prevention of illness, and they can improve their abilities to demand and receive services related to their needs (Simonds, Kay, and Regan 1984; Morgen 1982; Rusek 1978).

Feminist health activists add another dimension to the meaning of self-help: that collective learning and sharing of knowledge be practised with true equality among the providers and the consumers of alternative health services (O'Leary 1986). Furthermore, beyond the individual control over women's bodies, another aim is to control how services are provided to women. This control gives health centres a decisive role to play and a voice within the medicare system (Bégin 1989; Comité de lutte pour l'avortement libre et gratuit 1978).

More specifically, health centres in Quebec have articulated their aims as the three "Ds": *démédicalisation*, *déprofessionalisation*, and *désexisation*. The fundamental principles imbedded in the three "Ds" represent the health centres' orientation towards radical change in the relationships that women have with scientific medicine and the health-care system.[9] The three "Ds" express health centres' intentions to put in place alternative practices that mirror their feminist perspectives on health. They express a feminist denunciation of a system that victimizes women, as well as the willingness to transform that system by developing a feminist expertise that enhances women's autonomy (Centre de santé des femmes du quartier 1986a: 2).

The definition of each of these three elements reveals a feminist discourse that has considered health centres as a site for experiencing another way of practising medicine, a space in which different relations among women, based on their global lived experiences, become possible. From this specific location feminist health activists intend to transform how scientific medicine is practised in civil society. For instance, *déprofessionaliser* supposes the demystification of medical language, the transmission of maximum information on health, a relation based on collective exchange among providers and consumers of alternatives services, and:

L'insertion de chaque acte médical dans le contexte général, individuel et social, qui le motive, de façon à permettre aux femmes d'acquérir des informations en ce qui a trait à leur anatomie, à leur physiologie et à leur santé mentale. Cette information leur donne du contrôle sur leur corps et leur permet de choisir véritablement, parce que consciemment, les décisions concernant la résolution de leurs problèmes de santé (Centre de santé des femmes du quartier 1986a: 3).*

----

* "The integration of every medical act within the general context, individual or social, that motivated it, in a way which will allow women to acquire information concerning their autonomy, their physiology, and their mental health. This information gives them control over their bodies and allows them to really choose, because consciously, the decisions concerning the resolution of their health problems."

Each of the three "Ds" forms a close interrelation between the victimization of women by the medical system and the need to develop a practice that enhances women's consciousness and autonomy. In their intent to *démédicaliser* aspects of women's lives, feminist health activists aim to change women's perceptions of themselves, to transform their relations with their own bodies, and to give women their autonomy through collective means (Centre de santé des femmes du quartier 1986a: 3).

Finally, in the case of *désexisation*, the feminist analysis consists of a denunciation of a predominantly male system, whose consumers are mainly women. Scientific medicine has established not only a double standard of treatment for women and men, but enforces gynaecological violence through mutilations of reproductive organs by unnecessary surgeries, and even sometimes sexual violence (Centre de santé des femmes du quartier 1986a: 3).

Although not all health centres have articulated their aims with the same precision, each health centre encompasses the same shared vision.[10] Elements of *déprofessionalisation*, *démédicalisation*, and *désexisation* were given enough importance within their discourse that members of each centre continually questioned themselves on the space and the specific location these elements occupied within their organization and daily practices (Regroupement des centres de santé 1991: 5-8, s.d.).

The construction of such a feminist discourse has been developed concurrently with the existence of a widespread feminist movement in general and in health in particular (Bégin 1989; Saillant 1985). Moreover, at the end of the 1970s and the beginning of the 1980s, there existed an important network of feminist health professionals – nurses, social workers, women's doctors – who were active at many levels of the health-care system. The feminist discourse on the three "Ds" has been influential enough so that many feminist activists working in other women's groups or even within medical establishments can refer to it and make changes within their own practice. Furthermore, the nature of the services rendered to women by health centres forces the centres to establish links with parts of the health-care system, mainly CLSCs (Centres locaux de services communautaires), and to some extent local hospitals. From the beginning, the exchange of services was necessitated by possible situational emergencies and laboratory tests of all kinds; and some medical establishments referred women to health centres in their region for specific services.

Exchanges between health centres and the traditional medical establishments indicate that some sort of feminist knowledge and expertise were circulating between the two entities (Michaud 1992). This circulation of services, of feminist health-care providers and activists, of feminist knowledge and expertise, coming from both the alternative and the mainstream level of the health-care system, is real but very difficult to measure. Also, because a large number of women still relied on mainstream medicine (Bégin 1989) the health centres could not ignore the presence of the state-controlled health-care system. The "unavoidability of the state," as some authors put it, was part of the daily reality of health centres' practices (Regroupement provincial des maisons d'hébergement 1990: 140; see also Franzway, Court, and Connell 1989).

Women's health centres and a great number of feminist health activists have devoted their time and energies to filling a serious gap in the health-care system. Yet, to some extent, the health-care system has largely taken advantage of their expertise and knowledge without acknowledging the feminist critique that comes with it (O'Leary 1986). The issue of the integration/co-optation of feminist knowledge and expertise is important to consider, because it sheds light on how hegemony operates with alternative services that challenge its position of authority (Worcester and Whatley 1988: 18).

The Difficult Integration of Collective Identities in Feminist Health Discourse
Yet health centres' expertise was said to be based on the globality of women's lives (Morgen 1990, 1986, 1982; Thurston 1987; O'Leary 1986; Simmons, Kay, and Regan 1984; Fee 1983). The way in which feminist health activists integrated women's reality into their knowledge and expertise is the fundamental aspect in the formation of a powerful counterhegemony. In counterpoint to the mainstream definition of health – a definition that barely considers the social, the political, the economic, and the cultural contexts within which women and men live (Turner 1992: 136; Clarke 1990) – the health centres movement presents an approach that potentially takes into consideration issues of poverty, working conditions, housing situations, and overmedication. To continue to pose a real challenge to scientific medicine, health centres have to deepen and enlarge their main political platform by integrating marginalized elements of feminist politics and collective identities that propose a radical critique to hegemony in their own terms.

Nevertheless, beyond good intentions regarding health centres' desire to consider the globality of women's lives, how do they integrate different realities within their feminist political platform? How do they deal with the fact that poverty, racism, and homophobia have a significant impact not only on women's health but also on their own political platform? Issues such as ethnicity, class, and sexual orientation, for instance, are put forth by groups of women eager to demonstrate that their reality has a significant impact on their health and that feminist discourse should reflect it. The dynamic of consensual practices, in renegotiating the conditions for the integration of these issues, is confronted with the challenge to transform feminist counterhegemony in a way that is qualitative – which means that feminist discourse, to be inclusive, will do more than simply add issues as a mere appendix to its main political platform. The integration of issues through the challenging presence of constituted groups of women becomes the necessary condition for such transformation.

Take, for instance, the issue of sexual orientation. Lesbian politics made its way through the Montreal health centre first in demanding recognition and visibility and second in questioning former feminist discourses on sexuality. The lesbian clinic in the Montreal health centre (1982-85) – the first of its kind to provide a full range of health services specifically for lesbians (Centre de santé des femmes du quartier 1986b) – was an experience created through the initiative of some lesbian health activists within the centre.[11] However, it provoked misunderstandings among co-workers, who, at the beginning of the clinic, did not grant lesbian voices any specific relevance to the main issue of women's health. Some co-workers went as far as dismissing lesbian experience totally.

Already, lesbian identity and experience are hardly discussed within the broader women's movement (Femmes en tête 1990; Chamberland 1989). As far as the Montreal health centre is concerned, the issue of lesbians' health emerged, and still operates, at the margin of the health centre's alternative services (Centre de santé des femmes du quartier 1986b: 5-6). Nonetheless, the lesbian clinic became the point of entry for challenging feminist discourse within the entire health centres movement.[12] Lesbian activists in Montreal and some other health centres went beyond the first demand of naming their specific oppression and the demand for the recognition of their needs, their visibility, and their autonomy. Furthermore, they located themselves within the feminist counterhegemony and within the feminist tradition of self-help. Lesbian activists were among those who most challenged the expert/client relations. Their full engagement with the self-help feminist ideology inspired the health centre's practice (Centre de santé des femmes du quartier 1986b: 8-13). From this vantage point lesbian activists elaborated a lesbian critique about how sexuality was talked about within the health centre, and they demanded that their feminist co-workers transform their approach to allow every woman to express her lived reality, regardless of her sexual practice and resistance to compulsory heterosexuality (Michaud 1995: 291).

A discourse on class was more difficult to integrate within feminist core demands, although the necessity of providing alternative services to working-class women and women on welfare counted among the priorities of the first generation of feminist health activists.[13] Health centres had some success in reaching women who lived in poor economic conditions. However, the absence of a constituted group of women acting from within, as in the case of lesbian politics, resulted in the lack of integration of a class perspective into feminist self-help discourse itself (Michaud 1995: 299) – a class perspective that reflected how, why, and in which conditions a single mother, for instance, needs to have access to abortion, mental health care, or information about the biology and physiology of her body. If feminist discourse on health encompasses issues that influence women's health (O'Leary 1986) – such as access to affordable housing, violence, social isolation, being a single mother on welfare – many critics have pointed out many contradictions in self-help politics, which remains too narrow in its definition of women's health (Fee 1983; Rusek 1978) and fails to reach categories of women hurt by social and economic conditions as opposed to those who benefit from a white middle-class background (Morgen 1990, 1986; Foster 1989; Simmons, Kay, and Regan 1984).

Finally, if the presence of working-class women was knowingly problematic within the health centres, the question of race hardly became a real issue. If we have difficulty in measuring the extent to which issues of class have modified the feminist counterhegemony on health, the question of race remains practically invisible despite the significant number of women of colour requesting abortion services, especially in metropolitan cities like Montreal and Hull. If the question of race did become visible, it was treated at best as a question of equal access for all women to the health centres' alternative services (Michaud 1995: 299).

Racism is central to the specific reality of women and shapes their relations not only with Western scientific medicine (Anderson 1990) and the health-care system but also within the health centres movement and the women's movement as a whole.[14] There is a lack of representation of collective voices from within the health centres movement aiming at the transformation of the discourse on health from the perspective of ethnicity, which would point out the effect of racism and racist bias in scientific medicine on all the issues raised by health centres themselves. There is no such visibility or space given to groups of women with a collective identity that could make their issues central to the main discourse of abortion and self-help politics and contribute to the shape of current feminist counterhegemony on health generally. However, there are women's organizations constituted on the basis of race and ethnicity that are very active and pose a direct challenge to the centre of feminist discourse.[15]

Even with the apparent absence of questioning from within the health centres movement, as in the case of race and to a lesser extent with class, or with a partial integration of issues such as sexual orientation, collective identities are emerging at the margins of the main political platform. In the context in which the health centres movement continues to define health-related issues and has based its counterhegemonic discourse on women's experience globally, it is possible to envision the day when activism from groups of women with collective identities will force the renewal of feminist counterhegemony.

CONCLUSION

Because the women's health centres movement is engaged in all sorts of solidarity coalitions at the regional and provincial levels, and despite a sense of organizational autonomy they want preserved, they cannot remain hermetic to their environment and to the changing context within the larger community of women. The renewal of feminist counterhegemony on health is a dynamic process, and the challenge to its core discourse is happening from within as well as from outside women's organizations. Feminist strategies have attempted to create feminist counterhegemonic responses to infuse feminist politics into the welfare state system identified as the site of the organization of consent and the regulation of women's lives.

Counterhegemony operates not only in relation to state hegemony and to the hegemony of scientific medicine but also in relation to what is evolving outside the feminist consensus. The signs of movement towards the creation of a hegemony within the women's movement are visible, but the voices against its universality of speech in many areas of feminist politics are multiple as well. As we have seen, there are concrete examples of challenges that aim at feminist counterhegemony, from the margins to the centre – and this contestation has the potential to reshape the current counterhegemonic formation. But marginalized elements of feminist discourses that have the potential to achieve a greater feminist counterhegemony are still fragmented, as is feminist counterhegemonic formation in its discourse in relation to hegemony. Nevertheless, the potential for transformation remains: the action from the margins towards the centre exists, and the presence of collective identities is perceptible in the constant renewal of feminist discourse.

NOTES

1. Haraway (1990) includes a long list of references using the term "sexual politics." See also Flax (1990) on the lack of theoretical consensus among feminists concerning the definition of the concept of "gender."
2. Grant and Tancred (1991) argue that the structure of representation of "women's issues" within state bureaucracy ensures that women are concentrated in relatively powerless positions in those ministries and posts in which the need for "adjunct control" predominates.
3. See in particular the chapter on job market and parental practices in Secrétariat à la famille (1989). The gender-neutral language used in this policy sets general norms around parental practices, starting with the assumptions that equality in gender relations has become part of Quebec society and most parents today have to cope with the reality of balancing professional work and parental responsibilities. The real involvement of women and men in terms of their lived reality in parental work and domestic work is neither analysed nor described.
4. Marcil-Lacoste (1987: 200-6) indicates 140 ways of being equal in the twentieth century; see also Jaggar (1983) on the origin of the concept of equality.
5. According to Paquette (1989: 7), only 66 per cent of women will give birth in their life.
6. The work of Jenson (1986, 1989b, 1991) has some interest here as it relates to the dynamic of what she calls the "universe of political discourse," in which competitive collective identities are carrying their own meaning system, making alli-

ances with some collective identities while entering in confrontation with other, in all efforts to transform social paradigms.

7. The concept of women's service groups is given to women's organizations providing immediate services in response to women's specific needs. Shelters for women victims of family violence; centres for victims of sexual violence (CALACS), health centres for women, and women's centres are examples of women's services groups.

   The information in this section comes entirely from a group's documents and personal interviews undertaken with informants from five Quebec health centres (Montreal, Sherbrooke, Quebec City, Trois-Rivières, and Hull) and their provincial network (Regroupement des centres de santé des femmes du Québec). For more details about the methodology used for this research, see Michaud (1995).

8. In my chapter in the first edition of this book (1992), I analysed a specific document from the health centres movement that defended the position of non-participation in relation to the welfare state system, a position that appears to be countercurrent to other positions of participation within women's groups (see Relais-femmes 1985: 15). Although this position was at one time strongly debated within the Regroupement des centres de santé, it was confronted with other internal positions of participation similar to the orientation taken by other women's service groups.

9. See Centre de santé des femmes du quartier (1989), *Objectifs du centre de santé des femmes du quartier*, [s.l.] 4 pages; (1986a), *Représentation écrite présentée à la Commission d'enquête sur les services de santé et les services sociaux*, Montreal, 16 pages; [s.d.], *Présentation du centre du santé des femmes: Kit d'intégration des militantes*, Montreal, 19 pages; Regroupement des centres de santé des femmes (1986b), *Compte rendu du Forum, "Idéologie et financement des centres de santé pour femmes du Québec*, Montreal, 23 pages; (1985), *Le développement des centres de santé des femmes: une contribution importante à l'amélioration des conditions de vie des femmes*, 3 pages; [s.d.], *Documents de réflexion pour le forum idéologie*, 16 pages.

10. See, from the Regroupement des centres de santé des femmes du Québec (1991), *Cadre de référence des centres de santé des femmes du Québec*, [s.l.], 28 pages; (1987), *Un regard de l'intérieur: bilan des centres de santé des femmes du Québec*, Caroline Larue (rédaction), [s.l.], 83 pages; and (1986a), *Les centres de santé de femmes du Québec*, représentation écrite présentée à la Commission d'enquête sur les services de santé et les services sociaux, Hull, 18 pages. Also, Centre de santé des femmes de Sherbrooke Inc. (1986), *Document présenté à la Commission d'enquête sur les services de santé et les services sociaux du Québec*, préparé par le centre de santé des femmes de Sherbrooke inc., Sherbrooke, 11 pages; and Le centre de santé des femmes de Sherbrooke (1985), *Mouvement d'auto-santé*, rédigé pour le Regroupement des centres de santé des femmes du Québec, October, 17 pages.

11. The lesbian clinic ceased operation in 1985 but was immediately replaced by a self-help group on lesbian health.

12. For instance, the health centre in Sherbrooke followed the path of the Montreal health centre and set up a workshop on lesbian health and sexuality. See Carole Tatlock (Centre de santé des femmes de Sherbrooke) and Louise Picard (CALACS, Trève pour elles, Montreal) (1994), "Santé lesbienne, j'connais pas," 2 pages; followed by "La question lesbienne au centre de santé des femmes de Sherbrooke," 1 page, présentation, l'Association pour la santé publique du

Québec, *Forum sur la santé gaie*, Université du Québec à Montréal: October 27-28, 1994.

13. Centre de santé des femmes qu quartier (n.d.), "Historique: souper-causerie avec Louise Vandelac, Ginette Fortier, Lise Lapierre et Francine Dandurand, organisé par Catherine Germain," audiotape, Montreal. See also O'Leary and Toupin 1982, in which they underline the influence of neonationalism and neo-Marxist ideologies on the first generation of feminist activists at the end of the 1960s and beginning of the 1970s.

14. Concerning issues of racism within the women's movement in Quebec, see Ship 1991; Dûcheine 1986/1987.

15. See, for instance, Monique, Rosemary et Vivian (1982). This article lists (50-1) a number of Haitian women's groups created in relation to the lack of response from the Quebec women's movement to Haitian women's needs. See also Pole (1990).

MANAGING AIDS ORGANIZING: "CONSULTATION," "PARTNERSHIP," AND "RESPONSIBILITY" AS STRATEGIES OF REGULATION

Gary Kinsman

*DEDICATED – to the lives and memories of Michael Smith, 1958-91;
Michael Lynch, 1944-91; Doug Wilson, who died in 1992; George Smith,
1935-94; Kalpesh Oza, 1961-95; and Father Mike McDonald,
who died in 1995*

I attended the Atlantic AIDS Network meeting, in November 1990 in St. John's, Newfoundland, as an AIDS activist.[1] This Network brings "community-based" AIDS groups in the region together to address common concerns.[2]

Glancing at the agenda I realized there was going to be significant input from the federal government. As I experienced it, this meeting focused around a federal state-defined agenda. This included a talk by Judy Wright, then executive director of the AIDS Secretariat, the administrative centrepiece of the National AIDS Strategy. The Secretariat was set up to co-ordinate federal departments working on AIDS, to connect various other agencies with federal ones, and to co-ordinate relations with community-based groups. What I experienced was the articulation of AIDS groups to federal state agencies, with the AIDS Secretariat being offered as the "entry point" for community groups.

Another key speaker at the meeting was Kathy Coffin of Health Promotions (Atlantic Region), who co-ordinated federal AIDS Community Action Program (ACAP) funding for AIDS groups in this region.[3] People listened intently to what she said and asked questions regarding funding procedures. In a region where provincial governments generally provide little funding for

AIDS groups, ACAP funding is crucial. The AIDS Secretariat and ACAP were crucial aspects of a distinct AIDS bureaucracy constructed at the federal level.

Not everyone at the meeting felt comfortable with this federal state influence. There was a vague feeling of unease, which surfaced for some people as a sense of frustration that we were not dealing with the issues raised for us in our local AIDS work. It was an experience of frustration that was socially organized. How was it, then, that a meeting of community-based AIDS groups was less organized by our own local needs and more by the policies of the federal AIDS bureaucracy? How was it that, generally speaking, the needs of people living with AIDS/HIV (PLWA/HIVs) were marginalized in the actual accomplishment of this conference?

These were not simply problems produced by a badly organized meeting, for they were rooted in the extralocal practices of state management of AIDS groups. The meeting was organized in large part through the "national" relations in which local and regional AIDS organizing has become enmeshed, so that agencies based in Ottawa came to shape its direction. The actual organization and regulation of community-based groups become part of the work of state agencies.[4]

Two years later in Nova Scotia I was involved in lobbying efforts on the part of community-based AIDS groups during the formation of the provincial AIDS strategy. We attempted to get this strategy to meet the needs of PLWA/HIVs and those most affected by AIDS (Kinsman 1992). After almost a year of "consultation" and a series of meetings with two different ministers of health and health department representatives, the resulting strategy, while it embodied some advances, did not meet the objectives that community-based groups had set out. In particular it did not meet the needs of PLWA/HIVs. Again, "consultation" and "partnership" with a government did not lead to the meeting of crucial AIDS concerns. What I and others experienced in Nova Scotia on a provincial level had many similarities to the experience at the Atlantic AIDS Network meeting in St. John's.

AIDS ORGANIZING AS A SOCIAL MOVEMENT

AIDS organizing emerged as a social movement in the early 1980s. In North America AIDS groups first grew out of the gay and lesbian movements and began to involve progressive health-care workers. They developed as social movements in response to state inaction and indifference, problems with the medical profession, and social discrimination against gays, Haitians, injection drug users, and sex-trade workers. Community-based support and educational groups were set up in the early and mid-1980s (Patton 1986; Altman 1986, 1994).

By the later 1980s a new wave of AIDS activism had developed as state regulations, the medical profession, and drug corporations deterred access to badly needed treatments that could extend the lives of PLWA/HIVs (Crimp 1988; Crimp with Rolston 1990; Callen 1990). Treatment-based activism emerged out of the contradiction between the possibility that people could survive and resist AIDS and HIV infection longer and the medical, pharmaceutical, and state policies that continued to deny this possibility. This activism was initially based largely among white middle-class gay men, lesbians, and health activists and was defined largely around their concerns. Following the self-organization of a number of previously excluded groups, it has now been extended to other communities that had been excluded from the social response to AIDS, including people of colour, First Nations people, and women ("Living with HIV 1992; The ACT UP/New York Women and AIDS Book Group 1990; Rudd and Taylor 1992).

More recently activism has begun to focus on questions of poverty and the needed social supports regarding nutrition, adequate food, vitamins, and good housing that are preconditions for the survival of PLWA/HIVs (Mykhalovskiy and Smith 1994). This shift has directed concerns towards the lack of funding for needed treatments and lack of access to badly needed social services and supports for PLWA/HIVs, which has in turn raised important class questions that some AIDS groups have begun to address. AIDS activism has politicized questions of health and sexuality as informed by gay movement politics and the feminist health movement's emphasis on empowerment. PLWA/HIVs empowered themselves and challenged and transformed medical professional relations, even challenging how scientific and medical research is done (Epstein 1991; G. Smith: 1989).

The social organization of the AIDS crisis, which is a condensation of many social relations, has meant that AIDS activism has had to confront questions of sexuality, race, haemophilia, gender, and class in varying ways. AIDS organizing is one of the most profound social movements ever to emerge around health issues. In the United States and to a lesser extent in Canada this activist approach is now being used by feminist groups to combat breast cancer (Epstein 1991: 37). Still, research on AIDS in Canada has only begun to comprehensively address the state regulation of AIDS organizing.[5]

There is, then, an experience of rupture between the needs of community-based AIDS organizing and state and often professional regulatory practices on the federal and provincial levels. Where these experiences of disjuncture come from – looking at these social processes from the social standpoints of AIDS activists and PLWA/HIVs – is my main orienting question here.[6]

TEXTS AND REGULATION

A crucial aspect of how this regulatory relation has been put in place is the National AIDS Strategy, including how it continued to inform federal and provincial state practices regarding AIDS until at least 1996. This strategic framework informed the development of an AIDS strategy in Nova Scotia in 1992-93. In many areas this regulatory strategy clearly continues. By early 1997 aspects of this regulatory strategy were, however, being phased out, with further National AIDS Strategy funding uncertain.

In this case, an analysis of textually mediated social organization (D. E. Smith 1990b: 209-24) points us towards how texts such as government documents and policies play an important part in the organization of ruling in this society.

Government texts such as AIDS strategy documents are attempts to organize social policies regarding the AIDS crisis, one feature of which is the management of AIDS groups. They are not simply passive, "objective," or neutral knowledge, but actively co-ordinate social practices among various institutions (D. E. Smith 1990a: 61-104, 1990b: 120-58,209-24). As D. E. Smith puts it, texts "actively organize the social relations in which they are embedded" (1982: 46). Documents can be attempts at providing conceptual organization for the co-ordination of state and professional responses to "social problems" (Walker 1990). They organize knowledge in particular directions and from particular standpoints, which often include the containment of social movements.

Unfortunately, this examination of state and other official texts is not done enough in studies of social movements and state regulation. Regulation is often accomplished through these texts and how they are read and used. They are an important part of the social organization of hegemony, which counterhegemonic politics must address.[7] This investigation engages us not only "theoretically" but also very practically with the history and politics of AIDS.[8]

My research is political-activist ethnography (G. W. Smith 1990a) through my involvement in AIDS ACTION NOW! (AAN!) in Toronto in the summer of 1990 (and previously) and again in early 1994; in the Newfoundland AIDS Association in 1989-91; and in the Valley AIDS Concern Group and the Coalition of Nova Scotia AIDS Community Groups in 1992-93. This work combines "data" collected through attendance at meetings and conferences with textual analysis of preparatory and final federal and provincial AIDS strategy documents. I examine these AIDS strategies as attempted regulation-building upon previous policies with greater conceptual co-ordination around themes of "consultation" and "partnership." Such language is a vehicle for organizing the activities of people in institutional and community-based settings. I examine how the strategic approach articulated in the National AIDS Strategy was used and adapted in the Nova Scotian context to manage community-based AIDS groups in that province (Kinsman 1992). This exploration is part of a broader exploration of relations between movement organizing and state regulatory agencies and draws on insights from this work (Ng 1988; Ng, Walker, and Muller 1990; Morgan 1981).

A BRIEF HISTORY OF FEDERAL AIDS POLICY

Then federal Health Minister Perrin Beatty's (1988-91) AIDS strategy was released on June 28, 1990. This was more than eight years into the impact of the AIDS crisis in this country; after years of organizing by community-based AIDS groups, AIDS activists, and PLWA/HIVs – a history that is not visible in the strategy texts.

For the purpose of analysis the response of federal state agencies to the AIDS crisis can be roughly divided into five overlapping periods.[9] Between these "periods" there are elements of continuity as well as discontinuity.

Firstly, in the early 1980s federal agencies basically ignored AIDS, aside from the collection of epidemiological information by the Laboratory Centres for Disease Control in Ottawa, some job-creation funding for the first community-based groups, and some "public health" measures. In the face of this inaction badly needed community-based support and education groups emerged in a number of centres.

In the mid-1980s the second period began when the federal government provided more than job-creation funding and began to systematically fund community-based groups through Health Promotions. Under Health Minister Jake Epp (1984-88) there were major problems around lack of action on treatment delivery for PLWA/HIVs and lack of co-operation with community-based groups. State AIDS policies were completely defined by palliative care and public health concerns, basically assuming that PLWAs were going to die and defending the "general public" from "infection" from PLWAs and affected communities. During these years federal agencies began to do some educational work on prevention issues – but with major limitations.[10]

State agencies built their work in a piecemeal fashion on top of the previous responses of social agencies. A relation developed between AIDS organizing and state regulation, which was sometimes "consensual" but sometimes conflictual, as at the National AIDS conference in May 1988 in Toronto when AIDS activists burned an effigy of Epp at the end of a demonstration against federal AIDS policy.

In the third period the emergence of a new treatment-based activism, which gained wide support among the community-based groups, forced Beatty to take up a new orientation when he became health minister in 1988. The old strategies were no longer cogent and were producing growing problems. Beatty promised a new strategy based on a process of "consultation" in response to the concerns of community-based groups. This strategy, while it was still primarily based in discourses of public health and palliative care, was also based on a conceptualization of "partnership" with community-based groups and represented at least a partial and limited break with past policies in recognizing some of the treatment-information concerns of PLWA/HIVs.

This preparatory "third" period of "consultation" was largely tranquil, but it did include a demonstration on March 15, 1990, of three hundred people organized by AAN! demanding federal action on treatment delivery and a treatment registry. As AIDS activist George Smith (1990b: 1) wrote: "The national AIDS Strategy was designed basically to solve the political problems the Minister and the Department of Health and Welfare faced with regards to AIDS, rather than the specific problems faced by people with HIV infection. The strategy, in other words, was designed from the standpoint of the federal government."

The fourth period was marked by a continuation of the essential features of the National AIDS Strategy, with a falling off of AIDS activism on the federal level. The decline in this activity was partly because community-based groups and activists began to focus on questions under provincial and even municipal jurisdiction given the division of labour within Canadian state formation. This new focus encompassed social support policies, anonymous HIV testing,[11] and funding for treatments. During these years provincial AIDS strategies informed by the National AIDS strategy were developed in a number of provinces.

In its 1993 text "National AIDS Strategy, Phase II, Building on Progress," the federal government signalled the continuation of the main themes of the National AIDS strategy and claimed major progress in meeting some of the strategy's objectives. This second phase would have raised annual AIDS funding from $37.3 million to $42.2 million by 1997, a level still grossly inadequate in meeting AIDS needs. Actual funding never went above $40.7 million a year. The only major policy and funding shifts were in more clearly mandating funding and support for "Recognizing HIV Disease as a Chronic and Progressive Condition" and "Health Promotion for People Living with HIV Disease and AIDS" (Health and Welfare Canada 1993). The government also provided funding for a *Canadian Survey of Gay and Bisexual Men and HIV Infection* (Myers, Godin, Calzarara, Lambert, and Locker 1993) and for a number of woman and AIDS, Black outreach, and First Nations AIDS projects.

The falling off of activism on the federal level allowed state agencies to partially deprioritize AIDS questions, to not undertake new major AIDS initiatives, and to cut back on the level of total funding for community-based AIDS groups. The year 1995 can be seen as the start of a new fifth period opened up by the very success of the National AIDS Strategy in managing AIDS groups. This stage has created the basis for the federal government to demote and deprioritize AIDS funding and initiatives. In the realm of AIDS concerns it has now become more like business as usual. The federal government reshuffled responsibilities within Health Canada, effectively demoting the National AIDS Secretariat.[12] In February 1995 it became clear that then Health Minister Diane Marleau was not spending all the funds allocated under the National AIDS Strategy (Hannon 1995). Phase Two of the National AIDS Strategy would end in March 1998, with no commitment made for funding beyond that point or for a third phase of the National AIDS Strategy

(Pavelich 1996). The context of federal policies focusing on "deficit-reduc-tion," fiscal restraint, and cutbacks in transfer payments in health-care fund-ing to the provinces made it much more difficult for efforts to meet the needs of PLWA/HIVs; and the deterioration of health-care services and re-sources more generally will have a detrimental impact on PLWA/HIVs.

In response to this turn of affairs AIDS groups engaged in a partial but still limited remobilization. In July 1996, just before the opening of the Inter-national AIDS conference in Vancouver, a thousand AIDS activists marched against the AIDS policies of the Chrétien government and for the renewal of the National AIDS Strategy. Chrétien refused to attend the AIDS conference, even though the head of government usually opens these conferences. The protests did effectively embarrass the federal government – the actions tem-porarily captured media attention to partially frame the Canadian media cov-erage of the conference. Later that summer, when Chrétien appeared in Wolfville, Nova Scotia, almost a hundred people gathered to protest his AIDS policies. (He was there to open a Girl Guides conference.) AIDS ACTION NOW! co-ordinated a campaign of sending postcards to the government and initiated a full-page ad in *The Globe and Mail*. In late 1996 member groups of the Canadian AIDS Society were encouraging members and supporters to write and call their MPs about the need to extend the National AIDS Strategy.

One major federal initiative, the Krever Commission (1994-95), which had still not reported by early 1997, became the first federal commission of in-quiry into AIDS-related matters, focusing on how it was that more than a thousand haemophiliacs and others were infected through the blood supply and blood products of the early and mid-1980s. This commission was partly brought about through the self-organization of haemophiliacs and others in-fected through the blood supply. Canadian blood regulatory history reveals very real and major problems. In the case of haemophiliacs, the record shows decisions made to give some of them possibly unsafe blood on the grounds that they were most likely infected already; and that there were unnecessary delays in heat-treating blood products and in HIV screening of the blood supply.[13]

The Krever Commission and associated media coverage also had the pos-sibility of rewriting the history of the response to AIDS in Canada. The focus on those PLWA/HIVs who were infected through the blood supply and blood products tended to privilege their stories and experiences, further displacing other community-based groups and AIDS activists from their centrality in the narrative of responding to AIDS. It could establish an official history of AIDS that marginalizes the stories of gay men and community activists. This is especially the case given that some officials in the Red Cross have argued – in contrast to the actual safe sex and blood-donation responsibility efforts of early AIDS groups – that they could not properly screen the blood supply because of supposed "resistance" from the gay community; and that they could not implement HIV testing because they feared gay men would flood the testing with the possibility of infection because of the period between infection and the appearance of HIV antibodies. Fortunately, the main focus of criticism of the Krever process has remained on the Red Cross and official policies.

The media continue to elaborate on their earlier distinctions between "innocent" and "guilty" PLWA/HIVs. The announcement of financial assistance packages for those infected through the blood supply and blood products in Canada and other countries, given governmental responsibility for the safety of the blood supply, was also partly a result of the struggles of haemophiliacs and others infected through blood products. While this is a move forward, and the funding is badly needed, it also leads to the construction of divisions between different groups of PLWA/HIVs – dividing PLWA/HIVs on the basis of how they were infected – and poses the danger of reconstructing the distinction between "innocent" (infected through the blood supply) versus "guilty" (infected through sexual activities or injection drug use) PLWA/HIVs. This time the distinction carries with it important financial implications.

Some levels of "risk" – injection drug use, gay sex, "promiscuous" sex, and sexual contact more generally – are deemed to be a person's own responsibility (what some insurance companies classify as "self-inflicted"), while the risk of infection through the state-regulated blood supply is not constructed as the individual's responsibility in the same way. Those who acquired HIV infection through gay sexual activity or injection drug use are already considered to be more "irresponsible" than those infected through the blood supply. However, all PLWA/HIVs require financial and social support, which is the position that the Canadian AIDS Society and many AIDS activists have developed as they attempt to develop solidarity and unity among all PLWA/HIVs.

"CONSULTATION" – PREPARING THE AIDS STRATEGY

The federal AIDS Strategy was based on close to a year of "consultation." Sadinsky and Associates, Ottawa-based consultants, were contracted to facilitate this work. In October 1989 they prepared an initial working document that received widespread criticism from community-based groups and activists (Sadinsky and Berger 1989; Blott 1990: 3; Kinsman 1990: 1,5).

Its major problem as a text based on "consultation" with agencies and institutions was that it straddled conflicting interests between state agencies, professional associations, communities affected by AIDS/HIV, and PLWA/HIVs. Sadinsky and Associates were mandated to consult with numerous groups and draw up a consensus document on what a strategy should look like. In examining the Sadinsky report, along with the submissions of the Canadian AIDS Society (CAS), AAN!, and the report of the parliamentary Ad Hoc Committee on AIDS,[14] we begin to recover parts of the work process that went into the formation of the strategy – before the various pieces had fully entered into document or textual time (D. E. Smith 1990a: 74) in their final form, when they were stabilized in the "official" documents released in June 1990. To recover their process of social organization, the National Strategy documents must be analysed historically and "archaeologically."

In preparing their working document (October 1989) Sadinsky and Associates met with the provincial ministries of health, CAS, PLWA groups, AAN!, the Canadian Medical Association, the Canadian Life and Health Insurance Association, and various federal agencies including the Health Protection Branch. In attempting to mediate these different interests the document adopts the standpoint of government and administration and often that of "public health." It does not take up the standpoint of PLWA/HIVs or AIDS activists. The document develops a hegemonic administrative framework for incorporating community-based groups into a state regulatory strategy.

The text contains quite obvious contradictions, because parts of it were written under the influence of different agencies. It is especially limited in not dealing with treatment delivery and the needs of PLWA/HIVs. The process of consultation proved to be more difficult and time-consuming than anticipated. The social character of this work is in large part organized through conceptualizations of consultation, collaboration, and partnership – terms that were carried through into the final strategy texts as crucial organizing concepts. An analysis of this work reveals how the language used in documents can operate as a conceptual co-ordination for social action (G. W. Smith 1990a: 642).

The resulting strategy, released in June 1990, proved disappointing from the standpoint of AIDS activists. It had been preceded by almost a year in which valuable time went into speaking to government officials and consultants and not much pressure for badly needed action was put on the federal government. In retrospect, in the first five years of this strategy not that much was achieved either; and a bureaucratic, jurisdictional, and professional nightmare was produced around its best proposal – the AIDS/HIV treatment registry – which significantly delayed its implementation and put its credibility as a project in question. It became operational only in 1995.

The end result of this "consultation" was more of a ministerial statement of intention than an actual "national" strategy that would bind together various levels of government and others in a plan of action. Given the character of Canadian state formation, in which the provinces have considerable jurisdiction over health care and social services, this is a major problem with the strategy. It addressed important areas that are outside the direct mandate of the Ministry of Health and Welfare in terms of concerns rather than policy.[15]

At the time of the announcement, AAN! gave Beatty two out of ten as a score for the strategy. He received a pass on the treatment registry and on a commitment to have PLWA/HIVs on all boards and committees, but a failing grade on everything else.[16]

"COLLABORATION" AND "PARTNERSHIP" ON WHOSE TERMS?

Before examining the strategy texts, it is important to consider the different social contexts in which these documents are read: readers located differently accomplish different readings of the texts. One group of readers – including state officials, public-health officials, and health-care administrators – accomplishes the dominant, intended reading. For many of these readers, the documents provide a conceptual language for managing the AIDS crisis and AIDS groups. Another group of readers, the media, read the strategy for "coverage" and frames for their manufacturing of the news (Fishman 1980; G. Smith 1983).

Other readers include members of community-based AIDS groups, AIDS activists, and PLWA/HIVs. Some of us feel excluded from the dominant reading, which requires us to take up the social standpoint of federal state administration. AIDS activists read these texts for what is not there, for their limitations – as in the low score that AAN! gave in its appraisal. At the same time the use of consensual language and terms such as "partnership" tends to neutralize and moderate criticism.[17]

As a final text the strategy consisted of two documents. One was more generally about the Canadian response, and the second was more specifically the response of the Ministry of Health and Welfare and Beatty.[18] Much of the strategy was informed by the language of partnership and collaboration between the federal government, provincial governments, professional and medical groups, and community-based groups.[19] Terms like "co-ordination" and "collaboration" had been used in previous federal literature on AIDS, although largely in terms of the co-ordination of federal government initiatives.[20] In the strategy they came to be linked with conceptualizations of consultation and partnership. The federal government, according to the strategy, would play a crucial role in co-ordinating AIDS-related initiatives, bringing agencies and groups with very different access to social power together under its hegemony.

Partnership, Whose Partnership?

Beatty outlined the importance of "partnership" to the strategy in his June 1990 speech. The term was borrowed and transformed from the language of community-based groups in CAS that were talking about the need for a partnership with government in the fight against AIDS.[21] The various CAS submissions, the Sadinsky working document, and the final strategy texts revealed a process of struggle over the meaning and interpretation of partnership. When CAS speaks of partnership it means that governments need to recognize the leadership and contribution of community-based groups to the fight against AIDS – "We are the AIDS experts, we need to be listened to, we play a leading role being on the front-lines of dealing with AIDS."[22] Partnership has often been posed in the community-based groups as involving something close to an equal relation between government agencies and AIDS groups. An excerpt from a CAS document reveals this approach:

> All levels of government in Canada must recognize the essential contribution of the community-based sector and people living with AIDS/HIV, must form a partnership with this component and ensure that it has the necessary resources to participate in the National AIDS Strategy. This participation must include its development, implementation and management. (CAS 1989: 91)

In the final strategy documents the idea of partnership was worked over and lifted out of this context. There was a shift in usage as the documents outlined a "partnership" defined much more by the imperatives of ruling political and administrative agencies than by community-based groups and PLWA/HIVs. Part of this shifting and working over was accomplished through the entry of discourses developed in business administration, labour management, and policy and strategic planning, which deploy partnership from an administrative and ruling standpoint as a mechanism for integrating other groups under the hegemony of business, professional, and/or state agencies.

At the same time space was opened up through the rhetoric of partnership for pushing the government further in certain areas, and some space was provided for alternative readings. CAS members can see some of their own language taken up and used and could more easily identify with the strategy. This has been an active process of shifting and resituating interpretations of "partnership" so that the strategy documents could provide for the hegemony of a state-defined reading.

Beatty himself clarified this difference in usage. In announcing the strategy he declared, "The key to success lies in partnership," and "A central element of partnership is the power it gives us to reach specific audiences with the messages we know to be of critical importance" (1990: 5). But which "us" was Beatty speaking of? Given that Beatty was Minister of Health and Welfare, this "us" took up the social standpoint of federal state agencies – this "us" was not the standpoint of AIDS activists or of PLWA/HIVs. This strategy of partnership, then, allowed state messages and regulation to get through to hard-to-reach groups that would often be out of the reach of state agencies. A crucial aspect of this partnership strategy was to get other groups, including community-based groups, to do work for state agencies. This can be seen as subcontracting state work to "community-based" groups through specific funding projects, project guidelines, and the work of funding officers.[23] State agencies thus come to shape the deployment of resources and reshape the agendas of community-based groups.

Treatment Registry an Important if Delayed Victory

In the strategy the most positive proposal was for a treatment registry,[24] which would allow doctors and PLWA/HIVs across the country to access information about treatments (Taylor 1990). While the registry proposal would provide for more information on treatments it would not in and of itself provide for greater access to them. It is as if the treatment information project stands on its own in the strategy, without the necessary substructure that would allow the treatments it will list to be freely available. This is in part because the registry was given as a concession to demands by AIDS activists and PLWA/HIVs for a treatment registry: the strategy did not deal with managing or transforming medical and corporate relations to get them to meet the needs of PLWA/HIVs (G. Smith 1989; T. McCaskell 1989).

In Canada the treatment registry idea originated with AAN! and gained the support of other activists.[25] In this area AIDS activism did shape the AIDS strategy: the commitment to setting up a treatment-information system was something we fought for and won. This victory gives us an important insight into how "partnership" can be transformed and redefined.[26] Unfortunately, when problems in implementation of this proposal emerged this activism was not sustained. The project was almost destroyed by institutional and professional competition but finally, after pressure from community-based AIDS groups, it was located at the Community AIDS Treatment Information Exchange (CATIE) in 1995.

The analysis here is meant to provide a way of accounting for what happened at the Atlantic Network meeting and also for what occurred in the formation of the provincial AIDS strategy in Nova Scotia. The AIDS Network meeting was part of how the "partnership" was socially accomplished, on the ground, in regional settings. The supposed partnership was part of a more extended social relation; it was accomplished interactively and constructed to some extent jointly within the context of unequal social power relations. The relationship was not simply an imposition from the state, but rather a process of negotiation and acceptance on the part of community-based groups in the construction of this form of hegemony; and the concept of partnership was to hold this relation together in the strategy and play a key part in constructing this hegemony. A set of mutual dependencies were produced in which state agencies held the major power. At the same time the rhetoric and practice of "partnership" created a certain amount of dependency by state agencies upon the other "partners" or "stakeholders," providing space for community and activist groups to redefine partnership on our own terms – for building our own counterhegemony.

THE NOVA SCOTIA AIDS STRATEGY

A draft Nova Scotia AIDS strategy was released on August 6, 1992 (Nova Scotia Advisory Commission on AIDS, 1992), four years after the release of the report of the Nova Scotia Task Force on AIDS. The draft was prepared by the Nova Scotia Advisory Commission on AIDS, formed in 1989 to advise the provincial health minister. Many community AIDS groups and AIDS activists found major problems with this strategy, saying that it did not meet the needs of PLWA/HIVs or the communities most affected by AIDS. Many of the criticisms paralleled those made previously of the National AIDS strategy. Speaking at a community press conference, Eric Smith, a member of the 1988 Task Force, remarked, "The thing that most discourages me about this strategy is how similar it sounds to a lot of the recommendations that were made to the government four years ago.... Little progress has been made."[27] Smith also pointed out that the people consulted in the development of this strategy included only one visible PLWA (Kinsman 1992).

The draft strategy's major organizational proposal was for the formation of an interdepartmental committee to oversee the implementation of the strategy and to co-ordinate government departments. Those proposed as members of this committee were to be government officials and appointees, and there was no suggestion that PLWA/HIVs or the communities affected by AIDS were to be represented.

In response thirteen community-based groups doing work on AIDS-related concerns across the province formed the Coalition of Nova Scotia AIDS Community Groups to lobby the government to dramatically improve the draft strategy. This involved attempting to develop a common perspective on what should be in an AIDS strategy as well as initiating a series of meetings with health ministers and health department officials over the next year. The work included verbal and written submissions to the government, which took up a great deal of the time and energy of AIDS groups that could otherwise have spent the energy more directly in the fight against AIDS.

Taking advantage of the rhetoric of "partnership," and the government's commitment to it, we were able to make advances when we had a clearly defined agenda and were able to seize the dynamic of the process of consultation. We made the most progress when we were united, well prepared, and forceful. Unfortunately there were also points of division in the coalition, including questions about how accommodating to be with the government. The government was also able to use the rhetoric of "consultation" and "partnership" against us by emphasizing the atmosphere of compromise and consensuality while also talking about financial constraints. This tension prevented us from putting more pressure for action on the government during these crucial months.

On December 1, 1993, World AIDS Day, the Nova Scotia Liberal government finally released its AIDS strategy, revealing limited victories in two areas. The strategy gave some recognition to the importance of the experiences and work of the community-based AIDS groups, but made no commitment to provide badly needed funding to support the activities of community groups. It did, finally, make a commitment to establish one anonymous HIV testing site in Metro Halifax – a goal that community-based AIDS groups in Nova Scotia had been stressing for more than seven years – and this was an important victory. At the same time the coalition had been pushing for a series of local testing sites throughout the province so that people from other parts of the province did not have to travel all the way to Halifax to get tested anonymously.[28]

The coalition felt the strategy was totally inadequate in most areas. There was no progress in meeting the treatment and social-support needs of PLWA/HIVs and in meeting AIDS/HIV needs outside the Metro Halifax area, where almost all AIDS services and medical facilities are concentrated. Since the strategy was announced there has been little further progress. The provincial strategy has generally been more effective at managing AIDS groups than in meeting the needs of those most affected by AIDS.

An important victory did come in another provincial context. In December 1994, after years of lobbying and activism by AAN! the Ontario government finally announced its commitment to establish a program for catastrophic drug funding that would assist some PLWA/HIVs and others in catastrophic conditions to gain access to the expensive treatments they need (Giese 1994). The NDP government commitment only came after AAN! had announced plans to burn an effigy of Premier Bob Rae in the streets of Toronto on World AIDS Day. This was enough to apparently overcome remaining cabinet opposition to this move. Once again this demonstrated that activism can work, although there are now fears that the Harris Conservative government in Ontario will remove some of the badly needed AIDS/HIV treatments from the list of treatments covered by this Trillium Drug Plan.

THE SOCIAL RELATIONS OF STRUGGLE

The state is not a "thing" or an "entity" to which social movements and AIDS organizing are external. State formations are a condensation of, and coordinator of, social relations with which social movements must engage and transform (Corrigan and Sayer 1985). Ideological conceptualizations become part of how state agencies guide and organize their work. The study of ideology and social organization is, in an important way, a study of its language (G.W. Smith 1990a: 645). In deconstructing hegemonic language we can open up possibilities for counterhegemonic transformation.

In the AIDS strategy perspective, "partnership" and "collaboration" are the concepts used to develop a regulatory approach for bringing together different groups with divergent social interests. The strategy lays out a process of consultation and collaboration, allowing for a way of organizing state management of the AIDS crisis that is at the same time the regulation of AIDS groups. The strategy recognizes that within ruling relations the bureaucratic institutions and political apparatus that need to be co-ordinated in any AIDS "strategy" are not located simply within the federal Department of Health and Welfare, or provincial departments of health. Part of the effort of co-ordination includes work with other state agencies, whether federal or provincial, along with professional and community-based agencies. In this light, AIDS strategies are attempts to handle the peculiarities of Canadian state formation, including the federal/provincial divisions of powers. This strategy framework and the conceptual organization initially developed at the federal level can, then, be useful to provincial governments in attempting to manage their own work relating to AIDS.

At the same time this strategy does not engage with the management or co-ordination of the medical profession or the drug companies, because it presumes the continuation of hegemonic professional and capitalist relations. Access to treatments is still largely left up to private contractual agreements between physicians, patients, and drug companies, and defined by concerns over profit rates and professional careers.[29]

Dilemmas of Partnership

The concept of partnership sets up a common language between governments and AIDS groups that obscures underlying differences in social power and needs. "Partnership" has a nice neutral ring to it. It is difficult to question or oppose because it draws us into constructing a consensus. Partnership sounds consensual; it implies that everyone is being given an equal voice, that all partners are equal. It is therefore a useful conceptualization for the construction of hegemonic relations, and it has achieved a high degree of cogency (Kinsman 1995) for this kind of work.

In this conceptualization the community-based groups, AIDS activists, and PLWA/HIVs become just one of many "partners" with no special relation to defining responses to AIDS. The standpoint taken up is "above" these competing "interest groups," partners, and stakeholders. In the National AIDS Strategy it is the standpoint of federal state mediation, definition, and co-ordination. Federal state agencies mediate between the different "partners." In the Nova Scotia AIDS strategy the provincial state, especially the Department of Health, takes up this position. The language of partnership and collaboration smooths over the struggles and contradictions of the past, and with them disappears the history of community AIDS organizing and AIDS activism, which has led to most positive initiatives on AIDS. In part as a result of the achievement of this hegemony, activist campaigns have diminished in relation to the federal and many provincial governments, even while, from the standpoint of AIDS activists, positive results from this partnership have been limited. As problems emerge, the terrain of struggle becomes framed by the *terms* of partnership but not the *concept* of "partnership" itself. The struggle takes place within the shared discursive framework of "partnership" and does not burst its hegemonic boundaries.

FUNDING AND REGULATION

The National AIDS strategy outlined various policy initiatives – including funding priorities. This determines what resources are available to community-based groups. The *HIV and AIDS: Canada's Blueprint* text argues that community-based groups appear to provide "extremely cost-effective" services: "To ensure that community groups continue providing this support, governments must strengthen the partnership, stabilize the funding for community groups and continue to guide them" (Health and Welfare 1990b: 50-1).

State funding for community groups is a victory gained through political struggle. At the same time it is also part of how groups are "guided" by federal and sometimes by provincial agencies.[30] These funding regulations work to "depoliticize" groups, moving them away from contestative, progressive activities and connecting them to the relevancies of particular state bureaucracies. The groups must conform to certain constraints of the bureaucratic procedures that need to be followed, forms that need to be filled out, and the progress reports that need to be filed to maintain their funding. A good deal of these groups' time and energy is spent on securing more funding and ensuring that existing funding continues.[31]

Within these groups political and community mobilization from below can be deflected away from activism and transformed into demands for services. Within the context of service provision, PLWA/HIVs and others affected by AIDS get transformed into "clients" or "users." As Roxana Ng (1988: 69) suggests, state regulation is accomplished "not merely through coercive mechanisms, but also through ... [an] elaborate funding apparatus which penetrates into grassroots organizations and movements."

Groups originally set up to empower PLWA/HIVs and the communities most affected by AIDS can come to stand over these communities as part of a state-regulated process of management.[32] These policies also lead to the replication of forms of state and professional organization within these groups, with incorporation, boards of directors often dominated by professionals and managers, executive directors, and pay and status hierarchies among employees.[33]

PROFESSIONAL RELATIONS, "PUBLIC HEALTH," AND PALLIATIVE CARE

As a terrain of struggle, AIDS is highly medicalized and professionalized. AIDS/HIV is primarily defined in dominant discourses as a medical problem. This privileges the power and knowledge of the medical profession and its "expert" status. Professional relations are defined by forms of specialized knowledge and social power that are not allowed to people outside these professions; they are power/knowledge relations of exclusion.[34] These relations are tied into the extended social organization of class, gender, and race in contemporary capitalist patriarchal societies.

People on the boards of "community-based" groups often have close associations that tie them into the medical profession, to public health, and to social work. These provide common allegiances, standpoints, and ways of working for people inside AIDS groups and within professional groups. In some groups these tendencies towards "professionalization" are held in check, but they come to shape many community-based groups. If you do not have the right credentials or qualifications you can get "organized out" of the inner circles of these groups, or you become simply a "volunteer." As Ng (1988: 27) elaborates, "Professionalization is the process which transforms non-capitalist forms of organization into hierarchical ones." In these professional and state contexts it is difficult for AIDS groups and PLWA/HIVs to claim "expert" status. At the same time this is the very basis for the self-empowerment movement of PLWA/HIVs and AIDS activism.

The terrain of AIDS is also highly state-defined, in terms of "public health" (Sears 1992 1995). There is proposed, in these strategies, no fundamental transformation of the relations of "public health," which continue to be hegemonic state and professional approaches. Public health ideology and practice often make PLWA/HIVs into social problems while limiting treatment delivery (G. Smith 1989; Kinsman 1994: 179-81). Emphasis is put on the protection of "the general public" and not on the needs of those most affected by AIDS/HIV.[35] AIDS policies often marginalize and exclude the needs of many communities affected by AIDS and PLWA/HIVs, including the need to challenge sexism, racism, heterosexism, and poverty as central parts of the social response to AIDS.

"Irresponsible" and "Responsible" PLWA/HIVs

The National Strategy documents come close to branding some "irresponsible" PLWA/HIVs as a threat to "public health," a charge that once again counterposes the rights of the people most affected by AIDS to those of "society," perpetuating the frame that AIDS/HIV is spread through the actions of individual "deviants" (Health and Welfare 1990b: 39).

The regulatory site of the "responsibility" or "irresponsibility" of PLWA/HIVs has been produced most clearly in relation to HIV transmission questions. This regulatory site has been and is being constructed through public-health discourse and practice, criminal legal responses, professional medical and expert advice, and mass media framing (Kinsman, 1996b). The current conventional framing of the problem still focuses on the responsibility/irresponsibility and behaviour of the person who is already infected. It does not focus on the responsibilities of others in the same way – the mythical "general population" (of public health and media discourses) – or on the responsibilities of governments, the medical profession, researchers and drug companies. It constructs PLWA/HIVs as the "risk" and the "problem." The framing defines the issue as *their* responsibility not to engage in "risk" activities, even though the vast majority of HIV transmission occurs from people who have no knowledge they are HIV+ or are ignorant of how it is transmitted.[36]

Public-health and criminalizing practices and their media-framing focus in different ways on "irresponsible" PLWA/HIVs as the problem in the spread of HIV infection. The established approaches do not rely on other regulatory responses that have a very different character, and that have relied on community-based safer sex and safer activity education and organizing and have demonstrated their effectiveness. These alternatives approaches give a different social content to the notion of responsibility, associating it with forms of community and mutual responsibility regarding safe sex, relying on grassroots education and not coercive measures. These approaches have been the success stories in popular education regarding AIDS. The making of some PLWA/HIVs into the problem also obscures the responsibility of governments and public-health agencies for not providing adequate, effective, and explicit AIDS and safer activity education from a much earlier period.

Too much emphasis is still placed on palliative care – compassion while dying in dignity and AIDS as a necessarily fatal disease[37] – rather than on building the capacity of people to live longer and resist HIV/AIDS. But compassion is not enough, especially when there is the growing possibility for more people with AIDS and HIV infection to live longer and higher-quality lives. While the National AIDS strategy documents do mention the possibility of transforming AIDS/HIV into a chronic but manageable condition, they do not accept the principle of catastrophic rights for PLWA/HIVs – the right of PLWA/HIVs to have free access to promising treatments and therapies.[38] Treatment access and the lack of attention to problems of access to social services are central limitations of these strategies. They provide no greater access to therapies for PLWA/HIVs.[39] There is commitment to representation for PLWA/HIVs on bodies dealing with AIDS, but little commitment to their empowerment.

There has been a recent shift in the official language of AIDS/HIV: it is becoming a "chronic, manageable disease." Originally this term was developed from the standpoints of AIDS activists and PLWA/HIVs to get at the state, professional, and pharmaceutical practices that block access to needed treatments, suggesting that breaking through these blockages could open up possibilities for survival and resistance (G. Smith 1989). This approach was developed in response to earlier frames of understanding AIDS – "that everyone who is infected will die." Now it has been turned and shifted by some medical and government officials: AIDS/HIV has become a "chronic manageable condition," but without the state, medical, and corporate blockages being substantively addressed. Therefore the message is that there is not always a need for great urgency in addressing an individual's AIDS concerns and that, for instance, individual PLWA/HIVs may have no urgent need to see a specialist because they should be capable of managing their own health over long periods of time under the supervision of primary-care physicians.

The state and professions give individuals the responsibility for managing their own health but do not give them the resources, supports, or knowledge to do this. They are "free" to self-regulate within the confines of "expert" advice; and the message is that responsible PLWA/HIVs follow this expert advice. This strategy does not focus on problems such as the lack of necessary social supports for nutrition and maintaining immune systems (Mykhalovskiy and Smith 1994) and for the major problems that continue with the social organization of AIDS/HIV research and treatment delivery (G. Smith 1990).

Because of the struggles of PLWA/HIVs and AIDS activists, funding is now available through ACAP as well as through provincial funding for "health promotion" for PLWA/HIVs. The funding has led to the hiring of specific individuals to co-ordinate this work and to this aspect becoming part of the regular work of AIDS Service Organizations (ASOs). This approach is also part of an increasing transformation of community-based groups and activism into sites of service provision, a transformation in part emphasizing the *individual* responsibility of PLWA/HIVs to manage major aspects of their own health, including through the work of ASOs, which are taking over growing responsibility for managing PLWA/HIVs and the communities of people most affected by AIDS. Increasingly, the mandate of ASOs is to "empower" PLWA/HIVs in becoming responsible for their own self-management – to communicate to them the skills and languages of self-management and regulation. This shift can be seen in a growing number of self-help workshops and counselling sessions and in the production of manuals on proper diet, treatment, and care for PLWA/HIVs. What is involved is not only the transfer and communication of practical information and advice but also a transfer of responsibility for areas of managing their lives to individual PLWA/HIVs within the context of "expert" and ASO advice. The approach can open up important spaces for some PLWA/HIVs to gain more control over the circumstances of their lives and over their own health, but important problems can also arise with what Barbara Cruikshank (1994) calls the "will to empower" of governments and service organizations in this area.

This "will to empower" uses the language of choice and informed consent regarding medical care and treatment, but there are currently only limited treatment options available for PLWA/HIVs, and it remains difficult to challenge hegemonic medical relations, especially for individual PLWA/HIVs. The strategy of producing self-managing, self-regulating individuals with AIDS/HIV who will be much easier for social and medical agencies to handle is in part a twisting and shifting of demands for empowerment and for PLWA/HIVs to have control over their own health. Activists have pressured for this – an impetus "from below" – but, as in other areas, "empowerment" has been transformed from a critique of professional powers into a new mode of "professional" activity. These relations and practices of empowerment become sites of negotiation, compromise, resistance, and struggle.

There are advances here, but also major limitations. PLWA/HIVs are not given the necessary resources, access to treatments, knowledge, or control that would allow this approach to lead to them having more control over their own health care and lives. "Responsible" PLWA/HIVs, in this context, follow "expert" advice and do not create difficulties for medical or other regulatory agencies. PLWA/HIVs with less resources (poverty, lack of formal education, less familiarity with the operation of professional and governmental bureaucracies) are not able to participate in these practices of "taking responsibility" as well as others.

This tendency also shifts the focus away from problems with governmental, professional, and corporate responses to AIDS/HIV towards relocating the problem as an incapacity within individual PLWA/HIVs regarding lack of education, "apathy," not knowing about medical services, treatments and social programs, and not following medical and other advice. The focus becomes shifted from the actions or inactions of powerful social institutions onto the individual capacities and incapacities of PLWA/HIVs.

These strategies do not start from the standpoints of the experiences of people living with AIDS/HIV and the problems they experience that are organized through state, professional, and corporate relations. The major emphasis is not on meeting the needs of the people most affected by AIDS. Instead, emphasis is still placed on managing them and "protecting" the "general public."[40]

FROM "HEALTH FROM ABOVE" TO "HEALTH FROM BELOW" – BUILDING A COUNTERHEGEMONY

As parts of the relations of ruling, the practices of the state and professionals are largely oriented around notions of "health from above" and at times a professional "will to empower." Community-based groups and AIDS activists have begun to develop, however hesitantly and inconsistently, a different approach based on the effective empowerment of people living with AIDS/HIV and the communities most affected by AIDS. This has sometimes been referred to as "health from below" (Sears 1990). It entails a counterhegemonic, transformative politics.

Community-based groups originally used the notion of partnership with government agencies as an attempt to shift state policies more in the direction of "health from below," especially with community-based groups playing a leading role in the social response to AIDS. In these state strategies this notion of partnership has been resituated as part of a hegemonic regulatory strategy based on "health from above," which creates problems for PLWA/HIVs and AIDS activists.

The analysis developed here provides us with a way of accounting for the experiences of disjuncture. I have begun to unearth the extralocal and textually mediated social relations that organize state management of AIDS organizing and that marginalize, exclude, and shift the needs and concerns of PLWA/HIVs. But we face a dilemma. In the context of the fight against AIDS, we desperately need state and professional resources and initiatives, and getting them is always an important victory. At the same time we have to avoid the implications of state and professional regulatory strategies in limiting and constraining our abilities to organize in our communities and movements. We need increased funding and resources for social services, housing, education, treatments, community-based groups, and PLWA/HIVs, but we also have to preserve our independence and autonomy. The question of who controls and defines programs and initiatives becomes key. The question engages us necessarily with and within state and professional relations, but also requires an organizing direction *against* ruling relations. We have to begin to define AIDS policies much more on our own terms. We have to resituate notions of "partnership" to recognize our leadership and defining of issues and policies from below.

Key to this approach is a radical shift from reliance on public health and palliative care and professional strategies about personal responsibility to qualitatively improved treatment access and the creation of the actual social conditions for HIV/AIDS to be a chronic manageable condition. This shift is tied into broader social transformations in health care, sexuality, the medical profession, research, the drug corporations, and other areas – transformations that must put the needs and concerns of the people most affected by AIDS/HIV at the centre of social policy – and not profit rates or professional careers. We can only seriously address AIDS by dealing with fundamental features of the class society we exist within. AIDS organizing must be a politics of social transformation, including building coalitions with other marginalized and oppressed groups around health care and other concerns. Coalitions and solidarity between groups are especially needed given current cutbacks on health care. We must not allow the cutbacks to divide us, like they have tended to do regarding funding for cancer versus AIDS, but instead we must argue, as in the campaign for catastrophic drug funding, for optimal health care for everyone. This is what making our own hegemony is all about.

This counterhegemonic relation has to be accomplished at local community levels and at more extralocal levels. We have to remember that through our own activities and struggles we helped to create the basis for developing these AIDS strategies, we won the commitment to establish a treatment registry, the limited establishment of anonymous testing in Nova Scotia, and in Ontario a program for catastrophic drug funding. We have never simply been external to state policy developments; we have also been internal to them, participating in shaping the ground upon which state activities and initiatives take place. This chapter is intended to open up discussion on how we can accomplish relations between state agencies and AIDS groups differently, how we can transform this relation in a progressive, activist direction. This work involves gaining more control and space for empowerment and health from below. It requires moving beyond hegemonic discursive frameworks, including the frame embodied in the National AIDS strategy and its conceptualization of partnership. Part of the task is to transform and redefine partnership on our own terms, as part of building our own hegemony.

NOTES

* The original version of this chapter was presented in the joint session "Silence = Death, Action = Life: The Sociology and Politics of AIDS in Canada," Canadian Sociology and Anthropology Association and Socialist Studies meetings, Queen's University, Kingston, Ontario, June 3, 1991. It has now been substantially revised and updated. Thanks to Alan Sears, Patrick Barnholden, Brian Conway, William Carroll, Eric Mykhalovskiy, the late George Smith, Lorna Weir, Mariana Valverde, AIDS ACTION NOW!, the Newfoundland AIDS Association, the Valley AIDS Concern Group, and the Coalition of Nova Scotia AIDS Community Groups, although none of them bear any responsibility for what is written here.

1. This was the second of their meetings. See the minutes and proceedings published by the Newfoundland and Labrador AIDS Committee, 1991.
2. "Community-based" AIDS groups is the term commonly used to describe member groups of the Canadian AIDS Society (CAS), an organization of AIDS groups across the country. AIDS "community-based" groups are now often referred to in official discourse as AIDS service organizations (ASOs), which narrows their mandates to service provision. These groups were initially community-based groups initiated by gay men, lesbians, and community health activists that have received various levels of government funding to provide services and education to people living with AIDS/HIV and to the communities of people most affected by AIDS. They have largely (but not entirely) been transformed from advocacy into service provision organizations, as has also been the experience of groups emerging from other communities and movements. Some of these community-based groups are also people living with AIDS/HIV coalitions, and a few are AIDS activist groups. At the same time, "community-based" can be a misleading description, because many of these groups have tenuous relations with the communities and movements they emerged from, and "community" representation on their boards often includes only a professional/managerial elite. Those with professional and academic credentials come to stand in a managerial or administrative relation to the communities they claim to represent. There are also broader problems with the notion of "community," which tends to obscure class, gender, race, and other social inequalities and differences. On some of the limitations of "community-based" groups, especially in relation to "public health," see Sears (1990); G.W. Smith (1990a: 639-40). More recently the notion of an entity called the "AIDS community" has begun to emerge in professional and state AIDS discourse. Initially in the language of AIDS groups this referred to community-based AIDS groups, PLWA/HIVs, and primary-care physicians who advocated for the needs of their patients. Increasingly "AIDS community" is now being used to refer to all those institutions and agencies that have as part of their

mandate to work in relation to AIDS. This blurs major distinctions in social location and power between, on the one hand, People Living With AIDS and community AIDS workers and, on the other, government agencies, public health officials, insurance companies and pharmaceutical corporations. It also produces a consensual image of this AIDS "community" as if all the different "stakeholders" had equal defining power.

3. The Department of National Health and Welfare first provided funding to community-based AIDS groups in 1985. The National AIDS strategy documents describe the establishment of ACAP: "To consolidate these growing efforts at the community level, a designated funding stream, known as the AIDS Community Action Program (ACAP), was created in May 1989" (Health and Welfare Canada 1990a: 26). ACAP was formed shortly after Beatty became health minister and as the strategy of "consultation" was initiated.

4. The Newfoundland and Labrador AIDS Committee received a grant of $10,000 through ACAP to organize the meeting. Such funding is part of the ACAP mandate.

5. The most significant research and publications to engage with state regulation of AIDS in Canada, along with the 1992 version of this chapter, are Rayside and Lindquist (1992a, 1992b). While these articles contain much that is useful, they also tend to overemphasize the impact of community-based AIDS groups on state policy, which leads them to not adequately analyse the regulatory aspects of strategies adopted by state agencies. In this sense they are too uncritical of the language and rhetoric of "partnership." The work of Roy Cain also raises some similar concerns to mine. See his 1993 and 1994 articles. See also these early useful efforts: G. Smith's column "Talking Politics," in *Rites* 1988, and his 1990a: 639-40; in Sears (1990) and in a different way in Adam (1989: 1-14). On the U.S. context see C. Patton on the "AIDS Industry" (1988: 81-4, 1990: 5-23, 1996). On AIDS in the official and unofficial Canadian media see Emke (1991).

6. On social standpoint and taking up the standpoint of the oppressed see D.E. Smith (1987).

7. On my use of hegemony, see Kinsman (1996b: 37-40). There are difficulties with notions of "hegemony," especially if hegemony is construed as an explanatory category in and of itself. Some postmodernist/post-Marxist exponents of "hegemony" have also severed this notion from any grounding in class relations and class struggle (Laclau and Mouffe 1985), an approach that I reject. But hegemony can point us towards the relational character of social regulation in a clearer fashion than other terms. It suggests that social regulation is actively accomplished by individuals in diverse institutional sites and is always "problematic." It unites coercion and consent in the social organization of ruling. It points us towards the social organization of ruling relations while including within it the activities and resistances of the subordinated. Hegemony is always actively accomplished, never self-securing. It must be continuously struggled for, won, and maintained. It is never total, never exclusive, and there are always possibilities for subversion and transformation. It is these opportunities that we have to seize to resist dominant hegemonies and to construct our own.

8. On the sociology and politics of the AIDS crisis, see, among others, Patton (1986, 1990, 1996); Crimp (1988); Watney (1987, 1994); Aggleton and Homas (1988); Aggleton, Hart and Davies (1989); Huber and Schneider (1992); Altman (1994); Kinsman (1991, 1996a, 1996b); and Adam and Sears (1996).

9. On federal government policy towards AIDS see also Rayside and Lindquist (1992a, 1992b).

10. For instance, they provided funding to the Canadian Public Health Association to produce TV ads, which were widely criticized by community-based AIDS groups and AIDS activists for pushing monogamous heterosexuality as "safe" (Poirier 1987).

11. Anonymous HIV testing is when names and identities are not linked to the test and test result, thereby allowing people to come forward to be tested without fear of the government finding out who they are.

12. The AIDS secretariat has gone from reporting to the associate deputy minister to reporting to an assistant deputy minister to reporting to a director-general.

13. For an initial journalistic analysis that is not very informed by the experiences of AIDS activists, see Parsons (1995).

14. The Ad Hoc Committee was formed to make recommendations to the minister of health.

15. For instance, regarding the ending of immigration and travel restrictions on HIV-infected people, rather than taking a clear position Beatty asked the Immigration Medical Review Board "to review the current regulations" (1990: 9). It was not until April 1991 that he was able to announce that restrictions on HIV-infected visitors and visitors with AIDS had been dropped (1991: 9). Regarding the need for sexual orientation protection in federal human rights legislation, the strategy documents took no clear position despite the urging of the parliamentary Ad-Hoc Committee on AIDS, CAS, and others, in part because this fell under the jurisdiction of another ministry. On the federal level, despite court decisions arguing that sexual orientation should be read as being in the equality rights section of the Charter, the government only officially added sexual orientation protection to Canadian human rights legislation in June 1996. Other limitations include the following. While Beatty in his 1990 speech referred to the pioneering work of the gay community in response to AIDS, the strategy itself operates to deny the experiences of gays and others in developing safe sex education and organizing (Patton 1987: 67-78, 1996). Regarding prisoners, the strategy only makes reference to the need for concerns to be addressed and for research to be undertaken; there are no proposals for treatment for prisoners or on the need for condoms and clean needles in prisons. The distribution of condoms within prisons is finally being addressed, although officials are still refusing to officially admit that sex takes place within prison walls. Regarding women, the strategy argues that "stable monogamous relationships are the least risky," suggesting that monogamy is safer, a position that amounts to misleading misinformation (Health and Welfare 1990b: 42). In putting the emphasis on the number of partners and not the type of activities engaged in, the strategy denies the lessons of safe-sex organizing. While there is some concern shown in the strategy towards AIDS/HIV among Aboriginal peoples and other communities, the concerns of the "ethnocultural communities" are seen as separate from those of "the general population." The "general population," it seems, is presumed to be white; see Health and Welfare (1990a: 10). This is embedded in state/professional languages of race and ethnicity. There is no discussion about how racism is influencing the social organization of the AIDS crisis and no understanding of the need to challenge racism in responding to AIDS.

16. AAN! gave him a failing grade on lack of government testing of promising treatments; on lack of ethical access to treatments; on lack of attention to accelerated care; on lack of core funding for community-based groups; on lack of attention to special needs in terms of education, prevention, and treatment; for no action on sexual-orientation protection in human rights legislation; for no support for

anonymous HIV testing; and for no action on travel and immigration restrictions (G. Smith 1990b: 1-2).

17. This can be seen in the "Response of the Canadian AIDS Society to the Announcement of the National AIDS Strategy," CAS (1990a).

18. Health and Welfare Canada, *HIV and AIDS: Canada's Blueprint* (1990b), and *Building an Effective Partnership: The Federal Government's Commitment to Fighting AIDS* (1990a), and also four background papers, all June 1990.

19. "Partnership" is one of the key themes stressed in Sadinsky and Associates (October 1989: 9) as well as in the report of the Parliamentary Ad Hoc Committee on AIDS (1990).

20. See the brochure, Health and Welfare Canada, "AIDS in Canada: The Federal Government Responds" (1989).

21. See the first CAS submission to the "consultation" process, "Working Together" (Sept. 19, 1989).

22. In the "Response of the Canadian AIDS Society to the Announcement of the National AIDS Strategy," this continuing struggle over the use of terms goes on. Referring to community-based AIDS groups, they declare (2-3): "We are AIDS experts. We are experts because we live with AIDS. Because we have risen to this formidable challenge. Because we have felt the pain of loss, have experienced with anger the indifference to our needs.... We are the leaders in responding to AIDS. We are the leaders because we dare to challenge. Because we propose solutions. Because it is paramount that those closest to this issue advocate for necessary changes to how our institutions respond."

23. On the subcontractual relationships that can be developed between state-funded groups and state agencies through the constraints and criteria of funding programmes, see Ng (1988: 35-47).

24. At first called the Treatment Information System for AIDS/HIV (TISAH), it was later renamed the HIV/AIDS Treatment Information Network, a project of the Community AIDS Treatment Information Exchange.

25. The demand for an AIDS/HIV treatment registry in the Canadian context was first made in the seven-point policy adopted by AAN! at its annual general meeting in October 1988. See AIDS ACTION NOW! (1989, 1990); articles in *AIDS ACTION NEWS!* June 1990: 1-3, and CAS (1990b).

26. Although the establishment of a treatment registry represented an important victory, it was only four years after its announcement that plans really got going when the registry was relocated to the Community AIDS Treatment Information Exchange (CATIE). There have been struggles over different visions of what this information system should be, with AAN! and others pushing for an activist vision of a treatment registry that would be accessible, have community representation, produce optimal standards of care across Canada, support PLWA/HIVs and their physicians, and improve access to a wide range of effective treatments for AIDS/HIV. Part of these problems have been attempts by some medical professionals to reshape the treatment information proposal, to re-establish their professional hegemony as doctors over their "patients." They have been able to do this in part because of the lack of commitment to empowerment of PLWA/HIVs in the national strategy and because there was only ever a partial and inconsistent break in the strategy towards actual treatment delivery. The basic features of the original proposal, including provision of treatment information to PLWA/HIVs, have been carried forward in the HIV/AIDS Treatment Information Network, located at CATIE.

27. Eric Smith was a teacher in Cape Sable Island who was taken out of the class-

238   PART 2: SOCIAL MOVEMENTS IN PRACTICE

room in 1987 when his HIV status was leaked to the local community. He fought a long and unsuccessful battle to return to classroom teaching. See McCormick (1995).

28. The one site in Halifax is still the only one existing in Nova Scotia.

29. This leads to a series of continuing problems. For instance, in the summer of 1995 AAN! organized a campaign against Abbott Laboratories, which was refusing to release ABT 538, a protease inhibitor, which works differently from AZT/DDI and is less toxic. It can therefore be used in combination with them. Abbott was refusing to make it available to PLWA/HIVs on a compassionate basis. There are also major continuing problems with the lack of organization of research in Canada. See AAN! (1993). AAN! also released a report card in spring 1995 on the response of pharmaceutical corporations in Canada to AIDS research and treatment. The highest mark was a "B," and 3 out of 20 companies received "F." See *Wayves* (1995).

30. Certain of their possible activity areas are state-funded, others are not, and they tend to focus on those areas that can get funded. For instance, until recently Health Promotions (under which ACAP funding for community groups takes place) was not specifically mandated to deal with treatment-related concerns, but focused on education and prevention issues. It therefore prioritized the funding of certain types of proposals, which is one of the reasons why the needs of PLWA/HIVs were marginalized in some "community-based" groups. This has now been altered with mandated funding for "health promotion" for PLWA/HIVs. Because of the demands for funding from community-based groups, and the lack of increase in ACAP funding for community-based groups, ACAP in 1993-94 began to pressure groups in Nova Scotia with provincial mandates to merge if they wanted to continue to receive funding. In Nova Scotia, AIDS Nova Scotia and the PWA Coalition were actively encouraged to merge. As a result the Halifax-based AIDS Coalition of Nova Scotia was formed with the loss of the special mandate of the former PWA Coalition to organize and express the specific needs of PLWA/HIVs, and a series of tensions continue to exist in AIDS organizing in the city.

31. A particular problem for small AIDS groups not based in larger urban centres, such as the Valley AIDS Concern Group in the Annapolis Valley in Nova Scotia, is that continuous funding is not available. Project funding and continuously scrambling for more project funding can be very time-consuming and create a lack of resources, instability, and/or lack of continuity in community-based groups.

32. As George Smith (1990a: 639) suggests, through this process "community groups often end up functioning as the local extension of the management system of government; at least to the extent that government makes them party to its policies and funds their activities." See also Kinsman (1996b).

33. As Ng (1988: 32) points out, "the incorporation process is another extension of the state's ruling capacity into community activities." Many community-based groups also have charitable tax status to facilitate fundraising and adopt various interpretations of the prohibition on "political" activities for groups with this status. In some cases groups have refused to take up certain issues or to co-sponsor certain activities because they have felt that this will jeopardize their charitable status.

34. I borrow the notion of "power/knowledge" from the work of Michel Foucault. At the same time such valuable insights in Foucault's work are limited by lack of attention to social standpoint and the deletion of active subjects from his discourse analysis. At times it is almost as if power/knowledge relations are self-generating in Foucault's work. Notions of "power/knowledge" relations need to

be firmly grounded in social relations and must always be seen as social accomplishments. On some of the problems with Foucault's notion of "power/knowledge," see D.E. Smith (1990a: 70, 79-80).

35. As George Smith (1989: 2) puts it, "A fundamental feature of public health relations is that they focus on the protection of 'the public' and produce the sick or infected as 'dangerous.' Consequently, within the management of the AIDS pandemic, the public health relations co-ordinated by this conception operated to create policies that excluded communities with high rates of infection (for example, gay male, and IV-drug communities) as beyond the pale of 'the public.'"

36. In contrast gay and AIDS activists pioneered safe (and safer) sex organizing. This was the development of a new notion of social and mutual sexual responsibility based on community organizing and grassroots education. This form of sexual governance was based on a notion of responsibility to one's community, and to oneself, and not a "responsibility" defined by state, professional, or public-health practices. This early organizing came to be taken up and transformed by public health and other professionals, and also in the work of community AIDS groups themselves, into forms of "risk reduction" in relation to sexual activities and injection drug use practices. As this was transformed from political and community organizing to more public-health oriented education, risk reduction became a matter for the individual calculation and management of risk, rather than the construction of new practices of community and social sexualities.

37. This can be traced through the Report of the Expert Working Group on Integrated Palliative Care for Persons with AIDS, 1989.

38. We need this in a much broader sense than indicated in Dixon 1990. For instance, catastrophic rights must cover people living with HIV infection and not only those with official classifications of AIDS.

39. The basic infrastructure for the HIV clinical trials network was set up through funding mandated in the Strategy. A number of its clinical trials have posed ethical difficulties, forcing people who want treatment into product-testing research. The central focus of the clinical trials network is product-testing, *not* treatment delivery. AIDS activists won an important victory when the government allowed the federal Emergency Drug Release Program (EDRP), a body set up to allow for limited exemptions to (or relaxations of) the regulatory policies of the Health Protection Branch, to be used for the release of promising AIDS/HIV treatments in 1989. Unfortunately, problems quickly emerged as drug companies either refused to release promising treatments or set restrictions on their release. The EDRP and the Strategy (Health and Welfare 1990b: 50) basically enshrine the rights of manufacturers to determine when and where they will release promising therapies. This practice puts the needs and profits of private corporations ahead of the survival of PLWA/HIVs.

40. For useful comments on official AIDS policy and alternative proposals, see Lee (1991: 155-73).

FRAMING THE FORESTS: CORPORATIONS, THE B.C. FOREST ALLIANCE, AND THE MEDIA

Aaron Doyle, Brian Elliott, and David Tindall

Social movement activity may involve – crucially – a struggle over meanings. Collective processes of social change mean, in part, changing how people think. The importance of such interpretive or meaning work by social movements is sometimes neglected but has been stressed in recent analyses, including a series of prominent articles about the "framing" of meanings by social movements and their opponents (Snow et al. 1986; Snow and Benford 1988, 1992; Benford 1993a, 1993b; Hunt, Benford, and Snow 1994).

Social movements often take this contest over meanings to the news media. Similarly, corporations and other movement opponents may be forced to use the media to oppose movement claims. A passionate environmental struggle over a dwindling treasure – British Columbia's old-growth forests – has entailed such a contest, in the media and elsewhere. Environmental conflict over B.C. forests led to perhaps the largest set of mass arrests in Canadian history – police arrested more than 800 protesters at Clayoquot Sound on Vancouver Island in summer 1993. The controversy of meanings over these forests has also spread onto the global stage: to *The New York Times*, to Hollywood, to public meetings in England, to German television. Believing in the centrality of this image contest, forest companies have spent millions on a public relations operation, the B.C. Forest Alliance.

While environmentalists and their opponents struggle to communicate preferred meanings, media outlets construct stories using their own frames or systems of meanings (Gitlin 1980; Ericson et al. 1987). Certainly, the media may not adopt the particular frames desired by social movements, or by their opponents. Instead, news stories are created in a process of "negotiating control" (Ericson et al. 1989) involving the framing processes of media outlets and those of news sources such as the B.C. Forest Alliance.

This chapter looks at attempts by forest companies to use the B.C. Forest Alliance to "frame" their vision of the forests dispute, in the media and elsewhere, in order to thwart the environmental movement.[1] Previous research has explored the openness of the news media to the frames of various social movements (Gitlin 1980; Gamson and Modigliani 1989; Hackett 1991). We come at this situation from another direction, by examining how large corporations that are movement opponents fare in attempting to promote anti-movement frames in the media. Our case study is based on various sources of empirical data. We interviewed several key individuals working in public relations for the B.C. forest industry, including, most centrally, one communications professional working for the Forest Alliance. We examined Alliance promotional literature and television productions at length. We also made an extensive review of media coverage of B.C. forests issues over a period dating back about ten years. We considered hundreds of television and radio news and advertising items and newspaper and magazine clippings concerning environmental controversy about B.C. forests. These were drawn from several sources, including a sample of approximately one thousand articles collected for an ongoing content analysis of print-media coverage of B.C. forests issues.[2]

FRAMING, MEDIA, NEWS SOURCES, AND AUDIENCES

By "frame" we refer to a cognitive schema or system of structuring or imposing meaning on a set of symbols so those symbols are situated in relation to one another. "By rendering events or occurrences meaningful, frames function to organize experience and guide action" (Snow et al. 1986: 464). A frame can be distinguished from an ideology because "frames are more flexible and situationally influenced constructs than formal ideological systems and are more easily and rapidly communicated to target groups, adapted to change, and extended to blend with other frames" (Tarrow 1992: 190).

This concept of "frame" is adaptable enough to be useful to analysts in different theoretical traditions (for example, Snow et al. 1986; Gitlin 1980; Ericson et al. 1987). The idea of "framing" in social movements was introduced in a highly influential article by David Snow, Robert Benford, and others (1986), who present the concept as an attempt to bridge resource mobilization and social psychological perspectives on movement participation (464). The analysis cited Erving Goffman's work on frame analysis (1974) and drew on the social constructionist tradition more generally. This new "framing" approach thus tried to look at the interpretive aspect of people's grievances that lead to social movements. Resource mobilization theory had previously neglected this issue by focusing on structural factors and treating the grievances that led to mobilization as simple constants. The key argument was that "frame alignment" was a necessary prerequisite to movement participation. According to Snow and his co-authors, "By frame alignment, we refer to the linkage of individual and SMO (social movement organization) interpretations, such that some set of individual interests, values and beliefs and SMO activities, goals and ideologies are congruent and complementary" (1986: 464). Thus, the term means aligning the interpretive frames of the individual and the SMO.

Snow et al. (1986: 468) suggest that frame alignment can occur through the mass media, but the series of articles on framing has not yet considered this question in any detail.[3] However, Todd Gitlin's well-known book on the media and social movements, *The Whole World Is Watching*, also adopted Goffman's concept of framing to talk about "media frames." Gitlin (1980: 7) suggests: "*Media* frames, largely unspoken and unacknowledged, organize the world both for journalists who report it and, in some important degree, for us who rely on their reports. *Media frames are persistent patterns of cognition, interpretation, and presentation, of selection, emphasis, and exclusion, by which symbol handlers routinely organize discourse, whether verbal or visual*" (emphasis in original).

Gitlin suggests that news stories are created by "an *active* movement and *active* media pressing on each other, sometimes deliberately, sometimes not, in a process rich with contradiction" (14). Thus it may be argued that the "frames" in news stories are "negotiated" in an interaction between journalists and sources (Ericson et al. 1989).

Furthermore, looking at what is in the media does not tell us what sense audiences make of it. Thus, by looking at media content, we are only studying part of the framing process. Frame alignment is the result of an "interaction" between SMO frames and individual or audience frames (Snow et al. 1986: 464, 476). Similarly, William Gamson (1992) discusses media audiences and "collective action frames," adopting the concept of Snow and Benford (1992). Gamson's audience research suggests to us that we should be cautious about what inferences we make about audiences' acceptance of various frames. That is, we should not assume that audiences simply accept media frames. Gamson's book *Talking Politics* (1992) is excellent in that it actually examines the processes by which audiences make meanings, whereas much literature on the mass media and dominant ideology takes this as a given (see Ericson 1991, for a critique of this literature). Gamson's book argues that the mass media are not the only source of people's information. The key themes of Gamson's book are stated as, "People are not so passive; people are not so dumb; people negotiate with media messages in complex ways that vary from issue to issue." It thus disputes what it calls the conventional wisdom that "people are stupid about politics." Gamson argues that "people read media messages in complicated and sometimes unpredictable ways, and draw heavily on other resources as well in constructing meaning."[4]

Thus, frames are contested. Indeed, they are contested at sites of both source-journalist negotiations and audience-text interactions. As Anders Hansen (1991: 448) argues, "The social construction of environmental issues cannot be reduced to a question of information flowing from certain 'source' institutions through the mass media to a wider public and other institutions." Frames are not simply imposed on a passive public by the forest industry or environmental groups or the media. Instead, sources, media, and publics or audiences interact in complex and recursive ways to produce frames (Ericson, Baranek, and Chan 1989; Gamson and Modigliani 1989; Gamson 1992; Hansen 1991).

Here we can examine only part of this process, focusing on the production and content of media texts and leaving the question of how audiences make meanings from them for future research. We make claims about what framing attempts are evident from our perspective in media content and elsewhere, but not about what readings other audiences may give them.

THE MEDIA AND OPPOSITIONAL VIEWPOINTS

Some prominent accounts suggest that the reproduction of dominant ideology in the mass media is relatively seamless and uncontested; examples are Edward Herman and Noam Chomsky's book *Manufacturing Consent* (1988) and, surprisingly, given its neo-Gramscian roots, *Policing the Crisis* by Stuart Hall et al. (1978). Other authors argue that the mass media represent more of a contested space, offering potential for resistance (Hackett 1991; Bruck 1992). While the media may tend towards the reproduction of hegemony in their operations, hegemony is a process that is always contested and unfinished (Williams 1977). Thus the media are more open, pluralistic, and diverse than the more pessimistic dominant ideology accounts suggest (Ericson 1991; Doyle and Ericson 1996).

The media are frequently accused of framing stories in a way that reflects ideological bias towards capital (Herman and Chomsky 1988); alternately, others suggest that outlets such as the Canadian Broadcasting Corporation are biased to the left (Cooper 1994). More generally, though, the media must frame stories as part of their routine operations. That is, to construct a narrative that fits television, radio, or print formats, they must impose meaning on a jumble of chaotic symbols and events (Ericson et al. 1987).

More sophisticated, less conspiratorial analyses suggest that the media, through their routine operations, reproduce hegemony – through a structured overreliance on official sources, for example (Hall et al. 1978). The television format in particular may reduce politics to a spectacle (Postman 1985), inhibiting more complex forms of political discourse that could lead to a substantial critique of contemporary social relations. The media tend to frame stories in terms of distinct dramatic events in the immediate present, a quality known as "event orientation." This practice can displace a focus on broader social issues (Ericson et al. 1987, 1991).

Todd Gitlin (1980) argues that, under normal circumstances, social movements can exploit a desire in liberal-democratic ideology for media legitimacy and objectivity. He also suggests a contradiction between the desires of elites to maintain the system as a whole, and to pursue their own particular advantage (258-9). Thus, "The hegemonic routines of news coverage are vulnerable to the demands of oppositional and deviant groups" (270). However, social movements will be contained by the various aspects of media operations: "Discrepant statements about reality are acknowledged – but ... *domesticated* at the same time" (270). In times of crisis this process of domestication may break down. "When elites are themselves at odds ... opposition groups pressing for social and political change can exploit self-contradictions in hegemonic ideology." Gitlin ultimately refers to the mass media as "partially contested zones in which the hegemonic ideology meets its partial challenges and then adapts." He suggests, for example, that the anti-nuclear power movement was able to gain a foothold in the media after Three Mile Island, but the anti-nuclear weapons movement was not so successful in this regard.

Since the publication of Gitlin's book a number of other analysts have looked at social movements and the mass media with varying degrees of optimism. For example, Sean Cassidy (1992: 173) argues, "Greenpeace has had a great deal of success in exploiting the contradiction between the media's role as upholder of the status quo and their hunger for dramatic, though critical, stories with powerful visuals." Some analyses have argued for the key role of media coverage in the rise of the environmental movement in the 1980s (Corner and Schlesinger 1991) or for the importance of television in the advent of new social movements more generally (Tarrow 1994b). Robert Hackett (1991) conducted an extensive study of media coverage of the peace movement in Canada, offering an array of evidence that the media do provide at least some openings, as well as substantial obstacles, for social movements. Hackett (1991: 275-81) argues that key openings include contradictions in dominant discourse, a commercial requirement to be responsive to public concerns, and an "independent streak" in journalistic culture. His analysis parallels other more recent work attempting to provide a more qualified and nuanced intermediate position between classic pluralist and Marxist perspectives on the media (Curran 1990). Hackett encapsulates a view of the media and social movements neatly: "The media is not a level playing field but sometimes it is possible to win playing uphill."

If the media do provide openings for social movement framing, what of attempts by movement opponents to counter these frames?

CORPORATIONS AND FRAMING

Some authors suggest that corporations derive their power in part from staying out of the media (Ericson, Baranek, and Chan 1989: 287; Meyrowitz

1985). However, this may also serve to reduce their power in the negotiation of news, because journalists are not dependent on them for information, unlike the situation in other institutional realms, such as with the police (Hall et al. 1978).

Environmental organizations such as Greenpeace have become highly accomplished in using the media to achieve their goals (Hunter 1979; Cassidy 1992; Hansen 1993; Cracknell 1993; Yearley 1991). Some sources suggest environmental organizations may have outstripped business in the development of media skills. As George Froelich, the producer of Vancouver's UTV nightly news, told *B.C. Business* magazine (January 1994: 40): "We've been on panels and talked to business people about how to improve their press relations and all that. Do you realize in all the years I've been in journalism I've never had to do that with an environmental group? Special interest groups, when it comes to the media, are much smarter than CEOs.... They know how to have their voices heard, whereas CEOS hide out in the boardroom."

However, not all corporate interests "hide out in the boardroom." Increased social movement activity beginning in the 1960s meant that corporations, such as those in the nuclear industry, were often jarred from previously comfortable roles as entrenched insiders and forced to search for new strategies to recoup their standing (Useem and Zald 1987). Since the mid-1970s business has sought a variety of new modes of representation to reassert the interests of capital (Elliott et al. 1982; Elliott, McCrone, and Bechhofer 1988). In particular, social movement activity such as environmentalism may force corporations onto the news media stage. In keeping with the trend in other institutional realms (Ericson 1994), a number of corporations are taking a more proactive and professionalized approach to the news media. As Dan Schiller (1986: 26-8) points out, "At scores of major companies, in-house public affairs staffs routinely practise 'issues management,' by circulating the 'company side' of stories like Love Canal, Three Mile Island (and) Rely Tampons." Schiller continues: "The growing scale and sophistication of public relations has been matched by an increased willingness to experiment with new technologies to carry out corporate objectives.... Extensions of pre-packaged information may provide news media with nothing less than a complete presentation format....Video equivalents of written press releases now routinely appear on hundreds of local television broadcasts."

Frank Pearce and Steven Tombs (1993) discuss the "greening" of numerous multinational corporations. In recent years some corporations have devoted considerable resources to a more active public relations stance on environmental questions. For example, Allan Schnaiberg and Kenneth Gould (1994: 105) describe a recent television ad by Du Pont. The commercial features seals, dolphins, whales, sea otters, and penguins responding jubilantly to a soundtrack of Beethoven's "Ode to Joy." Why? A Du Pont subsidiary decided it would double-hull two medium-sized tankers it planned to build, a move that was inexpensive and made good business sense. Meanwhile Du Pont and its subsidiaries remained the worst corporate polluter in the United States, emitting more than 348 million pounds of industrial pollution in 1989, up 10 million from the previous year. Similarly, Donn J. Tilson (1993) details efforts to achieve favourable publicity for the nuclear industry. In the same vein, the corporations that are the major players in the B.C. forest industry have recently found it necessary to engage in "counterframing" in response to the critiques of environmentalists.

If the media are more open to resistance to hegemony than some accounts suggest, similarly they may be more closed to the ideological efforts of capital than some critics posit. The forest industry in British Colombia has strong links with global capital (Marchak 1983). Thus the relative successes of the Forest Alliance in achieving its aims in the news media permit an exploratory testing of the openness of these media to the framing activities of such capital.

THE B.C. FORESTS SITUATION

Forest companies, especially a handful of large corporations like MacMillan Bloedel, enjoyed decades of relatively unlimited access to vast stands of B.C. timber (Marchak 1983; Wilson 1990). Under a unique arrangement, although the great majority of forested land was publicly owned, the companies were able to log it on extremely favourable financial terms. But since the 1970s the future of British Columbia's old-growth forests has been a source of increasing political conflict and a focus of environmentalist activity, and the once-comfortable position of the forest companies has been threatened. Patricia Marchak (1983: 80) wrote about a "sudden discovery" that reforestation practices had not replenished the timber stands: "By the 1970s it was apparent that in several regions of the province reforestation had not kept pace with production." The specific problems of the B.C. forest industry coincided with the surge of the environmental movement globally, which highlighted new concerns such as biodiversity (Yearley 1991). Some key sites of conflict were the Stein Valley, Meares Island near Tofino, the Queen Charlotte Islands, and, as the 1980s drew to a close, the Walbran, the Tsitika, and the Carmanah (Tindall and Begoray 1993).

As the valley-by-valley struggle continued, the debate spilled onto a wider stage and drew international public and media attention. By the early 1990s Clayoquot Sound on Vancouver Island was a cauldron of dissent. In March 1993 an angry crowd of demonstrators stormed the B.C. legislature. A security guard fell and broke his hip, a window was shattered, and the throne speech was delayed. The provincial government announced its so-called Clayoquot compromise plan in April 1993. Under its terms about two-thirds of the old-growth rain forest in that area would be logged. An extended campaign of civil disobedience continued through the summer, as protesters violated a court order by a peaceful blockade of a logging road into the sound. More than 800 people were arrested. Some faced prison sentences: for example, six people convicted in October 1993 of criminal contempt were sentenced to 45 days in jail and fines of up to $3,000 (*Times-Colonist* [Victoria], Dec. 15, 1993: A3).

In early 1994 B.C. Premier Mike Harcourt travelled to Europe to promote the province's forestry industry, a move that continued an extended media duel between forestry companies and environmental organizations on the European front. Jack Munro of the B.C. Forest Alliance also travelled to Europe in early 1994 to counter an environmentalist publicity campaign that was getting more media attention there. Industry figures suggest that Western Europe is the second-largest market for B.C. pulp and paper after the United States (*The Globe and Mail*, April 11, 1994: B1).

While the framing literature focused initially on how social movements attract and keep potential adherents, it is worth noting that movement framing can have other targets. For example, SMOs sometimes focus framing activities on particular institutional audiences such as governments or corporations. SMOs such as Greenpeace may try to convince politicians or businesses that the public is accepting a certain frame, rather than targeting the public themselves (Doyle, Elliott, and Tindall 1995). In the European publicity campaign, environmentalists targeted various businesses. On March 1, 1994, *The Globe and Mail* reported (B5) that Scott Paper cancelled all contracts for pulp from companies operating in Clayoquot Sound. Later in March, Kimberly-Clark, the makers of Kleenex tissue, made a similar move. Greenpeace had apparently threatened to run negative ads linking the companies to clear-cutting in British Columbia.

It is not surprising that media coverage of the forestry dispute has been extensive within British Columbia, but even media outlets outside of Canada have also considered the forests dispute and sometimes given quite favourable coverage to the environmental movement. Critical stories about B.C. forest practices have appeared in the largest German news magazine and in Britain's *Observer* newspaper. *National Geographic*, traditionally shy of anything politically controversial, featured a photographic spread on clear-cuts. In summer 1991, *Time* magazine featured a two-page spread, "Canada's Troubled Trees," which talked about the "destruction" of British Columbia rain forests (*The Globe and Mail*, July 8, 1991). The article appeared in close to two million copies worldwide.

The extent to which framing contests played out in the international mass media have become a key element of the B.C. forests controversy is illustrated by the following episode, reported in the spring of 1995:

A war of words that began in Hollywood continues to escalate in the pages of major U.S. newspapers. The controversy over B.C. logging practises began when the San Francisco-based Rainforest Action Network took out full-page ads in Daily Variety, the Hollywood Reporter and the New York Times asking people in the U.S. film industry to help stop destruction of the very locations that have been bringing them north – although the fine print stopped short of explaining how that could be done. The Forest Alliance of British Columbia responded with its own full-pager in the New York Times and Daily Variety defending forestry practises and accusing the first group of deliberately discouraging Hollywood from calling. RAN then launched a fax blitz, claiming that the Alliance is only a front for MacMillan Bloedel and other provincial timber cutters, and that it even gets funds from the B.C. government. On April 18, RAN ran full-pagers once again in the New York Times and Daily Variety, this time suggesting that tourists to B.C. could "picnic in the clearcut forests" and "hike the eroded hillsides." On April 25, RAN followed with another full-page ad in the northeast edition of the New York Times, timed to coincide with Forests Minister Andrew Petter's visit to the United Nations Commission on Sustainable Development. The Alliance plans to reply on May 2 in the Seattle Post-Intelligencer and the national edition of the New York Times. (*Georgia Straight*, April 28-May 5, 1995: 35)

BURSON-MARSTELLER AND THE FOREST ALLIANCE

In recent years the B.C. forest industry has been one of those corporate interests that has recognized the need for a new public relations push. For several years starting in the late 1980s, the forest industry spent in the range of $1.5 to $2 million annually on the "Forests Forever" publicity campaign, much of it on television advertising (Wilson 1990: 154). As *B.C. Report* (April 29, 1991: 21) states, this campaign "is now widely regarded as a major blunder. Forests executives said that the campaign was too vague." Other observers felt the campaign was seen as shilling too transparently for the industry.

Perhaps seeking the need for proven professionalism after this apparent debacle, the embattled forest companies engaged the huge multinational public relations firm Burson-Marsteller in late 1990. The forest industry joined a rather grim list of previous and current B-M clients. B-M, was, as *The Financial Post* (April 11, 1991: 4) put it, "noted for its work both on the Bhopal poison gas disaster in India and the Tylenol deaths in the U.S."

Writer Joyce Nelson researched Burson-Marsteller extensively for her book on international public relations, *Sultans of Sleaze* (1989), as well as for a number of recent articles. According to Nelson, B-M, the world's largest public-relations firm, specializes in "crisis management." B-M has also worked for Hydro-Québec, on the Three Mile Island and Exxon Valdez environmental disasters, and on the Dalkon Shield IUD and the Dow-Corning breast implant controversies. B-M had also done public relations for the governments of Romania, Singapore, Indonesia, and Nigeria (during the Biafran war). The Salinas government in Mexico used B-M extensively to promote Mexico's cause in the NAFTA talks, and B-M remained helpful in managing negative publicity about the Chiapas revolt (*Georgia Straight*, Jan. 28-Feb. 4, 1994: 7). In 1981 B-M completed a five-year contract doing public relations for the junta in Argentina, which included managing negative international publicity about the widespread torture and disappearance of opponents of the regime (Nelson 1989: 22-39).

The B.C. Forest Alliance was also a Burson-Marsteller strategy, with thirteen B.C. forest industry chief executives guided by B-M launching the Alliance in April 1991. As one headline writer put it, the Alliance's aim was "stumping for B.C."

As an Alliance communications official told us, the organization was created specifically to counter environmentalist frames: "A recommendation was made to a group of forest companies who came together, who saw themselves as getting slaughtered in the PR battle. The suggestion was made to set up the Alliance. The goal was to achieve a group that had some independence from the industry. We have a thirty-member citizens board and it's them we take our direction from – although three quarters of our funding comes from seventeen forest companies." The Alliance had a start-up budget of $1 million and seven full-time staff. It was registered as a non-profit organization, though it was funded by the forest industry. The Alliance sold $20 memberships, which included a T-shirt. It set up a toll-free number (1-800-567-Tree) and began issuing press releases.

For its chairman the Alliance selected Jack Munro, perhaps British Columbia's best-known labour leader. Munro had been president of the loggers' union, IWA-Canada, for eighteen years. After he became involved with the Alliance, several union locals accused Munro of a conflict of interest. As of mid-1994 Munro was taking on close to a hundred speaking engagements a year for the Alliance.

On April 15, 1991, BCTV aired a half-hour Forest Alliance "documentary" on the industry. (While the show was presented as a documentary, it was actually a half-hour of paid advertising.) The Alliance released a proposed set of "guiding principles" for the forest industry in December 1991, which were ratified with considerable fanfare. The Alliance also plugged into the "information highway" and set up a twenty-four-hour on-line computer news service. It opened an Information Centre on Dunsmuir St. in the heart of Vancouver. Outside the Centre a neon sign featured a constantly updated "seedling count" of the millions of potential trees replanted in the province. Inside a green theme permeated the decor, right down to the coffee cups. In the public area the walls were adorned by "pro-environment" quotes from Thoreau and J.E. Lovelock's *Gaia: A New Look at Life on Earth*.

The Alliance has devoted a lot of attention to countering the environmentalist frame that described British Columbia as the "Brazil of the North" because of the depletion of its forests. The "Brazil of the North" label, originated by the Valhalla Wilderness Society from the Kootenay area of B.C., is a great example of what Snow et al. (1986: 468) call "frame-bridging," which occurs when a social movement organization taps into previously unconnected "ideologically consistent or frame compatible sentiment pools." In this case the movement hoped to win supporters by tapping into people's sentiments about the destruction of Brazilian rain forests. To address the Brazil of the North frame, the Alliance sent its own mission to Brazil for an eleven-day tour (as reported in the Alliance magazine *Choices*). The result was that "it soon became clear there was no basis for the slogan Brazil of the North." Ironically, the Alliance also argued that the Brazilian situation was not that bad, thus also becoming an apologist for Brazilian forest practices.[5]

In early 1994 the Alliance began its counterframing assault against the public relations offensive by Greenpeace and other SMOs in Europe. As *British Columbia Report* put it, the Alliance "launched an intensive campaign of lobbying, scientific briefings and public relations counter-attacks." The Alliance bought a full-page ad in a major German newspaper and funded a $200,000 local television advertising campaign, which began with a two-minute spot on the BCTV *Newshour* in April. The Alliance accused Greenpeace of blackmailing *The Times* of London into turning down a full-page ad, but *The Times* denied the accusation. "I see this as further evidence that blackmail is at the centre of [Greenpeace's] campaign," said Patrick Moore, former Greenpeace president, now turned Alliance spokesperson (*The Vancouver Sun*, April 8, 1994: B4).[6]

The Alliance has also directed its attention to the production of social scientific knowledge that advances its position. For example, in December 1994, the Alliance and the Vancouver Board of Trade released a report suggesting that one in six jobs in British Columbia's lower mainland depends on the forest industry (*The Vancouver Sun*, Dec. 10, 1994: H4).

As of mid-1994 the Alliance had ten full-time staff and a budget of about $2.5 million.[7] An Alliance source said at the time, "We have 240 corporate sponsors who would donate anywhere from $500 to a couple of grand and 7500 private members." Nevertheless, Munro appealed for financial help from the federal and provincial government for the Forest Alliance's continuing campaigns. Despite these appeals, it is worth noting that in addition to the Alliance, there is another heavily funded forest industry organization, the Council of Forest Industries (COFI), which is also engaged in the public relations struggle. A COFI spokesperson said on the CBC news (April 7, 1994) that the Council's office in Europe was spending virtually all of its time on the "image issue." Individual companies also conduct their own public relations initiatives. For example, MacMillan Bloedel has invested heavily in its own series of television ads suggesting that the company is "Making the Most of a Renewable Resource." In addition the federal and provincial governments also contribute millions of dollars towards publicity for the forest industry in other forms (as detailed in Nelson 1994).

Nevertheless, Glen Clark, B.C. investment minister at the time, also said a deal was in the works to give the Alliance "modest funding" from the government (*The Vancouver Sun*, April 30, 1994: A4). In late April 1994 B.C. Transit chair Eric Denhoff announced he was leaving the provincial government and joining the Alliance as a "senior adviser." The Alliance said he would be tackling publicity problems on the European front.

CLAIMING THE MIDDLE GROUND: IDENTITY-FRAMING

The attempts of the Alliance, as well as other forest company sources, to impose their preferred meanings on the forestry dispute show up in several key frames.[8] A key Alliance tactic is to claim validity for its position by framing the forestry dispute so that it represents the "middle ground" in the polarized debate. The Alliance attempts to impose a structure of meaning on the dispute that situates its position as a balance between industry and "eco-extremists." Framing by social movements and their opponents often centrally involves questions of identity (Cohen 1985). Identity-framing can also involve construction of the identities of opponents; the constructed "us" is often defined in relation to a constructed "them" (Gamson 1992; Hunt, Benford, and Snow 1994).

As Jack Munro said in March 1994 on a CBC *Newsworld* media segment, "The Forest Alliance was created and its role in life is to find a balance between the rhetoric on one side and the rhetoric on the other side." An Alliance publication, *Treeline*, suggests that "what's really happening in our forests is too often shrouded by sensational headlines, industry positions and environmental protests" – implying that the Alliance does not itself represent the industry position. The Alliance thus sometimes attempts to distance itself from the forest industry. For example, to quote an Alliance pamphlet: "Who's in charge? The Forest Alliance of B.C. is guided by Chairman Jack Munro and a Citizens' Board of community leaders from many regions." The pamphlet did not mention the fact that three-quarters of the Alliance's substantial budget came from seventeen forest companies and that the idea came from a multinational public relations firm. "We generated the idea of the Alliance, brought it to life and have been retained to keep things going," Kevin Gass of Burson-Marsteller said in April 1991. "The Alliance's paid working staff are Burson-Marsteller employees and although officially the Alliance is the producer of 'The Forest and the People,' the bottom line is we produced the show and bought the ad space on BCTV" (*B.C. Report*, April 29, 1991: 21). Thus, while Munro is "chairman," Gary Ley of the multinational P.R. firm became the Alliance's "executive director" (*The Vancouver Sun*, July 19, 1991: A11).

The Alliance's attempts to bring environmentalists on side have met with little success. "We've had a tough time trying to get environmentalists to sit on our board," an Alliance source told us. There is one big exception: former Greenpeace president and co-founder Patrick Moore became an Alliance board member and has been an active spokesman for the Alliance in the media. While his Alliance position is nominally voluntary, Moore also serves as a paid consultant for the forest industry through his Greenspirit environmental consultancy firm (*The Province* [Vancouver], Jan. 6, 1993: A42). Moore, who has a Ph.D. in ecology from the University of British Columbia, left Greenpeace Canada after an internal power struggle in the 1980s. When he joined the Alliance, he was accused of "selling out" by others in the environmental movement. Moore has also argued in the media that the Alliance represents the "middle ground" (*The Province*, Jan. 6, 1993: A42). He said the Alliance was "trying to find a balance between the needs of the environment and the needs of the people."

In an opinion piece in *The Vancouver Sun* (Feb. 5, 1994: A23) Moore accused those in the environmental movement of "eco-extremism" and argued that the environmental movement had swung to the left. This was partly because the fall of the Berlin Wall left peace movement and "pro-Communist" groups with nothing to do, Moore said, so that many of their members joined the environmental movement. Never identifying exactly whom he was referring to, Moore set up a straw man in the "eco-extremist" position, arguing that it valued trees and wildlife at the expense of human interests to the point where it was "anti-human." "The human species is characterized as a 'cancer' on the face of the earth. The extremists perpetuate the belief that all human activity is negative whereas the rest of nature is good" (*The Vancouver Sun*, Feb. 5, 1994: A23). By contrast, the Alliance represented the "middle ground."

Similarly, the Alliance Information Centre in downtown Vancouver placed a copy of a letter to the editor of the *Province* on display. The letter suggested that "hemp was the answer" to the forests dispute, and beside the letter the Centre had pinned a graphic of a marijuana plant. This seemed to be an attempt to play on the stereotype of environmentalists as "dope-smoking hippies" with "way-out" solutions to the wilderness debate, as opposed to the "balanced view" of the Alliance. Some B.C. environmentalists complain more generally that the news media tend to depict them as "young welfare hippies," although survey research shows B.C. environmental groups have a broad base of middle-class support (Forrest and Tindall 1994).[9]

Related to Moore's portrayal of "eco-extremists" are attempts to wrap environmental groups together in public perception with "eco-terrorists" like the organization Earth First! When a bridge over the Kennedy River near

Clayoquot Sound was burned in April of 1991, environmental movements quickly distanced themselves from the action. However, after an arrest in the incident, Munro attempted to frame the environmentalists as eco-terrorists based on the Kennedy River incident (*The Times-Colonist*, May 22, 1993). Environmentalist Paul George of the Western Canada Wilderness Committee (WC²) said that any kind of law-breaking created the possibility of this kind of frame being used by the forest companies: "They'd love to lump us together as radicals and law-breakers" (*The Globe and Mail*, Jan. 5, 1991: D1). Joe Foy of WC² even offered a $1,000 reward for information leading to the conviction of tree-spikers, and said that tree-spiking was a dangerous act that made it difficult for environmentalists and forestry workers to work together.[10]

The positions of the various social movement organizations vary considerably on the issue of direct action. Some, like the Western Canada Wilderness Committee, will not condone any illegal acts. Others support non-violent action in the classic liberal-democratic tradition of "civil disobedience." Then there are the "monkey-wrenchers" of Earth First! who believe in more violent opposition such as sabotaging equipment.

The *Province* newspaper gave substantial play to an "eco-terrorist" frame with its front-page "Greenfleece" story on Jan., 9, 1994. A story on page A5 began: "Greenpeace International has a new cause – fighting allegations it engages in sabotage." The *Province* reported comments by a private investigator, who was "hired in 1989 by several logging, mining and ranching companies to infiltrate Earth First." The *Province* gave the story big play, even though the links to Greenpeace were tenuous. For example, the private investigator "said he continually ran into Greenpeace members who also belong to Earth First."

One person who has attempted this tactic is Lindy Coady, a leader in the P.R. battle who has worked for MacMillan Bloedel and the Council of Forest Industries. She tried this approach in a speech to an audience of doctors at Vancouver's St. Paul's Hospital in October 1993, by linking environmentalists with anti-abortionists. She told the doctors: "We have each found ourselves coping with a radical minority intent on remaking society in their own image. Doctors have been followed to their homes by slogan-chanting anti-abortionists. Forest workers have found potentially lethal spikes driven into trees marked for cutting. And true believers have blockaded abortion clinics and logging roads" (*The Globe and Mail*, Nov. 5, 1993).

Another aspect of claiming the middle ground, then, is this emphasis that the Alliance's position is based on calm and reason as opposed to the irrational passion of environmentalists. As an Alliance communications official told us, "Our goal is to bring the debate to a rational level, where it's based on real information, and not the rhetoric."

TREES VERSUS JOBS; CITY VERSUS COUNTRY; PEOPLE VERSUS NATURE

A second key frame – perhaps the most powerful and crucial interpretive framework in the forests dispute – can be stated simply as "trees versus jobs." The forest companies have repeatedly deployed this frame. In the "tree versus jobs" frame, the economy will suffer severely if the environmentalists – or, as the Alliance calls them, preservationists – have their way. The companies have often claimed that half of every dollar generated in B.C. comes from the forest industry.[11] Other sources suggest that the industry represents about 25 per cent of the provincial GDP. The "trees versus jobs" frame involves the key belief that environmentalism, rather than economic factors, including harvesting at an unsustainable rate, is the primary threat to workers maintaining employment in this field. About 80,000 jobs in British Columbia are directly related to the forest industry, but forestry employment, particularly in some coastal communities, has been hit hard in recent years. Despite this, many forest companies have made record profits in the mid-1990s. Unemployment in the forest sector can be attributed to a variety of other factors besides environmentalist activity. As Trevor Barnes and Roger Hayter (1994) indicate, these factors include a "sea-change" in the forest industry, which shifted from "a regime of Fordism to one of flexible specialization" with new products, technologies, labour practices, and markets. This change has been combined with other difficulties, including aging equipment in coastal mills, plus the depletion of the resource base for a variety of reasons, including environmental concerns and First Nations' land claims as well as overharvesting and inadequate reforestation. While British Columbia has long been central in the world forest industry – the province provided about a third of the world's softwood lumber in 1991 – the long-term economic future of forestry in the province may be under serious threat from the restructuring of the global forest industry (Marchak 1991). In sum, in the "trees versus jobs" frame, environmentalists are scapegoated for employment difficulties in the industry, even though unemployment may be due to a variety of other factors.

Variations of the trees versus jobs frame also play on wider class and regional divisions between loggers and environmentalists. B.C. environmentalists have tended to be relatively affluent (Wilson 1990). Survey data from members of three B.C. environmental organizations (Tindall 1994) shows that many are members of what some sociologists call "the new middle class," consisting of a sector of young, educated, middle-class professionals. Some analysts argue that members of this social grouping, who have what are known as "postmaterialist values," have spearheaded new social movements such as environmentalism (Kriesi 1989). An ethnography of forest workers in Ontario (Dunk 1994) similarly suggests that rifts between loggers and environmentalists may often be rooted in wider class and regional divisions. We are not suggesting that the controversy in British Columbia can be reduced to one of class interests, but merely that class is one key variable in the dispute.

An Alliance communications professional described what we call the "trees versus jobs" frame:

> We start from the belief that there is a place for the forest industry in British Columbia, that it's worth protecting.... Particularly in the last couple of years the preservationists attacks against forestry are ... not just attacks against Clayoquot Sound, and not just against the practices of clearcut logging, but against forestry.... The issue is whether we should gain economic benefits from the forest resource or not. We believe that, yes, we should. Others believe that, no we shouldn't, we don't have that right.... It's true there's been offensive practices in our forests over the years – but that's not reason to abandon the industry. Greenpeace and others ... their goal today may be Clayoquot Sound and clearcut logging but we feel it's going to be every forest in British Columbia.

The use of the word "preservationists" rather than "environmentalists" is part of this framing attempt. The communications expert said, "We use the word preservationist when we talk about our opponents ... people who want to essentially preserve the land exactly as it is rather than who are concerned about any sort of stewardship of it." He argued that "real" environmentalists would not be opposed to every possible human industrial activity – as the "straw man" opponents of the Alliance are, according to him.

Many environmentalists would dispute these claims and say they are merely for some form of "sustainable development."[12] This "straw man" version of the environmentalists' position contrasts sharply with, for example, the view of the Western Canada Wilderness Committee's Joe Foy, who says: "You could turn the best technology towards a forest owned by many smaller manufacturers, and use it to turn out higher quality products. With higher quality products, more people would be employed. Then we won't have thousand-year-old trees used as studs hidden in a wall or in a piece of newsprint that's looked at once and thrown away" (*The Ubyssey*, Jan. 11, 1994: 3).

Environmentalists criticized the Alliance television program *The Forest and the People* for use of the "trees versus jobs" frame. "The program implied environmentalists are demanding a complete shutdown of forestry when in fact we are simply calling for a restructuring of it," observed Catherine Stewart, a director of Greenpeace. "The program depicted the usual job-versus-environment conflict; it never talked about jobs and environment-versus-corporate profit and dividends.... It also sidestepped many concerns shared by Greenpeace and loggers, such as the critical issue of creating value-added products to raise the value of our logged wood" (*B.C. Report*, April 29, 1991).

Similarly, Greenpeace attacked the "trees versus jobs" frame in a full-page ad in *The Globe and Mail* (Feb. 9, 1994: A7) "Clearcutting kills jobs. Over the past 40 years, clearcutting has enabled logging companies to increase the number of trees cut by nearly 400 per cent. Meanwhile, the work force has been slashed by nearly two-thirds. As the Pulp and Paper Workers of Canada state, 'not only do modern clearcutting methods use fewer people and bigger machines, they are also an environmental disaster.'"

The selection of a high-profile union leader, Jack Munro, as key spokesman for the Alliance was carefully considered and carries important symbolism. Munro, noted for his confrontational style, was perhaps a surprising choice for an organization trying to find the "middle ground," but he was an excellent choice for companies trying to frame the debate as a "trees versus jobs" division. Furthermore, he was selected partly because it is more difficult to read him as a mouthpiece for capital. As an Alliance communications professional told us, "I think with Jack what you've got is someone who is associated with the industry, but for the most part is perceived as taking an adversarial role to the industry, towards the companies, a spokesman for the worker.... Everyday British Columbians are represented." In other words, the image of a plain-spoken, leather-jacketed, rough-hewn union man meant "logger" and "worker," not "management" and "corporation." This captures in miniature a key aspect of the trees versus jobs frame: loggers are the public advocates of an anti-environmentalist frame, even though the frame ultimately serves the corporations. Indeed, another possibility, a former politician and prominent B.C. radio personality, was rejected as an alternative choice for the job of Alliance chair for similar reasons: "You get a right winger like that, who people associate with defending free enterprise, defending business – we have this perception problem that we're defending the industry anyway," said an Alliance source.

However, the presence of Munro as figurehead of the "jobs" side in this split has a sad resonance for British Columbians who recall the tumultuous events of 1983's Operation Solidarity movement. In that turbulent year, the right-wing populist government of Social Credit Premier Bill Bennett introduced massive public-sector and social-service slashing in the name of "restraint," but seriously miscalculated by underestimating the powerful public response to their "restraint" package. A potent alliance was formed between organized labour and various other interest groups, including civil servants and other urbanites who might be categorized as "new middle class."[13] In a series of escalating labour and protest actions, this alliance, Operation Solidarity, threatened to force the provincial government to undo the package. In a closed door deal with Munro – the "Kelowna Accord" – the Socred leadership managed to employ a divide-and-conquer strategy that undid the threatening alliance and drove a wedge between labour and other segments of the opposition (Carroll 1984: 104-7). With a horrible irony, a labour leader, Munro, became history's scapegoat for anger about the "new reality" program that served Social Credit and big capital. Perhaps the ultimate lesson of the Operation Solidarity period was the dynamic potential of a somewhat similar class alliance in B.C. between loggers – a key segment of organized labour – and environmentalists who may be members of the "new middle class." The trees versus jobs frame serves to prevent this potential convergence.

Despite the efforts of environmentalists and others, the trees versus jobs frame has remained prominent and seems to represent the "common sense" for many British Columbians. In June 1990, 2,000 loggers and supporters protested outside the legislature. One logger's placard summed this frame up as "Save A Worker – Spike A Tree Hugger" (*The Vancouver Sun*, June 16, 1990). Similarly, on March 21, 1994, a massive rally of thousands of "pro-jobs" loggers gathered at the B.C. legislature, with a sign at the rally offering the sentiment, "Screw The Environment – We Need Jobs." In September 1995 the Forest Alliance released another report it had commissioned suggesting the NDP government's forest policies could cost 46,000 jobs (*The Vancouver Sun*, Sept. 29, 1995: D1).

Bert Useem and Mayer N. Zald (1987) detail the U.S. nuclear industry's varied and sometimes secretive efforts at promoting "grassroots" community opposition to the anti-nuclear movement. These efforts included hiring a New York consulting firm to give media training to pro-nuclear community activists (282). A similar situation has occurred in British Columbia: the Forest Alliance has made its communications expertise available to loggers' groups in their battles against environmentalist "foes," helping to maintain the "trees versus jobs" split. An Alliance communications professional told us: "An IWA [loggers' union] group in the lower mainland recently called me, and essentially they want to organize themselves to keep their members focused on the issues and playing an active role... I've been meeting with them to give them communications strategies and my best advice."

As Jeremy Wilson (1990) notes, there has been considerable debate about the extent to which "grassroots" pro-logging groups such as Share B.C., often centred on loggers and their families, have been initiated or bankrolled by forest companies. For example, in 1988 the Share the Stein pro-logging group apparently received $200,000 from various forest company sources (Wilson 1990: 154). Similarly, Nelson (1994: 16) points out, "According to Share B.C.'s leader, Mike Morton, in 1991 sixty percent of his umbrella group's annual budget was provided by the forest industry." Pro-logging forces also work on the "trees versus jobs" split by playing up a parallel urban-rural rift between environmentalists and loggers, a division described by Thomas Dunk (1994). Forest industry spokespeople attempt to frame protesters as upper class, "cappuccino-sucking," "big city fools" (*The Vancouver Sun*, July 22, 1991, April 8, 1994). For example, "Heather Broughton, a director of Share Our Forests ... told the rally urban residents are deciding the fate of their rural cousins. 'Nearly every day I hear someone from the big city centres demanding we save another so-called "last wilderness"'" (*The Vancouver Sun*, June 16, 1990: A10).

The forest industry has even used its own survey data to play up this urban-rural split. MacMillan Bloedel president Robert Findlay told *The Globe and Mail* in 1991 that surveys, conducted by Decima Research, "indicate a gulf between opinions of city people and those who live in the logging communities. For the most part, the local people are more knowledgeable and more accepting of how the companies handle the forest 'because they live in it, they see it'" (*The Globe and Mail*, July 8, 1991).

Acceptance of the trees versus jobs frame – the belief that preserving the forests will be economically costly rather than an economically beneficial case of "sustainable development" – opens the door to another strongly related frame, which we call the "nature versus people" frame. For example, "The preservationists are like a new pagan religion, worshipping trees and animals and sacrificing people," says Charles Cushman of the Multiple-Use Land Alliance (*U.S. News and World Report*, Oct. 21, 1991). This frame makes a link between a love of nature and a kind of irrationality.[14] For example, "These groups take a religious approach to the environment," said Warren Newman, who, according to *The Globe and Mail*, was "head of corporate relations at General Utilities PLC and someone who has studied industry-environment conflicts in the past." Newman said, "The environmental debate is presented as a matter of faith rather than a matter of science" (*The Globe and Mail*, April 11, 1994: B3). Similarly, MacMillan Bloedel's Linda Coady said, "We have borne witness to contemporary science's vulnerability to mythology" (*The Globe and Mail*, Nov. 5, 1993).

On the PBS television special "Ancient Habitats," aired on April 25, 1994, a man who owns a logging company on the Olympic peninsula in Washington state said, "They forget that people are on earth too and people are a part of nature." Similarly, an official for a pulp and paper workers' union said, "Let's put the human element back into the Endangered Species Act."

The "trees versus jobs" frame portrays environmentalists' goals as harmful to humans and sets up this nature versus people split. The tendency pushes aside an alternative frame that might suggest some kind of beneficial harmony between humans and the rest of the environment.

THE B.C. MEDIA

While the news media are obviously only one context in which Alliance framing occurs, they are of central importance because of the added legitimacy usually attached to news media coverage.[15] Unlike the extensive paid advertising and promotional literature of the Alliance, the news supposedly offers a more disinterested account.

Media ownership in British Columbia is highly and increasingly concentrated in a handful of large corporations (Hackett, Pinet, and Ruggles, 1992).

The media have close ties to the business community, with some interlocking directorships between media corporations and forest companies. For example, as of 1978, Marchak (1983: 66-7) found, "The board of directors for Pacific Press, then jointly owned by Southam and Thompson companies, which between them controlled both the Vancouver newspapers, included a chairman of Cominco who was also a MacMillan Bloedel director; chairman of the board of Inland Natural Gas whose board, in turn, included a key executive officer of Crown Zellerbach; and ... the Southam board included an executive of Noranda and Northwood."

More recently, *B.C. Environmental Report* pointed out in March 1993 that the board of directors of Southam News featured key forest company executives, Noranda boss Adam Zimmerman, and Canfor director Ronald Cliff. Southam News owns the two largest B.C. newspapers, *The Vancouver Sun* and the *Province*, and more than a dozen other Canadian dailies.[16]

Still, we have to be careful to avoid a "black box" model of the political economy of news production in which ownership in and of itself is automatically equated with an ideological bias (Schudson 1989). As quoted in Goldberg (1993a: 15), former *Sun* forestry reporter Ben Parfitt, a critic of the *Sun*'s recent forestry coverage, said, "I don't think Adam Zimmerman [the Noranda head] has any direct control over what appears [in the *Sun*].... But the people who control Southam share a corporate philosophy that is similar to Noranda's.... Why else would you choose to have Adam Zimmerman on your board of directors unless you shared similar values?"

The variety of "alternative" B.C. media outlets such as the weekly Vancouver newspaper *Georgia Straight* and the Victoria newsweekly *Monday Magazine* may help sometimes to set the agenda for the other media.[17] However, even within the mainstream media some key journalists have given environmental questions a good deal of in-depth, critical coverage, including a fair amount of play for environmentalists' positions.

Many sociological analyses of the media tend to portray their operations as largely unitary and seamless and ignore the possibility of conflict within media outlets (for example, Herman and Chomsky 1988; Hall et al. 1978). This is true even of some analysts who portray the media as open to various forms of critical comment (Tumber 1993). Analysts sometimes suggest that social movements may be able to exploit contradictions in the media's role in capitalist society (Gitlin 1980; Cassidy 1992), yet they ignore the possibility of conflicting ideologies within media operations themselves. But there is often a good deal of political and ideological conflict within media outlets, particularly between the journalistic and commercial arms of the operation, but also sometimes within the newsroom itself. An in-depth ethnographic study of Toronto media outlets made a similar finding, demonstrating extensive conflict within news organizations (Ericson, Baranek, and Chan 1987).

We know from first-hand experience[18] that many B.C. journalists are young, university-educated people who may have "postmaterialist values" similar to those of many environmentalists in the province. As Hansen (1991: 451) notes, a number of researchers have suggested that reporters who cover environmental issues tend to be positive about environmental groups as news sources. In Britain, a "media charity" called Media Natura was established in 1988 whereby media personnel donated their public relations skills to help conservation groups (Anderson 1991: 474).

Anecdotal evidence about the political leanings of B.C. journalists is quite mixed. Some prominent broadcast journalists have slid into key communications positions with the right-wing Social Credit and Liberal parties. On the other hand, Robert Hunter, a founding member and former president of Greenpeace, was a *Vancouver Sun* journalist while he was involved in founding that organization. Hunter has since been "environmental reporter" for CITY-TV in Toronto. More recently, an award-winning environmental journalist for CBC-TV, Ian Gill, left that organization in November 1994 to become director of the environmental group Eco-Trust Canada, which has been working in Clayoquot Sound. Gill said he plans to set up a community bank in the area to invest in ecologically sensitive projects such as a small sawmill or sustainable fishery to "show you can create economic opportunity in a place like Clayoquot Sound without having to clearcut it all or fish it within an inch of its life" (*The Vancouver Sun*, Nov. 16, 1994: A3).

Thus some journalists themselves may be among "the young social and cultural specialists" whom some sociologists argue form the avant-garde of the new social movements such as environmentalism (Kriesi 1989: 1111). (Kriesi seems to state that journalists belong to his category of "social and cultural specialists" [1083]). While we can only speculate here about this point, it would be an interesting subject for further empirical research on the sociology of news production. For example, it might prove to be most probable in the more junior front-line journalist positions, and less true of the collection of largely older males further up the editorial hierarchy, who might perhaps be somewhat less likely to be university-educated. Those in the commercial and advertising areas might also prove more likely to be conservative and more likely to be oriented towards business. This may be one factor that sets up a situation of ideological conflict *within* media organizations.

We are certainly not arguing here that journalists or editors will allow their political leanings to cause them to violate their professional ethics. While any claims to "objectivity" may be philosophically faulty, we believe that news media organizations – and the vast majority of media workers – have a moral commitment both to factual accuracy and to a significant amount of balance in their coverage. But we also believe that within the traditional media framework of truth, stories can be factually accurate and still coloured in various ways by the inclinations of individual media workers – for example, in the choice of topics reporters use their discretion to report on, or the extent to which they develop close ties with various kinds of news sources. While some reporters simply concede this tendency, in other cases it may occur despite their efforts to remain "objective." The professional culture of journalism has always featured somewhat of a tension between the ideal of detached "objectivity" and other ideals linked to more active roles for the journalist as analyst and advocate (Weaver and Wilhoit 1996).

The ideological positions of media workers, then, can vary within news organizations and have a significant effect on coverage. Conflict among these positions means that hegemony can be contested within media outlets themselves. According to B.C. freelance journalist Kim Goldberg, this type of conflict was demonstrated in events at *The Vancouver Sun* newspaper. Goldberg notes that, ironically, the *Sun* itself also engaged the public relations firm Burson-Marsteller, choosing B-M in summer 1991 to promote its shift to a morning paper. Goldberg and others have charged that the B-M link has influenced the *Sun*'s forests coverage. A July 1991 meeting of five Alliance directors with the Sun's editorial board to complain about the papers' forestry coverage backfired somewhat in that B-M was the subject of further criticism in a column by Stephen Hume (*The Vancouver Sun*, July 22, 1991). In an article in the *Columbia Journalism Review* (CJR), Goldberg (1993b: 19) gives an account of events at the *Sun* since the ascension of B-M and the Alliance:

> Delegations of forest company officials and Alliance members became a common sight in the Sun's editorial offices. Senior reporter Mark Hume says he was called into his editor's office and grilled for more than an hour by a logging company official and an industry consultant about columns he had written examining the origins of a pro-logging coalition. Sun managing editor Scott Honeyman, Hume says, stood by in silence.
>
> Prior to the birth of the Forest Alliance, the Sun had five full-time reporters covering forestry, fisheries, native affairs, energy and mines, and the environment. Today only the environment beat remains. The rest were lumped into a category called "resources" and handed over to the business section.

In a rebuttal in the next issue of CJR, Honeyman said the changes were a result of economic troubles experienced by the newspaper.

In her article, Goldberg (1993b: 19-20) continued:

> Reporters who wrote critically about the forest industry's impact on the environment, fisheries, or tribal land claims – and those who probed the workings of the Forest Alliance and Burson-Marsteller itself – say they were subjected to pressure. The Sun's forestry reporter, Ben Parfitt, quit after Honeyman pulled him off his beat because, on a freelance basis, he

had written about Burson-Marsteller and the Forest Alliance for a Vancouver weekly (*Georgia Straight*). "He was declaring himself not a dispassionate reporter" with the article, Honeyman says. The paper's former native affairs reporter, Terry Glavin, who says the newspaper became "a bloody war zone" for reporters who wrote critically about the forest industry, also quit this year.

The *Sun* also discontinued the column of well-known environmentalist David Suzuki, host of CBC television's popular *The Nature of Things*.

Goldberg's account is grim, but it is important to note Glavin's description of the newsroom as a "bloody war zone" characterized by a great deal of internal conflict. The comment suggests that hegemony is contested, partial, and unfinished (Williams 1977) within media outlets. Some journalists may have enough political power within the organization to be able to resist the kind of pressures described by Goldberg. Furthermore, the media depend for their legitimacy and commercial viability on presenting a variety of alternative positions (Gitlin 1980; Ericson 1991). Even after the changes outlined by Goldberg, the *Sun* continued to provide critical coverage of the forests dispute, as a number of examples sprinkled throughout this chapter suggest.[19] Thus Hackett's (1991) metaphor may be apt: the media are not a level playing field, but it may be possible for social movement organizations to win even when they are playing uphill.

B.C. MEDIA COVERAGE OF THE ALLIANCE

One of the consequences of the forest industry's hiring of B-M is that a string of negative stories about the firm's connection with the forest industry appeared in *The Vancouver Sun, Times-Colonist, Georgia Straight, This Magazine*, and *Canadian Forum*. For example, *Sun* columnist Stephen Hume (Nov. 8, 1993) described B-M as "the firm paid to put a happy face on Argentina while the ruling regime was busily murdering high school kids and liquidating thousands of citizens." The *Sun* also ran several stories critical of the B-M in the straight "news" section of the paper.

In hiring B-M, the forest industry had inadvertently permitted a terrible kind of link to be made by the media. Journalists were able to draw a connection between forestry disputes in British Columbia and the other outrageous issues that B-M had worked to "put a happy face" on, such as torture and murder, nuclear disaster, and other environmental devastation. By allowing this connection to be made, hiring the public relations firm would, with considerable irony, prove to be somewhat of a public relations fiasco for the forest industry. According to Alliance sources, as of mid-1994 the Alliance "still had a consulting relationship" with B-M, although the relationship was "more removed than it had been."

As well, while the Alliance has tried to claim "the middle ground," our review of coverage suggests that the media have strongly tended not to ascribe such impartiality to the organization. Over and over again the media refer to the Alliance as a "pro-industry" or "pro-logging" group. *The Vancouver Sun* (July 18, 1991: E1) referred to it, for example, as a "company funded public relations campaign." Similarly, in an editorial (Dec. 15, 1993) the Victoria *Times-Colonist* referred to the Alliance as a "pro-logging group." Even the unabashedly right-wing *British Columbia Report* refers to the Alliance as "pro-industry" (though this magazine has given the Alliance positive coverage in general; see the cover story in the April 18, 1994, issue, for example). One difficulty the Alliance would have encountered here is the presence of a government-sanctioned alternative body that might also be seen as trying to find the "middle ground" – the CORE commission set up by the provincial government to find compromise solutions to land-use conflicts. Of course, a more parsimonious and straightforward explanation is that the Alliance's role as a mouthpiece for the forest companies is simply quite transparent.

Thus, while the Alliance has attempted to frame itself as representing the middle ground, it has achieved limited success in convincing the media this is so. As an Alliance communications professional told us: "Three-quarters of our funding comes from seventeen forest companies – so we're tied to them. It's difficult to deny. Personally I never claim we are a wholly independent group.... I've said to people in the past, personally I don't feel we've totally fulfilled our mandate to foster more rational discussion. It's because the minute we stepped out we were cast as apologists."

Other Alliance employees offer a different view. "The Alliance is an independent body," said Eric Denhoff, who left the B.C. government to work for the organization. "Sometimes it's critical of the government. Sometimes it's critical of the industry."

It is more difficult to assess the success of Alliance efforts to promote the trees versus jobs frame, partly because this frame is far from unique to the Alliance. Goldberg suggests that reporters are "forever foundering in the false dichotomy of jobs versus environment" (*Georgia Straight*, April 15-22, 1994: 9). She argues, "The media seldom report that of the 27,000 forestry jobs lost in B.C. between 1981 and 1991, only two per cent were sacrificed to parks (the remainder were lost as a result of mechanization and over-cutting)." Goldberg has made these kind of arguments a number of times, in different alternative media outlets. Thus, at least through these channels, the media are open to criticisms of this frame.

The early results of a content analysis[20] of print media coverage of B.C. forests issues suggest that the "trees versus jobs" frame does get substantial play. But at this point it is difficult to assess the extent to which this is a result of Forest Alliance efforts. A number of examples in our sample indicate that the mainstream media have explicitly rejected the trees versus jobs frame. For example, *The Vancouver Sun* reported (Jan. 14, 1992: D2),

"MacMillan Bloedel is using land-use debates in Clayoquot Sound as a convenient excuse for cutting 55 logging jobs it would have chopped anyway, says the IWA-Canada.... Last week, B.C.'s biggest forest company said continued uncertainty over future logging levels in old-growth forests surrounding Clayoquot Sound forced it to announce the cutbacks.... But IWA-Canada Local I-85 president Dave Haggard disagreed, saying MB is 'using it as an excuse to downsize their operations.'"

Similarly, the *Sun*'s Stephen Hume wrote a strong column countering the trees versus jobs dichotomy. Hume (April 8, 1994: A19) quoted Mayor Tom McCrae of Tahsis: "We have been one of the few communities that has been through major down-sizing.... We once had a community of over 2,500 people. We are now just over 1,000 people. We lost a cedar mill – a complete mill – that employed 250 people. Then our hemlock mill was modernized and we lost another 200 jobs. We've lost our bank, the hospital has been chewed at." However, the column continues: "There's a side note to down-sizing. There wasn't a tree-hugger or environmentalist for 500 miles."

Similarly, the Alliance's most recent efforts to frame a "trees versus jobs" split have not received very favourable coverage in the *Sun* and elsewhere. For example, a front-page account of a Forest Alliance report in the Sept. 29, 1995, *Vancouver Sun* was headlined "Forestry report felled by minister" – and took a critical tone. It began, "B.C. Forests Minister Andrew Petter took his axe Thursday to a forest-industry commissioned report showing NDP policies could cost 46,000 jobs, calling the study full or errors and 'purely political.' He said the report reflects the political agenda of some forest companies that want to create fear in forestry-based communities." Aside from these examples, however, the general frequency with which the media adopt the trees versus jobs frame – and the Alliance's role in this – is a topic for further research.

Beyond this, it is important to note the constraints of typical media frames, which are focused on distinct, dramatic events rather than underlying conditions (Ericson, Baranek, and Chan 1987). The media's focus on spectacle – such as the arrest of Clayoquot protesters – particularly in the television format, can displace the possibility of a more complex political discourse that is needed to refute the "common sense" (Gramsci 1971) of a trees versus jobs division.

CONCLUSIONS

The B.C. forest industry is controlled by corporations, including powerful multinationals, that have devoted considerable resources to a publicity operation in the form of the Forest Alliance. Although we have not explored in much detail what audiences make of Alliance frames, an Alliance official argued in 1994 that a poll showed the Alliance was winning the ideological struggle: "We do have a recent Marktrend poll which shows for the first time in five years – the first time since they started doing this sort of polling – which shows that more British Columbians feel forest companies are acting responsibly than feel environmentalists are acting responsibly. The approval rating for environmentalists fell from 79 per cent about a year and a half ago – November of 92 – to about 51 per cent now. We feel that we have begun to make British Columbians question what the environmentalists tell them." The forestry companies are now at a 56 per cent "approval rating," he said.

Further research is needed to judge the efficacy of these claims. Meanwhile, our assessment is that the Alliance has not been particularly successful in attempts to validate its statements by framing itself in the media as representing the "middle ground" in the forests controversy. Furthermore, the Alliance's connection with Burson-Marsteller has, ironically, proved to be a source of bad publicity. However, the key "trees versus jobs" frame serves to counteract a potentially powerful convergence between workers and environmentalists. This frame seems to remain the prominent one in the B.C. forests controversy, whether or not it is due in large part to the efforts of the Alliance. The trees versus jobs frame may be a key factor in preventing a different kind of "forest alliance" from emerging between workers and environmentalists – a class alliance with considerable counterhegemonic potential, as the events of the Operation Solidarity era demonstrate. Evelyn Pinkerton (1993) details how the Tin Wis coalition began to explore the potential of an alliance between environmentalists and labour, along with small businesses and First Nations in British Columbia. Laurie Adkin (1992) argues for the possibilities of an "eco-socialist discourse" in addressing environmental concerns; such a system of meaning might prove the antidote to the "trees versus jobs" frame.

One of Project Censored Canada's top ten unreported stories of 1993 was corporations subverting the environmental movement.[21] Project Censored Canada argued, "Multinational corporations and their handlers are employing new tactics in order to influence public opinion and corporate decisions. They have established moderate 'front groups' – ranging from the influential Business Council on Sustainable Development to so-called Share groups – that often have a common link in PR giant Burson-Marsteller, which set up our province's 'grassroots' B.C. Forest Alliance.... The pitting of workers against environmentalists is another new strategy" (*Georgia Straight*, April 15-22, 1994).

It is important to note, however, that the Project Censored Canada list does not mean that these stories were completely "censored" from the media. For example,we read about the Burson-Marsteller/Forest Alliance story in the media repeatedly. In fact, Project Censored Canada acknowledges at least two media sources for all but one of its top ten stories. The fact that the stories are "censored" but still make it into media outlets to some degree suggests that hegemony is unfinished and contested in the mass media.

Alternative media outlets like the *Georgia Straight* may be one important factor in this regard, allowing the publication of stories stifled by the mainstream media and in particular a critique of mainstream media outlets that helps keep them somewhat "honest." However, some of the mainstream media have also covered this story.

While social movement and countermovement organizations engage in framing (Snow et al. 1986), it is important to recognize that the media also frame. Gitlin (1980) argues that the media may limit the potential for resistance against hegemony by "clamping frames on insurgent movements." We suggest here that the news media have sometimes also shown resistance to the frames of the Forest Alliance, a corporate framing effort, and we have cited a good deal of material from the media that casts the Alliance in a bad light. While some critics may characterize the media's role simply as an "upholder of the status quo" (Cassidy 1992), our case study shows that big corporations have felt compelled to invest millions in a public relations battle over B.C. forests, only to meet quite mixed success in communicating their viewpoint through the news media. Nevertheless, the routine "framing" operations of the media, such as a focus on immediate events and the search for televisual spectacle, may inhibit the complex discourse needed to displace the "common sense" of trees versus jobs.

Goldberg's account of the dispute within the confines of *The Vancouver Sun* can be read as demonstrating how hegemony is reproduced within media outlets – but also how this is a contested process. Despite the political economy of the news media, they are far from being simply an ideological apparatus for capital, as some prominent accounts suggest. While such accounts portray news media operations as seamless, there is sometimes considerable conflict within media outlets themselves. Our analysis indicates that to the extent hegemony is achieved in the mass media it is always partial, contested, and unfinished, and the news media are more open, pluralistic, and diverse than some accounts suggest (Ericson 1991; Ericson and Doyle 1996). The news media thus offer valuable openings for social movements struggling to contest dominant meanings.

NOTES

1. We focus in this chapter primarily on framing activities by the Alliance. We do not provide a systematic account of framing by environmental organizations and other players, leaving this as a topic for further research.
2. In addition to clipping files maintained by the authors, we've also used files at the University of British Columbia's Sedgewick Library, the Vancouver Public Library, and those of veteran activist Doran Doyle (of the "Raging Grannies"). We are also indebted to the investigative work of several B.C. journalists, notably Joyce Nelson and Kim Goldberg, concerning the activities of the public relations firm Burson-Marsteller and the B.C. Forest Alliance.
3. Snow and Benford (1992: 137) note briefly, "The recent spate of research on the

media and newsmaking both documents and highlights [the] function of frames (Gans 1979; Gitlin 1980; Tuchman 1978)."

4. Gamson's work thus has affinities with "reception analysis" or "active audience theory." See Fiske (1987).

5. In a bizarre footnote to the "Brazil of the North" debate, *B.C. Report* noted in late 1993 that Colleen McCrory of the Valhalla Wilderness Society was apologetic for comparing forestry in British Columbia and Brazil. In fact, McCrory's apology (*Monday Magazine*, Dec. 9-15, 1993: 6), in its full context, read: "I owe Brazil an apology – B.C. isn't as bad as Brazil, it's worse."

6. The forest industry has also applied similar economic pressure. For example, in 1991 the Council of Forest Industries encouraged an advertiser boycott of CBC's *Nature of Things* because of its displeasure with David Suzuki's two-hour special "Voices In The Forest." The CIBC withdrew advertising from the program shortly afterwards, citing its "controversial" nature (Persky 1991: 158).

7. As Munro stated in a letter to the editor of *Georgia Straight*, April 29-May 6, 1994: 4.

8. These do not represent an exhaustive account of the Alliance's framing efforts. Rather, we seek merely to highlight key strands in their work.

9. The depiction of environmentalists is a subject for further empirical research, although it is our perception that instead many media accounts of the forests dispute tend to focus on a few established and "respectable" environmentalist sources from organizations like the Sierra Club and Western Canada Wilderness Committee.

10. Opponents have also intermittently committed a number of acts of violence against those in the environmental movement. For example, in October 1990, in the Carmanah, a research station was burned down and a wooden walkway built by environmentalists was chainsawed to pieces (*The Vancouver Sun*, Oct. 23, 1990: B1).

11. In a more candid moment, Dick Brym, Manager, Economics, Statistics and Energy, of the B.C. Council of Forest Industries, said, "You've probably heard of the old saying about 50 cents out of every dollar generated in B.C. coming from the forest industry. Well. That's not true today, and actually I'm not sure it ever was" (Nixon, 1990: 14).

12. Forester Merv Wilkinson's Wildwood tree farm near Chemainus on Vancouver Island provides an example that some environmentalists support. For an article discussing Wilkinson's alternative logging practices, see Loomis and Wilkinson (1991).

13. This term must be used with an awareness that there is considerable debate in the social movements literature about understandings of the "new middle class." See Bagguley (1992).

14. Taken literally, the nature versus people frame can be reduced to the absurd, as when *U.S. News and World Report* (Oct. 21, 1991) noted recently, "The spotted owl, widely blamed for rising unemployment among loggers in the Pacific Northwest, has become the lightning rod for much of the frustration over job losses," which seems to suggest the owl is to blame.

15. Our account is focused somewhat narrowly on the print media. This is because of the easy availability of print media texts for review, and also of various sources of knowledge about the internal politics of B.C. print media outlets.

16. More recently the newspapers were acquired by Conrad Black's growing Hollinger chain.

17. *Monday Magazine* offered extensive coverage of forestry issues for many years because the issue was given high priority by former editor Sid Tafler.

18. One of the authors (Aaron Doyle) draws on several years of experience as a staff journalist at two B.C. community newspapers and at Victoria's *Monday Magazine*.

19. For example, an article in the *Sun* (April 22, 1994: B4) demonstrates once again the use of frame-bridging:

    Left jobless by the collapse of the East Coast fishery, Bernard Martin joined the Clayoquot Express last fall to carry his message "from the ocean without fish to the forest without trees." ... "There is no difference between the use of dragger technology by Fishery Products International or National Sea and the MacMillan Bloedel practice of clear-cutting in the forests," said Martin.... Scott McFayden, 25, of Mississauga, Ont., said he watched the dumping of toxic chemicals into the Great Lakes and helped clean oil from the beach in the Shetland Islands, and what is happening at Clayoquot Sound is just another example of what is happening all over world.

20. Enquiries regarding this ongoing project can be directed to David Tindall or Aaron Doyle, Department of Anthropology and Sociology, University of British Columbia.

21. This project by a group in Simon Fraser University's communications department is led by Robert Hackett, whose work on the Canadian media and the peace movement we cite elsewhere.

AFTERWORD

MANY DAVIDS,
ONE GOLIATH

R.S. Ratner

I

"Globalization" is a phenomenon only alluded to in the preceding chapters, but no observer today would minimize its significance. One need only take note of how in a remarkably short period of time the theatre of world politics has shifted from the "spectre of communism" to the "mantra of globalization." Indeed, the global marketplace has become the site for a new type of normativity, one in which capital can reconstitute society on a daily, lived basis.

Globalization in this sense is not merely a passing metaphor, but may have become, as some now view it, the new God before which all must bow.[1] Certainly globalization has transformed the scope of modern social struggles, forcing social movements to rethink their objectives and modify their strategies for achieving social change, a situation that commands increasing critical attention.

The term globalization emerged in the 1980s and is now in wide use, but with a variety of meanings. In a technical sense, emphasizing strictly *economic* aspects, it refers to the "growing international integration of markets for goods, services, and capital" (Qureshi 1996: 30), spurred by quantum changes in computerized modes of communication. Politically, it is a neoliberal project propelled by transnational corporations (TNCs), a project in which all nations become "peripheral to the new supranational network of corporate power" (Kennedy 1988: 245). Historically globalization can be understood as the most recent manifestation of modernization waves that first emerged in Western Europe in the sixteenth and seventeenth centuries (Campanella 1990: 2) and have crested as a proximate "world system" in which powerful, interconnected stateless corporations are nullifying national boundaries and incorporating whole societies as cost-effective "sites of production" (Nelson and Fleras 1995: 430). In essence a globalization-from-above (Falk 1993) or so-called New World Order is taking shape under the direction of transnational business, sponsored overtly by the political elites of leading states. Key components of this global system, according to Leslie Sklair (1995: 500), are "the transnational corporation, the characteristic institutional form of economic transnational practices, a still-evolving transnational capitalist class in the political sphere, and in the culture-ideology sphere, the culture-ideology of consumerism."[2]

These TNCs represent a new phase of international *monopoly* in their paradoxical demands for "free trade," and are bolstered by supranational institutions (for example, OECD, IMF, World Bank) that sanction their expansionist agenda (Cowling and Sugden 1987).[3] Although they do not have direct military capacities, they rely on market power and control over finance and technology to establish their control (Gill and Law 1988: 192). As companies without a country (Barnet and Müller 1974: 16), TNCs regard their quest for global profit as enhancing the prosperity of all because of claimed efficiencies in organizing the world economy, notwithstanding critical estimates that the well-being of at least two-thirds of the world's population has been abandoned or marginalized by the architects of globalization.[4]

Nevertheless, the ostensible neo-laissez faire doctrine of global capital goes forward as the presumed wave of the future, justified by alleged *convergences* in productivity and wages between poor and developed countries and generating momentum under the righteous auspices of an "integrated global economy." In this conception, nation-states are disparaged as obstacles to "planetary" development; indeed, domestic nationalism is portrayed as being in terminal decline, its "solutions" already proven inadequate in the Fordist transition.

Yet despite the triumphant sweep of global capital, it must be wondered whether what is under way is merely the transfer of the wealth of the many to the few, and whether that sardonic reality is not veiled by the "myths" of globalization that apotheosize the importance of growth, the benevolence of capital, the benefits that will accrue to all, and the claimed inevitability of the now unfolding processes. Is there truly a world capitalism towards which all forces are inexorably moving, or, as some sceptical observers believe, is globalization only "inevitable" so long as corporations are allowed to buy the politicians and write the laws? As David Korten (1995: 4) notes:

> The idea that we are caught in the grip of irresistible historical forces and inherent human imperfections to which we have no choice but to adapt is pure fabrication. Economic globalization is being advanced by conscious choices made by those who see the world through the lens of the corporate interest.

Even so, there is no denying that global financial markets and corporations are fast becoming the governing institutions of the planet.[5] Liberal welfare states are now clearly subordinate to the market, deindustrialization in the First World has racheted down wages and working conditions, seriously weakening labour, and revenue-short governments have caved into the draconian social policies of corporate capital. In short, "money" is governing with relatively little interference, and those without it are increasingly left to fend for themselves. All that is solid does not melt into air, but flows into the coffers of the TNCs, which shape even the priorities of officially "global" institutions such as the International Monetary Fund and World Bank, now guided by a supranational system of governance (for example, NAFTA, EU, GATT) indentured to the corporations – a veritable global coup d'état. If there is not as yet any visibly cohesive international capitalist class, the silhouettes are unmistakeable. As Mark C. Kennedy (1988: 274) asserts, "The only world project that is currently succeeding is the expansion of the network of transnational economic power."

Given the growing compass of corporate hegemony, its merits might be thought substantial. But apart from pointing to its capacity as an agent of economic modernization and industrial development (Black, Blank, and Hanson 1978; Qureshi 1996), critics underscore how devotion to profits benefits few and penalizes many (Laxer 1995; Korten 1995; Panitch 1992). Progressive taxation is undermined, the private sector is heedlessly deregulated, government programs that provide social and economic security are dismantled, and what remains of the public-service agencies is transferred piecemeal to the colder lap of profiteering corporations. All of this has led to the displacement of political community by a consumerist-driven ideology that numbs potential resistance by preoccupying people with commodity turnover or unrelieved indigence. While a small number of countries move from "have not" to "have" status, the TNC powerhouses generate growing economic disparities among the world's nations and regions.

In a recent assessment of the benefits and costs of globalization, Pierre Pettigrew, the Canadian federal Minister for International Co-operation, reached the following conclusion:

> Development and international cooperation are taking place today in a context of rapid globalization, a situation in which high-technology, information and knowledge make boundaries less meaningful and prosperity potentially boundless. Nevertheless, the sunny promise of globalization has a dark side. They counterpoise a more integrated world economy and boundless prosperity against the risk that most of the world's people will fall by the wayside, impoverished and disgruntled spectators to the global revolution. And this exclusion may occur not only south from north, but within societies where knowledge and access to wealth may become the preserve of a privileged few. The yawning gap between rich and poor, including Canada, can only exacerbate current problems, such as crime,

terrorism and environmental degradation, all of which contribute to global and national instability.[6]

Pettigrew's mixed judgement is one of many that question whether market-driven trade will enhance living standards for the vast majority.[7] Clearly the *social* dimension of globalization lags far behind the economic attainments of capital mobility. Richard Barnet and Ronald Müller's (1974: 25) reservations of nearly twenty-five years ago are still apropos: "To establish their political legitimacy, the aspiring World Managers must be able to demonstrate that the maximization of global profits is compatible with human survival."

Despite uncertainties, developing and developed nation-states have compliantly dropped protective sanctions in order to attract foreign capital, on the prayer that this move will eliminate fiscal and social problems.[8] Ironically, the one irrefutable byproduct of trade liberalization has been the dramatically reduced authority of individual states. Usurped by corporate CEOs and state elites, contemporary politics has withdrawn into an antipolitics of resignation or sprung to life only in the sequestered realms of "identity politics." But this relative quiescence may only signal the onset of massive *instability*; indeed, the quandary of globalization is precisely that of effecting the transition from relatively closed societies to the global market while maintaining political *stability*. This entails reducing disparities in wealth and moderating the powerful inegalitarian forces that arise in the wake of globalization – a highly improbable outcome in view of the "democratic deficit" (Chomsky 1994: 7) caused by the weakening of public institutions and the diminished influence of elected agents. Nation-states, formerly the principal bulwarks of domestic welfare and human rights, have been downgraded to mere "transmission belts" from the global to the national economy – mechanisms for adjusting national economic practices and policies to the perceived exigencies of the global economy (Cox 1992: 31).[9] The principal losers in the redistribution of power (Cook, Pakulski, and Waters 1992), they symbolize the powerlessness of the powerful (Sakamoto 1995: 131) as territorial boundaries are blurred and eradicated by the global concentration of power.[10]

Consequently, state-based strategies of social reform are consigned to irrelevance, and transnational corporations decide the rules of the global game. As Richard Flacks (1995: 260) observes, "The capacities of states to do economic steering, allocate capital, and redistribute income have been largely superseded by global capital flow, transnational corporate organization and the dynamics of the world market."

At the same time as this shrinkage of the state's claim to manage society has occurred, corporate capital has come to rely on the state as its guarantor for the implementation of country-based global projects through the "disciplining" of potentially recalcitrant populations. Given its neoliberal restructuring mandate, the nation-state is therefore not completely without the power to influence the course of globalization, which suggests the possibility of rediscovering a positive role for it: of holding transnational corporations accountable for the consequences of their policies across all levels of citizen involvement. Indeed, prior to the advent of full-blown globalization, the international field was largely reserved for intervention by states and structured by interstate relations (Hegedus 1989). Globalization, however, has subordinated national-level processes and reforming strategies to the judgement of international markets and co-ordination by "global governance" – a variety of extrastate and suprastate actors pledged to the new phase of capitalist dominance.[11] As Andre Drainville (1996: 3) notes, "Global governance represents an attempt to move transnationally-constructed orders beyond the coercive enforcement of managerial devices towards a politically more enduring consensual global framework for actions and policies."

In this sense "global governance" represents the maturation of organized capitalism on a worldwide scale, reinventing social relations from above, and creating a "global civil society" under the banner of liberal cosmopolitanism. Yet, while such a movement may halt the threatened chaos stemming from a "deglobalization" of world politics, it remains a highly fragile and underdeveloped project (White 1995), disdained by oppositional groups or existing regimes unwilling to yield advantage through engulfment in remote international structures.

The supreme political task, then, is to reconstitute power across different levels of authority in ways that counter the despotic tides of globalization. While the TNC trajectory is not inexorable (the struggle for hegemonic control is never-ending), it is *social movements* that are increasingly looked to as the dynamo of an authentic sense of community able to reverse the atomizing trends of economic globalization: thus the emergence of the "abnormal" politics of new social movements, prompting a shift from national politics to local grassroots action and the formation of a vast and profound solidarity grounded in the validity of communal experience. Such movements, as they multiply and spread, represent a different sort of globalization, one tantamount to a "globalization-from-below" (Falk 1993; Brecher and Costello 1990), a communally activated expression of democracy that opposes the homogenizing tendencies of "globalization-from-above." While some observers regard these movements as the key to democratic transformation, others, such as Drainville (1996: 19), caution that they are liable to take the form of a collection of episodic moments of international solidarity with little programmatic, strategic or political coherence.

In any case, what are widely referred to as the new social movements (NSMs) emerge from the near-dissolution of traditional politics. They contain the double prospect of autonomy and consolidation, but also the possibility of descent into sectarianism and political impotence. Should they take root locally and develop strong cords of political connectedness, they may

turn out to be the one force capable of cracking the mould of corporate globalization. An important question for NSMs, as well as for more traditional
social movements (such as labour), is whether amalgamation or unfettered
diversity (a "politics of identity") is the most promising route to social
change. Certainly the labour movement is now more receptive to cross-
movement collective action (Waterman 1993) as it finds its long-standing
modes of contention (strikes, for instance) less effective in the context of
capital mobility and the exploitable masses of the Third World,[12] which in
turn suggests that actions against corporate capital cannot be successfully
waged unless understandings about the effects of globalization both inform
local struggles and encourage the search for commonalities.

On this score a major development over the last twenty years has been
the proliferation of social movements in the international arena (Hegedus
1989), a field traditionally closed to such movements. Leslie Paul Thiele
(1993: 280) defines these international movements as transnational in two
senses: their multinational membership and organizational structure, and
their explicitly global, rather than solely national or local, concerns and allegiances.[13] A professed advantage of *transnational movements* is that in pursuing movement solidarity on a global scale through direct group-to-group
contact, they avoid the constraining influences of state structures (Tarrow
1994b: 196)[14] and are therefore in a better position to challenge the TNC version of order that now dominates the global economy.

So while "globalization" may have paralyzed state strategies of reform, it
has also motivated attempts to discover workable democratic principles for
reconciling local, national, and global interests. Transnational social movements (TSMs), based upon the creation of human solidarity on a global
scale,[15] have emerged as an incipient counterforce to expose the myths of
globalization, showing it to be neither inevitable nor desirable, and invalidat-
ing the standard refrain that "there is no alternative." In doing so, TSMs,
through such tactics as international boycotts, media campaigns, and labour
solidarity, apply direct economic pressures where states refuse to intervene,
reminding the marginalized not to exaggerate their helplessness in the face
of corporate power and that the mobilizing potential and democratic
resonances of social movements organized globally may yet match the complex patterns of global integration. Of course it remains unclear as to just
how "globalization-from-below" can create the institutional mechanisms that
would restore authentic governing structures.

As of now, no mass-based social movement with the capacity to cut
through the neoliberal agenda has appeared on the political horizon (Workman 1996: 87).[16] The search continues for some form of economic order that
is efficient without being exploitative, and compatible with humanitarian
objectives. As Yoshikozu Sakamoto (1995: 141) intones, "Even though we
cannot see the visible signs of a great revolution which might change the

present world order to one that is more humane, equitable and sustainable, we can hear countless underground rumbles all over the world which presage a global transformation."

II

The implication of these contemporary trends is that the new project of the left must be the creation of a globalized civil society, one in which social movements play a leading role. Thus far *economic* globalization under the direction of corporate capital has dominated the international arena. As Martin Shaw (1995: 655) observes, "Global civil society is still more potential than actual, following very slowly on economic globalization which has gathered very rapid momentum." Nonetheless, international links recently established within the women's, indigenous, and environmental movements mark an expansion in the theatre of collective action, so that strategizing about *social* globalization has now entered a crucial formative phase.

With this in mind, I will now offer some reflections on the chapters in this book. Although most of the contributions do not explicitly address the theme of globalization, they do provide analytic resources for thinking about how social movements can promote a counterhegemonic politics. In drawing upon the chapters, my aim is not to reduce globalization to a strictly economic phenomenon, but rather to indicate how cultural and political struggles are important facets of strategies organized around *resistance to capital* (Rustin 1988: 171) – a scenario increasingly evident in the current conjuncture. I organize my commentary on the chapters in relation to three main themes germane to globalization and movement activism: the social change agent; the site of struggle; and the strategies of action.[17]

SOCIAL CHANGE AGENT

A core theoretical issue in the analysis of social movements is the relative importance of "political economy" and "culture" as forces for social change. Interpretations based on political economy are rooted in classical Marxist imagery of class struggle and working-class agency, emancipatory politics, and the dynamics of modern world systems. A troubling feature of this perspective, as Barry Adam notes, is its embeddedness in a metanarrative of change entailing pregiven theoretical problems and top-down theorizing, as well as a partiality to socialist thought, rendering it at times oblivious to the myriad flux of conflict in daily life. Consequently, political economy accounts are inclined to downgrade the significance of contemporary mobilizations of people around multiple categories of subordination, construing even the trajectory of new social movements as shaped by the enduring effects of advanced capitalism.

Bob Russell addresses the challenge of the new social movements to this privileging of "class" as the fundamental social cleavage, and to the labour movement as the principal agent of social change, questioning whether the labour movement has become as irrelevant to social change as many of its NSM critics claim. Russell acknowledges the disabling impact of post-Fordist transformations of labour, yet leans towards a revitalized social unionism, one that links labour with other social collectivities, as a possible solution to the current social-democratic impasse.

Against the hopes of those who champion the working class, the Marxism given historical currency through communism has unfortunately proven reductionist and blind to Stalinist deformations, and social democracy – its dubious bourgeois variant – has revealed the limits of "class-collaborationism" in the denouement of the welfare state.

A theoretical position that upholds the centrality of the working class without assuming either its universality or its inevitability is the Gramscian version of social change (Gramsci 1971). For Gramsci, the construction of an alternative hegemony, or counterhegemony, depended upon the formation of a "new historical bloc" organized around the mutual consent of various groups in civil society under working-class leadership. Although contemporary neo-Gramscians (Boggs 1986; Epstein 1990) reject the necessity of a leading role for the proletariat, they continue to stress the important role of labour and, like Gramsci, locate the hegemonic centre in the mode of production. So while neo-Gramscians acknowledge that consent is forged through discursive struggles (not by the mere enunciation of objective interests) in breaking with the culture of advanced capitalism, their adherence to the idea of one hegemonic centre renders their revisionist Marxism equally suspect amongst those who abhor the slightest hint of economism.

New social movement theorists, in their focus on the "cultural" dimension of social change, envision a confluence of autonomous group struggles in the pursuit of social justice. In this "politics of identity," socialism is but one nodal point in a continuously unfolding articulatory process, not the formula, endpoint, or even epitome of diverse struggles. Indeed, some variant of liberalism or "radical pluralism" (Laclau and Mouffe 1985) is thought to provide a more suitable context for building an alternative hegemony than any preordained socialist blueprint. Interrogating NSM theory, Adam cautions that in abandoning what is indispensable in Marxism – a critical analysis of capitalism – NSM activists may be limited to identitarian concerns and fail to organize meaningful resistance against the more unified forces of capital. At the same time he notes that NSMs include socialists as well as identitarian activists, just as Russell observes that many labour movement activists are also members of NSMs – so on both counts there is hope, presumably, for greater solidarity and renewal on the left.

Sharon Stone goes further in arguing, from the example of lesbian politics in Canada, that social change can be definitively achieved without the insistence on a unified voice and common goals. While Stone's defence of unfettered lesbian diversity has a cogency (that is, that its visibility threatens heteropatriarchal dominance), to mobilize an effective counterhegemonic politics, especially in battling the pervasive effects of TNC policies, the lesbian challenge to heterosexism may require consensus around strategic issues. So without discounting her "irreducible plurality" argument, it is equally important to consider Adam's reminder of the structural prerequisites of capitalist development, "which have made the NSMs not only possible, but also predictable."

In sum, we are faced with an array of doubts and reservations about all the major vectors of social change: erudite pessimism about the likelihood of a proletariat-driven upheaval of capitalism; fears that labour's chronically state-centric orientation may be irrecoverably outmoded so that "social-democratic" compacts may soon be a thing of the past; doubts about the generative capacities of a "new historical bloc" still dependent on a politically and culturally fissured working class no longer containing the most progressive forces in society; and theoretical disquiet over whether "identity politics" is hopelessly sectoral and self-serving (even reducible to the interests of a "new middle class") and ultimately incapable of engaging in more than a reformist politics that ensures the survival of capitalism in its preferred form.

Largely for these reasons, the remnants of progressive forces are in a quandary about the potential sources of social change – thus the many treatises probing the viability of the left and the fate of oppositional politics in general. In the midst of this confusion, two developments stand out: first, the historical tide of polarization and proletarianization concomitant with the globalization of capital, and a consequent increase in the world's working-class population; and second, especially in the advanced capitalist countries with a record of affluence, an increasing weariness felt by most people in their daily lives under global neoliberalism, along with the growing realization that current levels of consumerism cannot be sustained without global catastrophe.

These urgent realities have begun to persuade social activists that they can no longer restrict their focus to national priorities, that there may be no choice but to mobilize internationally, and that the "moment" of the transnational movement may well have arrived. Indeed, if the obstacles to mobilizing huge constituencies against their own impoverishment or derogation can be surmounted, a new type of social change agent is imminent.

SITE OF STRUGGLE

Whether transnational social movements emerge as a major catalyst of social change, the conditions of struggle involve a long-term "war of position" marshalled on a global terrain, but legitimated primarily through the institutions of nation-states and fought on communal levels. Certainly the state cannot be discounted because, as Warren Magnusson observes, however sceptically, its transformation is often taken to be "the ultimate objective of outward, political action." Even where the state frustrates local initiatives, as Gary Kinsman documents in relation to AIDS activism, it possesses the resources that social movements desperately require. Not surprisingly, the TNCs, not viewing themselves as part of the nation-state framework, seek to minimize state autonomy, holding the state ransom with threats of disinvestment and using it to maintain the Damocles's sword of austerity in order to subvert local economies.

If, indeed, states now function largely at the behest of corporate capital in reproducing relations of dominance, it should be clear that social movements require new methods against the changing mechanisms of subordination. Jacinthe Michaud describes how the Quebec welfare state restructures its hegemonic discourse to define women as a social category in need of protection, thereby offsetting a feminist counterhegemonic discourse aimed at gaining control over the regulation of women's lives. Similarly, Kinsman shows how the federal AIDS bureaucracy, replete with specious discourses of "partnership" and "consultation," actually marginalizes the very individuals and groups most hurt by AIDS. Like Michaud, Kinsman examines the tactics that might penetrate administrative frameworks, including the deconstruction of "hegemonic language" as an opening to counterhegemonic transformation (that is, a "health from below"). Kinsman also alludes to tacit co-operation between federal programs and private corporations (for example, the "rights" of manufacturers to determine the release of promising therapies, putting their needs and profits ahead of the survival of AIDS victims). While Kinsman only hints at the relation between state policies, professional medical practices, and corporate objectives, this example of "health from above" obviously calls for further scrutiny in the context of globalization.

Yet neither Michaud nor Kinsman argue that state structures are intrinsically malevolent and must be thoroughly displaced by the less formal configurations of civil society. In many instances, the ability to influence state discourses and fashion meaningful alliances between state functionaries and community groups, or replace state functionaries with people closely tied to or supportive of community groups, may prove satisfactory. In considering new directions for the labour movement, Russell also underlines the practical reality of the state, seeing it as a "determining presence that agencies of social change are bound, sooner or later, to come up against in their strategic calculations." Even Magnusson, in his reflections on the "illusory character of state sovereignty," expects that statism will proliferate rather than disappear in the foreseeable future, although he believes that the relationship between states, and between states and people, must be reconceived in the paradigm of a giant global city in which the boundaries between states are blurred and liminal. Magnusson invokes his metaphor as a clue to conceptualizing the global realities to which we must relate politically; however, such high-flown imagery is reminiscent of Drainville's "metropoles of liberal cosmopolitanism" and seems curiously distant from the conditions of social activism in the Third World, the potential bulwark of resistance to corporate capital.

In any case, it can be assumed that transnational social movements will need to function across four complementary spaces: local, national, international, and global. Clearly, the foundations of TSMs must exist at the local level because a premature broadening of the social movement base to the global level may only result in wider defeats. The early establishment of transcommunal networks can help to overcome identitarian sectoralism by engaging people in concrete but intertwining projects, gradually escalating to levels of mobilization and expertise that can influence state agendas and foster global co-operation.

At the state level there is a pressing need to restore confidence in the state as a positive force for change and to refute the view that the state is increasingly irrelevant in the globalized world, a view that the ideological brainwashing of the corporate agenda would have people believe. At national and international levels, it is only through or with the support of nation-states that change can come about, although politicians beholden to corporate donors are unlikely to initiate or endorse change without compelling support at the grassroots level. Social movements must also parley their objectives at the international table, both within the inimical institutions of "global governance" and in the traditional international structures of relatively progressive organizations.

Once a strong base of support is established locally and reverberates at the national and international levels, it becomes possible to adopt the habit of thinking and acting both globally and locally.[18] This is the propitious moment for activism on a genuinely global scale, involving not only informational exchanges and gatherings at "parallel conferences," but also the creation of new structures implementing the unique agendas of transnational social movements.

ACTION STRATEGY

As capital becomes stronger it becomes less and less plausible to rely on necessitarian formulas such as "inevitable contradictions" and capitalist implosion to instigate social change. If economic globalization is to come under democratic controls, social movements must plumb the state and ideological apparatuses, widening the traditional focus of political economy to encompass the social relations of everyday life. Contesting hegemony on local to global planes of action is therefore mandatory for a long-term "war of position," but not one in which the working class serves as the anointed nucleus of the "new historical bloc."

A first task, as Catriona Sandilands argues in identifying the prerequisites for sound environmentalist dialogue, is to resuscitate a heterogeneous and dynamic "public sphere" by properly translating personal issues into a specifically political language that avoids the ideological cul-de-sacs of professional, corporate, and bureaucratic discourses. Once a proper dialogical relation is established, it becomes possible to form coalitions of diversely situated communities to challenge the systemic relations that underlie environmental threats to health and safety.

Undoubtedly, the difficulties are compounded when social activists from *various* social movements are drawn into coalitions, especially without any clear perception of common interests and lack of agreement over leadership. With no dominant centre, such as a working-class centrality might afford, how is consensus attainable? What are to be the priorities of egalitarian coalitions, and who will organize them? Russell narrows these questions down somewhat by focusing on the possibilities for a revival of working-class syndicalism, a social unionism in which labour is still at the helm, but with more inclusion of community groups.

Peter Bleyer, through his study of the Action Canada Network (ACN), examines the potential and limitations of coalition-formation among a range of progressive social movements that constitute much of the "popular sector" and link "new social movements" with labour. While Bleyer finds that the ACN experience demonstrates the continuing relevance of working-class politics, his insistence upon the crucial place of an activist labour movement in any potentially transformative political project remains moot. Notwithstanding some partial successes in mobilizing public opinion against the corporate agenda, Bleyer shows that the ACN was vulnerable to a familiar problem afflicting coalitions – the inability to mount more than a "defensive" unity in response to a perceived general threat (the effects of the increasing globalization of capital), thus reducing the coalition's agenda to the lowest common denominator. Here, as in other instances, the failure of the ACN to realize its long-term objectives reveals the inability to win significant reforms from a "neoliberal" state and underscores the difficulty of pursuing a progressive project in one country.

If nothing else, the ACN experience points to the importance of internationalizing domestic struggles, wherever that is tactically possible, in order to pressure state action on behalf of popular interests and incite mass defections from the global economy. Yet despite their limitations, domestic coalitions are important building blocks in a global movement – developing networks and communication infrastructures, and pulling people out of the sectoralist myopia of a "politics of identity." But coalitions also invite "grassroots backlash," which is precisely why movements that join coalitions cannot afford to lose touch with their respective local bases. Coalitions are also expensive to maintain, draining meagre organizational resources, especially in times of cutbacks. Consequently they tend to fizzle out when a mobilizing crisis wanes or disappears. Moreover, the international goals and agendas of coalitions are often vague and inconsequential to rank-and-file members of locally based groups, underscoring, again, the need for concrete achievements at the local level.

Perhaps most problematic for coalitions, especially at the national and international levels, is, as Michaud notes, "the multiplicity of definitions on the politics of resistance and the large spectrum of political ideologies that aim at social change." Recalling the work of Laclau and Mouffe, Adam emphasizes that social antagonisms are "polysemic" in that they bear as many different significations (or meanings) as the discourses by which they can be constituted. The issue of "language" is therefore central, that is, the way discourse, primarily through language, reproduces dominance and exiles or reductively incorporates difference, enabling potential dissidents to "discover" only what has already been hegemonically constructed. In this vein, Dominique Masson stresses the need for a "politically oriented analysis of movement meaning-making practices," one that elucidates the relationship between language, sites of meaning construction, and the widening field of power relations and struggles. Indeed, finding ways to use the new communicative technologies to revitalize public spheres and make them more accessible (thus broadening the discourse on political alternatives) is a crucial challenge facing social movements in their global ideological struggles with corporate capital.

Masson also refers to the construction of meaning "frames" and how they are diffused within and among movements to make sense of reality and organize collective action, and in his study of the Lubicon Lake First Nation coalition David Long provides an example of framing in coalition politics. The Lubicon protest against government land policies and environmental degradation received support from over one hundred separate organizations in Canada and elsewhere. This support was developed around two globally based movements – indigenous rights and environmental protection – that provided the master-frames pivotal in organizing social protest and legal action. Internal dissension, however, wracked the Lubicon coalition, exposing the risks of organizing around social differences. The Lubicon experience, therefore, raises questions about the sustainability of coalitions that include groups committed to distinctive and incompletely resonant master-frames. While the outcome shows that support for counterhegemonic coalitions is indeed a "precarious phenomenon," the Lubicon experience also demonstrates the need (as Long recognizes) to give more attention to system-movement-actor interrelationships in expanding social movement networks. This focus could provide welcome guidance to TSMs in their early efforts to deflect the momentum of corporate capital.

Another account of framing that involves a crucial struggle over meanings is that offered by Aaron Doyle, Brian Elliott, and David Tindall, who query the role of the mass media in fortifying hegemony. They examine the media "counterframing" of a corporate-sponsored movement – the British Columbia Forest Alliance, engaged in its own "war of position" to debunk environmentalist criticism of the logging industry. Doyle, Elliott, and Tindall take pains to avoid a conspiratorial analysis of the news media, attributing editorial outcomes, instead, to the media's routinely structured overreliance on official sources and pointing, as well, to the *diversity* of views within media organizations. Their conclusion that "the media are more open, pluralistic, and diverse than the more pessimistic dominant ideology accounts suggest," is contradicted, however, by the enormous concentration of ownership of those very media outlets, which are often under the financial control of powerful corporations that are also major investors in resource industries (including the B.C. Forest industry). While the media outlets do exercise a degree of autonomy in applying their own professional "frames" or systems of meanings in the construction of "news," this possibility warrants neither sanguine pluralist conclusions nor simplistic conspiratorial scenarios. But it would be disingenuous to think that transnational corporations would not want to gain a controlling influence over the mass media in order to propagate consumerist ideology, and it should be obvious why social movement organizations are often frustrated in their attempts to "get ink" in the mass media, and why they must use up some of their limited resources on producing "alternative media."

In the face of these "framing" challenges and other noted difficulties, and granting that the specific priorities of social movements differ from place to place, structurally and culturally, a pressing need exists to create parallel linkages between social movements at local, national, and international levels. The presuppositions of this effort are several: that there can be no expectation that capital will retreat from its current mode of super-exploitation; that strictly localist strategies are insufficient ways of ensuring redistributive objectives; that politicians, by themselves, will not initiate change because the money of the multinationals is what keeps them in office; and that the labour movement cannot be counted on to provide leadership on behalf of radical change, given its reluctance to unhinge from a fading Fordist compact. Furthermore, coalitions that operate only within the limits of national boundaries, no matter how progressive, cannot seriously challenge the structures of global capital; at best they usher in the dubious reformist gains of "passive revolution" (Buci-Glucksmann 1979; Sassoon 1982). Even these benefits are increasingly tenuous, because the illusory promises of an eventual capitalist cornucopia serve to rationalize the dismantling of welfare states; this results in conditions of austerity that induce competitive relations in the social movement sector and lead to greater friction between ostensibly incommensurable discourses, however "anticapitalist." With this development, social movements join capital in pre-empting the possibilities for counterhegemony, an irony that emphasizes the futility of challenging global capital in any one country and underscores the importance of movement activism at international and global levels. Parenthetically, it raises the question of whether fundamental changes can be achieved outside the theoretical purview of "class struggle" and, indeed, whether it may be necessary to return to some still vital aspects of the revolutionary, internationalist, and democratic traditions of classical Marxism (Smith 1997).

Finally, to go back to the beginning of this book, in his introductory essay William Carroll raises, by implication, a number of important questions concerning the viability of social movement activism in the context of globalization: the necessity of reconceiving what is meant by "resource mobilization" in an ever-widening political arena; the changing structure of "political opportunity" and the waning possibilities of "self-realization" under the constraints of globalization; the reinforcement of corporate hegemony through the fragmenting effects of "identity politics"; and the disappearance of visionary politics in the manipulated absence of grand theory. He acknowledges the contributions of the various case studies here to the idiographic tradition of Canadian studies (documenting the struggle for Canadian historicity); but the need for broader theoretical boundaries in these same studies in order to grasp the dynamics of globalization suggests that a greater emphasis on nomothetic interpretations would be timely.

Taken together, then, the chapters in this book thoughtfully apply a range of concepts in the social movements literature that inform us about the hopes, contradictions, and frustrations of movement activism in Canada. The authors alert us to various questions about the phenomenon of globalization and its relevance to the struggles waged by social movement activists. We are brought, perhaps somewhat inadvertently, to the portals of an exhilarating field of investigation: the study of transnational social movements as the new (dare I say?) vanguard of emancipatory politics. My fondest hope is that the various pieces in this book will offer some guidance to the legion of social activists charged with the reputable burden of organizing dissent against the corporate goliath.

NOTES

1. Waters (1995: 1) observes, "Just as postmodernism was the concept of the 1980s, globalization may be the concept of the 1990s, a key idea by which we understand the transition of human society into the third millennium."
2. In a similar vein, Hirst and Thompson (1996: 1) write, "The world economy has internationalized in its basic dynamics, it is dominated by uncontrollable market forces, and it has as its principal economic actors and major agents of change truly transnational corporations that owe allegiance to no nation state and locate wherever in the globe market advantage dictates."
3. Collier (1995: 11-12) notes, "Assumptions behind the studies and the policies of international organizations like the IMF, World Bank and OECD hinge on driving down external debt and deficits, usually in relation to Gross Domestic Product; making sure maximum financing is available to the private sector; and pro-

moting the idea that government spending, especially social security and welfare spending, 'crowd out' private sector financing and consumption, which is seen as more 'necessary.'"

4. For example, the critical views on the impacts of globalization expressed by Ralph Nader, Vandana Shiva, John Cavanaugh, and David Korten, "A Report on the International Forum on Globalization," audiotape, New York City, November 10-12, 1995.

5. As Robinson (1995: 373) points out, there is a "shift from a world economy that is an aggregation of national market economies, quite varied in their regulatory and redistributive principles, to a global market economy governed by a uniform set of rules."

6. Excerpted from "In a Bad World, Canada Must Be Good (United)," *The Vancouver Sun*, Aug. 27, 1996: All.

7. Jones (1995: 213), for example, writes, "Experience and skeptical reflection have ... encouraged doubts about the robustness of the benign view of international interdependence and globalization."

8. In Collier's (1995: 18) pithy summation, "Government, Communism, and social programs are repetitiously drummed into our consciousness as being of one wholeness, to be despised."

9. Fuentes and Frank (1989: 187) offer only the barest qualification of the state's subordinated role: "Although state intervention should not be underestimated (as it is by free marketeers), its limitations are ever greater in a world economy whose cycles and trends are largely beyond control."

10. Indeed, as Held and McGraw (1993: 262) note, "Globalization has become associated with a crisis of the territorial nation-state."

11. The actual workings of "global governance" appear to represent an uneasy combination of the "sovereignty-at-bay" model, in which TNCs reign supreme in the interests of global economic efficiency while nation-states become anachronistic, and the "mercantilist" option, in which governments seek to manipulate economic arrangements in favour of national priorities, regardless of global considerations (Gilpin 1979).

12. As John Sweeny, the new AFL-CIO president, enjoined the Canadian Labour Congress at its 1996 convention in Vancouver (in *The Vancouver Sun*, May 16, 1996), "Here is a key ingredient of change. Just as our adversaries think and act globally, so must we. We must fight so that workers' wages throughout the world are not leveled down, but are leveled up."

13. Thiele (1993) identifies Greenpeace as an example of a social movement that is transnational in both senses of the term.

14. Examining social movements on a global scale, Ray (1993: xvii), comments, "In an age of globalization of economic and political structures, it is no longer appropriate to analyze social movements solely at the level of nationally defined space."

15. Examples of transnational social movements are the global networks developed amongst women's, environmental, and indigenous groups. Most are in germinal stages of formation. Many NGOs are of the transnational variety, but function unpredictably between social movement activism or domestic pacification on behalf of "global governance."

16. Especially in Canada, as Panitch (1996: 86) notes, "A clear alternative to free trade and unbridled capitalist competition remains to be articulated."

17. For analytic convenience, these overlapping themes are discussed separately.

18. This is the modus operandi, for example, of Greenpeace, which deploys mutually reinforcing strategies for social change at the global and local levels (see Wapner 1996).

REFERENCES

Acker, Joan
  1989 *Women, Families and Public Policy in Sweden*. Stockholm: The Swedish Center for Working Life.
Action Canada Network
  1992a *ACN Dossier* 35 (January-February).
  1992b *ACN Dossier* 36 (March-April).
  1992c "Election Strategies: A Working Document." June.
The ACT UP/New York Women and AIDS Book Group
  1990 *Women, AIDS and Activism*. Toronto: Between the Lines.
Adam, Barry D.
  1978 *The Survival of Domination*. New York: Elsevier/Greenwood.
  1987 *The Rise of a Gay and Lesbian Movement*. Boston: Twayne Publishers.
  1988 "The State, Public Policy, and AIDS Discourse." Presentation, Canadian Sociology and Anthropology Association (CSAA), annual meeting, Windsor, Ont. Also in *Contemporary Crisis* 13: 1-14 (1989).
  1995 *The Rise of a Gay and Lesbian Movement*. Rev. ed. New York: Twayne Publishers.
Adam, Barry and Alan Sears
  1996 *Experiencing HIV, Personal, Family and Work Relationships*. New York: Columbia University Press.
Adams, Howard
  1989 *Prison of Grass: Canada from a Native Point of View*. Rev. ed. Saskatoon: Fifth House Publishers.
Adamson, Nancy, L. Briskin, and M. McPhail
  1988 *Feminist Organizing for Change: The Contemporary Women's Movement in Canada*. Toronto: University of Toronto Press.
Adkin, Laurie E.
  1992 "Counter-hegemony and Environmental Politics in Canada." In W.K. Carroll (ed.), *Organizing Dissent: Contemporary Social Movements in Theory and Practice*. 1st ed. Toronto: Garamond Press.
Aggleton, Peter and Hilary Homans (eds.)
  1988 *Social Aspects of AIDS*. London: Falmer Press.
Aggleton, Peter, Graham Hart, and Peter Davies (eds.)
  1989 *AIDS: Social Representations, Social Practices*. London: Falmer Press.
AIDS ACTION NEWS! (AIDS ACTION NOW!), Toronto.
AIDS ACTION NOW! (AAN!)
  1989 "Towards a Comprehensive Federal/Provincial AIDS Policy." Policy proposals from AIDS ACTION NOW!, Toronto, Aug. 2.

287

1990 "A National Treatment Registry for HIV and AIDS: An Urgent Call To Action." Toronto, March 13.

1993 "Confronting the HIV Research Crisis: Treatment Activists' Perceptions of the Canadian Research Effort." Toronto.

Allen, Jeffner (ed.)

1990 *Lesbian Philosophies and Cultures.* Albany, N.Y.: State University of New York Press.

Altman, Dennis

1986 *AIDS in the Mind of America.* Garden City, N.Y.: Anchor Press/ Doubleday.

1994 *Power and Community, Organizational and Cultural Responses to AIDS.* London: Taylor and Francis.

Alvarez, Sonia E. and Arturo Escobar

1992 "Conclusion: Theoretical and Political Horizons of Change in Contemporary Latin American Social Movements." In Arturo Escobar and Sonia E. Alvarez (eds.), *The Making of Social Movements in Latin America: Identity, Strategy, and Democracy.* Boulder, Col.: Westview Press.

Anadón, Marta, Dominique Masson, Marielle Tremblay, and Pierre-André Tremblay

1991 "Les collectives de femmes: une démocratie sororale." *Nouvelles pratiques sociales* 3,2: 7-70.

Anderson, Alison

1991 "Source Strategies and the Communication of Environmental Affairs." *Media, Culture and Society* 13,4: 459–76.

1993 "Source–Media Relations: The Production of the Environmental Agenda." In A. Hansen (ed.), *The Mass Media and Environmental Issues.* Leicester, England: University of Leicester Press.

Anderson, Joan M.

1990 "Work and Health: Considerations for Immigrant Women." *Anthropology of Work Review,* Fall: 3-7.

Angenot, Marc

1989 *Ce que l'on dit des juifs en 1889: Antisémitisme et discours social.* Paris: Presses Universitaires de Vincennes.

Arato, Andrew and Jean Cohen

1989 *Civil Society and Democratic Theory.* Cambridge, Mass.: MIT Press.

Arendt, Hannah

1958 *The Human Condition.* Chicago: University of Chicago Press.

Armstrong, Pat and Hugh Armstrong

1978 *The Double Ghetto.* Toronto: McClelland and Stewart.

Aronowitz, Stanley

1973 *False Promises: The Shaping of American Working Class Consciousness.* New York: McGraw-Hill.

1987/88 "Postmodernism and Politics." *Social Text* 18: 113.

Ash-Garner, Roberta and Mayer Zald

1987 "The Political Economy of Social Movement Sectors. In Zald and McCarthy (1987).

Atkinson, J.
  1984 "Manpower Strategies for Flexible Organisations." *Personnel Management.*
Austin, John L.
  1962 *How to Do Things with Words.* Cambridge, Mass.: Harvard University Press.
Bagguley, Paul
  1992 "Social Change, the Middle Class and the Emergence of New Social Movements: A Critical Analysis." *Sociological Review*: 27–47.
Barker, E. (ed. and trans.)
  1962 *The Politics of Aristotle.* New York: Oxford University Press.
Barnes, Trevor J. and Roger Hayter
  1994 "Economic Restructuring, Local Development and Resource Towns: Forest Communities in Coastal British Columbia." *Canadian Journal of Regional Science* 17,3 (Autumn: 289–310.
Barnet, Richard and Ronald E. Müller
  1974 *Global Reach: The Power of the Multinational Corporations.* New York: Simon and Schuster.
Barrett, Michèle
  1988 *Women's Oppression Today.* Rev. Ed. London: Verso.
  1991 *The Politics of Truth: From Marx to Foucault.* Stanford, Cal.: Stanford University Press.
Bashevkin, Sylvia
  1989 "Free Trade and Canadian Feminism: The Case of the National Action Committee on the Status of Women." *Canadian Public Policy* 15,4: 363-75.
Bartholomew, Amy and Margit Mayer
  1992 "Nomads of the Present: Melucci's Contribution to 'New Social Movement' Theory." *Theory, Culture & Society* 9,4: 141–59.
Bearchell, Chris
  1983 "Why I'm a Gay Liberationist: Thoughts on Sex, Freedom, the Family and the State." *Resources for Feminist Research* 12,1: 57-60.
Beatty, Perrin
  1990 "The National AIDS Strategy." Speech announcing the strategy at the 81st Conference of the Canadian Public Health Association, June 28.
  1991 "The National Strategy on AIDS Revisited." Speech given at the National Conference on AIDS, Vancouver, April 14.
Bégin, Monique
  1989 "Les femmes et les sciences de la santé: une analyse politique." Colette Gendron and Micheline Beauregard (eds.), *L'avenir-santé au féminin.* Boucherville, Que.: Gaëtan Morin, éditeur.
Benford, Robert D.
  1987 "Framing Activity, Meaning, and Social Movement Participation: the Nuclear Disarmament Movement." Ph.D. thesis, University of Texas at Austin.

1993a "Frame Disputes within the Nuclear Disarmament Movement." *Social Forces* 71,3 (March: 677–701.

1993b " 'You Could Be the Hundredth Monkey': Collective Action Frames and Vocabularies of Motive within the Nuclear Disarmament Movement." *The Sociological Quarterly* 34,2: 195–216.

Benford, Robert D. and Scott A. Hunt
1995 "Dramaturgy and Social Movements: The Social Construction and Communication of Power." In Stanford M. Lyman (ed.), *Social Movements: Critiques, Concepts, Case–Studies*. London: Macmillan.

Benhabib, Seyla
1992 *Situating the Self: Gender, Community and Postmodernism in Contemporary Ethics*. New York: Routledge.

Bercuson, D.
1978 *Fools and Wisemen: The Rise and Fall of the One Big Union*. Toronto: McGraw-Hill Ryerson.

Berger, Peter and Thomas Luckmann
1967 *The Social Construction of Reality*. Garden City, N.Y.: Doubleday.

Berson, Ginny
1988 "The Furies." In Hoagland and Penelope (1988).

Black, Robert, Stephen Blank, and Elizabeth C. Hanson
1978 *Multinationals in Contention: Responses at Governmental and International Levels*. Multinational Corporate Responsibility Project, Conference Board, Public Affairs Division, U.S. Department of State.

Blott, Ken
1990 "Draft Report Rife with Contradictions: Five Years into AIDS, Ottawa Ponders National Policy." *Xtra* XS supplement, Toronto, January: 3.

Bocock, Robert
1986 *Hegemony*. London and New York: Ellis Horwood and Tavistock Publications.

Boggs, Carl
1976 *Gramsci's Marxism*. London: Pluto.
1986 *Social Movements and Political Power*. Philadelphia: Temple University Press.

Boldt, Menno
1993 *Surviving as Indians: The Challenge of Self-Government*. Toronto: University of Toronto Press.

Bookchin, Murray
1987 *The Modern Crisis*. Montreal: Black Rose Books.
1988 "Social Ecology Versus Deep Ecology." *Socialist Review* 18,3: 9–29.
1989 *Remaking Society*. Montreal: Black Rose Books.

Bopp, Judie, Michael Bopp, Lee Brown, and Phil Lane (compilers)
1984 *The Sacred Tree*. Lethbridge, Alta.: Four Worlds Development Publishers.

Bourdieu, Pierre
1991 *Language and Symbolic Power*. Cambridge, Mass.: Harvard University Press.

Bowles, Samuel and Herbert Gintis
 1986 *Democracy and Capitalism*. New York: Basic Books.
Brand, Karl-Werner
 1990 "Cyclical Aspects of New Social Movements." In Russell Dalton and
  Manfred Kuechler (eds.), *Challenging the Political Order*. New York:
  Oxford University Press.
Brecher, J. and T. Costello
 1990 *Building Bridges: The Emerging Grassroots Coalition of Labor and
  Community*. New York: Monthly Review Press.
Breines, Wini
 1982 *Community and Organization in the New Left*. South Hadley, Mass.:
  Bergin and Garvey.
Briskin, Linda
 1993 "Union Women and Separate Organizing." In L. Briskin and P.
  McDermott (eds.), *Women Challenging Unions: Feminism, Democracy,
  and Militancy*. Toronto: University of Toronto Press.
Brodie, Janine
 1990 *The Political Economy of Canadian Regionalism*. Toronto: Harcourt
  Brace Jovanovich.
 1992 "Choice and No Choice in the House." In Janine Brodie, Shelley A.M.
  Gavigan, and Jane Jenson, *The Politics of Abortion*. Toronto: Oxford
  University Press.
 1995 *Politics at the Margins: Restructuring and the Canadian Women's
  Movement*. Halifax: Fernwood Publishing.
Brodie, Janine, Shelley A.M. Gavigan, and Jane Jenson
 1992 *The Politics of Abortion*. Toronto: Oxford University Press.
Brody, D.
 1980 *Industrial Workers in America*. New York: Oxford University Press.
Bruck, Peter
 1992 "Discursive Movements and Social Movements: The Active Negotia-
  tion of Constraints." In Janet Wasko and Vincent Mosco (eds.), *Demo-
  cratic Communications in the Information Age*. Toronto: Garamond
  Press.
Brunet, Ariane and Louise Turcotte
 1988 "Separatism and Radicalism." In Hoagland and Penelope (1988).
Brym, Robert J.
 1978 "Regional Social Structure and Agrarian Radicalism in Canada:
  Alberta, Saskatchewan and New Brunswick." *Canadian Review of
  Sociology and Anthropology* 15: 339-51.
Brym, Robert and James Sacouman (eds.)
 1979 *Underdevelopment and Social Movements in Atlantic Canada*. Toronto:
  New Hogtown Press.
Buci-Glucksmann, Christine
 1979 "State Transition and Passive Revolution." In Chantal Mouffe (ed.),
  Gramsci and Marxist Theory. Boston: Routledge and Kegan Paul.

Buechler, Steven M.
   1993 "Beyond Resource Mobilization? Emerging Trends in Social Move-
      ment Theory." *The Sociological Quarterly* 34: 217–35.
Bullard, Robert
   1990 *Dumping in Dixie*. Boulder, Col.: Westview Press.
Bunch, Charlotte
   1987 *Passionate Politics: Feminism Theory in Action: Essays 1968-1986*. New
      York: St. Martin's Press.
Cain, Maureen
   1994 "Foucault, Feminism and Feeling: What Foucault Can and Cannot
      Contribute to Feminist Epistemology." In Caroline Ramazoglu (ed.), *Up
      Against Foucault*. London: Routledge.
Cain, Roy
   1993 "Community-Based AIDS Services: Formalization and
      Depoliticization." *International Journal of Health Services* 23,1.
   1994 "Managing Impressions of an AIDS Service Organization: Into the
      Mainstream or out of the Closet." *Qualitative Sociology* 17,1.
Calhoun, Craig
   1988 "Populist Politics, Communications Media and Large Scale Societal
      Integration." *Sociological Theory* 6 (Fall: 222.
   1993 "New Social Movements of the Early Nineteenth Century." *Social
      Science History* 17: 385–427.
Callen, Michael
   1990 *Surviving AIDS*. New York: HarperCollins.
Campanella, M.L.
   1990 "Globalization: Processes and Interpretations." *World Futures* 30,1-2: 1-
      16.
Canadian AIDS Society (CAS)
   1989 "Working Together: Towards A National AIDS Strategy in Canada."
      Sept. 19.
   1990a "Response of the Canadian AIDS Society to the Announcement of the
      National AIDS Strategy." June 28.
   1990b "Treatment Issues: Submission by the Canadian AIDS Society to the
      Parliamentary Ad-hoc Committee on AIDS." April 24.
Canadian Auto Workers Union (CAW)
   1993 "Hard Times, New Times." CAW Statement on Direction, mimeo.
   1994a "Transforming the CAW: Where Are the Changes in Our Union
      Taking Us?" Discussion paper, 4th Constitutional Convention, Quebec
      City.
   1994b "Labour and Politics: Rethinking, Redefining, Rebuilding." Discus-
      sion paper, 4th Constitutional Convention, Quebec City.
   1994c "Social Reform or Social Destruction? Expanding the Meaning of
      Citizenship." Discussion paper, 4th Constitutional Convention, Quebec
      City.
   1995 "Political Goals for the Leadership Tour and the CAW Area Action
      Groups: Some Ideas and Suggestions." Mimeo.

Canadian Conference of Catholic Bishops (CCCB)
1983 *Ethical Reflections on the Economic Crisis*. Ottawa: Concacan.
Canel, Eduardo
1992 "New Social Movement Theory and Resource Mobilization: The Need for Integration." In W.K. Carroll (ed.), *Organizing Dissent: Contemporary Social Movements in Theory and Practice*. 1st ed. Toronto: Garamond Press.
Card, Claudia
1995 *Lesbian Choices*. New York: Columbia University Press.
Cardinal, Harold
1969 *The Unjust Society*. Edmonton: Hurtig.
Caron, Michèle
1994 "Variations sur le thème de l'invisibilisation." *Canadian Journal of Women and the Law* 7,2: 271-85.
Carroll, William K.
1984 "The Solidarity Coalition." In W. Magnusson, W. Carroll, C. Doyle, M.Langer, and R.B.J. Walker (eds.), *The New Reality: The Politics of Restraint in British Columbia*. Vancouver: New Star Books.
1986 *Corporate Power and Canadian Capitalism*. Vancouver: University of British Columbia Press.
1990 "Restructuring Capital, Reorganizing Consent: Gramsci, Political Economy, and Canada." *Canadian Review of Sociology and Anthropology* 27: 390–416.
Carroll, William K. and R.S. Ratner
1989 "Social Democracy, Neo–Conservatism and Hegemonic Crisis in British Columbia." *Critical Sociology* 16,1: 29–53.
1994 "Between Leninism and Radical Pluralism: Gramscian Reflections on Counter-hegemony and the New Social Movements." *Critical Sociology* 20,2: 3–26.
1995 "Old unions and New Social Movements." *Labour/le travail* 35: 195–221.
1996a "Master Frames and Counter–hegemony: Political Sensibilities in New Social Movements." *Canadian Review of Sociology and Anthropology* 33: 407-35.
1996b "Master Framing and Cross–movement Networking in Contemporary Social Movements." *The Sociological Quarterly* 37, 4: 601-25.
Carroll, William K. and R. Warburton
1995 "Capital, Labour and the State: The Future of the Labour Movement." In B. Singh Bolaria (ed.), *Social Issues and Contradictions in Canadian Society*. 2nd ed. Toronto: Harcourt Brace Canada.
Carroll, William K., Linda Christiansen-Ruffman, Raymond F. Currie, and Deborah Harrison (eds.)
1992 *Fragile Truths: Twenty-Five Years of Sociology and Anthropology in Canada*. Ottawa: Carleton University Press.

Cassidy, Sean
  1992 "The Environment and the Media: Two Strategies for Challenging
      Hegemony." In Janet Wasko and Vincent Mosco (eds.), *Democratic
      Communications in the Information Age*. Toronto: Garamond Press.
Castells, M.
  1977 *The Urban Question*. London: Edward Arnold.
Centre de santé des femmes du Quartier
  1986a *Représentation écrite présentée à la commission d'enquête sur les
      services de santé et les services sociaux*. Montreal. 16 pages.
  1986b *Bilan pour la clinique pour lesbiennes du centre de santé des femmes de
      Montréal*. 51 pages.
Centre de santé des femmes de Sherbrooke
  1985 *Mouvement d'auto-santé*. Rédigé pour le Regroupement des centres de
      santé des femmes du Québec, octobre. 17 pages.
Chamberland, Line
  1989 "Le lesbianisme: continuum féminin ou marronage? Réflexions
      féministes pour une théorisation de l'expérience lesbienne." *Recherches
      féministes* 2,2: 135-45.
Chee, Alexander S.
  1991 "A Queer Nationalism." *Out/Look* 11 (Winter: 15-23.
Chomsky, Noam
  1994 *The Prosperous Few and the Restless Many*. Berkeley, Cal.: Odonian
      Press.
Clark, S.D.
  1968 *The Developing Canadian Community*. 2nd ed. Toronto: University of
      Toronto Press.
  1976 *Canadian Society in Historical Perspective*. Toronto: McGraw Hill-
      Ryerson.
Clark, Samuel D.
  1975 "General Introduction: The Nature of Social Movements." In Samuel
      D. Clark et al. (eds.), *Prophesy and Protest: Social Movements in Twenti-
      eth-Century Canada*. Toronto: Gage.
Clarke, Juanne Nancarrow
  1990 *Health, Illness, and Medicine in Canada*. Toronto: McClelland and
      Stewart.
Clement, W.
  1981 *Hardrock Mining: Industrial Relations and Technological Changes at
      Inco*. Toronto: McClelland and Stewart.
Cohen, J.L.
  1982 *Class and Civil Society: The Limits of Marxian Critical Theory*.
      Amherst: University of Massachusetts Press.
  1983 "Rethinking Social Movements." *Berkeley Journal of Sociology* 28: 97-
      113.
  1985 "Strategy or Identity: New Theoretical Paradigms and Contemporary
      Social Movements." *Social Research* 52,4: 663-716.

Cohen, J.L. and A. Arato
1992 *Civil Society and Political Theory.* Cambridge, Mass.: The MIT Press.
Collectif d'amazones d'hier, lesbiennes d'aujourd'hui
1986/87 "Lesbianisme radical." *Resources for Feminist Research* 15,40: 5-7.
Collier, Ken
1995 "Global Finance against State Intervention." *Socialist Studies Bulletin* 42: 8-23.
Collins, Patricia Hill
1990 *Black Feminist Thought: Knowledge, Consciousness, and the Politics of Empowerment.* Boston: Unwin Hyman.
Comeau, Pauline and Aldo Santin
1990 *The First Canadians: A Profile of Native People Today.* Toronto: James Lorimer and Company.
Comité de lutte pour l'avortement libre et gratuit.
1978 *C'est à nous de déciser.* Montreal: Les éditions du remue-ménage.
CDPQ [Commission des droits de la personne du Québec]
1994 *De l'illégalité à l'égalité: Rapport de la consultation publique sur la violence et la discrimination envers les gais et lesbiennes.* Quebec.
Connell, R.W.
1990 "The State, Gender, and Sexual Politics," *Theory and Society* 19,5: 507-44.
Connolly, W. E.
1983 *The Terms of Political Discourse.* 2nd ed. Princeton, N.J.: Princeton University Press.
Cook, Stephen, Jan Pakulski, and Malcolm Waters
1992 *Postmodernization: Change in Advanced Society.* London: Sage Publications.
Cooper, Barry
1994 *Sins of Omission: Shaping the News at CBC TV.* Toronto: University of Toronto Press.
Cooper, Davina
1994 "A Retreat from Feminism? British Municipal Lesbian Politics and Cross-Gender Initiatives." *Canadian Journal of Women and the Law* 7,2: 431-53.
Cornell, Drucilla
1991 "Gender Hierarchy, Equality, and the Possibility of Democracy." *American Imago* 48,2 (Summer).
Cornell, Stephen
1988 *The Return of the Native: American Indian Political Resurgence.* New York: Oxford University Press.
Corner, John and Philip Schlesinger
1991 "Introduction to Special Issue on Media and the Environment." *Media, Culture and Society* 13,4: 459–76.
Corrigan, Philip and Derek Sayer
1985 *The Great Arch: English State Formation as Cultural Revolution.* Oxford: Basil Blackwell.

Cosson, Steve
  1991 "Queer Nationalism." *Out/Look* 11 (Winter: 14, 16-18, 20-23.
Council of Canadians
  1986 "Goals and Priorities." Adopted by the Council of Canadians Board of
    Directors, March 3-4, Ottawa.
Cowling, Keith and Roger Sugden
  1987 *International Monopoly Capitalism.* New York: St. Martin's Press.
Cox, Robert
  1987 *Production, Power and World Order.* New York: Columbia University
    Press.
  1992 "Global Perestroika." In Ralph Miliband and Leo Panitch (eds.), *New
    World Order? Socialist Register 1992.* London: The Merlin Press.
Cracknell, Jon
  1993 "Issue Arenas, Pressure Groups and Environmental Agendas." In A.
    Hansen (ed.), *The Mass Media and Environmental Issues.* Leicester,
    England: University of Leicester Press.
Crick, Barnard
  1993 *In Defence of Politics.* 4th ed. Chicago: University of Chicago Press.
Crimp, Douglas (ed.)
  1988 *AIDS, Cultural Analysis, Cultural Activism.* Cambridge, Mass.: MIT
    Press.
Crimp, Douglas with Adam Rolston
  1990 *AIDSDEMOGRAPHICS.* Seattle, Wash.: Bay Press.
Crook, Stephen
  1991 *Modernist Radicalism and its Aftermath.* London: Routledge.
Crouch, C. and A. Pizzorno (eds.)
  1978 *The Resurgence of Class Conflict in Western Europe since 1968.* Vol. 1.
    New York: Holmes and Meier.
Crozier, M., S.P. Huntington, and J. Watanuki
  1975 *The Crisis of Democracy.* New York: New York University Press.
Cruikshank, Barbara
  1994 "The Will to Empower: Technologies of Citizenship and the War on
    Poverty." *Socialist Review* 23,4: 29-55.
Cunningham, F., S. Findlay, M. Kadar, A. Lennon, and E. Silva (eds.)
  1988 *Social Movements/Social Change: The Politics and Practice of Organiz-
    ing.* Toronto: Between the Lines.
Curran, James
  1990 "The New Revisionism in Mass Communication Research: A Reap-
    praisal." *European Journal of Communication* 5,2-3: 135-64.
Dalton, Russell J. and Manfred Kuechler (eds.)
  1990 *Challenging the Boundaries of Political Order: New Social and Political
    Movements in Western Democracies.* Cambridge, Mass.: Polity Press.
D'Anieri, Paul, Claire Ernst, and Elizabeth Kier
  1990 "New Social Movements in Historical Perspective." *Comparative
    Politics* 22,4: 445-58.

Davis, James C.
1969 "The J–Curve of Rising and Declining Satisfactions as a Cause of Some Great Revolutions and a Contained Rebellion." In H.D. Graham and Ted R. Gurr (eds.), *The History of Violence in America.* New York: Praeger.
Davis, Arthur K.
1974 [1971] "Canadian Society and History as Hinterland Versus Metropolis." In Michiel Horn and Ronald Sabourin (eds.), *Studies in Canadian Social History.* Toronto: McClelland and Stewart.
De Certeau, M.
1984 *The Practice of Everyday Life.* Berkeley: University of California Press.
Deleuze, Gilles and Felix Guattari
1987 *A Thousand Plateaus.* Minneapolis: University of Minnesota Press.
Demczuk, Irène
1994 "Derrière les coulisses de l'événement." *Treize*, March: 14-17.
D'Emelio, John
1983 *Sexual Politics, Sexual Communities: The Making of a Homosexual Minority in the Untied States, 1940-1970.* Chicago: University of Chicago Press.
De Roo, Remi
1983 "What's Wrong with Canada? Facing up to the Crisis." *Alternatives* 1,9.
Dickason, Olive Patricia
1993 *Canada's First Nations: A History of Founding Peoples from the Earliest Times.* Toronto: McClelland and Stewart.
Dietz, Mary G.
1991 "Hannah Arendt and Feminist Politics." In Mary Shandley and Carol Pateman (eds.), *Feminist Interpretations and Political Theory.* University Parks: Pennsylvania State University Press.
Dixon, John
1990 *Catastrophic Rights: Experimental Drugs and AIDS.* Vancouver: New Star Books.
Dominy, Michèle D.
1986 "Lesbian-Feminist Gender Conceptions: Separatism in Christchurch, New Zealand." *Signs*, 11,2: 274-89.
Donati, Paolo
1992 "Political Discourse Analysis." In Mario Diani and Ron Eyerman (eds.), *Studying Collective Action.* London: Sage Publications.
Donzelot, Jacques
1979 *The Policing of Families.* New York: Pantheon Books.
Doucette, Joanne
1990 "Redefining Difference: Disabled Lesbians Resist." In Stone (1990).
Doyle, Aaron, Brian Elliott, and David Tindall
1995 "Frames of Power and the Power of Framing: Re–Examining Culture, Power and Mobilization." Presentation, Canadian Sociology and Anthropology Association (CSAA), annual meeting, Montreal, June 1995.

Doyle, Aaron and Richard V. Ericson
  1996 "Breaking into Prison: News Sources and Correctional Institutions."
    Canadian Journal of Criminology 38,2: 155-90.
Drache, Daniel and Duncan Cameron (eds.)
  1985 *The Other Macdonald Report.* Toronto: James Lorimer and Company.
Drache, Daniel and Wallace Clement (eds.)
  1985 *The New Practical Guide to Canadian Political Economy.* Toronto:
    James Lorimer and Company.
Drache, D. and H. Glasbeek
  1992 *The Changing Workplace: Reshaping Canada's Industrial Relations
    System.* Toronto: James Lorimer and Company.
Drainville, Andre C.
  1996 "The Fetishism of Global Civil Society: Global Governance,
    Transnational Urbanism, and Sustainable Capitalism in the World
    Economy." Presentation, Society for Socialist Studies, annual meeting, St.
    Catherines, Ont.
Dubofsky, M.
  1994 *The State and Labor in Modern America.* Chapel Hill: University of
    North Carolina Press.
Dûcheine, Vivien
  1986/1987 "Les femmes haïtiennes au Québec." *RFR/DRF* (Numéro
    spécial: Les pratiques du féminisme au Québec) 15,4: 10-12.
Duggan, Lisa
  1992 "Making It Perfectly Queer." *Socialist Review* 22,1: 11-31.
Dunk, Thomas
  1994 "Talking about Trees: Environment and Society in Forest Workers'
    Culture." *Canadian Review of Sociology and Anthropology* 31,1: 14-34.
Durocher, Constance
  1990 "L'hétérosexualité: Sexualité ou système social?" *RFR/DRF* 19,3/4: 18-
    22.
Eagleton, Terry
  1991 *Ideology: An Introduction.* London: Verso.
Eckersley, Robyn
  1989 "Green Politics and the New Class." *Political Studies* 37,2: 205-23.
Eder, Klaus
  1985 "The 'New Social Movements': Moral Crusades, Political Pressure
    Groups, or Social Movements?" *Social Research* 52,4: 869-90.
  1993 *The New Politics of Class.* Newbury Park, Cal.: Sage Publications.
Egan, Carolyn
  1987 "Toronto's International Women's Day Committee: Socialist Feminist
    Politics." In Heather Jon Maroney and Meg Luxton (eds.), *Feminism and
    Political Economy: Women's Work, Women's Struggles.* Toronto: Methuen.
Egan, Carolyn, B. Lee, and Michele Robidoux
  1991 "Book Review of Brodie, Janine, Shelley A.M. Gavigan, and Jane
    Jenson, 'The Politics of Abortion.'" *Resources for Feminist Research* 20,3/
    4: 152-5.

Elliott, Brian, Frank Bechhofer, David McCrone, and Stewart Black
  1982 "Bourgeois Social Movements in Britain: Repertoires and Responses."
  Sociological Review 30,1: 71–96.
Elliott, Brian and Aaron Doyle
  1994 "Brazil of the North? Movement, Counter–movement and Contested
  Action Frames: Environmental Struggles in British Columbia." Paper
  presented at the 13th World Congress of Sociology, Bielefeld, Germany,
  18–23 July, 1994.
Elliott, Brian, David McCrone, and Frank Bechhofer
  1988 "Anxieties and Ambitions: The Petit Bourgeoisie and the New Right in
  Britain." In David Rose (ed.), *Social Stratification and Economic Change*.
  London: Hutchinson.
Ely, John
  1993 "Post–Fordist Restructuring in Germany: What Role for the New
  Social Movements?" *New Political Science* 25: 145–73.
Emke, Ivan
  1991 "Speaking of AIDS in Canada: The Texts and Contexts of Official,
  Counter-Cultural and Mass Media Discourses Surrounding AIDS." Ph.D.
  thesis, Sociology and Anthropology, Carleton University, Ottawa.
Epstein, B.
  1990 "Rethinking Social Movement Theory." *Socialist Review* 20,1: 35–65.
Epstein, Steven
  1991 "Democratic Science? AIDS Activism and the Contested Construction
  of Knowledge." *Socialist Review* 21,2 (April-June): 35-64.
Erasmus, Georges
  1989 "Epilogue." In Boyce Richardson (ed.), *Drum Beat: Anger and Renewal
  in Indian Country*. Toronto: Summerhill Press.
Ericson, Richard
  1991 "Mass Media, Crime, Law and Justice: An Institutional Approach."
  British Journal of Criminology 31,3: 219–49.
  1994 "An Institutional Perspective on News Media Access and Control." In
  M. Aldridge and N. Hewitt (eds.), *Controlling Broadcasting*. Manchester,
  England: University of Manchester Press.
Ericson, Richard, Patricia Baranek, and Janet Chan
  1987 *Visualizing Deviance: A Study of News Organizations*. Milton Keynes,
  England: Open University Press and Toronto: University of Toronto
  Press.
  1989 *Negotiating Control: A Study of News Sources*. Milton Keynes, England:
  Open University Press and Toronto: University of Toronto Press.
  1991 *Representing Order: Crime, Law and Justice in the News Media*.
  Buckingham, England: Open University Press and Toronto: University of
  Toronto Press.
Escobar, Arturo
  1992 "Culture, Economics, and Politics in Latin American Social Movements
  Theory and Research." In Arturo Escobar and Sonia E. Alvarez (eds.),

The Making of Social Movements in Latin America: Identity, Strategy, and Democracy. Boulder, Col.: Westview Press.

Escobar, Arturo and Sonia E. Alvarez
1992 "Introduction: Theory and Protest in Latin America Today." In Arturo Escobar and Sonia E. Alvarez (eds.), *The Making of Social Movements in Latin America: Identity, Strategy, and Democracy.* Boulder, Col.: Westview Press.

Escoffier, Jeffrey
1990 "Inside the Ivory Closet." *Out/Look* 10 (Fall): 40-48.

Evernden, Neil
1984 "The Environmentalist's Dilemma." In Neil Evernden (ed.), "The Paradox of Environmentalism," Symposium Proceedings, Faculty of Environmental Studies, York University, North York, Ont.

Expert Working Group on Integrated Palliative Care for Persons with AIDS
1989 *Caring Together.* Ministry of Supply and Services Canada, February. Available from the Federal Centre for AIDS.

Eyerman, R. and A. Jamison
1991 *Social Movements: A Cognitive Approach.* Cambridge: Polity Press.

Faderman, Lillian
1981 *Surpassing the Love of Men: Romantic Friendship and Love between Women from the Renaissance to the Present.* New York: Morrow.
1991 *Odd Girls and Twilight Lovers: A History of Lesbian Life in Twentieth-Century America.* New York: Columbia University Press.

Fairclough, Norman
1992 *Discourse and Social Change.* Cambridge: Polity Press.
1993 "Critical Discourse Analysis and the Marketization of Public Discourse: The Universities." *Discourse & Society* 4,2: 133-68.

Falk, Richard
1993 "The Making of Global Citizenship." In Jeremy Brecher, John Brown Childs, and Jill Cutler (eds.), *Global Visions: Beyond the New World Order.* Montreal: Black Rose Books.

Fanon, Frantz
1967 *Black Skin, White Masks.* New York: Grove.

Fantasia, R.
1988 *Cultures of Solidarity: Consciousness, Action, and Contemporary American Workers.* Berkeley: University of California Press.

Fee, Elisabeth
1983 "Women and Health Care: A Comparison of Theories." In Elisabeth Fee (ed.), *Women and Health: The Politics of Sex in Medicine.* 2nd ed. Farmingdale: Baywood Publishing Company.

Fields, A. Belden
1988 "In Defense of Political Economy and Systemic Analysis: A Critique of Prevailing Theoretical Approaches to the New Social Movements." In C. Nelson and L. Grossberg (eds.), *Marxism and the Interpretation of Culture.* Urbana: University of Illinois Press.

Felski, Rita
1989 "Feminist Theory and Social Change." *Theory, Culture and Society* 6,2: 230.

Femmes en tête
1990 *De travail et d'espoir: des groupes de femmes racontent le féminisme.* Montreal: Remue-ménage.

Ferguson, Ann
1991a *Sexual Democracy: Women, Oppression, and Revolution.* Boulder, Col.: Westview Press.
1991b "Patriarchy, Sexual Identity, and the Sexual Revolution." In her *Sexual Democracy: Women, Oppression, and Revolution.* Boulder: Westview Press.

Ferree, Myra Marx
1992 "The Political Context of Rationality: Rational Choice Theory and Resource Mobilization." In Aldon D. Morris and Carol McClurg Mueller (eds.), *Frontiers in Social Movement Theory.* New Haven, Conn.: Yale University Press.

Fillmore, Nick
1989 "The Big Oink." *This Magazine*, March/April.

Finkler, Lilith
1980 "A Dykey Kike, or a Kikey Dyke, Which Will It Be? Oy Vey." *Lesbian Perspective*, February: 2.

Fireman, B. and W.A. Gamson
1979 "Utilitarian Logic in the Resource Mobilization Perspective." In Zald and McCarthy (1979).

Fishman, Mark
1980 *The Manufacturing of News.* Austin: University of Texas Press.

Fiske, John
1987 *Television Culture.* London: Methuen.
1989 *Understanding Popular Culture.* Boston: Unwin Hyman.

Flacks, Richard
1995 "Think Globally, Act Politically: Some Notes toward New Movement Strategy." In Marcy Darnovsky, Barbara Epstein, and Richard Flacks (eds.), *Cultural Politics and Social Movements.* Philadelphia: Temple University Press.

Flax, Jane
1992 "The End of Innocence." In Judith Butler and Joan W. Scott (eds.), *Feminists Theorize the Political.* New York and London: Routledge.

Forrest, Cris J. and David B. Tindall
1994 "The Whole World is Watching: Constituency and Identity among Vancouver Island Environmental Activists." Presentation, Canadian Anthropology Society, annual meeting, Vancouver, May 1994.

Foster, Peggy
1989 "Improving the Doctor/Patient Relationship: A Feminist Perspective." *Journal of Social Policy* 18,3: 337-61.

Foucault, Michel

1980 *Power/Knowledge*. New York: Pantheon.

1982 "The Subject and Power." In H.L. Dreyfus and P. Rabinow (eds.), *Michel Foucault: Beyond Structuralism and Hermeneutics*. Chicago: University of Chicago Press.

1984 "The Order of Discourse." In Michael Shapiro (ed.), *Language and Politics*. New York: New York University Press.

Fowler, Roger

1991 *Language in the News: Discourse and Ideology in the Press*. London: Routledge.

Fox, Bonnie J.

1989 "The Feminist Challenge: A Reconsideration of Social Inequality and Economic Development." In Robert J. Brym with Bonnie J. Fox, *From Culture to Power: The Sociology of English Canada*. Toronto: Oxford University Press.

Franzway, Suzanne, Diane Court, and R.W. Connell

1989 *Staking a Claim: Feminism, Bureaucracy and the State*. Cambridge: Polity Press.

Fraser, Nancy

1989a "What's Critical about Critical Theory? The Case of Habermas and Gender." In Nancy Fraser, *Unruly Practices*. Minneapolis: University of Minnesota Press.

1989b *Unruly Practices: Power, Discourse, and Gender in Contemporary Social Theory*. Minneapolis: University of Minnesota Press.

1992a "Rethinking the Public Sphere: A Contribution to the Critique of Actually Existing Democracy." In Craig Calhoun (ed.), *Habermas and the Public Sphere*. Cambridge, Mass.: MIT Press.

1992b "The Uses and Abuses of French Discourse Theories for Feminist Politics." In Nancy Fraser and Sandra Lee Bartky (eds.), *Revaluing French Feminism: Critical Essays on Difference, Agency, and Culture*. Bloomington: Indiana University Press.

Freeman, R. and J. Medoff

1984 *What Do Unions Do?* New York: Basic Books.

Frideres, James

1988 *Native Peoples in Canada: Contemporary Conflicts*. 3rd ed. Scarborough, Ont.: Prentice Hall Canada.

Friedmann, John

1989 "The Dialectic of Reason." *International Journal of Urban and Regional Research* 13: 217–44.

Frye, Marilyn

1992 *Willful Virgin: Essays in Feminism*. Freedom, Cal.: Crossing Press.

Fudge, Judy

1987 "Voluntarism and Compulsion: The Canadian Federal Government's Intervention in Collective Bargaining from 1900 to 1946." Ph.D. thesis, University of Oxford.

Fuentes, Marta and Andre Gunder Frank
1989 "Ten Theses on Social Movements." *World Development* 17,2: 179-91.
Fuss, Diana
1989 *Essentially Speaking: Feminism, Nature and Difference.* New York: Routledge.
Galipeau, Claude
1989 "Political Parties, Interest Groups, and New Social Movements: Toward New Representation?" In Alain Gagnon and Brian Tanguay (eds.), *Canadian Politics in Transition.* Toronto: Nelson.
Gamble, Andrew
1988 *The Free Economy and the Strong State: The Politics of Thatcherism.* London: Macmillan.
Gamson, William
1992 *Talking Politics.* Cambridge: Cambridge University Press.
Gamson, William and Andre Modigliani
1989 "Media Discourse and Public Opinion: A Constructionist Approach." *American Journal of Sociology* 95,1 (July): 1–37.
Garner, Roberta
1994 "Transnational Movements in Postmodern Society." *Peace Review* 6,4: 427-33.
GATT-Fly
1987b "Free Trade or Self-Reliance: Report of the Ecumenical Conference on Free Trade, Self Reliance and Economic Justice." Toronto.
George, J.
1994 *Discourses of Global Politics: A Critical (Re)Introduction to International Relations.* Boulder, Col.: Lynne Rienner.
Gerhards, Jurgen and Dieter Rucht
1992 "Mesomobilization: Organizing and Framing in Two Protest Campaigns in West Germany." *American Journal of Sociology* 98: 555–95.
Germino, Dante
1990 *Antonio Gramsci: Architect of a New Politics.* Baton Rouge: Louisiana State University Press.
Giese, Rachel
1994 "Catastrophic Drug Plan Announced." *Xtra!* 264 (Dec. 9): 1.
Gill, Stephen
1990 *American Hegemony and the Trilateral Commission.* Cambridge: Cambridge University Press.
Gill, Stephen and David Law
1987 *The Global Political Economy.* Baltimore: The Johns Hopkins University Press.
1988 *The Global Political Economy: Perspectives, Problems, and Policies.* New York: Harvester/Wheatsheaf.
Gilpin, Robert
1979 "Three Models of the Future." In G. Modelski (ed.), *Transnational Corporations and the World Order.* San Francisco: W.H. Freeman.

Gitlin, Todd
    1980 *The Whole World is Watching: Mass Media and the Making and Unmaking of the New Left*. Berkeley: University of California Press.
Goddard, John
    1991 *Last Stand of the Lubicon Cree*. Vancouver: Douglas and McIntyre.
Goffman, Erving
    1974 *Frame Analysis*. Cambridge, Mass: Harvard University Press.
Goldberg, Kim
    1993a "Axed: How the Vancouver Sun Became a Black Hole for Environmental Reporting." *This Magazine*, August: 11–15.
    1993b *Columbia Journalism Review*, November–December
Goldfield, M.
    1987 *The Decline of Organized Labor in the United States*. Chicago: University of Chicago Press.
Gorz, André
    1982 *Farewell to the Working Class: An Essay on Post-Industrial Socialism*. London: Pluto Press.
    1989 *Critique of Economic Reason*. London: Verso.
Gouvernement du Québec
    1987 "La politique familiale: énoncé des orientations et de la dynamique administrative." Adopté par le Conseil des ministres. Quebec.
Government of Canada
    1969 *Statement on Indian Policy* ("The White Paper"). Ottawa: Supply and Services Canada.
Gramsci, Antonio
    1971 *Selections from the Prison Notebooks*. Quintin Hoare and Geoffrey Nowell Smith (eds. and trans.). New York: International Publishers.
Grant, Judith and Peta Tancred
    1991 "Un point de vue féministe sur la bureaucratie étatique." *Sociologie et sociétés* 23,1: 201-14.
Grenier, Marc
    1992 "The Centrality of Conflict in Native Indian Coverage by the Montreal Gazette: War Zoning the Oka Incident." In Marc Grenier (ed.), *Critical Studies of Canadian Mass Media*. Toronto: Butterworths.
Grevatt, Margaret
    1975 *Lesbian/Feminism: A Response to Oppression*. Ph.D. thesis, Case Western Reserve University.
Gurr, Ted R.
    1970 *Why Men Rebel*. Princeton, N.J.: Princeton University Press.
Gusfield, Joseph R.
    1994 "The Reflexivity of Social Movements: Collective Behavior and Mass Society Theory Revisited." In Enrique Larana, Hank Johnston, and Joseph R. Gusfield (eds.), *New Social Movements: From Ideology to Identity*. Philadelphia: Temple University Press.

Habermas, Jürgen
1974 "The Public Sphere: An Encyclopedic Article (1964)." *New German Critique* 1,3 (Fall).
1975 *Legitimation Crisis*. Boston: Beacon Press.
1981 *The Theory of Communicative Action*. Vol. 2. Boston: Beacon Press.
1987a *The Philosophical Discourse of Modernity*. Cambridge, Mass.: MIT Press.
1987b *The Theory of Communicative Action*. Vol. 2. Boston: Beacon Press.
1989 "The Public Sphere." In Steven Seidman (ed.), *Jurgen Habermas on Society and Politics: A Reader*. Boston: Beacon Press.
Hackett, Robert
1991 *News and Dissent: The Press and the Politics of Peace in Canada*. Norwood, N.J.: Ablex.
Hackett, Robert, Richard Pinet, and Myles Ruggles
1992 "From Audience Commodity to Audience Community: Mass Media in B.C." In Helen Holmes and David Taras (eds.), *Seeing Ourselves: Media Power and Policy in Canada*. Toronto: Harcourt Brace Jovanovich.
Haiven, Larry
1990 "Hegemony and the Workplace: The Role of Arbitration." In L. Haiven et al. (eds.), *Regulating Labour: The State Neo-Conservatism and Industrial Relations*. Toronto: Garamond Press.
Halfmann, Jost
1988 "Risk Avoidance and Sovereignty." *Praxis International* 8,1: 14-33.
Hall, Stuart
1986 "Gramsci's Relevance for the Study of Race and Ethnicity." *Journal of Communication Inquiry* 10,2: 5-27.
1988 *The Hard Road to Renewal: Thatcherism and the Crisis of the Left*. London: Verso.
Hall, Stuart, Chas Critcher, Tony Jefferson, John Clarke, and Brian Roberts
1978 *Policing the Crisis*. London: Macmillan.
Halliday, M.A.K.
1989 "Context of Situation"; "Functions of Language"; "Register Variation." In M.A.K. Halliday and Ruquaiya Hasan, *Language, Context, and Text: Aspects of Language in a Social-semiotic Perspective*. London: Oxford University Press.
Hamel, Peter
1994 "The Aboriginal Rights Coalition." In Christopher Lind and Joe Mihevc (eds.), *Coalitions for Justice: the Story of Canada's Interchurch Coalitions*. Ottawa: Novalis.
Hammersmith, Bernice
1992 "Aboriginal Women and Self-Government." In Diane Englestad and John Bird (eds.), *Nation to Nation: Aboriginal Sovereignty and the Future of Canada*. Toronto: Anansi Press.
Hannon, Philip
1995 "The Canadian AIDS Society Should Act Up." *Xtra!* 279 (July 7): 25.

Hansen, Anders
1991 "The Media and the Social Construction of the Environment." *Media, Culture and Society* 13,4: 451.
Haraway, Donna
1990 "Investment Strategies for the Evolving Portfolio of Primate Female." In Mary Jacobus, Evelyn Fox Keller, and Sally Shuttleworth (eds.), *Body/Politics: Women and the Discourse of Science.* New York and London: Routledge.
Hark, Sabine
1994 "Stakes in the Field of Power: On the Political Limitations of Lesbian Identity Discourses." Paper prepared for presentation at the conference "Organizing Sexuality: Gay and Lesbian Movements since the 1960s." Free University of Amsterdam, June 22–24.
Harries-Jones, Peter (ed.)
1991 *Making Knowledge Count: Advocacy and Social Science.* Montreal and Kingston: McGill-Queen's University Press.
Harris, H.
1982 *The Right to Manage.* Madison: University of Wisconsin Press.
Harrison, Deborah
1981 *The Limits of Liberalism: The Making of Canadian Sociology.* Montreal: Black Rose Books.
Harvey, D.
1989 *The Condition of Postmodernity.* Oxford: Basil Blackwell.
Health and Welfare Canada
1989 "AIDS in Canada: The Federal Government Responds."
1990a *Building an Effective Partnership, the Federal Government's Commitment to Fighting AIDS.* Ministry of Supply and Services Canada.
1990b *HIV and AIDS: Canada's Blueprint,* Ministry of Supply and Services Canada.
1993 *National AIDS Strategy, Phase II, Building On Progress,* Ministry of Supply and Services Canada.
Hegedus, Zsuzsa
1989 "Social Movements and Social Change in Self-Creative Society: New Civil Initiatives in the International Arena." *International Sociology* 4,1: 19-36.
Heilbrun, J.
1995 *The Rise of Social Theory.* Cambridge: Polity Press.
Held, David and Anthony McGraw
1993 "Globalization and the Liberal Democratic State." *Government and Opposition* 28,2: 261-88.
Hennessy, Rosemary
1993 "Queer Theory: A Review of the *Differences* Special Issue and Wittig's *The Straight Mind.*" *Signs* 18,4: 964-73.

Herman, Didi
1994a *Rights of Passage: Struggles for Lesbian and Gay Legal Equality.* Toronto: University of Toronto Press.
1994b "A Jurisprudence of One's Own? Ruthann Robson's Lesbian Legal Theory." *Canadian Journal of Women and the Law* 7,2: 509-22.
Herman, Edward S. and Noam Chomsky
1988 *Manufacturing Consent: The Political Economy of the Mass Media.* New York: Pantheon.
Hewitt, Martin
1993 "Social Movements and Social Need: Problems with Postmodern Political Theory." *Critical Social Policy* 13,1: 52–74.
Higgins, Paul
1980 *Outsiders in a Hearing World.* Beverly Hills, Cal.: Sage Publications.
Hirsch, Joachim
1988 "The Crisis of Fordism, Transformations of the 'Keynesian' Security State, and the New Social Movements." *Research in Social Movements, Conflicts and Change,* 10: 43–55.
Hirst, Paul and Grahame Thompson
1996 *Globalization in Question.* Cambridge: Polity Press.
Hoagland, Sarah Lucia
1988a "Introduction." In Hoagland and Penelope (1988).
1988b *Lesbian Ethics: Towards New Value.* Palo Alto, Cal.: Institute of Lesbian Studies.
Hoagland, Sarah Lucia and Julia Penelope (eds.)
1988 *For Lesbians Only: A Separatist Anthology.* London: Onlywomen Press.
Hobsbawm, Eric
1989 *Politics for a Rational Left.* London: Verso.
Hofley, John R.
1992 "Canadianization: A Journey Completed?" In Carroll et al. (1992)
Hofrichter, Richard
1993 *Toxic Struggles: The Theory and Practice of Environmental Justice.* Gabriola Is., B.C.: New Society Publishers.
Holmes, Helen and David Taras
1992 *Seeing Ourselves: Media Power and Policy in Canada.* Toronto: Harcourt Brace Jovanovich.
Holub, Renate
1992 *Antonio Gramsci: Beyond Marxism and Postmodernism.* New York: Routledge.
Honderich, Ted
1989 *Violence for Equality: Inquiries in Political Philosophy.* London and New York: Routledge.
Honig, Bonnie
1992 "Toward an Agonistic Feminism: Hannah Arendt and the Politics of Identity." In Judith Butler and Joan Scott (eds.), *Feminists Theorize the Political.* New York: Routledge.

1995 (ed.), *Feminist Interpretations of Hannah Arendt.* University Park: Pennsylvania State University Press.

hooks, bell

1990 *Yearning: Race, Gender, and Cultural Politics.* Toronto: Between the Lines.

Howard, D.

1989 *Defining the Political.* London: Macmillan.

Huber, Joan and Beth E. Schneider (eds.)

1992 *The Social Context of AIDS.* Newbury Park, Cal.: Sage Publications.

Huber, Joseph

1989 "Social Movements." *Technological Forecasting and Social Change* 35: 365-74.

Hughes, Nym, Yvonne Johnson, and Yvette Perrault

1984 *Stepping out of Line: A Resource Book on Lesbian Feminism.* Vancouver: Press Gang.

Hunt, Alan

1990 "Rights and Social Movements: Counter–hegemonic Strategies." *Journal of Law and Society* 17: 309–28.

Hunt, Scott A., Robert D. Benford, and David A. Snow

1994 "Identity Fields: Framing Processes and the Social Construction of Movement Identities." In Enrique Larana, Hank Johnston, and Joseph R. Gusfield (eds.), *New Social Movements: From Ideology to Identity.* Philadelphia: Temple University Press.

Hyman, R.

1986 "Reflections on the Mining Strike." In R. Miliband et al. (eds.), *Socialist Register 1985/86.* London: The Merlin Press.

Indian Association of Alberta

1970 *Citizens Plus.* Edmonton.

Ingalsbee, Timothy

1994 "Resource and Action Mobilization Theories: The New Social-psychological Research Agenda." *Berkeley Journal of Sociology* 38: 139–55.

Jeffreys, Sheila

1993 *The Lesbian Heresy.* Melbourne, Australia: Spinifex Press.

Jenkins, J.C.

1983 "Resource Mobilization Theory and the Study of Social Movements." *Annual Review of Sociology* 9: 527–53.

Jenson, Jane

1986 "Gender and Reproduction: Or, Babies and the State." *Studies in Political Economy* 20: 9-46.

1989a "Different but Not Exceptional: Canada's Permeable Fordism." *Canadian Review of Sociology and Anthropology* 26,1: 69–94.

1989b "Paradigms and Political Discourse: Protective Legislation in France and the United States Before 1914." *Canadian Journal of Political Science* 22,2: 235-58.

1991 "All the World's a Stage: Ideas, Space and Times in Canadian Political Economy." *Studies in Political Economy* 36 (Fall): 43-72.

1993 "Naming Nations: Making Nationalist Claims in Canadian Public Discourse." *Canadian Review of Sociology and Anthropology* 30,3: 337–58.

Jessop, Bob et al.

1988 *Thatcherism: A Tale of Two Nations*. Cambridge: Polity Press.

Johnson, C.

1966 *Revolutionary Change*. Boston: Little, Brown.

Johnston, Hank

1991 *Tales of Nationalism: Catalonia, 1939–1979*. New Brunswick, N.J.: Rutgers University Press.

1992 "'Fightin' Words': Discourse, Frames, and the Cultural Analysis of Social Movements." Paper prepared for the Plenary Session on Methodology, International Workshop on Social Movements and Culture, University of California, San Diego, June 18–20.

Jones, R.J. Barry

1995 *Globalization and Interdependence in the International Political Economy: Rhetoric and Reality*. London: Pinter Publishers.

Juteau, Danielle and Louis Mahue

1989 "Sociology and Sociologists in Francophone Quebec: Science and Politics." *Canadian Review of Sociology and Anthropology*: 26,3: 363-93.

Kaku, M.

1994 *Hyperspace: A Scientific Odyssey through Parallel Universes, Time Warps and the Tenth Dimension*. New York: Oxford University Press.

Katz, H.

1985 *Shifting Gears*. Cambridge, Mass.: MIT Press.

Kaufman, Cynthia

1994 "Postmodernism and Praxis." *Socialist Review* 24,3: 57–80.

Kauffman, L.A.

1990 "The Anti-Politics of Identity." *Socialist Review* 20, 1.

Kealey, G. and B. Palmer

1987 *Dreaming of What Might Be: The Knights of Labour in Ontario, 1880-1900*. Toronto: New Hogtown Press.

Keil, R.

1994 "Green Work Alliances: The Political Economy of Social Ecology." *Studies In Political Economy* 44.

Kellogg, P.

1989 "State, Capital and World–Economy: Bukharin's Marxism and the 'Dependency–Class' Controversy in Canadian Political Economy." *Canadian Journal of Political Science* 22,2.

Kennedy, Elizabeth Lapovsky and Madeline D. Davis

1993 *Boots of Leather, Slippers of Gold: The History of a Lesbian Community*. New York: Routledge.

Kennedy, Mark C.

1988 "The New Global Network of Corporate Power and the Decline of National Self-Determination." *Contemporary Crisis* 12,3: 245-76.

King, D.
  1987 *The New Right: Politics, Markets and Citizenship.* Chicago: The Dorsey
  Press.
Kinsman, Gary
  1987 *The Regulation of Desire.* Montreal: Black Rose Books.
  1990 "Feds Delay National AIDS Strategy, AIDS Activists Plan to Put on the
  Heat." *Rites* 6,8 (February): 1,5.
  1991 " 'Their Silence, Our Deaths': What Can the Social Sciences Offer to
  AIDS Research?" In Diane E. Goldstein (ed.), *Talking AIDS: Interdiscipli-
  nary Perspectives on Acquired Immune Deficiency Syndrome.* Institute for
  Social and Economic Research (ISER) Policy Papers 12, Memorial
  University of Newfoundland: 39-60.
  1992 "Provincial AIDS Strategy Fails To Deliver." *Gazette* Halifax, Septem-
  ber: 4-5.
  1994 "Constructing Sexual Problems: 'These Things May Lead to the
  Tragedy of Our Species.'" In Les Samuelson (ed.), *Power and Resistance:
  Critical Thinking About Canadian Social Issues.* Halifax: Fernwood
  Publishing.
  1995 "The Textual Practices of Sexual Rule: Sexual Policing and Gay Men."
  In Marie Campbell and Ann Manicom (eds.), *Knowledge, Experience and
  Ruling: Studies in the Social Organization of Knowledge.* Toronto:
  University of Toronto Press: 80-95.
  1996a *The Regulation of Desire: Homo and Hetero Sexualities.* 2nd rev. and
  expanded ed. Montreal: Black Rose Books.
  1996b " 'Responsibility' as a Strategy of Governance: Regulating People
  Living with AIDS and Lesbians and Gay Men in Ontario." *Economy and
  Society* 215,3 (August): 393-409.
Kitschelt, Herbert
  1985 "New Social Movements in West Germany and the United States."
  Political Power and Social Theory 5: 310.
Klandermans, Bert (ed.)
  1989 *International Social Movement Research*, vol. 2. London: JAI.
  1990 "Linking the Old and the New Movement Networks in the Nether-
  lands." In Dalton and Kuechler (1990).
Klare, K.
  1978 "Judicial Deradicalization of the Wagner Act and the Origins of
  Modern Legal Consciousness, 1937-1941." *Minnesota Law Review* 62.
Knox, P.L. and P.J. Taylor (eds.)
  1995 *World Cities in a World–System.* Cambridge: Cambridge University
  Press.
Knox, T. M. (ed. and trans.)
  1967 *Hegel's Philosophy of Right.* New York: Oxford University Press.
Kochan, T. et al.
  1986 *The Transformation of American Industrial Relations.* New York: Basic
  Books.

Korten, David
1995 "When Corporations Rule the World." *Noetic Sciences Review* 34: 4-10.
1995a *When Corporations Rule the World.* West Hartford, Conn.: Kumarian Press.
Kostash, Myrna
1980 *Long Way from Home: The Story of the Sixties Generation in Canada.* Toronto: James Lorimer and Company.
Krieger, Susan
1984 *The Mirror Dance: Identity in a Women's Community.* Philadelphia: Temple University Press.
Kriesi, Hanspeter
1989 "New Social Movements and the New Class in the Netherlands." *American Journal of Sociology* 94,5: 1078-116.
Krimerman, Len, and Frank Lindenfeld
1990 "Contemporary Workplace Democracy in the United States." *Socialism and Democracy* 11: 109-39.
Kuhn, Annette, and AnnMarie Wolpe
1978 *Feminism and Materialism.* London: Routledge and Kegan Paul.
Laclau, Ernesto
1992 "Universalism, Particularism, and the Question of Identity." *October* 61 (Summer).
Laclau, Ernesto and Chantal Mouffe
1985 *Hegemony and Socialist Strategy: Towards a Radical Democratic Politics.* London: Verso.
1987 "Post-Marxism without Apologies." *New Left Review* 166.
Lamoureux, Diane
1989 *Citoyennes? Femmes, droit de vote et démocratie.* Montreal: Les éditions du remue-ménage.
Langdon, Steven And Victoria Cross (eds.)
1994 *As We Come Marching: People, Power and Progressive Politics.* Windsor: Windsor Works Productions.
Langille, David
1988 "The Business Council on National Issues and the Canadian State." *Studies in Political Economy* 24.
Larana, Enrique
1994 "Continuity and Unity in New Forms of Collective Action: A Comparative Analysis of Student Movements." In Enrique Larana, Hank Johnston, and Joseph R. Gusfield (eds.), *New Social Movements: From Ideology to Identity.* Philadelphia: Temple University Press.
Laslett, P.
1983a *The World We Have Lost.* 3rd ed. London: Methuen.
Laxer, Gordon
1995 "Introduction." *Canadian Review of Sociology and Anthropology* (Special Issue on Globalization) 32,3: 247-51.

LEAF [Women's Legal Education and Action Fund]
    1993 *Litigating for Lesbians: LEAF's Report on Consultations with the Lesbian Community*. Toronto.
Lee, B.
    1991 "Living with AIDS: Towards an Effective and Compassionate Health Policy." In Christine Overall and William P. Zion (eds.), *Perspectives on AIDS: Ethical and Social Issues*. Toronto: Oxford University Press.
Lefèbvre, Henri
    1976 *The Survival of Capitalism*. London: Allison and Busby.
Lefort, Claude
    1988 *Democracy and Political Theory*. Minneapolis: University of Minnesota Press.
Leiss, William
    1979 *Ecology Versus Politics in Canada*. Toronto: University of Toronto Press.
Lemke, Jay L.
    1990 "Making Meaning: The Principles of Social Semiotics." In *Talking Science*. Norwood, N.J.: Ablex.
Lennarson, Fred
    1991 Lennarson Papers, personal collection.
Lesbians Making History
    1989 "People Think This Didn't Happen in Canada." *Fireweed* 28 (Spring): 81-94.
Lesbians of Colour
    1991 "Loving and Struggling: A Conversation between Three Lesbians of Colour." In Makeda Silvera (ed.), *Piece of My Heart: A Lesbian of Colour Anthology*. Toronto: Sister Vision Press.
Lewis, Sasha Gregory
    1979 *Sunday's Women: A Report on Lesbian Life Today*. Boston: Beacon Press.
Lichtenstein, N.
    1982 *Labor's War at Home: The CIO in World War II*. Cambridge: Cambridge University Press.
Lintula, Douglas
    1994 "Trends: Environmental Priorities Shift." *Earthkeeper* 4,4 (April/May).
Lipset, Seymour
    1950 *Agrarian Socialism*. Toronto: Oxford University Press.
"Living with HIV"
    1992 *Fuse* (Special issue) 15,5 (Summer).
Lockard, Denyse
    1985 "The Lesbian Community: An Anthropological Approach." *Journal of Homosexuality* 11,3-4: 83-95.
Long, David A.
    1992 "Culture, Ideology and Militancy: the Movement of Indians in Canada 1969-1991." In W.K. Carroll (ed.), *Organizing Dissent: Contemporary*

Social Movements in Theory and Practice. 1st ed. Toronto: Garamond Press.

1993 "Oldness and Newness in the Movement of Canada's Native Peoples." Paper presented to the Society for Socialist Studies, Learned Societies Conference, Carleton University, Ottawa.

1995 "On Violence and Healing: Native Experiences, 1969-1994." In Jeffrey Ian Ross (ed.), *Violence in Canada: Socio-political Perspectives.* Toronto: Oxford University Press.

Loomis, Ruth and Merv Wilkinson

1991 "Wildwood: A Forest For the Future." In C. Plant and J. Plant (eds.), *Green Business: Hope or Hoax?* Gabriola Island, B.C.: New Catalyst Publishers.

Luke, Tim

1993 "Green Consumerism: Ecology and the Ruse of Recycling." In Jane Bennett and William Chaloupka (eds.), *In the Nature of Things: Language, Politics, and the Environment.* Minneapolis: University of Minnesota Press.

Luxton, Meg

1980 *More Than a Labour of Love.* Toronto: Women's Press.

MacDonald, M.

1991 "Post-Fordism and the Flexibility Debate." *Studies in Political Economy* 36.

Macpherson, C.B.

1953 *Democracy in Alberta.* Toronto: University of Toronto Press.

Maggenti, Maria

1993 "Wandering through Herland." In Stein (1993).

Magnusson, Warren

1990 "Critical Social Movements: De–centring the State." In Alain Gagnon and James P. Bickerton (eds.), *Canadian Politics: An Introduction to the Discipline.* Peterborough, Ont.: Broadview Press.

1992 "Decentring the State, or Looking for Politics." In W.K. Carroll (ed.), *Organizing Dissent: Contemporary Social Movements in Theory and Practice.* 1st ed. Toronto: Garamond Press.

1994 "Social Movements and the Global City." *Millennium: Journal of International Studies* 23,3: 621–45.

1996 *The Search for Political Space.* Toronto: University of Toronto Press.

Magnusson, Warren and R. Walker

1988 "De–Centring the State: Political Theory and Canadian Political Economy." *Studies in Political Economy* 26: 37–71.

Maier, C.S. (ed.)

1987 *Changing Boundaries of the Political.* Cambridge: Cambridge University Press.

Maingueneau, Dominique

1991 *L'analyse du discours: Introduction aux lectures de l'archive.* Paris: Hachette.

Majury, Diane
1994 "Refashioning the Unfashionable: Claiming Lesbian Identities in the Legal Context." *Canadian Journal of Women and the Law* 7,2: 286-317.

Marchak, Patricia
1983 *Green Gold: The Forest Industry in British Columbia.* Vancouver: University of British Columbia Press.
1991 "For Whom the Tree Falls: Restructuring of the Global Forest Industry." *B.C. Studies* 90 (Summer): 3-24.

Marcil-Lacoste, Louise
1987 *La raison en procès: Essais sur la philosophie et le sexisme.* Hurtubise HMH, collection Brèches.

Maroney, Heather Jon
1988 "Using Gramsci for Women: Feminism and the Quebec State (1960-1980)." *RFR/DRF* 17,3: 26-30.

Maroney, Heather J. and M. Luxton
1987 *Feminism and Political Economy: Women's Work, Women's Struggles.* Toronto: Methuen.

Martin, Biddy and Chandra Talpade Mohanty
1986 In Teresa de Lauretis (ed.), *Feminist Studies/Critical Studies.* Bloomington: Indiana University Press.

Marx, Gary T. and Douglas McAdam
1994 *Collective Behavior and Social Movements.* Englewood Cliffs, N.J.: Prentice–Hall.

Marx, Karl
1968 "Theses on Feurbach." In *Karl Marx and Frederick Engels: Selected Works.* New York: International Publishers.

Masson, Dominique et Pierre–André Tremblay
1993 "Mouvement des femmes et développement local." *Revue canadienne des sciences régionales/Canadian Journal of Regional Science* 16,2: 165–83.

Mayer, Margit
1991 "Social Movement Research in the United States: A European Perspective." *International Journal of Politics, Culture, and Society* 4,4: 459-80.

Maynard, Steven
1991 "When Queer Is Not Enough: Identity and Politics." *Fuse* 15,1,2: 14-18.

McAdam, Douglas
1982 *Political Process and the Development of Black Insurgency: 1930–1970.* Chicago: University of Chicago Press.
1994 "Culture and Social Movements." In Enrique Larana, Hank Johnston, and Joseph R. Gusfield (eds.), *New Social Movements: From Ideology to Identity.* Philadelphia: Temple University Press.

McAdam, D., J.D. McCarthy, and M.N. Zald
1988 "Social Movements." In Neil Smelser (ed.), *Handbook of Sociology.* Newbury Park, Cal.: Sage Publications.

McCarney, Joseph
1990 *Social Theory and the Crisis of Marxism.* London: Verso.

McCarthy, John D.
1994 "Activists, Authorities, and Media Framing of Drunk Driving." In Enrique Larana, Hank Johnston, and Joseph R. Gusfield (eds.), *New Social Movements: From Ideology to Identity*. Philadelphia: Temple University Press.

McCarthy, J.D. and M.N. Zald
1973 *The Trend of Social Movements in America: Professionalization and Resource Mobilization*. Morristown, N.J.: General Learning Corporation.
1977 "Resource Mobilization and Social Movements: A Partial Theory." In Zald and McCarthy (1987).

McCaskell, Tim
1989 "AIDS Activism: The Development of a New Social Movement." *Canadian Dimension* 23,6 (September): 7-11.

McClurg Mueller, Carol
1992 "Building Social Movement Theory." In Aldon D. Morris and Carol McClurg Mueller (eds.), *Frontiers in Social Movement Theory*. New Haven, Conn.: Yale University Press.

McCormick, Chris
1995 "AIDS Fiends and High-risk Groups: Misrepresenting and Signifying a Disease" (talk by Eric Smith). In *Constructing Danger: The Mis/representation of Crime in the News*. Halifax: Fernwood Publishing.

McKay, Stan
1992 "Calling Creation into Our Family." In Diane Engelstad and John Bird (eds.), *Nation to Nation: Aboriginal Sovereignty and the Future of Canada*. Toronto: Anansi Press.

McLellan, David (ed.)
1977 *Karl Marx: Selected Writings*. Oxford: Oxford University Press.
1988 *Marxism: Essential Writings*. Oxford: Oxford University Press.

McLeod, Ian
1994 *Under Siege: The Federal NDP in the Nineties*. Toronto: James Lorimer and Company.

Melucci, Alberto
1980 "The New Social Movements." *Social Science Information* 19,2: 220.
1988 "Social Movements and the Democratization of Everyday Life." In John Keane (ed.), *Civil Society and the State: New European Perspectives*. London: Verso.
1989 *Nomads of the Present: Social Movements and Individual Needs in Contemporary Society*. Philadelphia: Temple University Press.
1992 "Liberation or Meaning? Social Movements, Culture and Democracy." *Development and Change* 23,3: 43–77.
1994 "Paradoxes of Post–industrial Democracy: Everyday Life and Social Movements." *Berkeley Journal of Sociology* 38: 185–92.

Merchant, Carolyn
1994 *Key Concepts in Critical Theory: Ecology*. Atlantic Highlands, N.J.: Humanities Press.

Meyrowitz, Joshua
   1985 *No Sense of Place: The Impact of Electronic Media on Social Behaviour.*
      New York: Oxford University Press.
Michaud, Jacinthe
   1992a "The Welfare State and the Problem of Counter–hegemonic Response
      within the Women's Movement." In W.K. Carroll (ed.), *Organizing
      Dissent: Contemporary Social Movements in Theory and Practice.* 1st ed.
      Toronto: Garamond Press.
   1992b "Le mouvement des Centres de santé: discours et pratiques de l'auto-
      santé et son impact sur le réseau institutionnel de santé au Québec."
      Communication inédite présentée au Congrès des Sociétés savantes.
      Association Canadienne des Études sur les femmes. Université de l'Ile
      du Prince Édouard.
   1995 "Angel Makers or Trouble Makers? The Health Centres Movement in
      Québec and the Conditions of Formation of a Counter-Hegemony on
      Health." Ph.D thesis, University of Toronto.
Michels, R.
   1949 *Political Parties.* Glencoe, Ill.: Free Press.
Milan Women's Bookstore Collective (The)
   1990 *Sexual Difference: A Theory of Social-Symbolic Practice.* Bloomington
      and Indianapolis: Indiana University Press.
Millar, D.
   1980 "Shapes of Power: The Ontario Labour Relations Board, 1944 to 1950."
      Ph.D. thesis, Department of History, York University, Toronto.
Miller, J.R.
   1991 "The Northwest Rebellion of 1885." In J.R. Miller (ed.), *Sweet Prom-
      ises: A Reader on Indian-White Relations in Canada.* Toronto: University
      of Toronto Press.
Milner, Sheilagh and Henry Milner
   1973 *The Decolonization of Quebec.* Toronto: McClelland and Stewart.
Mishler, Elliot G.
   1991 "Once Upon a Time ..." *Journal of Narrative and Life History* 1,2/3:
      101-8.
Mohanty, Chandra Talpade
   1992 "Feminist Encounters: Locating the Politics of Experience." In Michèle
      Barrett and Anne Phillips (eds.), *Destabilizing Theory: Contemporary
      Feminist Debates.* Stanford, Cal.: Stanford University Press.
Monique, Myrian, Rosemary et Vivian
   1982 "Femmes haïtiennes: noires, immigrantes et réfugées." *Les cahiers de
      la femme* 4,2: 48-51.
Montgomery, D.
   1979 *Workers' Control in America.* Cambridge: Cambridge University Press.
Mooers, Colin and Alan Sears
   1992 "The 'New Social Movements' and the Withering Away of State
      Theory." In W.K. Carroll (ed.), *Organizing Dissent: Contemporary Social
      Movements in Theory and Practice.* 1st ed. Toronto: Garamond Press.

Morgan, Patricia
  1981 "From Battered Wife to Program Client: The State's Shaping of Social
    Problems." *Kapitalistate* 9: 17-39.
Morgen, Sandra
  1982 "Ideology and Change in a Feminist Health Centre: The Experience
    and Dynamics of Routinization." Ph.D. thesis, Department of Anthropol-
    ogy, University of North Carolina at Chapel Hill.
  1986 "The Dynamic of Cooptation in A Feminist Health Clinic." *Social
    Science and Medicine* 23,2: 201-10.
  1990 "Contradiction in Feminist Practice: Individualism and Collectivism in
    a Feminist Health Center." In T.M.S. Evens and James L. Peacock (eds.),
    Comparative Social Research: A Research Annual. Greenwhich, Conn.
    and London: Jai Press.
Morris, Aldon
  1984 *The Origins of the Civil Rights Movement.* New York: Free Press.
Mouffe, Chantal
  1988a "Radical Democracy." *Social Text* 21: 35.
  1988b "Hegemony and New Political Subjects: Toward a New Concept of
    Democracy." In Cary Nelson and Lawrence Grossberg (eds.), *Marxism
    and the Interpretation of Culture.* Urbana: University of Illinois Press.
  1992 "Feminism, Citizenship, and Radical Democratic Politics." In Judith
    Butler and Joan W. Scott (eds.), *Feminist Theorize the Political.* New York
    and London: Routledge.
Mumford, L.
  1961 *The City in History.* New York: Harcourt Brace.
Myers, Ted, Gaston Godin, Liviana Calzavara, Jean Lambert, and David Locker
  in collaboration with the Canadian AIDS Society
  1993 *The Canadian Survey of Gay and Bisexual Men and HIV Infection:
    Men's Survey.* Ottawa: Canadian AIDS Society.
Mykhalovskiy, Eric and George W. Smith
  1994 *Hooking up to Social Services: A Report on the Barriers People Living
    with AIDS Face Accessing Social Services.* Toronto: Ontario Institute for
    Studies in Education and the Community AIDS Treatment Information
    Exchange.
Nadeau, Chantal
  1995 "Pret-à-porter: Queer Studies, représentation lesbienne et frénésie
    médiatique." Presentation, Canadian Women's Studies Association,
    annual meeting, Université du Québec à Montreal, June.
Nelson, E.D. and Augie Fleras
  1995 "Globalization." In E.D. Nelson and A. Fleras (eds.), *Social Problems in
    Canada: Issues and Challenges.* Scarborough, Ont.: Prentice Hall Canada.
Nelson, Joyce
  1989 *Sultans of Sleaze: Public Relations and the Media.* Toronto: Between
    the Lines.
  1994 "Pulp and Propaganda." *Canadian Forum* July/August: 14–19.

Nicholson, Linda
   1986 *Gender and History: The Limits of Social Theory in the Age of the
      Family.* New York: Columbia University Press.
   1994 "Interpreting Gender." *Signs* 20,1: 79–105.
Nixon, Bob
   1990 "The Death of Another Forestry Myth: Fifty Cents on the Dollar."
      Forest Planning Canada 6,4: 14.
Ng, Roxana
   1988 *The Politics of Community Services: Immigrant Women, Class and State.*
      Toronto: Garamond Press.
Ng, Roxana, Gillian Walker, and Jacob Muller (eds.)
   1990 *Community Organization and the Canadian State.* Toronto: Garamond
      Press.
Nova Scotia Advisory Commission on AIDS
   1992 "Nova Scotia AIDS Strategy."
O'Brien, Carol-Anne and Lorna Weir
   1995 "Lesbians and Gay Men Inside and Outside Families." In Nancy
      Mandell and Aunn Duffy (eds.), *Canadian Families: Diversity, Conflict
      and Change.* Toronto: Harcourt Brace Canada.
Offe, Claus
   1984 *Contradictions of the Welfare State.* Cambridge, Mass.: MIT Press.
   1985a *Disorganized Capitalism.* Cambridge: Polity Press.
   1985b "New Social Movements: Challenging the Boundaries of Institutional
      Politics." *Social Research* 52: 817–68.
O'Leary, Véronique
   1986 "Conception féministe de la santé." Mémoire d'un forum de femmes:
      questions pratiques en éducation, en santé et sur le pouvoir. Centrale de
      l'enseignement du Québec.
O'Leary, Véronique and Louise Toupin
   1982 "Nous sommes le produit d'un contexte." *Québécoises debouttes!* 1.
      Montreal: Les éditions du remue-ménage.
Olofson, Gunnar
   1988 "After the Working-class Movement? An Essay on What's 'New' and
      What's 'Social' in the New Social Movements." *Acta Sociologica* 31,1: 26.
Olson, M.
   1965 *The Logic of Collective Action.* Cambridge, Mass.: Harvard University
      Press.
Omi, Michael and Howard Winant
   1994 *Racial Formation in the United States.* 2nd ed. New York: Routledge.
Onstad, Katrina
   1994 "Queer Kids: High-School Sweethearts, Earnest Politics, and the
      Trouble with Trendy." *This Magazine* 28 (September/October): 24-28.
Ontario Federation of Labour
   1993 "Labour's Relationship with the New Democratic Party When the NDP
      Is in Government." 2nd Biennial Convention, Don Mills, Ont.

Osborne, Peter
  1991 "Radicalism without Limits? Discourse, Democracy and the Politics of Identity." In Peter Osborne (ed.), *Socialism and the Limits of Liberalism.* London: Verso.
Overbeek, Henk
  1990 *Global Capitalism and National Decline.* Boston: Unwin Hyman.
Paehlke, Robert
  1989 *Environmentalism and the Future of Progressive Politics.* New Haven, Conn.: Yale University Press.
Palmer, Bryan
  1987 *Solidarity: The Rise and Fall of an Opposition in British Columbia.* Vancouver: New Star Books.
  1992 *Working Class Experience: Rethinking the History of Canadian Labour, 1800-1991.* Toronto: McClelland and Stewart.
Panitch, Leo
  1979 "Corporatism in Canada." *Studies in Political Economy* 1: 43-92.
  1989 "The Ambiguous Legacy of the Free Trade Election." *Canadian Dimension* 23,1: 18-9.
  1992 "New World Order and the Socialist Agenda." In *Socialist Register 1992.* London: The Merlin Press.
  1996 "Globalization, States, and Left Strategies." *Social Justice* 23,1-2: 79-90.
Panitch, Leo and Donald Swartz
  1988 *The Assault on Trade Union Freedoms: From Consent to Coercion.* Toronto: Garamond Press.
  1993 *The Assault on Trade Union Freedoms: From Wage Controls to Social Contract.* Toronto: Garamond Press.
Paquette, Carmen
  1990 "Personal Reflections on Lesbian Organizing in Ottawa." In Stone (1990).
Paquette, Louise
  1989 "La situation socio-économique des femmes: faits et chiffres." Québec: Secrétariat à la condition féminine, Gouvernement du Québec.
Paris, Sherri
  1993 "Review of *A Lure of Knowledge* and *inside/out.*" *Signs* 18,4: 984-8.
Parliamentary Ad Hoc Committee on AIDS (Hon. David MacDonald, chairperson)
  1990 *Confronting a Crisis: The Report of the Parliamentary Ad Hoc Committee on AIDS.* Ottawa, June.
Parsons, Vic
  1995 *Bad Blood: The Tragedy of the Canadian Tainted Blood Scandal.* Toronto: Lester.
Passerin d'Entreves, Maurizio
  1994 *The Political Philosophy of Hannah Arendt.* New York: Routledge.
Patton, Cindy
  1985 *Sex and Germs: The Politics of AIDS.* Montreal: Black Rose Books.
  1987 "Resistance and the Erotic: Reclaiming History, Setting Strategy as We

Face AIDS." *Radical America* 20,6 (September): 68-78. Reprinted in Peter Aggleton, Graham Hart and Peter Davies (eds.), *AIDS: Social Representations, Social Practices*. London: Falmer Press, 1989.

1988 "The AIDS Industry." *Zeta Magazine* 1,5 (May): 81-4.

1990 *Inventing AIDS*. New York and London: Routledge.

1996 *Fatal Advice: How Safe Sex Went Wrong*. Durham, N.C.: Duke University Press.

Patton, Paul

1988 "Marxism and Beyond: Strategies of Reterritorialization." In Cary Nelson and Lawrence Grossberg (eds.), *Marxism and the Interpretation of Culture*. Urbana: University of Illinois Press.

Parajuli, Pramod

1991 "Power and Knowledge in Development Discourse: New Social Movements and the State in India." *International Social Science Journal* 43,1: 173–90.

Pavelich, Matthew D.

1996 "AIDS Strategy Won't Be Renewed." *Capital Xtra!* 34 (June 28): 13.

Pearce, Frank and Steven Tombs

1993 "U.S. Capital Versus the Third World: Union Carbide and Bhopal." In F. Pearce and M. Woodiwiss (eds.), *Global Crime Connections: Dynamics and Control*. London: Macmillan.

Penelope, Julia

1992 *Call Me Lesbian: Lesbian Lives, Lesbian Theory*. Freedom, Cal.: Crossing Press.

Persky, Stan

1991 *Mixed Media, Mixed Messages*. Vancouver: New Star Books.

Phelan, Shane

1994 *Getting Specific: Postmodern Lesbian Politics*. Minneapolis: University of Minnesota Press.

Pichardo, Nelson A.

1988 "Resource Mobilization: An Analysis of Conflicting Theoretical Variations." *The Sociological Quarterly* 29: 97-110.

Pinard, M.

1971 *The Rise of a Third Party: A Study in Crisis Politics*. Englewood Cliffs, N.J.: Prentice-Hall.

Pinkerton, Evelyn W.

1993 "Co–Management Efforts as Social Movements: The Tin Wis Coalition and the Drive for Practises Legislation in British Columbia." *Alternatives* 19,3 (May): 33–8.

Piore, M. and C. Sabel

1984 *The Second Industrial Divide*. New York: Basic Books.

Pitkin, Hannah

1981 "Justice: On Relating Private and Public." *Political Theory* 9,3 (August).

Plotke, D.

1990 "What's So New about New Social Movements?" *Socialist Review* 20,1: 81-102.

Poirier, Guy
1987 "Public Forum Votes Canadian Ads the Worst." *Rites* 4,1: 8.
Polanyi, Karl
1957 *The Great Transformation*. Boston: Beacon Press.
Pole, Nancy
1990 "Le féminisme a 50 ans: Vogue la galère (blanche) ou 50 ans et tout un chemin a faire." *Communiqu'Elle* 17,2: 7-11.
Ponting, J. Rick
1986 (ed.) *Arduous Journey: Canadian Indians and Decolonization*. Toronto: Butterworths.
1990 "Public Opinion on Aboriginal Issues in Canada." In Craig McKie and Keith Thompson (eds.), *Canadian Social Trends*. Toronto: Thompson Educational Publishing.
Postman, Neil
1985 *Amusing Ourselves to Death: Public Discourse in the Age of Show Business*. New York: Penguin.
Poynton, Cate
1993 "Grammar, Language and the Social: Poststructuralism and Systemic-functional Linguistics." *Social Semiotics* 3,1: 1-21.
Przeworski, Adam
1980 "Social Democracy as a Historical Phenomenon." *New Left Review* 122.
Pringle, Rosemary and Sophie Watson
1990 "Fathers, Brothers, Mates: The Fraternal State in Australia." In Sophie Watson (ed.), *Playing the State: Australian Feminist Interventions*. London: Verso.
Pro-Canada Network
1988 "Report of the Sixth Assembly of the Pro-Canada Network." Ottawa, December 3-5.
1989 "Canada's First Free Trade Budget: The PCN Response to the 1989 Federal Budget." Ottawa.
Purvis, Trevor and Alan Hunt
1993 "Discourse, Ideology, Discourse, Ideology, Discourse, Ideology ..." *The British Journal of Sociology* 44,3: 473-99.
Qureshi, Zia
1996 "Globalization: New Opportunities, Tough Challenges." *Finance & Development* 33,1: 30-3.
Ratner, R.S.
1992 "New Movements, New Theory, New Possibilities? Reflections on Counter–hegemony Today." In W.K. Carroll (ed.), *Organizing Dissent: Contemporary Social Movements in Theory and Practice*. 1st ed. Toronto: Garamond Press.
Ray, Larry J.
1993 *Rethinking Critical Theory: Emancipation in the Age of Global Social Movements*. Newbury Park, Cal.: Sage Publishing.

Rayside, David M. and Evert A. Lindquist
1992a "AIDS Activism and the State in Canada." *Studies in Political Economy* 39 (Autumn): 37-76.
1992b "Canada: Community Activism, Federalism, and the New Politics of Disease." In David L. Kirp and Ronald Bayer (eds.), *AIDS in the Industrialized Democracies: Passions, Politics, and Policies*. Montreal and Kingston: McGill-Queen's University Press.
"Rethinking Our Mission in Ontario: A Discussion Paper for Union Leaders" 1993 Mimeo (no author cited).
Regroupement provincial des maisons d'hébergement et de transition pour femmes victimes de violence conjugale.
1990 *Au grand jour*. Madeleine Lacombe (rédaction) Montreal: remue-ménage.
Regroupement des Centres de santé des femmes du Québec.
1986 "Les Centres de santé de femmes du Québec." Représentation écrite présentée à la Commission d'Enquête sur les services de santé et les services sociaux. Hull.
1987 "Un regard de l'intérieur: bilan des centres de santé de femmes du Québec." Caroline Larue (rédaction).
1991 "Cadre de référence des centres de santé des femmes du Québec."
Relais-femmes
1985 "Le Regroupement des centres de santé pour les femmes et la non-participation." Rédigé par Josée Belleau. Les rapports des groupes de femmes avec l'État. Compte rendu de la journée de réflexion organisée par Relais-femmes.
Rich, Adrienne
1980 "Compulsory Heterosexuality and Lesbian Existence." *Signs* 5 (Summer): 631-57.
Rich, E.E.
1991 "Trade Habits and Economic Motivation among the Indians of North America" In J.R. Miller (ed.), *Sweet Promises: A Reader in Indian-White Relations in Canada*. Toronto: University of Toronto Press.
Richardson, Mary, Joan Sherman, and Michael Gismondi
1993 *Winning Back the Words: Confronting Experts in an Environmental Public Hearing*. Toronto: Garamond Press.
Riley, Denise
1988 *"Am I That Name?" Feminism and the Category of "Women" in History*. Minneapolis: University of Minnesota Press.
Robbins, Bruce (ed.)
1993 *The Phantom Public Sphere*. Minneapolis: University of Minnesota Press.
Robertson, R.
1992 *Globalization: Social Theory and Global Culture*. London: Sage Publications.
Robinson, Ian
1995 "Globalization and Democracy." *Dissent* 42,3: 373-80.

Rorty, Richard
1995 "Movements and Campaigns." *Dissent*, Winter: 55–60.
Ross, Becki L.
1995 *The House That Jill Built: A Lesbian Nation in Formation*. Toronto: University of Toronto Press.
Rudd, Andrea and Darien Taylor
1992 *Positive Women: Voices of Women Living with AIDS*. Toronto: Second Story Press.
Rusek, Sheryl
1978 *The Women's Health Movement: Feminist Challenge to Medical Control*. New York: Praeger Publishers.
Rusk, James
1994 "Environmentalists Not Seen as Force in Next Ontario Election." *The Globe and Mail*, April 5.
Russell, Bob
1990 *Back to Work? Labour, State and Industrial Relations in Canada*. Scarborough, Ont.: Nelson Canada.
1995 "The Subtle Labour Process and the Great Skill Debate." *Canadian Journal of Sociology*.
1996. "Wagnerism in Canada at Fifty." In Cy Gonick, Paul Phillips, and Jesse Vorst (eds.), *Labour Gains, Labour Pains: Fifty Years of PC 1003*. Socialist Studies/Étude Socialistes, vol. 10. Winnipeg and Halifax: Society for Socialist Studies and Fernwood Publishing.
1997 "Rival Paradigms at Work: Work Reorganization and Labour Force Impacts in a Staple Industry." *Canadian Review of Sociology and Anthropology* 34,1.
Rustin, Michael
1988 "Absolute Voluntarism: Critique of a Post-marxist Concept of Hegemony." *New German Critique* 43: 146-71.
Saillant, Francine
1985 "Le mouvement pour la santé des femmes." In Jacques Dufresne, Fernand Dumont, Yves Martin (dir), *Traité d'anthropologie médicale: l'institution de la santé et de la maladie*. Québec: Presse de l'Université du Québec/Institut québécois de recherche sur la culture/Presses universitaires de Lyon.
Sandilands, Catriona
1993 "On 'Green' Consumerism: Environmental Privatization and 'Family Values.'" *Canadian Woman Studies* 13,3 (Spring).
1995 "From Natural Identity to Radical Democracy." *Environmental Ethics* 17,1 (Spring).
Sadinsky, Ian and Earl Berger and Associates
1989 *A Working Document for the Development of a National Strategy on HIV Infection and AIDS*. Ottawa: Sadinsky and Associates.

Sakamoto, Yoshikozu

1995 "Democratization, Social Movements, and the World Order." In Bjorne Hettne (ed.), *International Political Economy: Understanding Global Disorder.* Halifax: Fernwood Publishing.

Sassoon, Anne Showstack

1982 "Passive Revolution and the Politics of Reform." In *Approaches to Gramsci.* London: Readers and Writers Publishing Cooperative Society.

Schiller, Dan

1986 "Transformations of News in the U.S. Information Market." In P. Golding, G. Murdock and P. Schlesinger (eds.), *Communicating Politics: Mass Communications and the Political Process.* New York: Holmes and Meier.

Schloshberg, David

1995 "Communicative Action in Practice: Intersubjectivity and New Social Movements." *Political Studies* 63: 291–311.

Schnaiberg, Allan and Kenneth Gould

1994 *Environment and Society: The Enduring Conflict.* New York: St. Martin's Press.

Schudson, Michael

1989 "The Sociology of News Production." *Media Culture and Society* 11: 263–82.

Schulman, Sarah

1994 *My American History: Lesbian and Gay Life during the Reagan/Bush Years.* New York: Routledge.

Schwartz, Michael and Shuva Paul

1992 "Resource Mobilization Versus the Mobilization of People: Why Consensus Movements Cannot Be Instruments of Social Change." In Aldon D. Morris and Carol McClurg Mueller (eds.), *Frontiers in Social Movement Theory.* New Haven, Conn.: Yale University Press.

Scott, Alan

1990 *Ideology and the New Social Movements.* London: Unwin Hyman.

Seager, Joni

1993 *Earth Follies: Coming to Feminist Terms with the Global Environmental Crisis.* New York: Routledge.

Sears, Alan

1990 "AIDS and the Health of Nations: Public Health and the Politics of HIV Testing." Presentation, Canadian Sociology and Anthropology Association, annual meeting, Victoria, B.C. Later published as "AIDS and the Health of Nations," *Critical Sociology* 18,2 (1991): 31-50.

1992 "'To Teach Them How to Live': The Politics of Public Health from Tuberculosis to AIDS." *Journal of Historical Sociology* 5,1: 61-83.

1995 "Before the Welfare State: Public Health and Social Policy." *The Canadian Review of Sociology and Anthropology* 32,2 (May): 169-88.

Secrétariat à la famille

1989 *Famille en tête: plan d'action en matière de politique familiale 1989-1991.* Québec: Gouvernement du Québec.

Shapiro, Michael J.
  1981 *Language and Political Understanding: The Politics of Discursive Practices*. New Haven, Conn.: Yale University Press.
Shaw, Martin
  1994 "Civil Society and Global Politics: Beyond a Social Movements Approach." *Millenium: Journal of International Studies* 23,3: 647-67.
Shields, John
  1988 "British Columbia's New Reality: The Politics of Neo-Conservatism and Defensive Defiance." Ph.D. thesis, Department of Political Science, University of British Columbia, Vancouver.
Shields, John and Bob Russell
  1994 "Part-time Workers, the Welfare State, and Labour Market Relations." In A. Johnson et al. (eds.), *Continuities and Discontinuities: The Political Economy of Social Welfare and Labour Market Policy in Canada*. Toronto: University of Toronto Press.
Ship, Susan Judith
  1991 "Au-delà de la solidarité féminine." *Revue québécoise de science politique* 19: 5-36.
Silman, Janet
  1987 *Enough Is Enough: Aboriginal Women Speak Out*. Toronto: The Women's Press.
Simonds, Ruth, Bonnie K. Kay, and Carol Regan
  1984 "Women's Health Groups: Alternative to the Health Care System." *International Journal of Health Services* 14,4: 619-34.
Sinclair, Jim, ed.
  1992 *Crossing the Line*. Vancouver: New Star Books.
Sivanandan, A
  1989 "All That Melts into Air Is Solid." *Race and Class* 31,3: 11.
Sklair, Leslie
  1995 "Social Movements and Global Capitalism." *Sociology* 29,3: 495-512.
Skocpol, Theda
  1979 *States and Social Revolutions*. New York: Cambridge University Press.
Slater, David
  1994 "Power and Social Movements in the Other Occident: Latin America in an International Context." *Latin American Perspectives* 21,2: 11–37.
Smart, Barry
  1986 "The Politics of Truth and the Problem of Hegemony." In David C. Hoy (ed.), *Foucault: A Critical Reader*. London: Basil Blackwell.
Smelser, N.J.
  1963 *The Theory of Collective Behaviour*. New York: Free Press.
Smith, Dorothy E.
  1975 "Women, the Family and Corporate Capitalism." In M. Stephenson (ed.), *Women in Canada*. Toronto: New Press.
  1982 "The Active Text." Presentation, World Congress of Sociology, Mexico City.

1987 *The Everyday World as Problematic: A Feminist Sociology.* Toronto: University of Toronto Press.

1990a *The Conceptual Practices of Power: A Feminist Sociology of Knowledge.* Toronto: University of Toronto Press.

1990b *Texts, Facts and Femininity: Exploring the Relations of Ruling.* London and New York: Routledge.

Smith, George W.

1983 "Media Frames: How Accounts Are Produced and Read." *Fuse* 6,5 (January/February): 279-83.

1988 "Talking Politics." *Rites* 5.

1989 "AIDS Treatment Deficits: An Ethnographic Study of the Management of the AIDS Epidemic, the Ontario Case." Presentation, V International Conference on AIDS, Montreal, June.

1990a "Political Activist as Ethnographer." *Social Problems* 37,4 (November): 629-48.

1990b "AIDS ACTION NOW! Responds to Federal AIDS Strategy." *AIDS ACTION NEWS! AIDS ACTION NOW!* (Toronto), October: 1-2.

Smith, M.P.

1979 *The City and Social Theory.* New York: St. Martin's Press.

Smith, Murray

1997 "Revisiting Trotsky: Reflections on the Stalinist Debacle and Trotskyism as Alternative." *Rethinking Marxism* (forthcoming).

Smyth, Cherry

1992 *Lesbians Talk Queer Notions.* London: Scarlet Press.

Snow, David A. and Robert D. Benford

1988 "Ideology, Frame Resonance and Participant Mobilization." *International Social Movement Research* 1: 197–218.

1992 "Master Frames and Cycles of Protest." In Aldon D. Morris and Carol McClurg Mueller (eds.), *Frontiers in Social Movement Theory.* New Haven, Conn.: Yale University Press.

Snow, David A. and Richard Machalek

1984 "The Sociology of Conversion." *Annual Review of Sociology* 10: 367-80.

Snow, David A., E.B. Rochford, S.K. Worden, and R.D. Benford

1986 "Frame Alignment Process, Micromobilization, and Movement Participation." *American Sociological Review* 51: 464–481.

"Social Coalitions Versus Social Democracy"

1993 Mimeo (no author cited).

Stacey, Judith

1983 "The New Conservative Feminism." *Feminist Studies* 9: 559–83.

Starn, Orin

1992 "'I Dreamed of Foxes and Hawks': Reflections on Peasant Protest, New Social Movements and the Rondas Campesinas of Northern Peru." In Arturo Escobar and Sonia E. Alvarez (eds.), *The Making of Social Movements in Latin America: Identity, Strategy, and Democracy.* Boulder, Col.: Westview Press.

Stein, Arlene

1992 "Sisters and Queers: The Decentering of Lesbian Feminism." *Socialist Review* 22,1: 33-55.

1993 (ed.) *Sisters, Sexperts, Queers: Beyond the Lesbian Nation*. New York: Penguin Books.

Steinmetz, George

1994 "Regulation Theory, Post–Marxism, and the New Social Movements." *Comparative Studies in Society and History* 36: 176–212.

Stinson, J. and Penni Richmond

1993 "Women Working for Unions: Female Staff and the Politics of Transformation." In L. Briskin and P. McDermott (eds.), *Women Challenging Unions: Feminism, Democracy, and Militancy*. Toronto: University of Toronto Press.

Stone, Sharon Dale

1990 (ed.) *Lesbians in Canada*. Toronto: Between the Lines.

1991 "Lesbians against the Right." In Janice L. Ristock and Jeri Dawn Wine (eds.), *Women and Social Change: Feminist Activism in Canada*. Toronto: James Lorimer and Company.

Stone, Sharon D. and Joanne Doucette

1988 "Organizing the Marginalized: The DisAbled Women's Network." In Frank Cunningham, Sue Findlay, Marlene Kadar, Alan Lennon, and Ed Silva (eds.), *Social Movements/Social Change: The Politics and Practice of Organizing*. Toronto: Between the Lines.

Stonechild, Blair A.

1991 "The Indian View of the 1885 Uprising." In J.R. Miller (ed.), *Sweet Promises: A Reader on Indian-White Relations in Canada*. Toronto: University of Toronto Press.

Svensson, Frances

1979 "Liberal Democracy and Group Rights: The Legacy of Individualism and Its Impact on American Indian Tribes." *Political Studies* 27,3.

Swan, Peter

1993 "Communicative Rationality or Political Contestation in Environmental Rights." *ARSP-Beiheft* 52.

Symons, Thomas H.B.

1975 *To Know Ourselves*. Ottawa: Association of Universities and Colleges in Canada.

Tarrow, Sidney

1988 "National Politics and Collective Action: A Review of Recent Research in Western Europe and the United States." *Annual Review of Sociology* 14: 421-40.

1989 "Struggle, Politics and Reform: Collective Action, Social Movements, and Cycles of Protest." *Cornell Studies in International Affairs Western Societies Papers* 21.

1992 "Mentalities, Political Cultures, and Collective Action Frames: Constructing Meanings through Action." In Aldon D. Morris and Carol

McClurg Mueller (eds.), *Frontiers in Social Movement Theory*. New Haven, Conn.: Yale University Press.

1994a "Framing Collective Action." *In Power in Movement: Social Movements, Collective Action and Politics*. Cambridge: Cambridge University Press.

1994b *Power in Movement: Social Movements, Collective Action and Politics*. Cambridge: Cambridge University Press.

Taylor, John Leonard
1991 "Canada's Northwest Indian Policy in the 1870s: Traditional Promises and Necessary Innovations." In J.R. Miller (ed.), *Sweet Promises: A Reader in Indian-White Relations in Canada*. Toronto: University of Toronto Press.

Taylor, Dr. Kathryn M.
1990 *National Centre For Treatment Information System for AIDS/HIV infection (TISAH): Report for the Federal Centre for AIDS*. Health Protection Branch, Health and Welfare Canada, Health and Welfare Canada/University of Toronto.

Tennant, Paul
1990 *Aboriginal Peoples and Politics: The Indian Land Question in British Columbia, 1849-1989*. Vancouver: University of British Columbia Press.

Thiele, Leslie Paul
1993 "Making Democracy Safe for the World: Social Movements and Global Politics." *Alternatives* 18: 273–305.

Thompson, E.
1966 *The Making of the English Working Class*. London: Vintage Books.

Threadgold, Terry
1989 "Talking about Genre: Ideologies and Incompatible Discourses." *Cultural Studies* 3,1: 101-27.

Thurston, Maxine Amelia
1987 "Strategies, Constraints, and Dilemmas of Alternative Organizations: A Study of Women's Health Centers." Ph.D thesis, School of Social Work, Florida State University.

Tilly, Charles
1978 *From Mobilization to Revolution*. Reading, Mass.: Addison–Wesley.

1985 "Models and Realities of Popular Collective Action." *Social Research* 52: 4.

1988 "Social Movements, Old and New." *Research in Social Movements, Conflicts and Change* 10: 1–18.

Tilson, Donn J.
1993 "The Shaping of Eco–Nuclear Publicity: The Use of Visitors' Centres in Public Relations." *Media, Culture and Society* 15: 419–35.

Tindall, David B.
1994 "Collective Action in the Rainforest: Personal Networks, Collective Identity and Participation in the Vancouver Island Wilderness Preservation Movement." Ph.D. thesis, Department of Sociology, University of Toronto.

Tindall, David B. and Noreen Begorary
1993 "Old Growth Defenders: The Battle For the Carmanah Valley." In Sally Lerner (ed.), *Environmental Stewardship: Studies in Active Earth Keeping*. Waterloo, Ont.: University of Waterloo Geography Series.

Tomlins, C.
1985 *The State and the Unions: Labor Relations, Law, and the Organized Labor Movement in America, 1880-1960*. Cambridge: Cambridge University Press.

Torrance, Judy
1977 "The Response of Canadian Governments to Violence." *Canadian Journal of Political Science* 3: 473-96.

Touraine, Alain
1981 *The Voice and the Eye: An Analysis of Social Movements*. Trans. Alan Duff. Cambridge: Cambridge University Press.
1985 "An Introduction to the Study of Social Movements." *Social Research* 52,4: 776.
1988 *Return of the Actor: Social Theory in Postindustrial Society*. Minneapolis: University of Minnesota Press.
1995 *Critique of Modernity*. Oxford: Basil Blackwell.

Tucker, Kenneth
1991 "How New Are the New Social Movements?" *Theory, Culture and Society* 8,2: 75-98.

Tully, J.
1995 *Strange Multiplicity: Constitutionalism in an Age of Diversity*. Cambridge: Cambridge University Press.

Tumber, Howard
1993 "Selling Scandal: Business and the Media." *Media, Culture and Society* 18: 345–62.

Turner, Bryan S.
1992 *Regulating Bodies: Essays in Medical Sociology*. London and New York: Routledge.

United Steelworkers of America
1991 "Empowering Workers in the Global Economy: A Labour Agenda for the 1990s." Background and Conference Proceedings, Toronto, Ont.
1992 "Steelworker Guidelines For Participation In Work Reorganization." Conference Congress, Toronto, Ont.

Urry, John
1981 *The Anatomy of Capitalist Societies*. London: Macmillan.

Ursel, Jane
1992 *Privates Lives, Public Policy*. Toronto: Women's Press.

Useem, Bert and Mayer N. Zald
1987 "From Pressure Group to Social Movement: Efforts to Promote Use of Nuclear Power." In Zald and McCarthy (1987).

Vance, Carole (ed.)
1984 *Pleasure and Danger: Female Sexuality Today*. London: Routledge and Kegan Paul.

Van Dijk, Teun A.
   1985a "Introduction: Discourse Analysis as a New Cross-discipline." In T.A.
      Van Dijk (ed.), *Handbook of Discourse Analysis*, vol. 1, *Disciplines of
      Discourse*. London: Academic Press.
   1985b "Introduction: Dialogue as Discourse and Interaction." In T.A. Van
      Dijk (ed.), *Handbook of Discourse Analysis*, vol. 3, *Discourse and Dialogue*.
      London: Academic Press.
   1993 "Principles of Critical Discourse Analysis." *Discourse and Society* 4,2:
      249-83.
Vernon, Raymond
   1971 *Sovereignty at Bay: The Multinational Spread of U.S. Enterprises*. New
      York: Basic Books.
Vickers, Jill McCalla
   1989 "Feminist Approaches to Women in Politics." In Linda Kealy and Joan
      Sangster (eds.), *Beyond the Vote: Canadian Women and Politics*. Toronto:
      University of Toronto Press.
Vincent, A.
   1987 *Theories of the State*. Oxford: Basil Blackwell.
Volosinov, V.N.
   1973 [1929] *Marxism and the Philosophy of Language*. New York and
      London: Seminar Press.
Walker, Gillian A.
   1990 *Family Violence and the Women's Movement: The Conceptual Politics of
      Struggle*. Toronto: University of Toronto Press.
Walker, R.B.J.
   1993 *Inside/Outside: International Relations as Political Theory*. Cambridge:
      Cambridge University Press.
Wallerstein, Immanuel
   1989a *The Modern World-System*. Vols. 1-3. San Diego, Cal.: Academic Press.
   1989b "1968, Revolution in the World-System." *Theory and Society* 18: 431-
      49.
   1990 "Culture as the Ideological Battleground of the Modern World-
      System." *Theory, Culture and Society* 7,2-3: 31-55.
Wapner, Michael
   1989 "What's Left: Marx, Foucault and Contemporary Problems of Social
      Change." *Praxis International* 9,1/2: 88–111.
Wapner, Paul
   1996 *Environmental Activism and World Politics*. Albany: State University of
      New York Press.
Warnock, John
   1987 *Free Trade and the New Right Agenda*. Vancouver: New Star Books.
Warrian, Peter
   1986 "'Labour Is Not a Commodity': A Study of the Rights of Labour in the
      Canadian Postwar Economy, 1944-48." Ph.D. thesis, Department of
      History, University of Waterloo, Waterloo, Ont.

Waterman, Peter
  1993 "Social Movement Unionism: A New Union Model for a New World
    Order?" *Review* 16,3: 245-78.
Waters, Malcolm
  1995 *Globalization*. London: Routledge.
Watney, Simon
  1987 *Policing Desire: Pornography, AIDS and the Media*. London: Comedia.
  1994 *Practices of Freedom: Selected Writings on HIV/AIDS*. Durham, N.C.:
    Duke University Press.
Wayves (Halifax)
  1995 "Making The Grade." *Wayves* 1,3 (April): 18.
Weaver, David H. and Wilhoit, G. Cleveland
  1996 *The American Journalist in the 1990s: U.S. News People at the End of
    an Era*. Mahwah, N.J.: Lawrence Eribaum Associates.
Weaver, Sally
  1981 *Making Canadian Indian Policy*. Toronto: University of Toronto Press.
Weiler, P.
  1990 *Governing the Workplace*. Cambridge, Mass.: Harvard University
    Press.
Weir, Lorna
  1993a "Limitations of New Social Movement Analysis." *Studies in Political
    Economy* 48: 73-102.
  1993b "The Wanderings of the Linguistic Turn in Anglophone Historical
    Writing." *Journal of Historical Sociology* 6,2: 227-45.
  1993c "What's So New in the New Social Movements?" *Studies In Political
    Economy* 40.
  1995 "PC Then and Now: Resignifying Political Correctness." In Stephen
    Richer and Lorna Weir (eds.), *Beyond Political Correctness: Toward the
    Inclusive University*. Toronto: University of Toronto Press.
Weissman, Aerlyn and Lynne Fernit (directors)
  1992 *Forbidden Love: The Unashamed Stories of Lesbian Lives*. Montreal:
    National Film Board of Canada.
Weitz, Rose
  1984 "From Accommodation to Rebellion: The Politicization of Lesbianism."
    In Trudy Darty and Sandee Potter (eds.), *Women-Identified Women*. Palo
    Alto, Cal.: Mayfield Publishing.
Wells, Don
  1995 "The Impact of the Postwar Compromise on Canadian Unionism: The
    Formation of an Auto Worker Local in the 1950s." *Labour/Le Travail* 36
    (Fall): 147-73.
White, Randall
  1995 *Global Spin: Probing the Globalization Debate*. Toronto: Dundurn
    Press.
Williams, Raymond
  1977 *Marxism and Literature*. Oxford: Oxford University Press.
  1983 *Towards 2000*. London: The Hogarth Press.

Wilson, Jeremy
1990 "Wilderness Politics in B.C.: The Business Dominated State and the Containment of Environmentalism." In William Coleman and Grace Skogstad (eds.), *Policy Communities and Public Policy in Canada: A Structural Approach*. Missisauga, Ont.: Copp Clark Pittman.
Wirth, L.
1937 "Urbanism as a Way of Life." *American Journal of Sociology* 44: 1–24.
Whitaker, Reg
1987 "Neo–conservatism and the State." In Ralph Miliband, Leo Panitch and John Saville (eds.), *Socialist Register 1987*. London: Merlin Press.
Whiteside, Kerry
1994 "Hannah Arendt and Ecological Politics." *Environmental Ethics* 16 (Winter).
Wilde, Lawrence
1990 "Class Analysis and the Politics of New Social Movements." *Capital and Class* 42: 55-78.
Wilson, William Julius
1980 *The Declining Significance of Race*. 2nd ed. Chicago: University of Chicago Press.
Wittig, Monique
1992 *The Straight Mind and Other Essays*. Boston: Beacon Press.
Wolf, Deborah Goleman
1979 *The Lesbian Community*. Berkeley: University of California Press.
Wolfe, D.
1992 "Technology and Trade: Finding the Right Mix." In D. Drache (ed.), *Getting on Track: Social Democratic Strategies for Ontario*. Montreal and Kingston: McGill-Queen's University Press.
Wood, E. Meiksins
1986 *The Retreat from Class*. London: Verso.
Wood, James L. and Maurice Jackson
1982 *Social Movements: Development, Participation, and Dynamics*. Belmont, Cal.: Wadsworth.
Working Committee for Social Solidarity, The (Ottawa)
1987 "A Time to Stand Together: A Time for Social Solidarity."
1990 "Background Paper."
Workman, Thom
1996 *Banking on Deception: The Discourse of Fiscal Crisis*. Halifax: Fernwood Publishing.
Wrenn, R.
1985 "The Decline of American Labor." *Socialist Review* 15.
Wright, E. et al.
1992 *Reconstructing Marxism*. London: Verso.
Yates, C.
1993 *From Plant To Politics: The Autoworkers Union in Postwar Canada*. Philadelphia: Temple University Press.

Yearley, Steven
  1991 *The Green Case: A Sociology of Environmental Issues, Arguments and Politics.* London: HarperCollins.
Yeatman, Anna
  1990 *Bureaucrats, Technocrats, Femocrats: Essays on the Contemporary Australian State.* Sydney, Australia: Allen and Unwin.
York, Geoffrey
  1989 *The Dispossessed: Life and Death in Native Canada.* London: Vintage Press.
York, Geoffrey and Loreen Pindera
  1992 *The People of the Pines.* Toronto: Little, Brown and Company (Canada).
Young, Iris Marion
  1989 "Polity and Group Difference: A Critique of the Ideal of Universal Citizenship." *Ethics* 99,2: 250-74.
  1990 *Justice and the Politics of Difference.* Princeton, N.J.: Princeton University Press.
Zukin, S.
  1991 *Landscapes of Power: From Detroit to Disneyworld.* Berkeley, Cal.: University of California Press.
Zald, Mayer N. and John D. McCarthy (eds.)
  1979 *The Dynamics of Social Movements.* Cambridge, Mass.: Winthrop Publishers.
  1987 *Social Movements in an Organizational Society.* New Brunswick, N.J.: Transaction Books.